Network Quality of Service

Volume Editor: Adrian Farrel, Old Dog Consulting, UK

Network Quality
of Service
Know It All

Gerald Ash

Bruce Davie

John Evans

Adrian Farrel

Clarence Filsfils

Pete Loshin

Deepankar Medhi

Monique Morrow

Rogelio Martinez Perea

Larry L. Peterson

Karthik Ramasamy

John Strassner

Kateel Vijayananda

Zheng Wang

ELSEVIER

AMSTERDAM • BOSTON • HEIDELBERG • LONDON
NEW YORK • OXFORD • PARIS • SAN DIEGO
SAN FRANCISCO • SINGAPORE • SYDNEY • TOKYO

Morgan Kaufmann is an imprint of Elsevier

M K

MORGAN KAUFMANN PUBLISHERS

Morgan Kaufmann Publishers is an imprint of Elsevier.
30 Corporate Drive, Suite 400,
Burlington, MA 01803

This book is printed on acid-free paper. ∞

Library of Congress Cataloging-in-Publication Data
Farrel, Adrian.
    Network quality of service : know it all / Adrian Farrel et al.
        p.   cm. — (Morgan Kaufmann know it all series)
    Includes bibliographical references and index.
    ISBN 978-0-12-374597-2 (alk. paper)
    1. Computer networks—Quality control.   2. Computer networks—Reliability.
    I. Title.
TK5105.5956.F37 2008
004.6—dc22   2008040329

For information on all Morgan Kaufmann publications, visit
our Website at *www.mkp.com or www.books.elsevier.com*

Printed and bound by CPI Group (UK) Ltd, Croydon, CR0 4YY

Transferred to Digital Print 2011

Contents

Preface

Introduction

It has often been said that the more comfortable people's lives are, the more likely they are to complain and the more demanding they will become. This certainly seems to be the case for the average Internet user. In the past, slow dial-up access was seen as the zenith of computer networking, providing email exchange and slow-but-steady file transfer. But now the demands are for high-bandwidth links and seamless, real-time exchange of voice and video traffic, and users complain if their online games freeze for even the briefest moment.

From a user's point of view, therefore, quality of service (QoS) can be quantified according to their expectations and the programs that are being run. Interactive or real-time applications are judged according to their ability to send and receive data so that users do not notice any transmission issues, but other Internet uses, such as file transfer or Web browsing, have less stringent requirements.

People's perception of the way applications use the Internet can be categorized in terms of the way Internet protocol (IP) packets are delivered. We can measure behavioral characteristics such as delay (the time to deliver packets), jitter (the variation in delay), throughput (the rate of delivery), and packet loss or re-ordering. Each of these properties of an end-to-end traffic flow has a different effect on different applications. For example, file transfer is sensitive to packet loss, but a voice stream can tolerate a certain amount of packet loss without significant degradation of the user's experience. On the other hand, real-time multimedia (voice and video) conferencing applications are difficult to operate with large delays, and jitter may make audio or video streams difficult for human users to follow. This means that there is a real need to match the QoS delivered by a network with specific application requirements.

The end-to-end quality experienced by an application (and so by a user) depends on the network equipment that the data packets must traverse within the network. Low-speed links add to end-to-end delay. Variable loads on routers may introduce jitter. Overloading of routers or links may cause packet loss, delay, and jitter. Network QoS, therefore, is all about managing the network resources to ensure that data is delivered in an acceptable way so as to meet the requirements of applications.

One approach to delivering network QoS is simply to ensure that all of the links and routers in the network are sufficiently well provisioned so that there is never any congestion. To some extent, this is the case today and many users of popular voice over IP (VoIP) services are able to place host-to-host phone calls over the Internet without any issues. However, with increasing demands for video streaming and audio (e.g., live TV and radio feeds and video-on-demand services), and a dramatic increase in the number of people using VoIP or multimedia conferencing, we cannot expect the core of the Internet to remain congestion free. Further, overprovisioning represents wasted capital expenditure (CAPEX) because, by definition, an overprovisioned link or router contains resources that are not being used.

This book examines the following variety of alternative mechanisms to provide acceptable levels of service delivery over IP-based networks without having to rely on overprovisioning.

- Policing of traffic that is input to a network can be crucial to ensuring that the right quality of service guarantees can be met for a specific application and for other users of the network. If an application exceeds its prearranged rate of data generation, it may be impossible to meet promised delivery targets, and attempting to do so may impact other traffic flows in the network.

- Differentiating between traffic that exists for various services and applications allows traffic to be treated in different ways within the network. This means that packets that are high priority, or where the applications are sensitive to delay, can be expedited, while other packets may be queued. Alternatively, packets for applications that cannot tolerate data loss can be handled carefully, whereas other packets can be discarded by congested routers.

- Resources can be preallocated or reserved within the network for use by specific traffic flows. This can ensure that there will always be adequate provision for the needs of specific applications so that their QoS needs can be met.

- Measurement and monitoring of the level of service provided by the network is an important way to understand network QoS and to ensure that users' needs and expectations are met. By recording and reporting the behavior of the network, it is possible to gather information that can be used to tune it and to optimize both users' experience and the use made of the network resources.

- Network planning and traffic engineering (TE) are tools to ensure that sufficient network capacity and resources are in place to support the demands of user traffic, and that the traffic is placed within the network in such a way as to make best use of the available resources while continuing to meet QoS commitments.

The purpose of this book is to give a broad introduction to the subject of network QoS and the mechanisms that can be used to satisfy application requirements for traffic delivery in today's Internet. By drawing on material from books by many experts in the field, we hope to provide many views and opinions on the same subject, allowing readers to build solid foundations in the topic.

A Note about the Internet Engineering Task Force

The Internet Engineering Task Force (IETF) is the main body responsible for standardizing protocols and procedures for use of the Internet. As such, the IETF has developed most of the network QoS solutions described in this book. It publishes its standards as Request For Comment (RFC) documents, and you will see plenty of these referenced throughout the book. Each is identified by a separate document number, so, for example, RFC 2205 is the document that specifies the Resource Reservation Protocol (RSVP). All of the RFCs can be downloaded free of charge from the IETF's web site at *www.ietf.org/rfc.html*.

The IETF is not a membership organization and encourages contributions from everyone and anyone who has something to add in any of the areas in which it works. Although most participants are sponsored (i.e., paid) by a company, the IETF minimizes the emphasis on corporate affiliations and focuses on what individuals have to add to the process of developing new standards. Most of the work of the Internet Engineering Task Force is carried out informally on mailing lists dedicated to working groups set up to deal with specific topics. To find out more, visit the IETF's web site at *www.ietf.org*.

This Book's Contents

This book contains eleven chapters arranged so as to introduce the material starting with the basics and leading through different interpretations of the term *quality of service* as well as different mechanisms to provide the network user with suitable traffic-delivery characteristics to make the network usage experience fit with the demands of the applications being run. Most chapters include a further reading section from the original text to give readers advice about where to go for more information and details about the topics introduced in the chapter.

Chapter 1 sets the scene for the rest of the book by painting the big picture of network Internet QoS. It presents a high-level description of the problems with the current Internet, the rationales behind the new technologies being developed for deployment, and the approaches these technologies use to address QoS issues. The chapter introduces four technologies that have emerged in the past few years as the core building blocks for enabling QoS in the Internet.

Chapter 2 reviews some of the key traffic engineering and QoS optimization (TQO) technologies: MPLS, GMPLS, QoS mechanisms, IntServ, RSVP, DiffServ, and MPLS-based QoS mechanisms. The chapter is intended as a refresher or a brief introduction for those unfamiliar with these technologies. Ample references are provided for more detailed coverage of these important topics. A focus of TQO protocol design is the development of MPLS- and GMPLS-based networks, where

MPLS and GMPLS are used at the MPLS label switched path (LSP) and GMPLS LSP design layers, respectively.

Chapter 3 examines quality of service application requirements with special focus on real-time applications. It goes on to describe the mechanisms developed for use in today's Internet to help meet the requirements and deliver QoS to users.

Chapter 4 details some popular mechanisms for categorizing packets, for describing flows, and for reserving resources. Although packet categorization can be implemented differently in each router, for the provision of services within a network it is important that there is a common understanding of the service level being applied to the packets within a flow. This chapter provides the details of how various service management techniques are achieved in data and control protocols, and compares the costs and benefits of the various mechanisms.

Chapter 5 discusses what QoS routing means and how different routing algorithms may be extended to fit the QoS routing framework. It also presents a representative set of numerical studies so that we can understand the implications of routing schemes and roles played by different network controls.

Chapter 6 examines the techniques and protocols used to meet QoS expectations of IP network users. The mechanisms discussed can help service providers to enhance and add new IP-based services to their portfolios to meet the additional requirements of their customers. The demand for QoS in an IP network is increasing every day. With the rapid emergence of applications, such as VoIP and video-on-demand (VOD), customers' expectations are also increasing. Separate sections describe QoS and various applications.

Chapter 7 provides a brief retrospective of how Policy-Based Network Management (PBNM) has been conceived in the past. *Policy management* means many things to many people, and this chapter presents the fundamentals. The material points out two basic problems of previous solutions: the lack of an information model and the inability to use business rules to drive configuration of devices, services, and networks. A path forward, and benefits resulting from this improved approach, are described.

Chapter 8 contains several examples of how policy is used in different situations in PBNM systems. The policy continuum figures prominently in the recommended approach for building PBNM systems because it enables business, system, and implementation views to be seamlessly integrated. The chapter shows how policy can be used to provide QoS for IP services and examines how two contrasting views of policy can be harmonized: that policy is a way to change lines in the configuration file of a device and that policy is only appropriate for expressing rules in the business world.

Chapter 9 covers the IPv6 approach to quality of service, including the use of the DiffServ field in IPv6, and a discussion of IPv6 Flow Labels and the use of Explicit Congestion Notification with IPv6.

Chapter 10 introduces the QoS topic as applicable to IP communication scenarios where the Session Initiation Protocol (SIP) is in use. It describes some basic

QoS ideas that allow the reader to understand the mechanisms and protocols that exist to provide quality of service. Starting by looking at some of the available architectures at the IP transport level to provide QoS, the chapter introduces the framework for policy control, and then shows how these constructs are applied in a SIP-based communication scenario.

Chapter 11 addresses core capacity planning and how TE can be used as a tool to make more efficient use of network capacity. Core network capacity planning is the process of ensuring that sufficient bandwidth is provisioned such that the committed core network service level agreement (SLA) targets of delay, jitter, loss, and availability can be met. In the core network where link bandwidths are high and traffic is highly aggregated, the SLA requirements for a traffic class can be translated into bandwidth requirements, and the problem of SLA assurance can effectively be reduced to that of bandwidth provisioning. Therefore, the ability to guarantee SLAs is dependent on ensuring that core network bandwidth is adequately provisioned, which is in turn depends on core capacity planning.

Source Material

Of course, many of the topics covered here have already been described at length in other books. The Morgan Kaufmann Series in Networking includes a comprehensive range of titles that deal with many aspects of network QoS. However, each book in the series has as its main focus a particular function or technology. In some cases source texts are entirely devoted to the subject, while other chapters are included from more general works in which network management is presented as one aspect of some specific technology.

What we have done in this book, therefore, is to bring together material from ten sources to provide you with a thorough grounding in what is meant by quality of service within the Internet. When necessary we have edited the source material; however, on the whole the original text provides a rounded view of particular authors' thoughts on the subject and is simply reproduced here. This results in a single reference that introduces network QoS and explains the basics. Readers wanting to know more about a particular topic are encouraged to go to the sources and read more.

There is some intentional overlap in the subject matter presented in this book. Each of the contributing authors has their own specific take on how to present the problems of network quality of service, and their own views on how issues should be solved. By providing readers with the full text from the selected chapters, we hope that this provides you with a broad view of the problem-space to allow you to make up your own mind about the challenges that must be addressed.

In producing *Network Quality of Service: Know It All*, we have drawn on material from the following Morgan Kaufmann books.

Internet QoS: Architectures and Mechanisms by Wang—This book provides a guide to Internet quality-of-service techniques, addressing the special challenges unique to QoS in an Internet environment. It includes personal insights from the author who served time as a Bell Labs engineer, and it emphasizes integrated services, MPLS, traffic engineering, and differentiated services.

***Traffic Engineering and QoS Optimization of Integrated Voice and Data Networks* by Ash**—This book describes, analyzes, and recommends traffic engineering and quality-of-service optimization methods for integrated voice/data dynamic routing networks. These functions control a network's response to traffic demands and other stimuli such as link failures or node failures. TE and QoS optimization is concerned with measurement, modeling, characterization, and control of network traffic, and the application of techniques to achieve specific performance objectives.

***Computer Networks, 4e,* by Peterson and Davie**—This is the fourth edition of a popular book written by two authors who have had firsthand experience designing and using networking protocols and designing today's computer networks. The focus is on the why of network design, not just the specifications comprising today's systems but also how key technologies and protocols actually work in the real world to solve specific problems. Emphasis is given both to the lower network layers, where established technologies have been deployed for many years, and to higher levels in the protocol stack, where there is generally more innovative and exciting work going on at the application and session layers than at the link and physical layers.

***The Internet and Its Protocols: A Comparative Approach* by Farrel**—This book covers all the common IP-based protocols and shows how they combine to create the Internet in its totality. Each protocol, including the various MPLS and GMPLS protocols, is described completely, with an examination of the requirements that each protocol addresses and the exact means by which it does its job.

***Network Routing* by Medhi and Ramasamy**—Network routing can be broadly categorized into Internet routing, PSTN routing, and telecommunication transport network routing. This book systematically considers these routing paradigms, as well as their interoperability. The authors discuss how algorithms, protocols, analysis, and operational deployment impact the various approaches.

***Developing IP-Based Services* by Morrow and Vijayananda**—This book meets the challenge of uniting business and technical perspectives to provide a cohesive view of the MPLS development and deployment process to enable networking organizations to leverage IP and MPLS to drive traffic and boost revenue.

***Policy-Based Network Management* by Strassner**—PBNM systems enable business rules and procedures to be translated into policies that configure and control the network and its services. This book cuts through the hype surrounding PBNM and makes it approachable for those who really need to understand what it has to offer. It discusses system requirements, information models, and system components for policy-based management.

***IPv6: Theory, Protocols, and Practice* by Loshin**—By presenting a close and unbiased look at why so much time and effort has been expended on revising IPv4, this book guides readers through the fundamental requirements of IPv6 and introduces implementation and deployment issues.

***Internet Multimedia Communications Using SIP* by Martinez**—Internet telephony, Internet multimedia in general, is the latest revolution to hit the Internet. The Session Initiation Protocol (SIP) is the key that allows this phenomenon to grow by enabling the provision of advanced services over the core networks that make up the Internet. This book explains the underlying technologies that facilitate real-time IP multimedia communication services in the Internet (e.g., voice, video, presence, instant messaging, online picture sharing, white-boarding).

***Deploying IP and MPLS QoS for Multiservice Networks: Theory and Practice* by Evans and Filsfils**—Quality of service is one of the most important goals a network designer or administrator will have. Ensuring that the network runs at optimal precision with accurate data that is traveling fast to the correct user is the main objective of QoS. The authors provide a comprehensive treatise on this subject, including topics such as traffic engineering, capacity planning, and admission control. This book provides real-world QoS case studies about multiservice networks. The studies remove the mystery behind QoS by illustrating the how, what, and why of implementing QoS within networks. Readers will be able to learn from the successes and failures of actual working designs and configurations.

Adrian Farrel

Contributing Authors

Gerald Ash (Chapter 2) is from Glen Roc, New Jersey. He graduated from grammar school, high school, Rutgers, and Caltech, but got sent to Vietnam instead of being able to attend his Caltech graduation. He spent the first 20 years of his AT&T career as "the consummate BellHead" (as one colleague put it), but for the next 5 years sought to be a blossoming NetHead. He has been happliy married for more than 40 years, has three children, and four grandchildren.

Bruce Davie (Chapter 3) joined Cisco Systems in 1995, and was awarded recognition as a Cisco Fellow in 1998. For many years he led the team of architects responsible for Multiprotocol Label Switching (MPLS) and IP quality of service (QoS). He recently joined the Video and Content Networking Business Unit in the Service Provider group. Bruce has 20 years of networking and communications industry experience and has written numerous books, journal articles, conference papers, and networking standards. Prior to joining Cisco, Bruce was director of internetworking research and chief scientist at Bell Communications Research. Bruce holds a Ph.D. in computer science from Edinburgh University and is a visiting lecturer at MIT.

John Evans (Chapter 11) is a Distinguished Systems Engineer with Cisco Systems, where he has been instrumental in the engineering and deployment of QoS and policy control. His current areas of focus include policy/resource control, admission control, QoS, and traffic management with associated work in the DSL Forum, the Multiservice Forum, and ETSI/TISPAN. Before joining Cisco in 1998, John worked for BT where he was responsible for the design and development of large-scale networks for the financial community. Prior to BT, he worked on the design and deployment of battlefield communications networks for the military. He received a B.Eng. degree with honors in electronic engineering from the University of Manchester Institute of Science and Technology (UMIST—now part of the University of Manchester), UK, in 1991 and an M.Sc. in communications engineering from UMIST in 1996. He is a Chartered Engineer and Cisco Certified Internetwork Expert.

Adrian Farrel (Chapter 4) has more than two decades of experience designing and developing portable communications software. At Old Dog Consulting, he is an industry-leading freelance consultant on MPLS, GMPLS, and Internet routing. Formerly he worked as MPLS Architect for Data Connection Ltd. and as Director of Protocol Development for Movaz Networks Inc. He is active within the Internet Engineering Task Force, where he is co-chair of the CCAMP working group responsible for GMPLS, the Path Computation Element (PCE) working group, and the Layer One VPN (L1VPN) working group. Adrian has coauthored and contributed to numerous Internet Drafts and RFCs on MPLS, GMPLS, and related technologies.

Clarence Filsfils (Chapter 11) is a Cisco Distinguished System Engineer and a recognized expert in routing and QoS. He has been playing a key role in engineering, marketing, and deploying the Quality of Service and Fast Routing Convergence technology at Cisco Systems. Clarence is a regular speaker at conferences, has published several journal articles, and holds more than 30 patents on QoS and routing mechanisms.

Pete Loshin (Chapter 9), writer and technology consultant, started working as a TCP/IP network engineer is 1988 in a research lab in Cambridge, MA. Since then he has written about TCP/IP networking for *BYTE Magazine*, *ComputerWorld*, *Information Security Magazine*, *PC World*, *PC Magazine*, and many other publications.

Deepankar Medhi (Chapter 5) is professor of computer networking in the Computer Science and Electrical Engineering Department at the University of Missouri–Kansas City. He has worked extensively with network providers in the deployment and operations of network routing and design for different technologies. His research has been funded by NSF, DARPA, and various industries.

Monique Morrow (Chapter 6) is currently CTO Consulting Engineer at Cisco Systems. She has 20 years of experience in IP internetworking, including design implementation of complex customer projects and service deployment. Morrow has been involved in developing managed network services such as remote access and LAN switching in a service provider environment. She has worked for both enterprise companies and service providers in the United States and in Europe and, in 1999, led the Engineering Project team for one of the first European MPLS-VPN deployments. Morrow has an M.S. in telecommunications management and an M.B.A. in marketing and is a Cisco Certified Internetworking Expert.

Rogelio Martinez Perea (Chapter 10) holds an M.Sc. degree in telecommunications engineering from Universidad Politecnica de Madrid in Spain. He has worked for the Vodafone Group for more than 12 years leading a team of technical specialists devoted to mobile applications design and implementation. Rogelio has also been extensively involved in the deployment of SIP-based technology for operators all around the world.

Larry L. Peterson (Chapter 3) is professor and chair of Computer Science at Princeton University. He is the director of the Princeton-hosted PlanetLab Consortium and chair of the planning group for NSF's GENI Initiative. His research focuses on the design and implementation of networked systems. Peterson is a Fellow of the ACM.

Karthik Ramasamy (Chapter 5) has 10 years of industrial experience working in companies such as Juniper Networks, Desana Systems, and NCR. His technical expertise is in networking and database management. In addition to several published papers, Karthik holds 7 patents.

John Strassner (Chapters 7 and 8), chief security officer of Intelliden Corporation, has occupied high-level roles for a number of prominent IT companies. At Cisco, where he held the distinguished title of Cisco Fellow, he was responsible for defining the overall direction and strategy for creating and deploying intelligent networks and policy-driven networked applications. Strassner has led or served on several standards committees, currently including the DMTF Working Group. He is frequently an invited speaker at conferences and regularly teaches PBNM tutorials.

Kateel Vijayananda (Chapter 6) is currently a design consultant at Cisco Systems, has 10 years of experience in data networking, featuring design, implementation, management of IP networks, and software development devoted to OSI protocol stack implementation. He has also been involved in developing managed network service, such as LAN switching and LAN interconnect, in a service provider environment. Vijayananda has worked as a network engineer/architect for a European service provider where he was part of teams that designed and implemented an MPLS network and developed and managed IP-based services on top of an MPLS network. He holds an M.S. and a Ph.D. in computer science and is a CCIE.

Zheng Wang (Chapter 1) has been involved in Internet-related research and development for the last 14 years. He is currently with Bell Labs–Lucent Technologies working on high-speed routers and optical transport systems. He has been published in many journals and magazines and holds patents in IP routing, QoS mechanisms, differentiated services, MPLS, traffic engineering, and optical networking.

Network QoS: The Big Picture

In this first chapter, taken from Chapter 1 of *Internet QoS: Architectures and Mechanisms for Quality of Service* by Zheng Wang, we present a high-level description of the problems in the current Internet, the rationales behind these new technologies, and the approaches used in them to address QoS issues.

The current Internet has its roots in the ARPANET, an experimental data network funded by the U.S. Defense Advanced Research Projects Agency (DARPA) in the early 1960s. An important goal was to build a robust network that could survive active military attacks such as bombing. To achieve this, the ARPANET was built on the *datagram model,* where each individual packet is forwarded independently to its destination. The datagram network has the strength of simplicity and the ability to adapt automatically to changes in network topology.

For many years the Internet was primarily used by scientists for networking research and for exchanging information among themselves. Remote access, file transfer, and email were among the most popular applications, and for these applications the datagram model works well. The World Wide Web, however, has fundamentally changed the Internet. It is now the world's largest public network. New applications, such as video conferencing, Web searching, electronic media, discussion boards, and Internet telephony, are coming out at an unprecedented speed. E-commerce is revolutionizing the way we do business. At the beginning of the twenty-first century, the Internet is destined to become the ubiquitous global communication infrastructure.

The phenomenal success of the Internet has brought us fresh new challenges. Many of the new applications have very different requirements from those for which the Internet was originally designed. One issue is *performance assurance.* The datagram model, on which the Internet is based, has few resource management capabilities inside the network and so cannot provide any resource guarantees to users—you get what you get! When you try to reach a Web site or to make an Internet phone call, some parts of the network may be so busy that your packets cannot get through at all. Most real-time applications, such as video conferencing, also require some minimal level of resources to operate effectively. As the Internet becomes indispensable in our life and work, the lack of predictable performance is certainly an issue we have to address.

Another issue is *service differentiation*. Because the Internet treats all packets the same way, it can offer only a single level of service. The applications, however, have diverse requirements. Interactive applications such as Internet telephony are sensitive to latency and packet losses. When the latency or the loss rate exceeds certain levels, these applications become literally unusable. In contrast, a file transfer can tolerate a fair amount of delay and losses without much degradation of perceived performance. Customer requirements also vary, depending on what the Internet is used for. For example, organizations that use the Internet for bank transactions or for control of industrial equipment are probably willing to pay more to receive preferential treatment for their traffic. For many service providers, providing multiple levels of services to meet different customer requirements is vital for the success of their business.

The capability to provide resource assurance and service differentiation in a network is often referred to as *quality of service* (QoS). Resource assurance is critical for many new Internet applications to flourish and prosper. The Internet will become a truly multiservice network only when service differentiation can be supported. Implementing these QoS capabilities in the Internet has been one of the toughest challenges in its evolution, touching on almost all aspects of Internet technologies and requiring changes to the basic architecture of the Internet. For more than a decade the Internet community has made continuous efforts to address the issue and developed a number of new technologies for enhancing the Internet with QoS capabilities.

Four technologies have emerged in the last few years as the core building blocks for enabling QoS in the Internet. The architectures and mechanisms developed in these technologies address two key QoS issues in the Internet: resource allocation and performance optimization. Integrated Services and Differentiated Services are two resource allocation architectures for the Internet. The new service models proposed in them make possible resource assurances and service differentiation for traffic flows and users. Multiprotocol Label Switching (MPLS) and traffic engineering, on the other hand, give service providers a set of management tools for bandwidth provisioning and performance optimization; without them, it would be difficult to support QoS on a large scale and at reasonable cost.

Before we get down to the details, however, it is useful to look at the big picture. The next sections of this chapter present a high-level description of the problems in the current Internet, the rationales behind these new technologies, and the approaches used in them to address QoS issues.

1.1 RESOURCE ALLOCATION

Fundamentally, many problems we see in the Internet come down to the issue of *resource allocation*—packets get dropped or delayed because the resources in the network cannot meet all the traffic demands. A network, in its simplest form, consists of shared resources such as bandwidth and buffers, serving traffic from competing users. A network that supports QoS needs to take an active role in the resource allocation process and decides who should get the resources and how much.

The current Internet does not support any forms of active resource allocation. The network treats all individual packets exactly the same way and serves the packets on a first-come, first-served (FCFS) basis. There is no admission control either—users can inject packets into the network as fast as possible.

The Internet currently relies on the Transmission Control Protocol (TCP) in the hosts to detect congestion in the network and reduce the transmission rates accordingly. TCP uses a window-based scheme for congestion control. The window corresponds to the amount of data in transit between the sender and the receiver. If a TCP source detects a lost packet, it slows the transmission rate by reducing the window size by half and then increasing it gradually in case more bandwidth is available in the network.

TCP-based resource allocation requires all applications to use the same congestion control scheme. Although such cooperation is achievable within a small group, in a network as large as the Internet, it can be easily abused. For example, some people have tried to gain more than their fair share of the bandwidth by modifying the TCP stack or by opening multiple TCP connections between the sender and receiver. Furthermore, many UDP-based applications do not support TCP-like congestion control, and real-time applications typically cannot cope with large fluctuations in the transmission rate. The service that the current Internet provides is often referred to as *best effort*. Best-effort service represents the simplest type of service that a network can offer; it does not provide any form of resource assurance to traffic flows. When a link is congested, packets are simply pushed out as the queue overflows. Since the network treats all packets equally, any flows could get hit by the congestion.

Although best-effort service is adequate for some applications that can tolerate large delay variation and packet losses, such as file transfer and email, it clearly does not satisfy the needs of many new applications and their users. New architectures for resource allocation that support resource assurance and different levels of service are essential for the Internet to evolve into a multiservice network.

In recent years the Internet community came up with Integrated Services and Differentiated Services, two new architectures for resource allocation in the Internet. The two architectures introduced a number of new concepts and primitives that are important to QoS support in the Internet:

- Frameworks for resource allocation that support resource assurance and service differentiation
- New service models for the Internet in addition to the existing best-effort service
- Language for describing resource assurance and resource requirements
- Mechanisms for enforcing resource allocation

Integrated Services and Differentiated Services represent two different solutions. Integrated Services provide resource assurance through resource reservation for individual application flows, whereas Differentiated Services use a combination of edge policing, provisioning, and traffic prioritization.

1.1.1 **Integrated Services**

Although the problems with the best-effort model have long been recognized, the real push for enhanced service architectures came in the early 1990s after some large-scale video conferencing experiments over the Internet. Real-time applications such as video conferencing are sensitive to the timeliness of data and so do not work well over the Internet, where the latency typically is unpredictable. The stringent delay and jitter requirements of these applications require a new type of service that is able to provide some level of resource assurance to the applications.

In early 1990 the Internet Engineering Task Force (IETF) started the Integrated Services working group to standardize a new resource allocation architecture and new service models. At that time the World Wide Web, as we know it today, did not yet exist, and multimedia conferencing was seen by many people as a potential killer application for the Internet. Thus the requirements of the real-time applications had major impacts on the architecture of Integrated Services.

The Integrated Services architecture is based on *per-flow resource reservation*. To receive resource assurance, an application must make a reservation before it can transmit traffic onto the network. Resource reservation involves several steps. First, the application must characterize its traffic source and the resource requirements. The network then uses a routing protocol to find a path based on the requested resources. Next a reservation protocol is used to install the reservation state along that path. At each hop, admission control checks whether sufficient resources are available to accept the new reservation. Once the reservation is established, the application can start to send traffic over the path for which it has exclusive use of the resources. Resource reservation is enforced by packet classification and scheduling mechanisms in the network elements, such as routers.

The Integrated Services working group proposed two new service models that a user can select: the *guaranteed service* and the *controlled load service* models. The guaranteed service model provides deterministic worst-case delay bound through strict admission control and fair queuing scheduling. This service was designed for applications that require absolute guarantees on delay. The other service model, the controlled load service, provides a less firm guarantee—a service that is close to a lightly loaded best-effort network. The Resource Reservation Setup Protocol (RSVP) was also standardized for signaling an application's requirements to the network and for setting up resource reservation along the path.

The Integrated Services model was the first attempt to enhance the Internet with QoS capabilities. The research and development efforts provided valuable insights into the complex issues of supporting QoS in the Internet. The resource allocation architecture, new service models, and RSVP protocol were standardized in the late 1990s.

But deployment of the Integrated Services architecture in the service provider's backbone has been rather slow for a number of reasons. For one, the Integrated Services architecture focused primarily on long-lasting and delay-sensitive applications. The World Wide Web, however, significantly changed the Internet landscape. Web-based applications now dominate the Internet, and much of Web traffic is short-lived transactions. Although per-flow reservation makes sense for long-lasting sessions, such as video conferencing, it is not appropriate for Web traffic. The overheads for setting up a reservation for each session are simply too high. Concerns also arose about the scalability of the mechanisms for supporting Integrated Services. To support per-flow reservation, each node in a network has to implement per-flow classification and scheduling. These mechanisms may not be able to cope with a very large number of flows at high speeds.

Resource reservation requires the support of accounting and settlement between different service providers. Since those who request reservation have to pay for the services, any reservations must be authorized, authenticated, and accounted. Such supporting infrastructures simply do not exist in the Internet. When multiple service providers are involved in a reservation, they have to agree on the charges for carrying traffic from other service providers' customers and settle these charges among them. Most network service providers are currently connected through bilateral peering agreements. To extend these bilateral agreements to an Internet-wide settlement agreement is difficult given the large number of players.

The Integrated Services architecture may become a viable framework for resource allocation in corporate networks. Corporate networks are typically limited in size and operated by a single administrative domain. Therefore many of the scaling and settlement issues we discussed above vanish. Integrated Services can support guaranteed bandwidth for IP telephony, video conferencing over corporate intranets. RSVP can also be used for resources allocation and admission control for traffic going out to wide area networks.

The ideas, concepts, and mechanisms developed in Integrated Services also found their way into later work on QoS. For example, controlled load service has influenced the development of Differentiated Services, and similar resource reservation capability has been incorporated into MPLS for bandwidth guarantees over traffic trunks in the backbone networks.

1.1.2 Differentiated Services

The Differentiated Services architecture was developed as an alternative resource allocation scheme for service providers' networks. By mid-1997 service providers felt that Integrated Services were not ready for large-scale deployment, and at the same time the need for an enhanced service model had become more urgent. The

Internet community started to look for a simpler and more scalable approach to offer a *better than best-effort* service.

After a great deal of discussion, the IETF formed a new working group to develop a framework and standards for allocating different levels of services in the Internet. The new approach, called Differentiated Services, is significantly different from Integrated Services. Instead of making per-flow reservations, Differentiated Services architecture uses a combination of edge policing, provisioning, and traffic prioritization to achieve service differentiation.

In the Differentiated Services architecture, users' traffic is divided into a small number of *forwarding classes*. For each forwarding class, the amount of traffic that users can inject into the network is limited at the edge of the network. By changing the total amount of traffic allowed in the network, service providers can adjust the level of resource provisioning and hence control the degree of resource assurance to the users.

The edge of a Differentiated Services network is responsible for mapping packets to their appropriate forwarding classes. This packet classification is typically done based on the *service level agreement* (SLA) between the user and its service provider. The nodes at the edge of the network also perform traffic policing to protect the network from misbehaving traffic sources. Nonconforming traffic may be dropped, delayed, or marked with a different forwarding class.

The forwarding class is directly encoded into the packet header. After packets are marked with their forwarding classes at the edge of the network, the interior nodes of the network can use this information to differentiate the treatment of the packets. The forwarding classes may indicate drop priority or resource priority. For example, when a link is congested, the network will drop packets with the highest drop priority first.

Differentiated Services do not require resource reservation setup. The allocation of forwarding classes is typically specified as part of the SLA between the customer and its service provider, and the forwarding classes apply to traffic aggregates rather than to individual flows. These features work well with transaction-orientated Web applications. The Differentiated Services architecture also eliminates many of the scalability concerns with Integrated Services. The functions that interior nodes have to perform to support Differentiated Services are relatively simple. The complex process of classification is needed only at the edge of the network, where traffic rates are typically much lower.

The Differentiated Services approach relies on provisioning to provide resource assurance. The quality of the assurance depends on how provisioning is carried out and how the resources are managed in the network. These issues are explored in the next section, where we discuss performance optimization in the networks. Because of the dynamic nature of traffic flows, precise provisioning is difficult. Thus it is generally more difficult, and certainly more expensive, to provide deterministic guarantees through provisioning rather than reservation.

1.2 PERFORMANCE OPTIMIZATION

Once the resource allocation architecture and service models are in place, the second issue in resource allocation is performance optimization: that is, how to organize the resources in a network in the most efficient way to maximize the probability of delivering the commitments and minimize the cost of delivering the commitments.

The connection between performance optimization and QoS support may seem less direct compared with resource allocation. Performance optimization is, however, an important building block in the deployment of QoS. Implementing QoS goes way beyond just adding mechanisms such as traffic policing, classification, and scheduling; fundamentally, it is about developing new services over the Internet. Service providers must make a good business case so that customers are willing to pay for the new services and the new services will increase the return of their investment in the networks. The cost-effectiveness of the new services made possible by QoS capabilities is a major factor in the rollout of these services.

The Internet's datagram routing was not designed for optimizing the performance of the network. Scalability and maintaining connectivity in the face of failures were the primary design objectives. Routing protocols typically select the shortest path to a destination based on some simple metrics, such as hop count or delay. Such simple approaches are clearly not adequate for supporting resource allocation. For example, to make a reservation, we need to find a path with certain requested resources, such as bandwidth, but IP routing does not have the necessary information to make such decisions. Simply using the shortest-path algorithm for selecting paths is likely to cause high rejection rate and poor utilization. The shortest-path routing does not always use the diverse connections available in the network. In fact, traffic is often unevenly distributed across the network, which can create congestion hot spots at some points while some other parts of the network may be very lightly loaded.

Performance optimization requires additional capabilities in IP routing and performance management tools. To manage the performance of a network, it is necessary to have explicit control over the paths that traffic flows traverse so that traffic flows can be arranged to maximize resource commitments and utilization of the network. MPLS has a mechanism called *explicit routing* that is ideal for this purpose. MPLS uses the label switching approach to set up virtual circuits in IP-based networks. These virtual circuits can follow destination-based IP routing, but the explicit routing mechanism in MPLS also allows us to specify, hop by hop, the entire path of these virtual circuits. This provides a way to override the destination-based routing and set up traffic trunks based on traffic-engineering objectives.

The process of optimizing the performance of networks through efficient provisioning and better control of network flows is often referred to as *traffic engineering.* Traffic engineering uses advanced route-selection algorithms to provision traffic trunks inside backbones and arrange traffic flows in ways that maximize the overall efficiency of the network. The common approach is to calculate traffic trunks based on flow distribution and then set up the traffic trunks as explicit routes with the MPLS protocol. The combination of MPLS and traffic engineering provides IP-based networks with a set of advanced tools for service providers to manage the performance of their networks and provide more services at less cost.

1.2.1 Multiprotocol Label Switching

MPLS was originally seen as an alternative approach for supporting IP over ATM. Although several approaches for running IP over ATM were standardized, most of the techniques are complex and have scaling problems. The need for more seamless IP/ATM integration led to the development of MPLS in 1997. The MPLS approach allows IP routing protocols to take direct control over ATM switches, and thus the IP control plane can be tightly integrated with the rest of the IP network.

The technique that MPLS uses is known as *label switching.* A short, fixed-length label is encoded into the packet header and used for packet forwarding. When a *label switch router* (LSR) receives a labeled packet, it uses the incoming label in the packet header to find the next hop and the corresponding outgoing label. With label switching, the path that a packet traverses through, called the *label switched path* (LSP), has to be set up before it can be used for label switching.

In addition to improving IP/ATM integration, MPLS may also be used to simplify packet forwarding. Label lookup is much easier compared with prefix lookup in IP forwarding. With MPLS, packet forwarding can be done independent of the network protocols, and so forwarding paradigms beyond the current destination-based one can be easily supported. However, the driving force behind the wide deployment of MPLS has been the need for traffic engineering in Internet backbones. The explicit route mechanism in MPLS provides a critical capability that is currently lacking in the IP-based networks. MPLS also incorporates concepts and features from both Integrated Services and Differentiated Services. For example, MPLS allows bandwidth reservation to be specified over an LSP, and packets can be marked to indicate their loss priority. All these features make MPLS an ideal mechanism for implementing traffic-engineering capabilities in the Internet.

The purpose of MPLS is not to replace IP routing, but rather to enhance the services provided in IP-based networks by offering scope for traffic engineering, guaranteed QoS, and virtual private networks (VPNs). MPLS works alongside the existing routing technologies and provides IP networks with a mechanism for explicit control over routing paths. MPLS allows two fundamentally different data-networking approaches, datagram and virtual circuit, to be combined in IP-based networks. The datagram approach, on which the Internet is based, forwards packets hop by hop, based on their destination addresses. The virtual circuit approach, used in ATM and Frame Relay, requires connections to be set up. With MPLS, the two approaches can be tightly integrated to offer the best combination of scalability and manageability.

MPLS control protocols are based on IP addressing and transport and therefore can be more easily integrated with other IP control protocols. This creates a unified IP-based architecture in which MPLS is used in the core for traffic engineering and IP routing for scalable domain routing. In several recent proposals, extending the MPLS protocols to the optical transport networks has even been considered. MPLS may well become the standard signaling protocol for the Internet.

1.2.2 Traffic Engineering

The basic problem addressed in traffic engineering is as follows: Given a network and traffic demands, how can traffic flows in the network be organized so that an optimization objective is achieved? The objective may be to maximize the utilization of resources in the network or to minimize congestion in the network. Typically the optimal operating point is reached when traffic is evenly distributed across the network. With balanced traffic distribution, both queuing delay and loss rates are at their lowest points.

Obviously these objectives cannot be achieved through destination-based IP routing; there simply is not sufficient information available in IP routing to make possible such optimization. In traffic engineering, advanced route selection techniques, often referred to as *constraint-based routing* in order to distinguish them from destination routing, are used to calculate traffic trunks based on the optimization objectives. To perform such optimization, the traffic-engineering system often needs network-wide information on topology and traffic demands. Thus traffic engineering is typically confined to a single administrative domain.

The routes produced by constraint-based routing are most likely different from those in destination-based IP routing. For this reason these constraint-based routes cannot be implemented by destination-based forwarding. In the past, many service providers used ATM in the backbone networks to support constraint-based routing. ATM virtual circuits can be set up to match the traffic patterns; the IP-based network is then overlaid on top of these virtual circuits. MPLS offers a better alternative since it offers similar functions yet can be tightly integrated with IP-based networks.

The existing Internet backbones have used the so-called *overlay model* for traffic engineering. With the overlay model, service providers build a virtual network comprising a full mesh of logical connections between all edge nodes. Using the traffic demands between the edge nodes as input, constraint-based routing selects a set of routes for the logical connections to maximize the overall resource utilization in the network. Once the routes are computed, MPLS can be used to set up the logical connections as LSPs, exactly as calculated by constraint-based routing.

The downside of the overlay model is that it may not be able to scale to large networks with a substantial number of edge nodes. To set up a full-mesh logical network with N edge nodes, each edge node has to connect to the other $(N-1)$ edge nodes, resulting in $N \times (N-1)$ logical connections. This can add significant messaging overheads in a large network. Another problem is that the full-mesh logical topology increases the number of peers, neighbors that routers talk to, that a routing protocol has to handle; most current implementations of routing protocols cannot support a very large number of peers. In addition to the increased peering requirements, the logical topology also increases the processing load on routers during link failures. Because multiple logical connections go over the same physical link, the failure of a single physical link can cause the breakdown of multiple logical links from the perspective of IP routing.

Traffic engineering without full-mesh overlaying is still a challenge. One heuristic approach that some service providers have used is to adjust traffic distribution by changing the link weights in IP routing protocols. For example, when one link is congested, the link weight can be increased in order to move traffic away from this link. Theoretically one can achieve the same traffic distribution as in the overlay model by manipulating the link weights in the Open Shortest Path First (OSPF) routing protocol. This approach has the advantage that it can be readily implemented in existing networks without major changes to the network architecture.

1.3 SUMMARY

The need for QoS capabilities in the Internet stems from the fact that best-effort service and datagram routing do not meet the needs of many new applications, which require some degree of resource assurance in order to operate effectively. Diverse customer requirements also create a need for service providers to offer different levels of services in the Internet.

The Internet community has developed a number of new technologies to address these issues. Integrated Services and Differentiated Services provide new architectures for resource allocation in the Internet. Integrated Services use reservation to provide guaranteed resources for individual flows. The Differentiated Services architecture takes a different approach. It combines edge policing, provisioning, and traffic prioritization to provide different levels of services to customers.

MPLS and traffic engineering address the issues of bandwidth provisioning and performance optimization in Internet backbones. The explicit route mechanism in MPLS adds an important capability to the IP-based network. Combined with constraint-based routing in traffic engineering, MPLS and traffic engineering can help network providers make the best use of available resources and reduce costs.

1.4 **RESOURCES**

The basic principles of datagram networks and a detailed design were first described by Paul Baran in his 1964 RAND report "On Distributed Communications." Although the report was discovered after the ARPANET had already started, the current Internet is remarkably close to what Paul Baran originally had in mind. This 12-volume historical report is now available on-line at *www.rand.org/publications/RM/baran.list.html.*

For a general introduction about data networking and the Internet, we recommend Peterson, L., and B. Davie, *Computer Networks: A Systems Approach* (Morgan Kaufmann, 1999).

Traffic Engineering and QoS Optimization Technology

This chapter, originally Appendix A in *Traffic Engineering and QoS Optimization of Integrated Voice and Data Networks* by Gerald Ash, reviews some of the key Traffic Engineering and QoS Optimization (TQO) technologies: MPLS, GMPLS, QoS mechanisms, IntServ, RSVP, DiffServ, and MPLS-based QoS mechanisms. This is intended as a refresher and/or a brief introduction for those unfamiliar with these technologies. Ample references are provided for more detailed coverage of these important topics. A focus of TQO protocol design is the development of MPLS- and GMPLS-based networks, where MPLS and GMPLS are used at the MPLS label switched path (LSP) and GMPLS LSP design layers, respectively. MPLS and GMPLS are revolutionary new network control capabilities designed and standardized in the Internet Engineering Task Force (IETF). Networks are rapidly evolving toward converged MPLS/GMPLS-based technologies, and the technologies described in this chapter are key building blocks.

2.1 MULTIPROTOCOL LABEL SWITCHING

In this section we give an overview of MPLS technology and begin with a brief history on the evolution of MPLS and then summarize some of the benefits and technical details. Work on MPLS is carried out in the IETF under the auspices of the MPLS working group. The charter of the IETF MPLS working group and a list of working documents and request for comments (RFCs) that have been issued are listed on the MPLS home page at *www.ietf.org/html.charters/mpls-charter.html.*

MPLS groups packets to be forwarded in the same manner into forwarding equivalence classes (FECs), and labels are used to mark the packets to identify the forwarding path. The assignment of a packet to an FEC is done once, at the entry point to the network. MPLS capable label switching routers (LSRs) then use the label to make packet forwarding decisions. MPLS packets are able to carry a number of labels in a last-in first-out stack, which is very useful where two levels of routing are taking place across transit routing domains, such as in widely deployed MPLS virtual private networks (VPNs). A sequence of LSRs defines a label switched path, which can be hop by hop, where each node independently decides the next hop, and explicitly routed where the ingress node specifies the path to be taken. MPLS is able to work with any data link technology, connection oriented and connectionless.

In the mid-1990s, Internet service providers were often using an overlay model to run IP over ATM, but this posed scalability problems. Vendors started to develop means to take advantage of both high-speed ATM switching and lower-cost (but then slower) IP routing, with developments such as:

- IP switching—Ipsilon (1996)
- Tag switching—Cisco (1996)
- Aggregate route-based IP switching (ARIS)—IBM
- IP navigator—Cascade/Ascend/Lucent
- Cell switched router (CSR)—Toshiba (1995)
- IPSOFACTO

These solutions attempted to improve the throughput and delay performance of IP by using standard routing protocols to create "paths" between end points. Packets would follow a particular path based on the packet characteristics, wherein ATM switches would switch the packets along the path. Tag switching is considered by some to be the "pre-standard" implementation of the MPLS architecture.

These mid-1990s initiatives led to the development of MPLS in the IETF, starting in March 1997: "multiprotocol" because it can be transported over many different link layer protocols; "label" because the protocols are transported with a label changed at each hop; "switching" because labels are of local significance. By 2001, the IETF MPLS working group issued the first set of proposed standards for MPLS, and many more RFCs have been issued since then (the RFCs are listed on the MPLS home page at *www.ietf.org/html.charters/mpls-charter.html*).

Because today's IP-based routers perform at comparable speeds to ATM switches, this negates the original motivation for MPLS. However, MPLS provides important new networking capabilities, such as QoS, traffic engineering, fast reroute, and VPNs. AT&T was one of the early implementers of an MPLS-based service, with the highly successful development of IP-enabled Frame Relay (FR), which implements an MPLS-VPN solution.

Now we turn to the technical details of MPLS. In conventional packet networks, such as those that use IP and open shortest path first (OSPF) routing, a packet travels from one router to the next and each router makes an independent forwarding decision for that packet. Each router analyzes the packet's header and independently chooses a next hop for the packet based on the packet header and routing algorithm. The router periodically runs a network layer routing algorithm, such as OSPF, and the results are stored in the routing table for rapid lookup. For example, in conventional IP forwarding, a router will map an address prefix X in its routing tables based on the "longest match" for each packet's destination address. As the packet traverses the network, each hop in turn reexamines the packet and assigns it to a next hop.

The integration of layer 3 datagram forwarding and layer 2 transport switching uses label lookups to allow more efficient packet classification, and a flurry of vendor-specific approaches appeared between 1994 and 1997, as listed above. Because these approaches were proprietary and not interoperable, the IETF formed the MPLS working group to address routing scalability, provision of more flexible routing services, improved performance, and simplified integration of layer 3 routing and packet/connection switching technologies, with the overall goal of providing a standard label-swapping architecture.

In MPLS, the ingress router first classifies the packet into an FEC based on header information and then maps the FEC to a next hop based on the routing algorithm. The assignment of a packet to an FEC is done just once, and the FEC to which the packet is assigned is encoded as a 4-byte fixed length value known as a "label." The MPLS label formats, also known as a "shim" header, are illustrated in Figure 2.1. When a packet is forwarded to its next hop, the label is sent along with it. At subsequent hops, there is no further analysis of the packet's network layer header. Rather, the label is used as an index into a table, which specifies the next hop and a new label. The old label is replaced with the new label, called "label swapping" and the packet is forwarded to its next hop.

MPLS is able to be transported over any link layer protocol, including IP, ATM, Frame Relay, and Ethernet, as also illustrated in Figure 2.1, and hence the "multiprotocol" terminology is used. We make a clear distinction here between "multiprotocol," meaning MPLS over any link layer (layer 2) technology, and "multiprotocol," meaning anything over MPLS, which is sometimes used to also include pseudowire technology carrying encapsulated ATM, Frame Relay, and Ethernet packets over an MPLS network. A router that supports MPLS is known as a "label switching router" or LSR.

Each MPLS packet has a shim header that is encapsulated between the link layer and the network layer. A virtual path identifier/virtual channel identifier (VPI/VCI) pair is a label used in ATM networks to identify bandwidth channels (or circuits). Note that even though ATM uses the VPI/VCI as the MPLS label, an MPLS shim header is still used. Conversely, even though a Frame Relay frame carries a shim header, the label is present in the data link connection identifier (DLCI). As illustrated in Figure 2.1, the MPLS header contains a label, time-to-live (TTL) field, class-of-service (CoS) field, and stack indicator. Note that the CoS field is also known as the EXP bits field, as these three bits were originally designated as EXPerimental bits. MPLS defines a fundamental separation between the grouping of packets that are to be forwarded in the same manner (i.e., the FECs), and the labels used to mark the packets. At any one node, all packets within the same FEC could be mapped onto the same locally significant label, given that they have

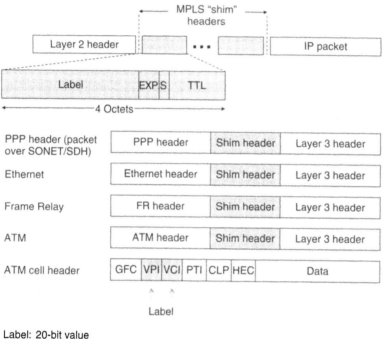

Label: 20-bit value
 EXP: 3-bits class-of-service
   S: 1-bit bottom of stack
 TTL: 8-bits time-to-live

FIGURE 2.1

MPLS "shim" header formats.

the same requirements. The assignment of a particular packet to an FEC is done once, at the entry point to the network. MPLS-capable LSRs then use only the label and CoS field to make packet forwarding and classification decisions. Label merging is possible where multiple incoming labels are to receive the same FEC.

MPLS packets are able to carry a number of labels, organized in a last-in first-out stack. This can be very useful in a number of applications, such as where two levels of routing are taking place across transit routing domains or where an MPLS-based VPN is implemented. Regardless of the existence of the hierarchy, in all instances the forwarding of a packet is based on the label at the top of the stack. In order for a packet to travel through a tunnel, the node at the transmitting side of the tunnel pushes a label relating to the tunnel onto the stack and sends the packet to the next hop in the tunnel. An ordering of LSRs defines an LSP. Two options are defined for the selection of a route for a particular forwarding class. Hop-by-hop routing defines a process where each node independently decides the next hop of the route. Explicit routing is where a single node, most often the ingress node of a path, specifies the route to be taken in terms of the LSRs in the path. Explicit routing may be used to implement traffic engineering (TE) algorithms to balance the traffic load.

There are two approaches to label path control. Independent path control means that LSRs are able to create label bindings and distribute these bindings to their peers independently. This is useful when bindings relate to information distributed by routing protocols such as OSPF. In this case, MPLS distributes labels using the label distribution protocol (LDP), where paths relate to certain routes. Ordered path control is used to ensure that a particular traffic class follows a path with a specified set of QoS properties. In this case, labels are distributed as part of the reservation protocol RSVP-TE, which allocates labels to packets of a specific flow or to an aggregated set of flows. Within the MPLS architecture, label distribution binding decisions are generally made by the downstream node, which then distributes the bindings in the upstream direction. This implies that the receiving node allocates the label. However, there are instances where upstream allocation may also be useful. In terms of the approach to state maintenance used within MPLS, a soft-state mechanism is employed, implying that labels will require refreshing to avoid time-outs. Approaches to this include the MPLS peer keep-alive mechanism and the time-out mechanisms inherent within routing and reservation protocols (in instances where they are used to carry out label distribution).

MPLS forwarding has a number of advantages over conventional network forwarding:

- can be done by traffic routers capable of label swapping but not capable of analyzing network layer headers; how an FEC is assigned can be complicated but does not affect label swapping
- an ingress router may use any information it has to determine the FEC; for example, the port on which the packet arrives (conventional forwarding can only consider information that travels with the packet in the packet header)
- a packet can be labeled differently based on the ingress router, and forwarding decisions can then depend on the ingress router (cannot be done with conventional forwarding, as the ingress router identity does not travel with the packet)
- a packet can be forced to follow an explicit path rather than being chosen by the routing algorithm to support TE
- class of service can be inferred from the label, and routers may then apply different scheduling and discard disciplines to different packets

2.2 GENERALIZED MULTIPROTOCOL LABEL SWITCHING

GMPLS is an extension of MPLS to include the packet layer as well as the transport layer, with its optical network elements. As with MPLS, the GMPLS standard focuses on both routing and signaling parts of the control plane. By providing a common control plane for packet and transport layers, GMPLS enables end-to-end, dynamic bandwidth provisioning, and optical transport networks, and thereby is a key enabler of intelligent optical networking.

Work on GMPLS is carried in the IETF under the auspices of the CCAMP working group and, to some extent, the L1 VPN working group. The charter of the IETF CCAMP working group and a list of working documents and RFCs that have been issued are listed on the CCAMP home page at *www.ietf.org/html. charters/ccamp-charter.html*. The charter of the IETF L1 VPN working group and a list of working documents and RFCs that have been issued are listed on the L1VPN home page at *www.ietf.org/html.charters/l1vpn-charter.html*.

GMPLS differs from MPLS in that it supports multiple types of transport switching, including TDM, lambda, and fiber (port) switching. Support for additional transport switching types requires GMPLS to extend MPLS, which includes how labels are requested and communicated, how errors are propagated, and other extensions. Interfaces on label switching routers can be subdivided into the following classes.

Packet Switch Capable (PSC): Interfaces that recognize packet boundaries and can forward data based on the packet header. Examples include interfaces on routers that forward data based on the IP header and the MPLS label.

Layer 2 Switch Capable (L2SC): Interfaces that recognize frame/cell boundaries and can switch data based on the frame/cell header. Examples include Ethernet bridges that switch data based on the content of the MAC header and ATM-LSRs that forward data based on the ATM VPI/VCI.

Time Division Multiplex Capable (TDM): Interfaces that switch data based on the time slot in a repeating cycle. Examples include SONET/SDH cross-connects, terminal multiplexers, or add-drop multiplexers.

Lambda Switch Capable (LSC): Interfaces that switch data based on the wavelength. Examples include optical cross-connects (OXCs) that can operate at the individual wavelength level.

Fiber-Switch Capable (FSC): Interfaces that switch data based on real-world physical spaces. Examples include an OXC that can operate at the single or multiple fiber level.

In MPLS, LSRs recognize either packet or cell boundaries and are able to process packet or cell headers. With GMPLS, non-PSC LSRs recognize neither packet nor cell boundaries and therefore cannot forward data based on the information carried in either packet or cell headers. Instead, GMPLS non-PSC LSRs include devices where the transport switching decision, in addition to packet switching decisions, is based on time slots, wavelengths, or physical ports. However, note that GMPLS PSC LSRs do recognize packet and cell boundaries and therefore can forward data based on the information carried in either packet or cell headers.

A bandwidth channel, or circuit, can be established only between, or through, interfaces of the same type. Depending on the particular technology being used for each interface, different channel names can be used (e.g., SDH circuit, optical trail, and light path). In GMPLS, all these channels are LSPs. The concept of nested LSP (LSP within LSP) in MPLS facilitates building a forwarding hierarchy of LSPs. This hierarchy of LSPs can occur on the same interface or between interfaces. For example, a hierarchy can be built if an interface is capable of multiplexing several LSPs from the same technology—for example, a lower-order SONET/SDH LSP (e.g., VT2/VC-12) nested in a higher-order SONET/SDH LSP (e.g., STS-3c/VC-4).

The nesting can also occur between interface types (e.g., at the top of the hierarchy are FSC interfaces), followed by LSC interfaces, followed by TDM interfaces, followed by L2SC interfaces, and followed by PSC interfaces. This way, an LSP that starts and ends on a PSC interface can be nested into an LSP that starts and ends on an L2SC interface, which in turn can be nested into an LSP that starts and ends on a TDM interface, which in turn can be nested into an LSP that starts and ends on an LSC interface, which in turn can be nested into an LSP that starts and ends on an FSC interface.

MPLS defines the establishment of LSPs that span only PSC or L2SC interfaces; GMPLS extends this control plane to support each of the five classes of interfaces defined above. GMPLS is based on extensions to MPLS-TE. In order to facilitate constraint-based routing of LSPs, nodes need more information about the links in the network than standard intranetwork routing protocols provide. These TE attributes are distributed using the transport mechanisms in routing protocols such as OSPF (e.g., flooding) and are taken into consideration by the LSP routing algorithm. GMPLS extends routing protocols and algorithms to carry TE link information and extends signaling protocols to carry explicit routes.

Transport technologies supported by GMPLS can have a very large number of parallel links between two adjacent nodes. For scalability purposes, multiple data links can be combined to form a single TE link, and the management of TE links can be done using the out-of-band link management protocol (LMP). LMP runs between adjacent nodes and provides mechanisms to maintain control channel connectivity, verify the physical connectivity of the data links, correlate link information, suppress downstream alarms, and localize link failures for protection/restoration purposes. Traditional IP routing requires that each link connecting two adjacent nodes must be configured and advertised. Having such a large number of parallel links does not scale well; for example, link state routing information must be flooded throughout the network.

GMPLS adapts the MPLS control plane to address this issue with the concept of link bundling and automated configuration and control with LMP. In some cases a combination of <TE link identifier, label> is sufficient to unambiguously identify the appropriate resource used by an LSP. In other cases, a combination of <TE link identifier, label> is not sufficient: for example, a TE link between a pair of

SONET/SDH cross-connects, where this TE link is composed of several fibers. In this case the label is a TDM time slot; moreover, this time slot is significant only within a particular fiber. Thus, when signaling an LSP over such a TE link, one needs to specify not just the identity of the link, but also the identity of a particular fiber within that TE link, as well as a particular label (time slot) within that fiber. Such cases are handled by using the link bundling construct, which is described in *RFC 4201*. Link bundling addresses the issues of configuration and scalability of advertisement.

GMPLS extends MPLS to control TDM, LSC, and FSC layers, as follows:

- An MPLS LSP can include a mix of links with heterogeneous label encoding (e.g., links between routers, links between routers and ATM-LSRs, and links between ATM-LSRs). GMPLS extends this by including links where the label is encoded as a time slot, a wavelength, or a position in physical space.
- An MPLS LSP that carries IP has to start and end on a router. GMPLS extends this by requiring an LSP to start and end on similar types of interfaces.
- The type of a link-layer protocol transported by a GMPLS LSP is extended to allow such payloads as SONET/SDH, G.709, 1-Gb or 10-Gb Ethernet, and so on.
- MPLS LSPs are unidirectional, and GMPLS supports the establishment of bidirectional LSPs.

Note that both MPLS and GMPLS bandwidth allocation can be performed only in discrete units, which is a function of the lower layer technology. That is, bandwidth can only be assigned in units that the physical medium can handle, and in PSC routers this is usually bytes per second; sometimes 1000s of bytes per second. At the transport layer, one could assign bandwidth, for example, in fractions of a wavelength, which could have some advantages on end-system equipment.

2.3 QOS MECHANISMS

In this section we discuss QoS mechanisms, including IntServ, DiffServ, and MPLS combined with DiffServ. We will not attempt to review queuing theory basics, as the topic is vast and there are many excellent books, papers, and other references on the topic. Some of my favorite books on the topic include those by Cooper and Kleinrock as listed in the References section at the end of this chapter. You should also consult my book on Dynamic Routing in Telecommunications Networks for some applications of queuing theory to tele-traffic-related topics, such as derivation of the Erlang B formula, Neal-Wilkinson theory, and other topics.

QoS is usually associated with hard, quantifiable metrics related to bandwidth, delay, jitter, and so on. To achieve QoS requires the definition of service classes, signaling, and connection admission control (CAC). QoS mechanisms include (a) conditioning, for example, policing, shaping, or dropping; (b) queue management, for example, random early detection (RED); (c) queue scheduling, for example, weighted fair queuing (WFQ); and (d) link-layer mechanisms.

2.3.1 Traffic Shaping and Policing Algorithms

Traffic shaping controls network traffic in order to optimize or guarantee performance, low latency, and/or bandwidth. Traffic shaping entails packet classification, queue disciplines, enforcing policies, congestion management, QoS, and fairness. It provides a mechanism to control the volume of traffic being sent into the network and the rate at which the traffic is being sent. For this reason, traffic shaping is implemented at the network edges to control the traffic entering the network. It may also be necessary to identify traffic flows that allow the traffic-shaping mechanism to shape them differently. Traffic shaping works by smoothing, or debursting, traffic flows by smoothing the peaks and troughs of data transmission. A before-and-after example of how traffic shaping works is as follows. Before traffic shaping: 10 packets in one second, 0 packets in the next second, 10 packets in the next second, 0 packets the next second. After traffic shaping: 1 packet per 0.2 s.

Shaping removes jitter at the expense of some latency. Two predominant methods for shaping traffic are the leaky-bucket and token-bucket mechanisms. Both of these algorithms have different properties and are used for different purposes. The leaky bucket imposes a hard limit on the data transmission rate, whereas the token bucket allows a certain amount of burstiness while imposing a limit on the average data transmission rate.

In contrast to traffic shaping, traffic policing is a method of marking/dropping packets in excess of the committed traffic rate and burst size. Policing may be performed at network ingress or logical policing points. Next we give an example of traffic policing.

Leaky-Bucket Algorithm

The leaky-bucket algorithm is used to control the rate at which traffic is sent to the network and provides a mechanism by which bursty traffic can be shaped to present a steady stream of traffic to the network, as opposed to traffic with erratic bursts of low-volume and high-volume flows. An analogy for the leaky bucket is a scenario in which four lanes of automobile traffic converge into a single lane. A regulated admission interval into the single lane of traffic flow helps the traffic move. The benefit of this approach is that traffic flow into the major arteries (the network) is predictable and controlled. The major liability is that when the volume of traffic is vastly greater than the bucket size, in conjunction with the drainage-time interval, traffic backs up in the bucket beyond bucket capacity and is discarded.

The algorithm is as follows:

- Arriving packets are placed in a bucket with a hole in the bottom.
- The bucket can queue at most b bytes.
- A packet that arrives when the bucket is full is discarded.
- Packets drain through the hole in the bucket into the network at a constant rate of r bytes per second, thus smoothing traffic bursts.

The size b of the bucket is limited by the available memory of the system.

The leaky bucket may use available network resources efficiently when traffic volume is low and network bandwidth is available. The leaky-bucket mechanism does not allow individual flows to burst up to port speed, effectively consuming network resources at times when there would not be resource contention in the network. The token-bucket implementation does, however, accommodate traffic flows with bursty characteristics. The leaky-bucket and token-bucket implementations can be combined to provide maximum efficiency and control of the traffic flows into a network.

Token-Bucket Algorithm

The token bucket is similar in some respects to the leaky bucket, but the primary difference is that the token bucket allows bursty traffic to continue transmitting while there are tokens in the bucket, up to a user-configurable threshold. It thereby accommodates traffic flows with bursty characteristics. The token-bucket mechanism dictates that traffic can be transmitted based on the presence of tokens in the bucket. Tokens each represent a given number of bytes, and when tokens are present, a flow is allowed to transmit traffic up to its peak burst rate if there are adequate tokens in the bucket and if the burst threshold is configured appropriately. The algorithm is as follows (assume each token = 1 byte):

- A token is added to the bucket every $1/r$ seconds.
- The bucket can hold at the most b tokens.
- If a token arrives when the bucket is full, it is discarded.
- When a packet of n bytes arrives, n tokens are removed from the bucket, and the packet is sent to the network.
- If fewer than n tokens are available, no tokens are removed from the bucket, and the packet is considered to be nonconformant.

The algorithm allows bursts of up to b bytes, but over the long run the output of conformant packets is limited to the constant rate, r. Nonconformant packets can be treated in various ways:

- Dropped
- Queued for subsequent transmission when sufficient tokens are in the bucket
- Transmitted but marked as nonconformant and possibly to be dropped subsequently if the network is overloaded

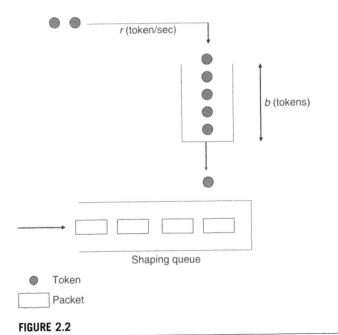

FIGURE 2.2

Token-bucket algorithm.

Policing checks conformance to a configured (or signaled) traffic profile. As illustrated in Figure 2.2, a token-bucket algorithm enforces behavior such that in-profile traffic is injected into the network and out-of-profile traffic may be marked, delayed, or discarded. The treatment of a series of packets leaving the shaping queue depends on the size of the packet and the number of bytes remaining in the conform bucket. These packets are policed based on the following rules. Tokens are updated in the conform bucket at the token arrival rate r. If the number of bytes in the conform bucket b is greater than or equal to the packet bytes p, the packet conforms and the conform action is taken on the packet. If the packet conforms, p bytes are removed from the conform bucket and the conform action is completed for the packet. If the number of bytes in the conform bucket b is fewer than p, the exceed action is taken.

For example, if the token bucket is configured with the average rate r of 1000 bytes/second and the normal burst size is 1000 bytes, if the initial token bucket starts full at 1000 bytes, and a 450-byte packet arrives, the packet conforms because enough bytes are available in the conform token bucket. The conform action (send) is taken by the packet and 450 bytes are removed from the token bucket (leaving 550 bytes). If the next packet arrives 0.25 s later, 250 bytes are added to the token bucket (0.25*1000), leaving 800 bytes in the token bucket. If the next packet is 900 bytes, the packet exceeds and the exceed action (drop) is taken. No bytes are taken from the token bucket.

2.3.2 Queue Management and Scheduling

Queue management and queue scheduling can improve on traditional FIFO queuing, which provides no service differentiation and can lead to network performance problems. QoS requires routers to support some form of queue scheduling and management to prioritize packets and control queue depth to minimize congestion. Queue management is important to prevent full queues, which are problematic because (a) new connections cannot get through, called lock-out; (b) it can lead to all packets from existing flows being dropped, resulting in across-the-board TCP slow starts (called congestive collapse); and (c) it causes inability to handle bursts of traffic.

Approaches to queue management include random early detection. As illustrated in Figure 2.3, RED monitors average queue length (*AvgLen*) and drops arriving packets with increasing probability as *AvgLen* increases. No action is taken if *AvgLen* < *MinTH*; however, all packets are dropped if *AvgLen* > *MaxTH*. Variants of RED include flow RED (FRED), which implements per-flow RED queues, and weighted RED (WRED), which provides per-class RED queues. RED is somewhat heavy handed in its sometimes over-control and should be used with caution.

Queue scheduling decides which packet to send out next and is used to manage bandwidth. There are different approaches to queue scheduling, as there are no standard mechanisms. Most router implementations provide some sort of priority queuing mechanism. Fair queuing objectives are to provide fair access to bandwidth and other resources and ensure that no one flow receives more than its fair share of resources. Fair queuing assumes that queues are serviced in a bit-by-bit round-robin fashion in which one bit is transmitted from each queue (in actuality bits are not interleaved from different queues). As illustrated in Figure 2.4, the scheduler computes when the packet would have left the router using bit-by-bit round-robin as follows:

$P(i)$ = packet length of flow i
$S(i)$ = when router begins sending packet
$F(i)$ = when router finishes sending packet
$A(i)$ = when packet arrives at router

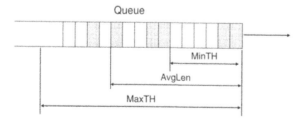

FIGURE 2.3

Queue management using random early detection.

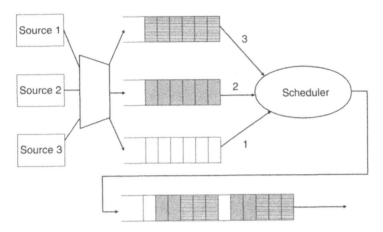

FIGURE 2.4

Weighted fair queuing.

Therefore,

$$F(i) = S(i) + P(i)$$

or

$$F(i) = \text{MAX}(F(i-1), A(i)) + P(i)$$

Each $F(i)$ (time stamp) is computed for each packet and the one with the smallest $F(i)$ value is transmitted.

Fair queuing assumes equal service for all flows, wherein each flow gets $1/N$th of bandwidth for N flows. That is, each flow has a weight = 1. Weighted fair queuing enables more than a fair share of bandwidth to be provided to a given flow based on a "weight" assigned to the flow. In WFQ, the bandwidth allocation is in proportion to the sum S of the weights of the flow sources. For example, if a flow has weight of 4 and $S = 8$, then the flow gets 4/8 or 50 percent of the bandwidth.

WFQ is work-conserving; that is, a router will always transmit packets if they are present in the queue. This means that the link is never idle as long as packets have arrived and are ready for transmission. In the example illustrated in Figure 2.4, the WFQ scheduler orders packets for departure based on the weights assigned to each source. Source 1 gets 50 percent, source 2 gets 33 percent, and source 3 gets 16.67 percent of the bandwidth. WFQ provides flow protection and can be used to bound delay.

Voice requires low latency and jitter, and queuing strategies are augmented with strict priority queues for voice. However, voice must be a small percentage of traffic or other queues will get "starved" (i.e., they will not be served adequately and will drop packets).

Link efficiency mechanisms address the problem that big packets can get in the way of small voice packets on slow speed links. To address this, big packets can be fragmented and interleaved with voice packets, which is known as link fragment interleaving. Of course, segmentation and reassembly create additional processing overhead.

2.4 INTEGRATED SERVICES

Integrated Services (IntServ) QoS mechanisms modify the basic IP model to support real-time and best-effort flows, in which a flow can be host to host or application to application. IntServ is achieved by performing admission control and installing per-flow state along the path. IntServ uses a setup protocol, the Resource Reservation Protocol (RSVP), so that applications can signal their QoS requirements into the network. IntServ/RSVP signaling maintains per-flow state in the core network, and thereby IntServ scalability has posed several challenges; however, these have been addressed by mechanisms discussed later in this section.

In the IntServ architecture, three classes of service are used based on an application's delay requirements:

- *Guaranteed-service class,* which provides for delay-bounded service agreements
- *Controlled-load service class,* which provides for a form of statistical delay service agreement (nominal mean delay) that will not be violated more often than in an unloaded network
- *Best-effort service,* which is further partitioned into three categories: interactive burst (e.g., Web), interactive bulk (e.g., FTP), and asynchronous (e.g., email)

Guaranteed service and controlled load classes are based on quantitative service requirements and both require signaling and admission control in network nodes. These services can be provided either per flow or per flow aggregate, depending on flow concentration at different points in the network. Best-effort service, on the other hand, does not require signaling. Guaranteed service is particularly well suited to the support of real-time, delay-intolerant applications. However, critical, tolerant applications and some adaptive applications can generally be efficiently supported by controlled load services. Other adaptive and elastic applications are accommodated in the best-effort service class. Because IntServ leaves the existing best-effort service class mostly unchanged (except for a further subdivision of the class), it does not involve any change to existing applications.

2.5 **RESOURCE RESERVATION PROTOCOL**

The Resource Reservation Protocol provides traffic control by supporting the following functions: (a) admission control, which determines if a QoS request can be granted; (b) packet classifier, which maps packets to a service class by looking at the contents of the IP header; and (c) packet scheduling, which forwards packets based on service class using queuing mechanisms such as WFQ. Admission control is supported by RSVP Path messages, which mark a path and deliver the path QoS information to the receiver, and Resv messages, which flow upstream to the sender and mark the QoS state. RSVP uses a "soft-state" mechanism, in which Path and Resv refresh messages flow periodically to refresh the flow state in each router.

Any continuing work on RSVP is carried in the IETF under the auspices of the TSVWG working group. The charter of the IETF TSVWG working group and a list of working documents and RFCs that have been issued are listed on the TSVWG home page at *www.ietf.org/html.charters/tsvwg-charter.html.*

RSVP is based on the concept of a session, which is composed of at least one data flow defined in relation to the 5-tuple source address, source port, destination address, destination port, and protocol id. Path messages are sent periodically toward the destination and establish a path state per flow in the routers. RESV messages are periodically sent toward the sources and establish the required reservations along the path followed by the data packets. The style of reservation in RSVP is receiver oriented, as receivers initiate the requests for resources to be reserved. Teardown messages (PathTear and ResvTear) are used for immediate release of the path state and reservations. Teardown requests can be initiated by a sender or receiver, or any intermediate RSVP router upon state time-out or service preemption.

A lifetime L is associated with each reserved resource, and the timer is reset each time an Resv message confirms the use of the resource. If the timer expires, the resource is freed. This principle of resource management based on timers is called soft state. Soft state is also applied to the path state in the routers; in this case, the timer is reset upon reception of a Path message. By default, L is 2 min 37.5 secs. Because RSVP messages are delivered unreliably and acknowledgements are not used, RSVP uses the soft state protocol mechanism to ensure reliable state information in the routers.

Although it is recognized that the support of per-flow guarantees in the core of the Internet poses severe scalability problems, various enhancements have allowed RSVP to be far more scalable than the original design. These include RSVP aggregation mechanisms and refresh reduction mechanisms. With RSVP aggregation, hosts generate normal end-to-end RSVP messages, which are ignored in the aggregated region, where routers generate aggregate RSVP messages creating single aggregate reservations from ingress to egress. The aggregate reservation should equal the sum of all the RSVP flows, and a policy dictates how often aggregated RSVP messages flow. In order to reduce RSVP overhead with refresh reduction, a bundle message reduces overall message handling load, an identifier identifies an unchanged message more readily, a message acknowledge supports reliable message delivery, and a summary refresh message enables refreshing state without the transmission of whole refresh messages.

2.6 DIFFERENTIATED SERVICES

DiffServ mechanisms use edge-based packet marking, local per-class forwarding behaviors, and resource management to support multiple service levels over an IP-based network. DiffServ terminology is as follows:

- *Per-hop behavior (PHB)*: the DiffServ treatment (scheduling/dropping) applied by a router to all the packets that are to experience the same DiffServ service
- *Differentiated services code point (DSCP)*: the value in the IP header indicating which PHB is to be applied to the packet
- *Behavior aggregate (BA)*: the set of all packets that has the same DSCP (and thus that will receive the same PHB)
- *Ordered aggregate (OA)*: the set of BAs that has an ordering constraint and must go into the same queue
- *PHB scheduling class (PSC)*: the set of PHBs applied to an OA, which uses the same queue

DSCPs in the packet header indicate how packets should be serviced at each hop and are marked at the ingress based on analysis of the packet. Intermediate routers service the packets based on the DSCPs. The DiffServ architecture specifies the DSCP format for each PHB. DiffServ is designed to be simpler and more scalable than RSVP/IntServ, as no signaling or per-flow state needs to be maintained in the core network. DiffServ requires no change to applications and is efficient for core routers, as just a few bits indicate the forwarding treatment and the complex classification work is done at the network edge. Furthermore, the network transport can be IP, ATM, Frame Relay, MPLS, or a mixture. Different packet handling services and mappings are possible, for example, the service class indicator (e.g., premium and best-effort) can indicate congestion control priority where low-priority packets are discarded first.

The DSCP was formerly the IPv4 type of service (TOS) field and IPv6 traffic class field. Six bits of the TOS byte are allocated to the DSCP, and two bits are allocated to the explicit congestion notification (ECN). DiffServ per-hop behaviors are defined as follows:

- *Default*: best effort
- *Expedited forwarding (EF)*: low delay, latency, jitter service
- *Assured forwarding (AF)*: four "relative" classes of service
- *Class selectors*: backward-compatible with IP precedence

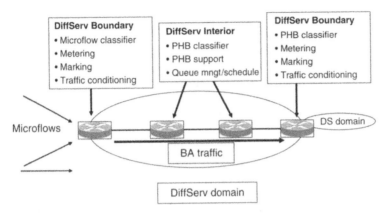

FIGURE 2.5

DiffServ processing.

As illustrated in Figure 2.5, routers at the edge of the DiffServ domain classify flows and mark packets with the DSCP. Edge route also measures traffic, compares to a traffic profile, and performs traffic conditioning (shape/drop as needed). Routers in the core of a DiffServ domain identify the PHB and implement PHB functionality by queue management/scheduling techniques.

By recognizing that most of the data flows generated by different applications can be ultimately classified into a few general categories (i.e., traffic classes), the DiffServ architecture provides simple and scalable service differentiation. It does this by discriminating and treating the data flows according to their traffic class, thus providing a logical separation of the traffic in the different classes. DiffServ achieves scalability and flexibility by following a hierarchical model for network resource management:

- *Interdomain resource management*: service levels, and hence traffic contracts, are agreed at each boundary point between a customer and a provider for the traffic entering the provider network.
- *Intradomain resource management*: the service provider is solely responsible for the configuration and provisioning of resources and policies within its network.

Therefore DiffServ is based on local service agreements at customer/provider boundaries, and end-to-end services are built by concatenating such local agreements at each domain boundary along the route to the final destination. Service providers build services with a combination of traffic classes and traffic conditioning, to ensure that traffic characteristics conform to a traffic profile and that traffic contracts are respected, and billing.

Provisioning and partitioning of both boundary and interior resources are the responsibility of the service provider and, as such, outside the scope of DiffServ.

DiffServ does not impose either the number of traffic classes or its characteristics on a service provider, and although traffic classes are nominally supported by interior routers, DiffServ does not impose any requirement on interior resources and functionalities. Traffic conditioning (metering, marking, shaping, or dropping) in the interior of a network is left to the discretion of the service providers.

The net result of the DiffServ approach is that per-flow state is avoided within the network, as individual flows are aggregated in classes. Compared with IntServ, traffic classes in DiffServ are accessible without signaling, which means they are readily available to applications without any setup delay. Consequently, traffic classes can provide qualitative or relative services to applications but not quantitative requirements. The only functionality imposed by DiffServ on interior routers is packet classification. This classification is simplified from that in RSVP because it is based on a single IP header field containing the DSCP rather than multiple fields from different headers. This has the potential of allowing functions performed on every packet, such as traffic policing or shaping, to be done at the boundaries of domains, so forwarding is the main operation performed within the network.

Simultaneously providing several services with differing qualities within the same network is a difficult task. Despite its apparent simplicity, DiffServ does not make this task any simpler. Instead, in DiffServ it was decided to keep the operating mode of the network simple by pushing as much complexity as possible onto network provisioning and configuration. Provisioning requires knowledge of traffic patterns and volumes traversing each node of the network, which also requires a good knowledge of network topology and routing. Provisioning is performed on a much slower timescale than the timescales at which traffic dynamics and network dynamics (e.g., route changes) occur, which means it is impossible to guarantee that overloading of resources will be avoided. This is caused by two factors:

1. Packets can be bound to any destination and thus may be routed toward any border router in the domain; in the worst case, a substantial proportion of the entering packets might all exit the domain through the same border router.
2. Route changes can suddenly shift vast amounts of traffic from one router to another.

Therefore, even with capacity overprovisioned at both interior and border routers, traffic and network dynamics can cause congestion and violation of service agreements. In addition, capacity overprovisioning results in a very poor statistical multiplexing gain and is therefore inefficient and expensive. Bandwidth is a class property shared by all the flows in the class, and the bandwidth received by an individual flow depends on the number of competing flows in the class as well as the fairness of their respective responses to traffic conditions in the class. Therefore, to receive some quantitative bandwidth guarantees, a flow must reserve its share of bandwidth along the data path, which involves some form of end-to-end signaling and admission control among logical entities called DiffServ band-width brokers (TQO processors). This end-to-end signaling should also track network dynamics (i.e., route changes) to enforce the guarantees, which can prove very complex.

However, delay and error rates are class properties that apply to every flow of a class. This is because in every router visited, all the packets sent in a given class share the queue devoted to that class. Consequently, as long as each router manages its queues to maintain a relative relationship between the delay and/or error rate of different classes, relative service agreements can be guaranteed without any signaling. However, if quantitative delay or error rate bounds are required, end-to-end signaling and admission control are also required. End-to-end signaling and admission control would increase the complexity of the DiffServ architecture. The idea of dynamically negotiable service agreements has also been suggested as a way of improving resource usage in the network. Such dynamic service-level agreements would require complex signaling, as the changes might affect the agreements a provider has with several neighboring networks.

Therefore in its simplest and most general form, DiffServ can efficiently provide pure relative service agreements on delay and error rates among classes. However, unless complex signaling and admission control are introduced in the DiffServ architecture or robustness is sacrificed to some extent, guarantees on bandwidth, as well as quantitative bounds on delay and error rates, cannot be provided. It should be noted that from a complexity point of view, a DiffServ scenario with dynamic provisioning and admission control is very close to an IntServ scenario with flow aggregation. The difference is that precise delay and error rate bounds might not be computed with DiffServ, as the delays and error rates introduced by each router in the domain may not be available to the DiffServ bandwidth broker/TQO processor.

DiffServ alone, therefore, does not represent the ultimate solution for QoS support for all types of applications, and combining DiffServ and IntServ capa-bilities could combine their individual advantages and mitigate some of their individual drawbacks. Figure 2.6 illustrates an approach to the integration of Diff-Serv and IntServ. RSVP messages flow end to end, which are ignored by DiffServ routers in the core of the network. Edge routers in this configuration perform both IntServ and DiffServ QoS mechanisms, while backbone routers only perform DiffServ QoS functions. An IntServ flow is tunneled through the core DiffServ domain in this configuration.

As detailed in *RFC 2998*, significant benefits can be achieved by combining IntServ and DiffServ to support dynamic provisioning and topology-aware admis-sion control, including aggregated RSVP reservations, per flow RSVP, or a DiffServ bandwidth broker/TQO processor. The advantage of using aggregated RSVP res-ervations is that it offers dynamic, topology-aware admission control over the DiffServ region without the scalability burden of per-flow reservations and the associated level of RSVP signaling in the DiffServ core. *RFC 3175* describes an architecture where multiple end-to-end RSVP reservations share the same ingress

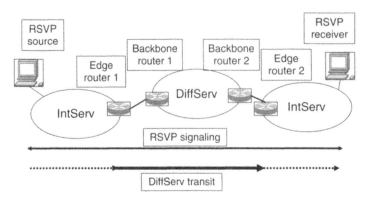

FIGURE 2.6

Integration of IntServ and DiffServ.

router (aggregator) and the same egress router (deaggregator) at the edges of an aggregation region and can be mapped onto a single aggregate reservation within the aggregation region. This considerably reduces the amount of reservation state that needs to be maintained by routers within the aggregation region. Furthermore, traffic belonging to aggregate reservations is classified in the data path purely using DiffServ marking.

2.7 MPLS-BASED QOS MECHANISMS

The DSCP field is not directly visible to an MPLS LSR, as the LSR forwards packets based only on the MPLS header and the DSCP is contained in the IP header. As such, information on DiffServ QoS treatment is made visible to the LSR using the CoS/EXP field and/or label in the MPLS header, as illustrated in Figure 2.1 and explained in the following paragraphs.

DiffServ routers forward packets to the next hop and egress interface based only on the destination IP address, which is independent of the packet's DiffServ PHB treatment. As discussed above, packet scheduling is based only on the DSCP. In contrast, MPLS routers that also implement DiffServ make a forwarding and scheduling decision based on the label and DiffServ information conveyed in the MPLS header in one of two ways:

1. *E-LSP*, where the queuing treatment and drop priority are inferred from the CoS/EXP field
2. *L-LSP*, where the queuing treatment is inferred from the label and the drop priority is inferred from the CoS/EXP field

Therefore the MPLS CoS/EXP field enables different service classes to be offered for individual labels. E-LSPs can be set up with existing, non-DiffServ-aware signaling (LDP, RSVP). The CoS/EXP bits to PHB mapping is configured on every router. However, L-LSPs require extensions to LDP and RSVP to bind the queuing treatment to the MPLS label. For more fine-grained QoS treatment, a separate label can be used for each class where, in this instance, the label would represent both the forwarding and the service classes.

More analysis of the benefits of per-flow QoS support versus aggregated per-VNET QoS support in terms of network performance, control load overhead, and capacity design implications, can be found in Chapters 3, 4, and 6, respectively, of *Traffic Engineering and QoS Optimization of Integrated Voice and Data Networks* by Gerald Ash. We conclude that the incremental benefits of per-flow QoS support, in terms of small or no improvement in performance and/or capacity design efficiencies, are not worth the significant additional control processing load such an approach would entail.

2.8 FURTHER READING

This chapter makes reference to the following sources.

Acharya, A., et al., *A Framework for IP Switching over Fast ATM Cell Transport (IPSO-FACTO)*. Conference on Broadband Networking Technology, vol. 3233, Chapter 36, 1997.

Ash, G. *Dynamic Routing in Telecommunications Networks*. McGraw-Hill, 1998.

Cooper, R. B., *Introduction to Queuing Theory*. Macmillan, 1972.

Farrel, A., *The Internet and Its Protocols: A Comparative Approach*. Morgan Kaufmann, 2004.

Farrel, A., and I. Bryskin., *GMPLS: Architecture and Applications*. Morgan Kaufmann, 2005.

Kleinrock, L. I., *Queuing Systems, Vol. I: Theory*. John Wiley & Sons, 1975.

Kleinrock, L. I., *Queuing Systems, Vol. II: Computer Applications*. John Wiley & Sons, 1976.

Newmann, P., IP Switching: ATM Under IP. *IEEE/ACM Transactions on Networking*, 6(2), 1998.

Rekhter, Y., et al., Tag Switching Architecture Overview. *Proceedings of the IEEE*, 85(12), 1997.

Viswanathan, A., Aggregate Route-Based IP Switching (ARIS). *IBM Technical Report TR29*, 2353, 1998.

IETF RFC Resources

RFC 1633, Integrated Services in the Internet Architecture: An Overview, R. Braden, D. Clark, and S. Shenker, IETF, 1994.

RFC 1990, The PPP Multilink Protocol (MP), K. Sklower et al., IETF, 1996.

RFC 2098, Toshiba's Router Architecture Extensions for ATM: Overview, Y. Katsube et al., IETF, 1998.

RFC 2205, Resource ReSerVation Protocol (RSVP)—Version 1: Functional Specification, R. Braden et al., IETF, 1997.

RFC 2207, RSVP Extensions for IPSEC Data Flows, L. Berger and T. O'Malley, IETF, 1997.

RFC 2210, The Use of RSVP with IETF Integrated Services, J. Wroclawski, IETF, 1997.

RFC 2309, Recommendations on Queue Management and Congestion Avoidance in the Internet, R. Braden et al., IETF, 1998.

RFC 2328, OSPF Version 2, J. Moy, IETF, 1998.

RFC 2474, Definition of the Differentiated Services Field (DS Field) in the IPv4 and IPv6 Headers, K. Nichols et al., IETF, 1998.

RFC 2475, An Architecture for Differentiated Services, S. Blake et al., IETF, 1998.

RFC 2597, Assured Forwarding PHB Group, J. Heinanen et al., IETF, 1999.

RFC 2702, Requirements for Traffic Engineering Over MPLS, D. Awduche et al., IETF, 1999.

RFC 2961, RSVP Refresh Overhead Reduction Extensions, L. Berger et al., IETF, 2001.

RFC 2998, A Framework for Integrated Services Operation over Diffserv Networks, Y. Bernet et al., IETF, 2000.

RFC 3031, Multiprotocol Label Switching Architecture, E. Rosen et al., IETF, 2001.

RFC 3032, MPLS Label Stack Encoding, E. Rosen et al., IETF, 2001.

RFC 3175, Aggregation of RSVP for IPv4 and IPv6 Reservations, F. Baker et al., IETF, 2001.

RFC 3209, RSVP-TE: Extensions to RSVP for LSP Tunnels, D. Awduche et al., IETF, 2001.

RFC 3246, An Expedited Forwarding PHB (Per-Hop Behavior), B. Davie et al., IETF, 2002.

RFC 3270, Multi-Protocol Label Switching (MPLS) Support of Differentiated Services, F. Le Faucheur et al., IETF, 2002.

RFC 3945, Generalized Multi-Protocol Label Switching (GMPLS) Architecture, E. Mannie et al., IETF, 2004.

RFC 4201, Link Bundling in MPLS Traffic Engineering (TE), K. Kompella, Y. Rekhter, and L. Berger, IETF, 2005.

RFC 4202, Routing Extensions in Support of Generalized Multi-Protocol Label Switching (GMPLS), K. Kompella and Y. Rekhter, IETF, 2005.

RFC 4364, BGP/MPLS IP Virtual Private Networks (VPNs), E. Rosen and Y. Rekhter, IETF, 2006.

RFC 4847, Framework and Requirements for Layer 1 Virtual Private Networks, T. Takeda et al., IETF, 2007.

RFC 5036, LDP Specification, L. Andersson et al., IETF, 2007.

RFC 5212, Requirements for GMPLS-Based Multi-Region and Multi-Layer Networks (MRN/MLN), K. Shiomoto et al., IETF, 2008.

Internet-Draft draft-ietf-ccamp-gmpls-mln-eval, Evaluation of Existing GMPLS Protocols against MultiLayer and MultiRegion Networks (MLN/MRN), J-L. Le Roux et al., IETF, 2008 (work in progress).

Quality of Service

3

This chapter, taken from Section 6.5 of Chapter 6 of *Computer Networks* (4th edition) by Larry Peterson and Bruce Davie, examines application requirements for Quality of Service with special focus on real-time applications. It goes on to describe the mechanisms developed for use in today's Internet to help meet the requirements and deliver QoS to the user.

For many years, packet-switched networks have offered the promise of supporting multimedia applications—that is, the ones that combine audio, video, and data. After all, once digitized, audio and video information becomes just another form of data—a stream of bits to be transmitted. One obstacle to the fulfillment of this promise has been the need for higher-bandwidth links. Recently, however, improvements in coding have reduced the bandwidth needs of audio and video applications, while at the same time link speeds have increased.

There is more to transmitting audio and video over a network than just providing sufficient bandwidth, however. Participants in a telephone conversation, for example, expect to be able to converse in such a way that one person can respond to something said by the other and be heard almost immediately. Thus, the timeliness of delivery can be very important. We refer to applications that are sensitive to the timeliness of data as *real-time applications*. Voice and video applications tend to be the canonical examples, but there are others such as industrial control—you would like a command sent to a robot arm to reach it before the arm crashes into something. Even file transfer applications can have timeliness constraints, such as a requirement that a database update complete overnight before the business that needs the data resumes on the next day.

The distinguishing characteristic of real-time applications is that they need some sort of assurance *from the network* that data is likely to arrive on time (for some definition of "on time"). Whereas a non-real-time application can use an end-to-end retransmission strategy to make sure that data arrives *correctly*, such a strategy cannot provide timeliness: Retransmission only adds to total latency if data arrives late. Timely arrival must be provided by the network itself (the routers), not just at the network edges (the hosts).

We therefore conclude that the best-effort model, in which the network tries to deliver your data but makes no promises and leaves the cleanup operation to the edges, is not sufficient for real-time applications. What we need is a new service model in which applications that need higher assurances can ask the network for them. The network may then respond by providing an assurance that it will do better or perhaps by saying that it cannot promise anything better at the moment. Note that such a service model is a superset of the current model: Applications that are happy with best-effort service should be able to use the new service model; their requirements are just less stringent. This implies that the network will treat some packets differently from others—something that is not done in the best-effort model. A network that can provide these different levels of service is often said to support quality of service (QoS).

3.1 APPLICATION REQUIREMENTS

Before looking at the various protocols and mechanisms that may be used to provide quality of service to applications, we should try to understand what the needs of those applications are. To begin, we can divide applications into two types: real-time and non-real-time. The latter are sometimes called "traditional data" applications, since they have traditionally been the major applications found on data networks. They include most popular applications like Telnet, FTP, email, Web browsing, and so on. All of these applications can work without guarantees of timely delivery of data. Another term for this non-real-time class of applications is *elastic*, since they are able to stretch gracefully in the face of increased delay. Note that these applications can benefit from shorter-length delays, but they do not become unusable as delays increase. Also note that their delay requirements vary from the interactive applications like Telnet to more asynchronous ones like email, with interactive bulk transfers such as FTP in the middle.

3.1.1 A Real-Time Audio Example

As a concrete example of a real-time application, consider an audio application similar to the one illustrated in Figure 3.1. Data is generated by collecting samples from a microphone and digitizing them using an analog-to-digital $(A \rightarrow D)$ converter. The digital samples are placed in packets, which are transmitted across the network and received at the other end. At the receiving host, the data must be *played back* at some appropriate rate. For example, if the voice samples were collected at a rate of one per 125 μs, they should be played back at the same rate. Thus, we can think of each sample as having a particular *playback time*: the point in time at which it is needed in the receiving host. In the voice example, each sample has a playback time that is 125 μs later than the preceding sample. If data arrives after its appropriate playback time, either because it was delayed in the network or because it was dropped and subsequently retransmitted, it is

FIGURE 3.1

Audio application.

essentially useless. It is the complete worthlessness of late data that characterizes real-time applications. In elastic applications, it might be nice if data turns up on time, but we can still use it when it does not.

One way to make our voice application work would be to make sure that all samples take exactly the same amount of time to traverse the network. Then, since samples are injected at a rate of one per 125 µs, they will appear at the receiver at the same rate, ready to be played back. However, it is generally difficult to guarantee that all data traversing a packet-switched network will experience exactly the same delay. Packets encounter queues in switches or routers and the lengths of these queues vary with time, meaning that the delays tend to vary with time, and as a consequence, are potentially different for each packet in the audio stream.

The way to deal with this at the receiver end is to buffer up some amount of data in reserve, thereby always providing a store of packets waiting to be played back at the right time. If a packet is delayed a short time, it goes in the buffer until its playback time arrives. If it gets delayed a long time, then it will not need to be stored for very long in the receiver's buffer before being played back. Thus, we have effectively added a constant offset to the playback time of all packets as a form of insurance. We call this offset the *playback point*. The only time we run into trouble is if packets get delayed in the network for such a long time that they arrive after their playback time, causing the playback buffer to be drained.

The operation of a playback buffer is illustrated in Figure 3.2. The left-hand diagonal line shows packets being generated at a steady rate. The wavy line shows when the packets arrive, some variable amount of time after they were sent, depending on what they encountered in the network. The right-hand diagonal line shows the packets being played back at a steady rate, after sitting in the playback buffer for some period of time. As long as the playback line is far enough to the right in time, the variation in network delay is never noticed by the application. However, if we move the playback line a little to the left, then some packets will begin to arrive too late to be useful.

For our audio application, there are limits to how far we can delay playing back data. It is hard to carry on a conversation if the time between when you speak and when your listener hears you is more than 300 ms. Thus, what we want from the network in this case is a guarantee that all our data will arrive within

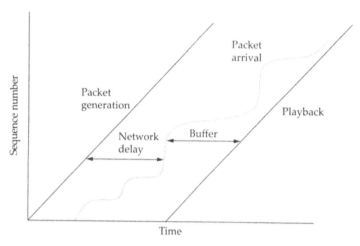

FIGURE 3.2

Playback buffer.

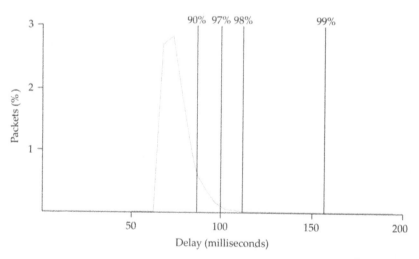

FIGURE 3.3

Example distribution of delays for an Internet connection.

300 ms. If data arrives early, we buffer it until its correct playback time. If it arrives late, we have no use for it and must discard it.

To get a better appreciation of how variable network delay can be, Figure 3.3 shows the one-way delay measured over a certain path across the Internet over the course of one particular day. While the exact numbers would vary depending on the path and the date, the key factor here is the *variability* of the delay, which is consistently found on almost any path at any time. As denoted by the cumulative percentages given across the top of the graph, 97 percent of the packets in this case had a latency of 100 ms or less. This means that if our example audio application were to set the playback point at 100 ms, then on average, 3 out of every 100 packets would arrive too late to be of any use. One important thing to notice about this graph is that the tail of the curve—how far it extends to the right—is very long. We would have to set the playback point at over 200 ms to ensure that all packets arrived in time.

3.1.2 Taxonomy of Real-Time Applications

Now that we have a concrete idea of how real-time applications work, we can look at some different classes of applications, which serve to motivate our service model. The following taxonomy owes much to the work of Clark, Braden, Shenker, and Zhang (1992), whose papers on this subject can be found in the Further Reading section at the end of this chapter. The taxonomy of applications is summarized in Figure 3.4.

The first characteristic by which we can categorize applications is their tolerance of loss of data, where "loss" might occur because a packet arrived too late to be played back as well as arising from the usual causes in the network.

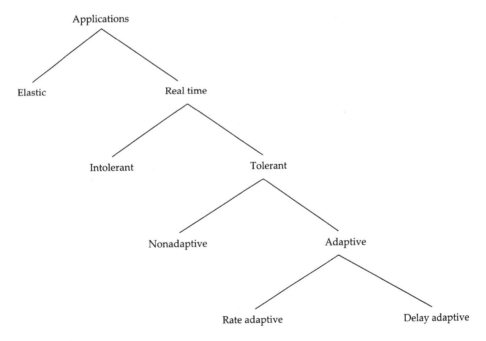

FIGURE 3.4

Taxonomy of applications.

On the one hand, one lost audio sample can be interpolated from the surrounding samples with relatively little effect on the perceived audio quality. It is only as more and more samples are lost that quality declines to the point that the speech becomes incomprehensible. On the other hand, a robot control program is likely to be an example of a real-time application that cannot tolerate loss—losing the packet that contains the command instructing the robot arm to stop is unacceptable. Thus, we can categorize real-time applications as *tolerant* or *intolerant* depending on whether they can tolerate occasional loss. (As an aside, note that many real-time applications are more tolerant of occasional loss than non-real-time applications. For example, compare our audio application to FTP, where the uncorrected loss of one bit might render a file completely useless.)

A second way to characterize real-time applications is by their adaptability. For example, an audio application might be able to adapt to the amount of delay that packets experience as they traverse the network. If we notice that packets are almost always arriving within 300 ms of being sent, then we can set our playback point accordingly, buffering any packets that arrive in less than 300 ms. Suppose that we subsequently observe that all packets are arriving within 100 ms of being sent. If we moved up our playback point to 100 ms, then the users of the application would probably perceive an improvement.

The process of shifting the playback point would actually require us to play out samples at an increased rate for some period of time. With a voice application, this can be done in a way that is barely perceptible simply by shortening the silences between words. Thus, playback point adjustment is fairly easy in this case, and it has been effectively implemented for several voice applications such as the audio teleconferencing program known as vat. Note that playback point adjustment can happen in either direction, but that doing so actually involves distorting the played-back signal during the period of adjustment, and that the effects of this distortion will very much depend on how the end user uses the data.

Observe that if we set our playback point on the assumption that all packets will arrive within 100 ms and then find that some packets are arriving slightly late, we will have to drop them, whereas we would not have had to drop them if we had left the playback point at 300 ms. Thus, we should advance the playback point only when it provides a perceptible advantage and only when we have some evidence that the number of late packets will be acceptably small. We may do this because of observed recent history or because of some assurance from the network.

We call applications that can adjust their playback point *delay-adaptive* applications. Another class of adaptive applications are *rate adaptive*. For example, many video coding algorithms can trade-off bit rate versus quality. Thus, if we find that the network can support a certain bandwidth, we can set our coding parameters accordingly. If more bandwidth becomes available later, we can change parameters to increase the quality.

3.1.3 **Approaches to QoS Support**

Considering this rich space of application requirements, what we need is a richer service model that meets the needs of any application. This leads us to a service model with not just one class (best effort), but with several classes, each available to meet the needs of some set of applications. Toward this end, we are now ready to look at some of the approaches that have been developed to provide a range of qualities of service. These can be divided into two broad categories:

- *Fine-grained* approaches, which provide QoS to individual applications or flows
- *Coarse-grained* approaches, which provide QoS to large classes of data or aggregated traffic

In the first category we find Integrated Services, a quality-of-service architecture developed by the Internet Engineering Task Force (IETF) and often associated with the Resource Reservation Protocol (RSVP). ATM's approach to QoS was also in this category. In the second category lies Differentiated Services, which is probably the most widely deployed QoS mechanism. These in turn are discussed in the next two subsections.

Finally, adding QoS support to the network isn't necessarily the entire story about supporting real-time applications. We conclude our discussion by revisiting what the end host might do to better support real-time streams, independent of how widely deployed QoS mechanisms like Integrated or Differentiated Services become.

3.2 **INTEGRATED SERVICES AND RSVP**

The term *Integrated Services* (often called IntServ for short) refers to a body of work that was produced by the IETF around 1995–1997. The IntServ working group developed specifications of a number of *service classes* designed to meet the needs of some of the application types described earlier. It also defined how RSVP could be used to make reservations using these service classes. The following paragraphs provide an overview of these specifications and the mechanisms that are used to implement them.

3.2.1 **Service Classes**

One of the service classes is designed for intolerant applications. These applications require that a packet never arrive late. The network should guarantee that the maximum delay any packet will experience has some specified value; the application can then set its playback point so that no packet will ever arrive after its playback time. The assumption is that early arrival of packets can always be handled by buffering. This service is referred to as the *guaranteed* service.

In addition to the guaranteed service, the IETF considered several other services, but eventually settled on one to meet the needs of tolerant, adaptive applications. The service is known as *controlled load* and was motivated by the observation that existing applications of this type run quite well on networks that are not heavily loaded. The audio application vat, for example, adjusts its playback point as network delay varies, and produces reasonable audio quality as long as loss rates remain on the order of 10 percent or less.

The aim of the controlled load service is to emulate a lightly loaded network for those applications that request the service, even though the network as a whole may in fact be heavily loaded. The trick to this is to use a queuing mechanism such as weighted fair queuing (WFQ) to isolate the controlled load traffic from the other traffic, and some form of admission control to limit the total amount of controlled load traffic on a link such that the load is kept reasonably low. We discuss admission control in more detail later.

Clearly, these two service classes are a subset of all the classes that might be provided. It remains to be seen as Integrated Services are deployed whether these two are adequate to meet the needs of all the application types described earlier.

3.2.2 Overview of Mechanisms

Now that we have augmented our best-effort service model with some new service classes, the next question is how we implement a network that provides these services to applications. This section outlines the key mechanisms. Keep in mind while reading this section that the mechanisms being described are still being hammered out by the Internet design community. The main thing to take away from the discussion is a general understanding of the pieces involved in supporting the service model outlined earlier.

First, whereas with a best-effort service we can just tell the network where we want our packets to go and leave it at that, a real-time service involves telling the network something more about the type of service we require. We may give it qualitative information such as "use a controlled load service," or quantitative information such as "I need a maximum delay of 100 ms." In addition to describing what we want, we need to tell the network something about what we are going to inject into it, since a low-bandwidth application is going to require fewer network resources than a high-bandwidth application. The set of information that we provide to the network is referred to as a *flowspec*. This name comes from the idea that a set of packets associated with a single application and that share common requirements is called a *flow*.

Second, when we ask the network to provide us with a particular service, the network needs to decide if it can in fact provide that service. For example, if 10 users ask for a service in which each will consistently use 2 Mbps of link capacity, and they all share a link with 10-Mbps capacity, the network will have to say no to some of them. The process of deciding when to say no is called *admission control*.

Third, we need a mechanism by which the users of the network and the components of the network itself exchange information such as requests for service, flowspecs, and admission control decisions. This is sometimes called *signaling*, but since that word has several meanings, we refer to this process as *resource reservation*, and it is achieved using a resource reservation protocol.

Lastly, when flows and their requirements have been described, and admission control decisions have been made, the network switches and routers need to meet the requirements of the flows. A key part of meeting these requirements is managing the way packets are queued and scheduled for transmission in the switches and routers. This last mechanism is *packet scheduling*.

3.2.3 Flowspecs

There are two separable parts to the flowspec: the part that describes the flow's traffic characteristics (called the *TSpec*) and the part that describes the service requested from the network (the *RSpec*). The RSpec is very service-specific and relatively easy to describe. For example, with a controlled load service, the RSpec is trivial: The application just requests controlled load service with no additional parameters. With a guaranteed service, you could specify a delay target or bound. (In the IETF's guaranteed service specification, you specify not a delay but another quantity from which delay can be calculated.)

The TSpec is a little more complicated. As our previous example showed, we need to give the network enough information about the bandwidth used by the flow to allow intelligent admission control decisions to be made. For most applications, however, the bandwidth is not a single number; it is something that varies constantly. A video application, for example, will generally generate more bits per second when the scene is changing rapidly than when it is still. Just knowing the long-term average bandwidth is not enough, as the following example illustrates.

Suppose that we have 10 flows that arrive at a switch on separate input ports and that all leave on the same 10-Mbps link. Assume that over some suitably long interval each flow can be expected to send no more than 1 Mbps. You might think this presents no problem. However, if these are variable bit rate applications, such as compressed video, then they will occasionally send more than their average rates. If enough sources send at above their average rates, then the total rate at which data arrives at the switch will be greater than 10 Mbps. This excess data will be queued before it can be sent on the link. The longer this condition persists, the longer the queue will get. Packets might have to be dropped, and even if it doesn't come to that, data sitting in the queue is being delayed. If packets are delayed long enough, the service that was requested will not be provided.

Exactly how we manage our queues to control delay and avoid dropping packets is something we discuss later. However, note here that we need to know something about how the bandwidth of our sources varies with time. One way to describe the bandwidth characteristics of sources is called a *token-bucket* filter.

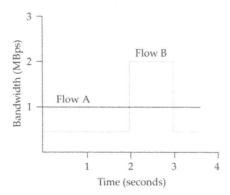

FIGURE 3.5

Two flows with equal average rates but different token-bucket descriptions.

Such a filter is described by two parameters: a token rate r, and a bucket depth B. It works as follows. To be able to send a byte, I must have a token. To send a packet of length n, I need n tokens. I start with no tokens and I accumulate them at a rate of r per second. I can accumulate no more than B tokens. What this means is that I can send a burst of as many as B bytes into the network as fast as I want, but over a sufficiently long interval, I can't send more than r bytes per second. It turns out that this information is very helpful to the admission control algorithm when it tries to figure out whether it can accommodate a new request for service.

Figure 3.5 illustrates how a token bucket can be used to characterize a flow's bandwidth requirements. For simplicity, assume that each flow can send data as individual bytes rather than as packets. Flow A generates data at a steady rate of 1 MBps, so it can be described by a token-bucket filter with a rate $r = 1$ MBps and a bucket depth of 1 byte. This means that it receives tokens at a rate of 1 MBps but that it cannot store more than 1 token—it spends them immediately. Flow B also sends at a rate that averages out to 1 MBps over the long term, but does so by sending at 0.5 MBps for 2 seconds and then at 2 MBps for 1 second. Since the token-bucket rate r is, in a sense, a long-term average rate, flow B can be described by a token bucket with a rate of 1 MBps. Unlike flow A, however, flow B needs a bucket depth B of at least 1 MB, so that it can store up tokens while it sends at less than 1 MBps to be used when it sends at 2 MBps. For the first 2 seconds in this example, it receives tokens at a rate of 1 MBps but spends them at only 0.5 MBps, so it can save up $2 \times 0.5 = 1$ MB of tokens, which it then spends in the third second (along with the new tokens that continue to accrue in that second) to send data at 2 MBps. At the end of the third second, having spent the excess tokens, it starts to save them up again by sending at 0.5 MBps again.

It is interesting to note that a single flow can be described by many different token buckets. As a trivial example, flow A could be described by the same token bucket as flow B, with a rate of 1 MBps and a bucket depth of 1 MB. The fact that it never actually needs to accumulate tokens does not make that an inaccurate description, but it does mean that we have failed to convey some useful information to the network—the fact that flow A is actually very consistent in its bandwidth needs. In general, it is good to be as explicit about the bandwidth needs of an application as possible, to avoid over-allocation of resources in the network.

3.2.4 Admission Control

The idea behind admission control is simple: When some new flow wants to receive a particular level of service, admission control looks at the TSpec and RSpec of the flow and tries to decide if the desired service can be provided to that amount of traffic, given the currently available resources, without causing any previously admitted flow to receive worse service than it had requested. If it can provide the service, the flow is admitted; if not, it is denied. The hard part is figuring out when to say yes and when to say no.

Admission control is very dependent on the type of requested service and on the queuing discipline employed in the routers; we discuss the latter topic later in this section. For a guaranteed service, you need to have a good algorithm to make a definitive yes/no decision. The decision is fairly straightforward if weighted fair queuing is used at each router. For a controlled load service, the decision may be based on heuristics, such as "The last time I allowed a flow with this TSpec into this class, the delays for the class exceeded the acceptable bound, so I'd better say no," or "My current delays are so far inside the bounds that I should be able to admit another flow without difficulty."

Admission control should not be confused with *policing*. The former is a per-flow decision to admit a new flow or not. The latter is a function applied on a per-packet basis to make sure that a flow conforms to the TSpec that was used to make the reservation. If a flow does not conform to its TSpec—for example, because it is sending twice as many bytes per second as it said it would—then it is likely to interfere with the service provided to other flows, and some corrective action must be taken. There are several options, the obvious one being to drop offending packets. However, another option would be to check if the packets really are interfering with the service of other flows. If they are not interfering, the packets could be sent on after being marked with a tag that says, in effect, "This is a nonconforming packet. Drop it first if you need to drop any packets."

Admission control is closely related to the important issue of *policy*. For example, a network administrator might wish to allow reservations made by his or her company's CEO to be admitted while rejecting reservations made by more lowly employees. Of course, the CEO's reservation request might still fail if the requested resources aren't available, so we see that issues of policy and resource availability may both be addressed when admission control decisions are made. The application of policy to networking is an area that has received much attention.

3.2.5 **Reservation Protocol**

While connection-oriented networks have always needed some sort of setup protocol to establish the necessary virtual circuit state in the switches, connectionless networks like the Internet have had no such protocols. As this section has indicated, however, we need to provide a lot more information to our network when we want a real-time service from it. While there have been a number of setup protocols proposed for the Internet, the one on which most current attention is focused is called the Resource Reservation Protocol. It is particularly interesting because it differs so substantially from conventional signaling protocols for connection-oriented networks.

One of the key assumptions underlying RSVP is that it should not detract from the robustness that we find in today's connectionless networks. Because connectionless networks rely on little or no state being stored in the network itself, it is possible for routers to crash and reboot and for links to go up and down while end-to-end connectivity is still maintained. RSVP tries to maintain this robustness by using the idea of *soft state* in the routers. Soft state—in contrast to the hard state found in connection-oriented networks—does not need to be explicitly deleted when it is no longer needed. Instead, it times out after some fairly short period (say, a minute) if it is not periodically refreshed. We will see later how this helps robustness.

Another important characteristic of RSVP is that it aims to support multicast flows just as effectively as unicast flows. This is not surprising, since many of the first applications that could benefit from improved quality of service were also multicast applications—vat and vic, for example. One of the insights of RSVP's designers is that most multicast applications have many more receivers than senders, as typified by the large audience and one speaker for a lecture. Also, receivers may have different requirements. For example, one receiver might want to receive data from only one sender, while others might wish to receive data from all senders. Rather than having the senders keep track of a potentially large number of receivers, it makes more sense to let the receivers keep track of their own needs. This suggests the *receiver-oriented* approach adopted by RSVP. In contrast, connection-oriented networks usually leave resource reservation to the sender, just as it is normally the originator of a phone call who causes resources to be allocated in the phone network.

The soft state and receiver-oriented nature of RSVP give it a number of nice properties. One of these is that it is very straightforward to increase or decrease the level of resource allocation provided to a receiver. Since each receiver periodically sends refresh messages to keep the soft state in place, it is easy to send a new reservation that asks for a new level of resources. In the event of a host crash, resources allocated by that host to a flow will naturally time out and be released. To see what happens in the event of a router or link failure, we need to look a little more closely at the mechanics of making a reservation.

Initially, consider the case of one sender and one receiver trying to get a reservation for traffic flowing between them. There are two things that need to happen before a receiver can make the reservation. First, the receiver needs to know what traffic the sender is likely to send so that it can make an appropriate reservation. That is, it needs to know the sender's TSpec. Second, it needs to know what path the packets will follow from sender to receiver, so that it can establish a resource reservation at each router on the path. Both of these requirements can be met by sending a message from the sender to the receiver that contains the TSpec. Obviously, this gets the TSpec to the receiver.

The other thing that happens is that each router looks at this message (called a Path message) as it goes past, and it figures out the *reverse path* that will be used to send reservations from the receiver back to the sender in an effort to get the reservation to each router on the path. Building the multicast tree in the first place is done by mechanisms such as multicast extensions to existing link-state and distance-vector routing protocols, or through new routing protocols specifically formulated to support multicast distribution.

Having received a Path message, the receiver sends a reservation back "up" the multicast tree in an Resv message. This message contains the sender's TSpec and an RSpec describing the requirements of this receiver. Each router on the path looks at the reservation request and tries to allocate the necessary resources to satisfy it. If the reservation can be made, the Resv request is passed on to the next router. If not, an error message is returned to the receiver who made the request. If all goes well, the correct reservation is installed at every router between the sender and the receiver. As long as the receiver wants to retain the reservation, it sends the same RESV message about once every 30 seconds.

Now we can see what happens when a router or link fails. Routing protocols will adapt to the failure and create a new path from sender to receiver. Path messages are sent about every 30 seconds, and may be sent sooner if a router detects a change in its forwarding table, so the first one after the new route stabilizes will reach the receiver over the new path. The receiver's next Resv message will follow the new path and (hopefully) establish a new reservation on the new path. Meanwhile, the routers that are no longer on the path will stop getting Resv messages, and these reservations will time out and be released. Thus, RSVP deals quite well with changes in topology, as long as routing changes are not excessively frequent.

The next thing we need to consider is how to cope with multicast, where there may be multiple senders to a group and multiple receivers. This situation is illustrated in Figure 3.6. First, let's deal with multiple receivers for a single sender. As an Resv message travels up the multicast tree, it is likely to hit a piece of the tree where some other receiver's reservation has already been established. It may be the case that the resources reserved upstream of this point are adequate to serve both receivers. For example, if receiver A has already made a reservation that provides for a guaranteed delay of less than 100 ms, and the new request

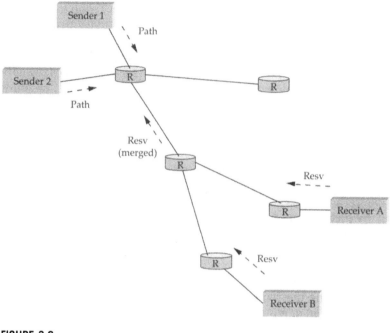

FIGURE 3.6

Making reservations on a multicast tree.

from receiver B is for a delay of less than 200 ms, then no new reservation is required. On the other hand, if the new request were for a delay of less than 50 ms, then the router would first need to see if it could accept the request, and if so, it would send the request on upstream. The next time receiver A asked for a minimum of a 100-ms delay, the router would not need to pass this request on. In general, reservations can be merged in this way to meet the needs of all receivers downstream of the merge point.

If there are also multiple senders in the tree, receivers need to collect the TSpecs from all senders and make a reservation that is large enough to accommodate the traffic from all senders. However, this may not mean that the TSpecs need to be added up. For example, in an audio conference with 10 speakers, there is not much point in allocating enough resources to carry 10 audio streams, since the result of 10 people speaking at once would be incomprehensible. Thus, we could imagine a reservation that is large enough to accommodate two speakers and no more. Calculating the correct overall TSpec from all the sender TSpecs is clearly application-specific. Also, we may only be interested in hearing from a subset of all possible speakers; RSVP has different reservation "styles" to deal with such options as "Reserve resources for all speakers," "Reserve resources for any *n* speakers," and "Reserve resources for speakers A and B only."

3.2.6 **Packet Classifying and Scheduling**

Once we have described our traffic and our desired network service and have installed a suitable reservation at all the routers on the path, the only thing that remains is for the routers to actually deliver the requested service to the data packets. There are two things that need to be done:

- Associate each packet with the appropriate reservation so that it can be handled correctly, a process known as *classifying* packets.
- Manage the packets in the queues so that they receive the service that has been requested, a process known as packet *scheduling*.

The first part is done by examining up to five fields in the packet: the source address, destination address, protocol number, source port, and destination port. (In IPv6, it is possible that the FlowLabel field in the header could be used to enable the lookup to be done based on a single, shorter key.) Based on this information, the packet can be placed in the appropriate class. For example, it may be classified into the controlled load classes, or it may be part of a guaranteed flow that needs to be handled separately from all other guaranteed flows. In short, there is a mapping from the flow-specific information in the packet header to a single class identifier that determines how the packet is handled in the queue. For guaranteed flows, this might be a one-to-one mapping, while for other services, it might be many to one. The details of classification are closely related to the details of queue management.

It should be clear that something as simple as a first-in, first-out (FIFO) queue in a router will be inadequate to provide many different services and to provide different levels of delay within each service. Several more sophisticated queue management disciplines exist, and some combination of these is likely to be used in a router.

The details of packet scheduling ideally should not be specified in the service model. Instead, this is an area where implementers can try to do creative things to realize the service model efficiently. In the case of guaranteed service, it has been established that a weighted fair queuing discipline, in which each flow gets its own individual queue with a certain share of the link, will provide a guaranteed end-to-end delay bound that can be readily calculated. For controlled load, simpler schemes may be used. One possibility includes treating all the controlled load traffic as a single, aggregated flow (as far as the scheduling mechanism is concerned), with the weight for that flow being set based on the total amount of traffic admitted in the controlled load class. The problem is made harder when you consider that in a single router, many different services are likely to be provided concurrently, and that each of these services may require a different scheduling algorithm. Thus, some overall queue management algorithm is needed to manage the resources between the different services.

3.2.7 **Scalability Issues**

While the Integrated Services architecture and RSVP represented a significant enhancement of the best-effort service model of IP, many Internet service providers felt that it was not the right model for them to deploy. The reason for this reticence relates to one of the fundamental design goals of IP: scalability. In the best-effort service model, routers in the Internet store little or no state about the individual flows passing through them. Thus, as the Internet grows, the only thing routers have to do to keep up with that growth is to move more bits per second and to deal with larger routing tables. But RSVP raises the possibility that every flow passing through a router might have a corresponding reservation. To understand the severity of this problem, suppose that every flow on an OC-48 (2.5-Gbps) link represents a 64-Kbps audio stream. The number of such flows is

$$2.5 \times 10^9 / 64 \times 10^3 = 39,000$$

Each of those reservations needs some amount of state that needs to be stored in memory and refreshed periodically. The router needs to classify, police, and queue each of those flows. Admission control decisions need to be made every time such a flow requests a reservation. And some mechanisms are needed to "push back" on users so that they don't make arbitrarily large reservations for long periods of time. (For example, charging per reservation would be one way to push back, consistent with the telephony model of billing for each phone call. This is not the only way to push back, and per-call billing is believed to be one of the major costs of operating the phone network.) These scalability concerns have, at the time of writing, prevented the widespread deployment of IntServ. Because of these concerns, other approaches that do not require so much per-flow state have been developed. The next section discusses a number of such approaches.

3.2.8 RSVP and IntServ Deployment

RSVP and the Integrated Services architecture have, at the time of writing, not been very widely deployed, in large part because of scalability concerns described at the end of this section. In fact, it is common to assert that they are "dead" as technologies. However, it may be premature to write the obituaries for RSVP and integrated services just yet.

Separated from IntServ, RSVP has been quite widely deployed as a protocol for establishing MPLS paths for the purposes of traffic engineering. For this reason alone, most routers in the Internet have some sort of RSVP implementation. However, that is probably the full extent of RSVP deployment in the Internet at the time of writing. This usage of RSVP is largely independent of IntServ, but it does at least demonstrate that the protocol itself is deployable.

There is some evidence that RSVP and IntServ may get a second chance more than 10 years after they were first proposed. For example, the IETF is standardizing extensions to RSVP to support aggregate reservations—extensions that directly address the scalability concerns that have been raised about RSVP and IntServ in the past. And there is increasing support for RSVP as a resource reservation protocol in commercial products.

Various factors can be identified that may lead to greater adoption of RSVP and IntServ in the near future. First, applications that actually require QoS, such as voice over IP and real-time video conferencing, are much more widespread than they were 10 years ago, creating a greater demand for sophisticated QoS mechanisms. Second, admission control—which enables the network to say "no" to an application when resources are scarce—is a good match to applications that cannot work well unless sufficient resources are available. Most users of IP telephones, for example, would prefer to get a busy signal from the network than to have a call proceed at unacceptably bad quality. And a network operator would prefer to send a busy signal to one user than to provide bad quality to a large number of users. A third factor is the large resource requirements of new applications such as high-definition video delivery: because they need so much bandwidth to work well, it may be more cost-effective to build networks that can say "no" occasionally than to provide enough bandwidth to meet all possible application demands. However this is a complex trade-off and the debate over the value of admission control, and RSVP and IntServ as tools to provide it, is likely to continue for some time.

3.3 DIFFERENTIATED SERVICES—EF AND AF

Whereas the Integrated Services architecture allocates resources to individual flows, the Differentiated Services model (often called DiffServ for short) allocates resources to a small number of classes of traffic. In fact, some proposed approaches to DiffServ simply divide traffic into two classes. This is an eminently sensible approach to take: If you consider the difficulty that network operators experience just trying to keep a best-effort Internet running smoothly, it makes sense to add to the service model in small increments.

Suppose that we have decided to enhance the best-effort service model by adding just one new class, which we'll call "premium." Clearly we will need some way to figure out which packets are premium and which are regular old best-effort. Rather than using a protocol like RSVP to tell all the routers that some flow is sending premium packets, it would be much easier if the packets could just identify themselves to the router when they arrive. This could obviously be done by using a bit in the packet header—if that bit is a 1, the packet is a premium packet; if it's a 0, the packet is best-effort. With this in mind, there are two questions we need to address:

- Who sets the premium bit, and under what circumstances?
- What does a router do differently when it sees a packet with the bit set?

There are many possible answers to the first question, but a common approach is to set the bit at an administrative boundary. For example, the router at the edge of an Internet service provider's network might set the bit for packets arriving on an interface that connects to a particular company's network. The ISP might do this because that company has paid for a higher level of service than best-effort. It is also possible that not all packets would be marked as premium; for example, the router might be configured to mark packets as premium up to some maximum rate, and to leave all excess packets as best-effort.

Assuming that packets have been marked in some way, what do the routers that encounter marked packets do with them? Here again there are many answers. In fact, the IETF standardized a set of router behaviors to be applied to marked packets. These are called *per-hop behaviors* (PHBs), a term that indicates that they define the behavior of individual routers rather than end-to-end services. Because there is more than one new behavior, there is also a need for more than 1 bit in the packet header to tell the routers which behavior to apply. The IETF decided to take the old type-of-service (TOS) byte from the IP header, which had not been widely used, and redefine it. Six bits of this byte have been allocated for DiffServ code points (DSCP), where each DSCP is a 6-bit value that identifies a particular PHB to be applied to a packet.

3.3.1 Expedited Forwarding PHB

One of the simplest PHBs to explain is known as *expedited forwarding* (EF). Packets marked for EF treatment should be forwarded by the router with minimal delay and loss. The only way that a router can guarantee this to all EF packets is if the arrival rate of EF packets at the router is strictly limited to be less than the rate at which the router can forward EF packets. For example, a router with a 100-Mbps interface needs to be sure that the arrival rate of EF packets destined for that interface never exceeds 100 Mbps. It might also want to be sure that the rate will be somewhat below 100 Mbps, so that it occasionally has time to send other packets such as routing updates.

The rate limiting of EF packets is achieved by configuring the routers at the edge of an administrative domain to allow a certain maximum rate of EF packet arrivals into the domain. A simple, albeit conservative, approach would be to ensure that the sum of the rates of all EF packets entering the domain is less than the bandwidth of the slowest link in the domain. This would ensure that, even in the worst case where all EF packets converge on the slowest link, it is not over-loaded and can provide the correct behavior.

There are several possible implementation strategies for the EF behavior. One is to give EF packets strict priority over all other packets. Another is to perform weighted fair queuing between EF packets and other packets, with the weight of EF set sufficiently high that all EF packets can be delivered quickly. This has an advantage over strict priority: The non-EF packets can be assured of getting some access to the link, even if the amount of EF traffic is excessive. This might mean that the EF packets fail to get exactly the specified behavior, but it could also prevent essential routing traffic from being locked out of the network in the event of an excessive load of EF traffic.

3.3.2 **The Quiet Success of DiffServ**

As recently as 2003, many people were ready to declare that DiffServ was dead. At that year's ACM SIGCOMM conference, one of the most prestigious networking research conferences, a workshop with the provocative title "RIPQoS" was held—the official name of the workshop was "Revisiting IP QoS" but the implication that QoS might be ready to rest in peace was clear in the workshop announcement. However, just as Mark Twain quipped that reports of his death were greatly exaggerated, it seems that the demise of IP QoS, and DiffServ in particular, was also overstated.

Much of the pessimism about DiffServ arose from the fact that it had not been deployed to any significant extent by Internet service providers. Not only that, but the fact that real-time applications such as IP telephony and video streaming appear to be working so well over the Internet without any QoS mechanisms in place makes one wonder if any QoS will ever be needed. In part this is the result of aggressive deployment of high-bandwidth links and routers by many ISPs, especially during the "boom" years of the late 1990s.

To see where DiffServ has succeeded, you need to look outside the ISP backbones. For example, corporations that have deployed IP telephony solutions—and there are over ten million "enterprise class" IP phones in use at the time of writing—routinely use "EF" behavior for the voice media packets to ensure that they are not delayed when sharing links with other traffic. The same holds for many residential voice over IP solutions: Just to get priority on the upstream link out of the residence (e.g., the "slow" direction of a DSL link), it is common for the voice endpoint to set the DSCP to EF, and for a consumer's router connected to the broadband link to use DiffServ to give low latency and jitter to those packets. There are even some large national telephone companies that have migrated their traditional voice services onto IP networks, with DiffServ providing the means to protect the QoS of the voice.

There are other applications beside voice that are benefiting from DiffServ, notably business data services. And no doubt the maturing of IP-based video in the coming years will provide another driver. In general, two factors make DiffServ deployment worthwhile: a high demand for QoS assurance from the application, and a lack of assurance that the link bandwidth will be sufficient to deliver that QoS to *all* the traffic traversing the link. It is important to realize that DiffServ, like any other QoS mechanism, cannot create bandwidth—all it can do is ensure that what bandwidth there is gets preferentially allocated to the applications that have more demanding QoS needs.

3.3.3 **Assured Forwarding PHB**

The *assured forwarding* (AF) PHB has its roots in an approach known as "RED with In and Out" (RIO) or "Weighted RED," both of which are enhancements to the basic RED algorithm. Figure 3.7 shows how RIO works; we see drop

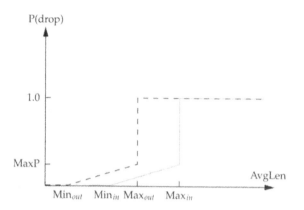

FIGURE 3.7

RED with "in" and "out" drop probabilities.

probability on the y-axis increasing as average queue length increases along the x-axis. For our two classes of traffic, we have two separate drop probability curves. RIO calls the two classes "in" and "out" for reasons that will become clear shortly. Because the "out" curve has a lower MinThreshold than the "in" curve, it is clear that, under low levels of congestion, only packets marked "out" will be discarded by the RED algorithm. If the congestion becomes more serious, a higher percentage of "out" packets are dropped, and then if the average queue length exceeds Min_{in}, RED starts to drop "in" packets as well.

The reason for calling the two classes of packets "in" and "out" stems from the way the packets are marked. We already noted that packet marking can be performed by a router at the edge of an administrative domain. We can think of this router as being at the boundary between a network service provider and some customer of that network. The customer might be any other network, for example, the network of a corporation or of another network service provider. The customer and the network service provider agree on some sort of profile for the assured service (and perhaps the customer pays the network service provider for this profile). The profile might be something like "Customer X is allowed to send up to y Mbps of assured traffic," or it could be significantly more complex. Whatever the profile is, the edge router can clearly mark the packets that arrive from this customer as being either in or out of profile. In the example just mentioned, as long as the customer sends less than y Mbps, all his packets will be marked "in," but once he exceeds that rate, the excess packets will be marked "out."

The combination of a profile meter at the edge and RIO in all the routers of the service provider's network should provide the customer with a high assurance (but not a guarantee) that packets within his profile can be delivered. In particular, if the majority of packets, including those sent by customers who have not paid extra to establish a profile, are "out" packets, then it should usually be the case that the RIO mechanism will act to keep congestion low enough that "in" packets are rarely dropped. Clearly, there must be enough bandwidth in the network so that the "in" packets alone are rarely able to congest a link to the point where RIO starts dropping "in" packets.

Just like RED, the effectiveness of a mechanism like RIO depends to some extent on correct parameter choices, and there are considerably more parameters to set for RIO. Exactly how well the scheme will work in production networks is not known at the time of writing.

One interesting property of RIO is that it does not change the order of "in" and "out" packets. For example, if a TCP connection is sending packets through a profile meter, and some packets are being marked "in" while others are marked "out," those packets will receive different drop probabilities in the router queues, but they will be delivered to the receiver in the same order in which they were sent. This is important for most TCP implementations, which perform much better when packets arrive in order, even if they are designed to cope with misordering. Note also that mechanisms such as fast retransmit can be falsely triggered when misordering happens.

The idea of RIO can be generalized to provide more than two drop probability curves, and this is the idea behind the approach known as weighted RED (WRED). In this case, the value of the DSCP field is used to pick one of several drop probability curves, so that several different classes of service can be provided.

A third way to provide Differentiated Services is to use the DSCP value to determine which queue to put a packet into in a weighted fair queuing scheduler. As a very simple case, we might use one code point to indicate the "best-effort" queue and a second code point to select the "premium" queue. We then need to choose a weight for the premium queue that makes the premium packets get better service than the best-effort packets. This depends on the offered load of premium packets. For example, if we give the premium queue a weight of one and the best-effort queue a weight of four, that ensures that the bandwidth available to premium packets is

$$B_{premium} = \frac{W_{premium}}{\left(W_{premium} + W_{best\_effort}\right)} = 1/(1+4) = 0.2$$

That is, we have effectively reserved 20 percent of the link for premium packets, so if the offered load of premium traffic is only 10 percent of the link on average, then the premium traffic will behave as if it is running on a very underloaded network and the service will be very good. In particular, the delay experienced by the premium class can be kept low, since WFQ will try to transmit premium packets as soon as they arrive in this scenario. On the other hand, if the premium traffic load were 30 percent, it would behave like a highly loaded network, and delay could be very high for the "premium" packets—even worse than the so-called best-effort packets.

Thus, knowledge of the offered load and careful setting of weights is important for this type of service. However, note that the safe approach is to be very conservative in setting the weight for the premium queue. If this weight is made very high relative to the expected load, it provides a margin of error and yet does not prevent the best-effort traffic from using any bandwidth that has been reserved for premium but is not used by premium packets.

Just as in WRED, we can generalize this WFQ-based approach to allow more than two classes represented by different code points. Furthermore, we can combine the idea of a queue selector with a drop preference. For example, with 12 code points we can have four queues with different weights, each of which has three drop preferences. This is exactly what the IETF has done in the definition of assured service.

3.3.4 ATM Quality of Service

ATM is a rather less important technology today than it was 10 years ago, but one of its real contributions was in the area of QoS. In some respects, the fact that ATM was designed with fairly rich QoS capabilities was one of the things that spurred interest in QoS for IP. It also helped the early adoption of ATM.

In many respects, the QoS capabilities that are provided in ATM networks are similar to those provided in an IP network using Integrated Services. However, the ATM standards bodies came up with a total of five service classes compared to the IETF's three (we count best-effort as a service class along with controlled load and guaranteed service). The five ATM service classes are:

- Constant bit rate (CBR)
- Variable bit rate–real-time (VBR-rt)
- Variable bit rate–nonreal-time (VBR-nrt)
- Available bit rate (ABR)
- Unspecified bit rate (UBR)

Mostly the ATM and IP service classes are quite similar, but one of them, ABR, has no real counterpart in IP. More on ABR in a moment. VBR-rt is very much like the guaranteed service class in IP Integrated Services. The exact parameters that are used to set up a VBR-rt virtual circuit (VC) are slightly different than those used to make a guaranteed service reservation, but the basic idea is the same. The traffic generated by the source is characterized by a token bucket, and the maximum total delay required through the network is specified. CBR is also similar to guaranteed service except that sources of CBR traffic are expected to send at a constant rate. Note that this is really a special case of VBR, where the source's peak rate and average rate of transmission are equal.

VBR-nrt bears some similarity to IP's controlled load service. Again, the source traffic is specified by a token bucket, but there is not the same hard delay guarantee of VBR-rt or IP's guaranteed service. UBR is ATM's best-effort service.

Finally, we come to ABR, which is more than just a service class; it also defines a set of congestion-control mechanisms. It is rather complex, so we mention only the high points.

The ABR mechanisms operate over a virtual circuit by exchanging special ATM cells called resource management (RM) cells between the source and destination of the VC. The goal of sending the RM cells is to get information about the state of congestion in the network back to the source so that it can send traffic at an appropriate rate. In this respect, RM cells are an explicit congestion feedback mechanism. This is similar to the DECbit, but contrasts with TCP's use of implicit feedback, which depends on packet losses to detect congestion. It is also similar to the new "quick start" mechanism for TCP.

Initially, the source sends the cell to the destination and includes in it the rate at which it would like to send data cells. Switches along the path look at the requested rate and decide if sufficient resources are available to handle that rate, based on the amount of traffic being carried on other circuits. If enough resources are available, the RM cell is passed on unmodified; otherwise, the requested rate is decreased before the cell is passed along. At the destination, the RM cell is turned around and sent back to the source, which thereby learns what rate it can send at. RM cells are sent periodically and may contain either higher or lower requested rates.

Given the relative decline of ATM in real networks today, the interesting point of ATM QoS is how many mechanisms are common across different technologies. Mechanisms that are found in both ATM and IP QoS include admission control, scheduling algorithms, token-bucket policers, and explicit congestion feedback mechanisms.

3.4 EQUATION-BASED CONGESTION CONTROL

We conclude our discussion of QoS by returning full circle to TCP congestion control, but this time in the context of real-time applications. Recall that TCP adjusts the sender's congestion window (and hence, the rate at which it can transmit) in response to ACK and timeout events. One of the strengths of this approach is that it does not require cooperation from the network's routers; it is a purely host-based strategy. Such a strategy complements the QoS mechanisms we've been considering, because (a) applications can use host-based solutions today, before QoS mechanisms are widely deployed, and (b) even with DiffServ fully deployed, it is still possible for a router queue to be oversubscribed, and we would like real-time applications to react in a reasonable way should this happen.

While we would like to take advantage of TCP's congestion control algorithm, TCP itself is not appropriate for real-time applications. One reason is that TCP is a reliable protocol, and real-time applications often cannot afford the delays introduced by retransmission. However, what if we were to decouple TCP from its congestion control mechanism, that is, add TCP-like congestion control to an unreliable protocol like UDP? Could real-time applications make use of such a protocol?

On the one hand, this is an appealing idea because it would cause real-time streams to compete fairly with TCP streams. The alternative (which happens today) is that video applications use UDP without any form of congestion control, and as a consequence, steal bandwidth away from TCP flows that back off in the presence of congestion. On the other hand, the sawtooth behavior of TCP's congestion control algorithm is not appropriate for real-time applications: It means that the rate at which the application transmits is constantly going up and down. In contrast, real-time applications work best when they are able to sustain a smooth transmission rate over a relatively long period of time.

Is it possible to achieve the best of both worlds: compatibility with TCP congestion control for the sake of fairness, while sustaining a smooth transmission rate for the sake of the application? Recent work suggests that the answer is yes. Specifically, several so-called "TCP-friendly" congestion control algorithms have been proposed. These algorithms have two main goals. One is to slowly adapt the congestion window. This is done by adapting over relatively longer time periods (e.g., a round-trip time—RTT) rather than on a per-packet basis. This smoothes out the transmission rate. The second is to be TCP-friendly in the sense of being fair to competing TCP flows. This property is often enforced by ensuring that the flow's behavior adheres to an equation that models TCP's behavior. Hence, this approach is sometimes called *equation-based congestion control*.

Both simplified and full TCP rate equations exist to help manage congestion control. The interested reader is referred to the papers cited at the end of this chapter for details about the full model. For our purposes, it is sufficient to note that the equation takes this general form:

$$Rate = \frac{1}{RTT \times \sqrt{\rho}}$$

which says that to be TCP-friendly, the transmission rate must be inversely proportional to the round-trip time and the square root of the loss rate (ρ). In other words, to build a congestion control mechanism out of this relationship, the receiver must periodically report the loss rate it is experiencing back to the sender (e.g., it might report that it failed to receive 10 percent of the last 100 packets), and the sender then adjusts its sending rate up or down, such that this relationship continues to hold. Of course, it is still up to the application to adapt to these changes in the available rate, but many real-time applications are quite adaptable.

3.5 SUMMARY

As we have just seen, the issue of resource allocation is not only central to computer networking, it is also a very hard problem. This chapter has examined two aspects of resource allocation. The first, congestion control, is concerned with preventing overall degradation of service when the demand for resources by hosts exceeds the supply available in the network. The second aspect is the provision of different qualities of service to applications that need more assurances than those provided by the best-effort model.

Most congestion-control mechanisms are targeted at the best-effort service model of today's Internet, where the primary responsibility for congestion control falls on the end nodes of the network. Typically, the source uses feedback—either implicitly learned from the network or explicitly sent by a router—to adjust the load it places on the network; this is precisely what TCP's congestion-control mechanism does. Independent of exactly what the end nodes are doing, the routers implement a queuing discipline that governs which packets get transmitted and which packets get dropped. Sometimes this queuing algorithm is sophisticated enough to segregate traffic (e.g., WFQ), and in other cases, the router attempts to monitor its queue length and then signals the source host when congestion is about to occur (e.g., RED gateways and DECbit).

Emerging quality-of-service approaches aim to do substantially more than just control congestion. Their goal is to enable applications with widely varying requirements for delay, loss, and throughput to have those requirements met through new mechanisms inside the network. The Integrated Services approach allows individual application flows to specify their needs to the routers using an explicit signaling mechanism (RSVP), while Differentiated Services assigns packets into a small number of classes that receive differentiated treatment in the routers. While the signaling used by ATM is very different from RSVP, there is considerable similarity between ATM's service classes and those of Integrated Services.

3.5.1 Open Issue: Inside versus Outside the Network

Perhaps the larger question we should be asking is how much can we expect from the network and how much responsibility will ultimately fall to the end hosts? The emerging reservation-based strategies certainly have the advantage of providing for more varied qualities of service than today's feedback-based schemes; being able to support different qualities of service is a strong reason to put more functionality into the network's routers. Does this mean that the days of TCP-like end-to-end congestion control are numbered? This seems very unlikely. TCP and the applications that use it are well entrenched, and in many cases have no need of much more help from the network.

Furthermore, it is most unlikely that all the routers in a worldwide, heterogeneous network like the Internet will implement precisely the same resource reservation algorithm. Ultimately, it seems that the endpoints are going to have to look out for themselves, at least to some extent. The end-to-end principle argues that we should be very selective about putting additional functionality inside the network. How this all plays out in the next few years, in more areas than resource allocation, will be very interesting indeed.

In some sense, the Differentiated Services approach represents the middle ground between absolutely minimal intelligence in the network and the rather significant amount of intelligence (and stored state information) that is required in an Integrated Services network. Certainly most Internet service providers have balked at allowing their customers to make RSVP reservations inside the providers' networks. One important question is whether the Differentiated Services approach will meet the requirements of more stringent applications. For example, if a service provider is trying to offer a large-scale telephony service over an IP network, will Differentiated Services techniques be adequate to deliver the quality of service that traditional telephone users expect? It seems likely that yet more QoS options, with varying amounts of intelligence in the network, will need to be explored.

3.6 FURTHER READING

The recommended reading list for this chapter is long, reflecting the breadth of interesting work being done in congestion control and resource allocation. It includes the original papers introducing the various mechanisms discussed in this chapter. In addition to a more detailed description of these mechanisms, including thorough analysis of their effectiveness and fairness, these papers are must reading because of the insights they give into the interplay of the various issues related to congestion control. In addition, the first paper gives a nice overview of some of the early work on this topic, while the last is considered one of the seminal papers in the development of QoS capabilities in the Internet.

Clark, D., S. Shenker, and L. Zhang, "Supporting Real-Time Applications in an Integrated Services Packet Network: Architecture and Mechanism." *Proceedings of the SIGCOMM '92 Symposium*, pp. 14–26, August 1992.

Demers, A., S. Keshav, and S. Shenker, "Analysis and Simulation of a Fair Queuing Algorithm." *Proceedings of the SIGCOMM '89 Symposium*, pp. 1–12, September 1989.

Floyd, S., and V. Jacobson, "Random Early Detection Gateways for Congestion Avoidance." *IEEE/ACM Transactions on Networking* 1(4):397–413, 1993.

Gerla, M., and L. Kleinrock, "Flow Control: A Comparative Survey." *IEEE Transactions on Communications* COM-28(4):553–573, 1980.

Jacobson, V., "Congestion Avoidance and Control." *Proceedings of the SIGCOMM '88 Symposium*, pp. 314–329, August 1988.

Parekh, A., and R. Gallager, "A Generalized Processor Sharing Approach to Flow Control in Integrated Services Networks: The Multiple Node Case." *IEEE/ACM Transactions on Networking* 2(2):137–150, 1994.

Beyond these recommended papers, there is a wealth of other valuable material on resource allocation. For starters, two early papers set the foundation for using power as a measure of congestion-control effectiveness:

Jaffe, J. M., "Flow Control Power Is Nondecentralizable." *IEEE Transactions on Communications* COM-29(9), 1981.

Kleinrock, L., "Power and Deterministic Rules of Thumb for Probabilistic Problems in Computer Communications." *Proceedings of the International Conference on Communications*, 1979.

A thorough discussion of various issues related to performance evaluation, including a description of Jain's fairness index can also be found in Jain, R., *The Art of Computer Systems Performance Analysis: Techniques for Experimental Design, Measurement, Simulation, and Modeling*. John Wiley & Sons, 1991.

More details about TCP Vegas can be found in Brakmo, L. S., and L. L. Peterson, "TCP Vegas: End-to-End Congestion Avoidance on a Global Internet." *IEEE Journal of Selected Areas in Communications (JASC)* 13(8), 1995. Similar congestion-avoidance techniques can be found in Wang, Z., and J. Crowcroft, "Eliminating Periodic Packet Losses in 4.3-Tahoe BSD TCP Congestion Control Algorithm." *Communications Review* 22(2), 1992. This paper gives an especially nice overview of congestion avoidance based on a common understanding of how the network changes as it approaches congestion. Some issues with and proposed modifications to the RED algorithm including "Flow RED" (FRED) are described in Lin, D., and R. Morris, "Dynamics of Random Early Detection." *Proceedings of the SIGCOMM '97 Symposium*, 1997.

The proposed ECN standard is spelled out in Ramakrishnan, K., S. Floyd, and D. Black, "The Addition of Explicit Congestion Notification (ECN) to IP." *RFC 3168*, IETF, 2001. Efforts to generalize this idea in the form of active queue management are put forth in many sources including Katabi, D., M. Handley, and C. Rohrs, "Congestion Control for High Bandwidth-Delay Product Networks." *Proceedings of the ACM SIGCOMM '02*, 2002. This paper introduces XCP, one of the proposed new transport protocols that tackles the issue of improving on TCP's throughput in high bandwidth-delay product networks.

There is a considerable body of work on packet scheduling that has extended the original fair queuing and processor sharing papers just cited. Excellent examples include the following.

Bennett, T., and H. Zhang, "Hierarchical Packet Fair Queuing Algorithms." *Proceedings of the SIGCOMM '96 Symposium*, 1996.

Goyal, P., H. Vin, and H. Chen, "Start-Time Fair Queuing: A Scheduling Algorithm for Integrated Services Packet Switching Networks." *Proceedings of the SIGCOMM '96 Symposium*, 1996.

Stoica, I., and H. Zhang, "A Hierarchical Fair Service Curve Algorithm for Link-Sharing and Priority Services." *Proceedings of the SIGCOMM '97 Symposium*, 1997.

Many additional articles have been published on the Integrated Services architecture, including:

Clark, D., "Internet Cost Allocation and Pricing." In *Internet Economics* edited by L. Knight and J. Bailey, MIT Press, 1997: the first paper to address the topic of Differentiated

Services. It introduces the RIO mechanism as well as the overall architecture of Differentiated Services.

Clark, D., and W. Fang, "Explicit Allocation of Best-Effort Packet Delivery Service." *IEEE/ACM Transactions on Networking* 6(4), 1998: follow-on paper that presents some simulation results.

RFC 1633—Integrated Services in the Internet Architecture: An Overview, R. Braden, D. Clark, and S. Shanker, IETF, 1994: provides an overview of Integrated Services.

RFC 2475—An Architecture for Differentiated Services, S. Blake et al., IETF, 1998: defines the Differentiated Services architecture.

RFC 3246—An Expedited Forwarding PHB (Per-Hop Behavior), B. Davie, et al., IETF, 2002: defines the EF per-hop behavior.

Zhang, L. et al., "RSVP: A New Resource Reservation Protocol." *IEEE Network*, 1993: provides a description of RSVP.

IP Service Management

We do not live in an egalitarian society and it is, therefore, no surprise that with finite limits on the availability of Internet resources such as processing power and bandwidth, there is a desire to offer grades of service within the Internet. For example, a bronze standard of service might be the cheapest for a user, simply promising "best-effort" data delivery—the data may arrive, or it may not, and if it does, it may take some time. Silver and gold service levels might make increasing pledges as to the timeliness and quality of data delivery. The platinum service might guarantee the user reliable and instant delivery of any amount of data.

To apply levels of service to the traffic flows passing through a router, it is necessary to classify or categorize the packets so that they can be given different treatments and get preferential access to the resources within the router. This chapter, taken from *The Internet and Its Protocols: A Comparative Approach* by Adrian Farrel, examines some popular mechanisms for categorizing packets, for describing flows, and for reserving resources.

Although packet categorization can be implemented differently in each router, it is important for the provision of services within a network that there is a common understanding of the service level applied to the packets within a flow. This is achieved by *Differentiated Services* (DiffServ), which allows individual packets to be labeled according to the service the originator has contracted. *Integrated Services* (IntServ) provides a standardized way to describe packet flows in terms of the amount of traffic that will be generated and the resources needed to support them. The *Resource Reservation Protocol* (RSVP) is a signaling protocol designed to install reserved resources at routers to support packet flows.

In considering how to achieve grades of service within an IP host or router it is helpful to examine a simplified view of the internal organization of such a device. Figure 4.1 shows a router with just two interfaces. Packets are received from the interfaces and moved to the Inwards Holding Area where they are held in buffers until they can be routed. This is an important function because the rate of arrival of packets may be faster than the momentary rate of packet routing—in other words, although the routing component may be able to handle packets at the same aggregate rate as the sum of the line speeds, it is possible that two

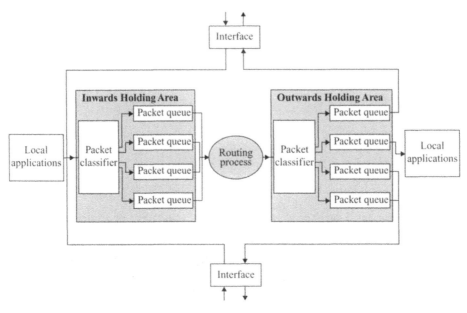

FIGURE 4.1

Simplified view of the internals of a router showing packet queues.

packets will arrive at the same time. After each packet has been routed, it is moved to an Outwards Holding Area and stored in buffers until it can be sent on the outgoing interface.

These holding areas offer the opportunity for prioritizing traffic. Instead of implementing each as a simple first-in, first-out (FIFO) queue, they can be constructed as a series (or queue) of queues—the packets pass through a packet classifier which determines their priority and queues them accordingly.

The queues in the holding areas obviously use up system resources (memory) to store the packets and it is possible that the queues will become full when there are no more resources available. The same categorization of packets can be used to determine what should happen next. The simple approach says that when a packet can't be queued it should simply be dropped (recall that this is acceptable in IP), but with prioritized queues it is also possible to discard packets from low-priority queues to make room for more important packets. A balance can also be implemented that favors discarding packets from the Inwards Holding Area before discarding from the Outwards Holding Area so that work that has been done to route a received packet is less likely to be wasted.

The queues in the holding areas can also be enhanced by limiting the amount of the total system resources that they can consume. This effectively places upper thresholds on the queue sizes so that no one queue can use more than its share, which is particularly useful if the queues are implemented per interface since it handles the case in which an outgoing interface becomes stuck or runs slowly. This introduces the concept of an upper limit to the amount of resources that a queue can consume, and it is also possible to dedicate resources to a queue—that is, to pre-allocate resources for the exclusive use by a queue so that the total system resources are shared out between the queues. With careful determination of the levels of pre-allocation it is possible to guarantee particular service levels to flows within the network.

4.1 CHOOSING HOW TO MANAGE SERVICES

The traditional operation model of IP networks was based on *best-effort* service delivery. No guarantees were made about the quality of service provided to applications or network users, and each packet was treated as a separate object and forwarded within the network with no precedence or priority over other packets. Additionally, a fundamental design consideration of IP and the Internet was to make simplicity more important than anything else.

But the Internet was not conceived for the sophisticated real-time exchange of data for applications that are sensitive not only to the quality of the delivered data, but also to the timeliness and smoothness of that delivery. New applications have left background, bulk data transfer far behind and make more sophisticated demands on the quality of service delivered by the network.

Quality of service is a concept familiar in the telecommunications industry. Developed principally to carry voice traffic, the modern telecommunications network is sensitive to the aspects of noise, distortion, loss, delay, and jitter that make the human voice unintelligible or unacceptably difficult to decipher. Nevertheless, the industry is dominated by proprietary protocols notwithstanding the existence of standardized solutions and the regulatory requirements to converge on interoperable approaches. Attempts to manage services in IP networks, therefore, are able to draw on plenty of experience and concepts, but no clear operational solution.

Further, some key differences exist between the structure of IP networks and telecommunications networks. Perhaps most obvious among these differences is the way that telecommunications networks are connection-oriented or virtual-circuit-based so that traffic for a given flow reliably follows the same path through the network. IP traffic is, of course, routed on a packet-by-packet basis. Other differences lie in the decentralized management structure of IP networks, and emphasis in IP networks on the management of elements (i.e., nodes, links, etc.) and not of data flows.

It is important in this light to examine what needs to be managed in order to provide service management and to attempt to address only those issues that are relevant to an IP framework. The first point to note is that in an IP network the distribution framework that is being managed (i.e., the network elements that forward IP traffic) is identical to the management framework. In other words, the

IP network is the tool that is used to manage the IP network. This raises several questions about the effect of service management activities on the services being managed. For example, a service management process that relied on regular and detailed distribution of statistical information to a central management point would significantly increase the amount of network traffic and would reduce the ability to provide the highest levels of throughput for applications. Thus, one of the criteria for service management in an IP network is to retain a high level of distributed function with individual network elements responsible for monitoring and maintaining service levels. This distributed model only becomes more important when we consider that IP networks are typically large (in terms of the number of network elements and the connectivity of the network).

Early attempts at service management have focused on traffic prioritization (see the type of service, or ToS, field in the IP header) and on policing the traffic flows at the edge of the network or on entry to administrative domains. This is not really service management so much as a precautionary administrative policy designed to reduce the chances of failing to meet service level agreements. It doesn't address any of the questions of guaranteeing service levels or of taking specific action within the network to ensure quality of service. Only by providing mechanisms to quantify and qualify both requested service and actual traffic is it possible to manage the traffic flows so that quality of service is provided.

In fact, an important requirement of IP service management is that any process that is applied should extend across management domains. This means that it should be possible for an application in one network to specify its quality of service requirements and have them applied across the end-to-end path to the destination even if that path crosses multiple networks. It is not enough to meet the service requirements in one network: they must be communicated and met along the whole path.

This consideration opens up many issues related to charging between service providers and the ultimate billing to the end user, because the provision of a specific quality of service is most definitely a chargeable feature. In a competitive world, service providers will vie with each other to provide service management features and traffic quality at different price points, and will want to pass on the costs. The bottom line is that it must be possible to track service requests as they cross administrative boundaries. Techniques to measure the services actually provided are a follow-up requirement for both the end user and for service providers that are interconnected.

It is only a short step from these requirements to the desire to be able to route traffic according to the availability and real, financial cost of services. This provides further input to constraint-based path computation algorithms.

Not all of these issues are handled well by the service management techniques described in this chapter. As initial attempts to address the challenges, they focus largely on the classification of traffic and services, and techniques to make service requests. Some of these considerations do not begin to be properly handled until traffic engineering concepts are introduced.

4.2 **DIFFERENTIATED SERVICES**

Differentiated Services (DiffServ) is an approach to classifying packets within the network so that they may be handled differently by prioritizing those that belong to "more important" data flows and, when congestion arises, discarding first those packets that belong to the "least important" flows. The different ways data is treated within a DiffServ network are called *policies*. For different policies to be applied to traffic it is necessary to have some way to differentiate the packets. DiffServ reuses the ToS byte in the IP header to flag packets as belonging to different classes which may then be subjected to different policies. The assignment of packets to different classes in DiffServ is sometimes referred to as *coloring*.

The policies applied to packets of different colors is not standardized. It is seen as a network implementation or configuration issue to ensure that the meaning of a particular color is interpreted uniformly across the network. DiffServ simply provides a standard way of flagging the packets as having different colors.

4.2.1 **Coloring Packets in DiffServ**

The ToS interpretation of the ToS field in the IP packet header has been made obsolete and redefined by the Internet Engineering Task Force (IETF) for DiffServ. In its new guise it is known as the Differentiated Services Code Point (DSCP), but it occupies the same space within the IP header and is still often referred to as the ToS field. Old network nodes that used the ToS field cannot interbreed successfully with nodes that use the DSCP since the meaning of the bits may clash or be confused. In particular, the bits in the ToS field had very specific meanings whereas those in the DSCP simply allow the definition of 64 different colors which may be applied to packets. However, some consideration is given to preserving the effect of the precedence bits of the ToS field. The precedence bits are the most significant 3 bits in the ToS field, and DiffServ-capable nodes are encouraged to assign their interpretation of DSCPs to meet the general requirements of these queuing precedences. Figure 4.2 reprises the IPv4 message header and shows the 6 bits designated to identify the DSCP.

As previously stated, the meanings of the DSCP values are not standardized, but are open for configuration within a network. Specifically, this does not mean that a packet with DSCP set to 1 is by definition more or less important than a packet with DSCP 63. The DSCP of zero is reserved to mean that no color is applied to the packet and that traffic should be forwarded as "best-effort," but how this is handled with respect to other packets that are colored remains an issue for configuration within the network. In fact, the interpretation of the DSCP at each node can be varied according to the source and destination of the packets, or other fields of the IP header such as the protocol. The rule that governs how packets are handled within a DiffServ network is called the *per-hop behavior* (PHB).

The encoding of the DSCP field in the IP header is defined in *RFC 2474*. This RFC also describes the backwards compatibility with the precedence field of the

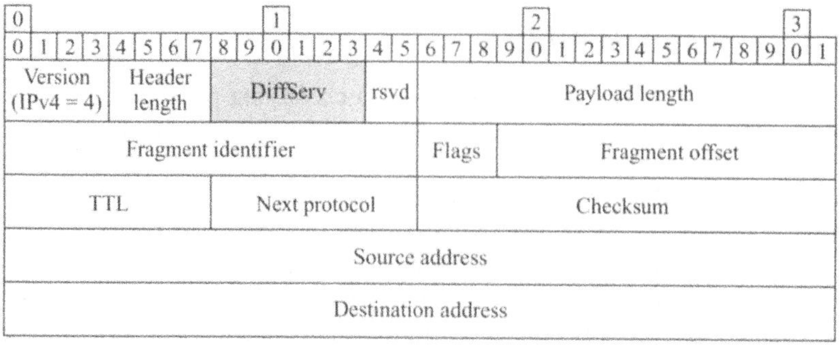

0										1										2										3	
0	1	2	3	4	5	6	7	8	9	0	1	2	3	4	5	6	7	8	9	0	1	2	3	4	5	6	7	8	9	0	1

Version (IPv4 = 4)	Header length	DiffServ	rsvd	Payload length
Fragment identifier			Flags	Fragment offset
TTL		Next protocol	Checksum
Source address				
Destination address				

FIGURE 4.2

IPv4 message header showing DSCP.

Table 4.1 DSCP Restricted Definitions

DSCP Bit Settings	Meaning
000000	Best effort
bbb000	Conforms to the requirements of ToS queuing precedence
bbbbb0	Available for standardization
bbbb11	For experimental or local network usage
bbbb01	For experimental or local network usage, but may be taken for standardization

ToS byte so that PHBs are defined to support the general properties controlled by IP precedence. This process creates PHBs (one for each combination of the top 3 bits) of the form bbb000 to match the precedence behaviors and leaves the other DSCP values open where each b may take the value zero or 1. However, it further restricts the meaning of the DSCP values according to Table 4.1. The RFC clearly states that care should be taken before applying any further restrictions to the meaning of DSCP values unless very clear and necessary uses are identified, since otherwise the restricted set of values will quickly be depleted.

The Internet Assigned Numbers Authority (IANA) is responsible for managing the allocation of DSCP values. In addition to the value for best effort, and the seven values that match the ToS queuing precedence, a further 13 values are defined. Twelve of the values are used to represent the *assured forwarding* (AF) PHBs that are defined by *RFC 2597*. Four AF classes are defined, and within each class there are three drop precedences defined. Each class groups packets for common treatment and sharing of resources and the drop precedence (low, medium, or high) indicates the likelihood of dropping a packet when congestion

Table 4.2 DSCP Values for Assured Forwarding PHBs

	AF Class 1	AF Class 2	AF Class 3	AF Class 4
Low Drop Precedence	001010	010010	011010	100010
Medium Drop Precedence	001100	010100	011100	100100
High Drop Precedence	001110	010110	011110	100110

occurs. An AF PHB is indicated by a 2-digit number showing its class and its drop precedence so that the AF PHB from class 2 with low drop precedence is represented as AF21. The AF PHBs are encoded in the DSCP as shown in Table 4.2.

Each router allocates a configurable set of resources (buffering, queuing space, etc.) to handle the packets from each class. Resources belonging to one class may not be used for packets from another class, except that it is permissible to borrow unused resources from another class so long as they are immediately released should that class need them. The drop precedence is applied only within a class, so that packets from one class may not be dropped simply because another class is congested.

The thirteenth standardized DSCP value (101110) is defined in *RFC 3246* (which replaces *RFC 2598*) to represent an *expedited forwarding* (EF) PHB. The intention is that EF packets should be handled at least at a configured rate regardless of the amount of non-EF traffic in the system. That is, packets carrying the EF DSCP should be prioritized over other traffic at least until the configured service rate has been delivered. There are, however, two issues with this requirement. First, packets cannot be serviced faster than they arrive, meaning that a router cannot deliver the service rate if it does not receive the data quickly enough. Second, the time period over which the rate is measured and the act of measuring the rate itself will affect the apparent rate. *RFC 3246* presents formal equations to define the behavior of a router that supports EF traffic—the bottom line is simply that when an EF packet arrives it should be given priority over other traffic unless the required rate has already been delivered.

4.2.2 DiffServ Functional Model

The DiffServ functional model is based on the packet classification shown in Figure 4.1. However, some details are added to help provide and distinguish between different qualities of service. Packet classification function can now be split into two stages. In the first stage (sometimes called *traffic conditioning*) traffic is assigned to a particular DiffServ class by setting the DSCP on the packets—this will most likely be done based on customer or application requirements and is performed when the traffic enters the network. The second stage is more akin to that shown in Figure 4.1, and involves the ordering and classifying of received packets based on the DSCP values they carry.

The required quality of service is maintained within a network by managing and avoiding congestion. Congestion is managed by assigning into queues the packets classified on receipt at a node. The queues can be scheduled for processing according to a priority-based or throughput-based algorithm, and limits on the queue sizes can also serve as a check on the amount of resources used by a traffic flow. Congestion can be avoided, in part, by preemptively discarding (*dropping*) packets before congestion is reached. The heuristics for avoiding congestion may be complex if they attempt to gather information from the network, or may be simple if applied to a single node, but in any case the algorithm for picking which packets should be dropped first and which should be protected is based on the DSCP values in the packets.

Reclassification of traffic may be beneficial in the core of networks where traffic is aggregated or when one Service Provider uses another's network. The reclassification process is similar to that originally applied at the edge of the network, and new DSCP values are assigned for the aggregated traffic flows. Note, however, that it is usually important to restore the original DSCP value to each packet as it exits the aggregated flow. Since it is impossible to restore the original classification of traffic if the DSCP is simply changed (how would we know the original value?), reclassification is best achieved by using IP tunneling, where a new IP header with a new DSCP value is used to encapsulate each end-to-end packet. When the packet emerges from the tunnel, the encapsulating IP header is removed to reveal the original IP header, complete with DSCP value.

At various points in the network it may be useful to monitor and police traffic flows. Levels of service are easiest to maintain when the characteristics of traffic flows are well understood, and it may be possible to use information fed back from monitoring stations to tune the PHB at nodes in the network to improve the quality of service delivered. The customers, too, are interested in monitoring the performance of the network to be certain that they are getting what they pay for—the wise service provider will also keep a careful watch on the actual service that is delivered and will take remedial action before a customer gets upset. But the flip side of this is that performance and tuning in the network may be based on commitments to upper bounds on traffic generation—no one traffic source should swamp the network. Traffic policing can ensure that no customer or application exceeds its agreements and may work with the traffic conditioning components to downgrade or discard excess traffic.

4.2.3 Choosing to Use DiffServ

The motivation for using DiffServ is twofold. It provides a method of grading traffic so that applications that require more reliable, smooth, or expeditious delivery of their data can achieve this. At the same time, it allows service providers to offer different classes of service (at different prices), thereby differentiating their customers.

As with all similar schemes, the *prisoner's dilemma* applies and it is important to avoid a situation in which all data sources simply classify their packets as the most important with the lowest drop precedence. In this respect, the close tie between policy and classification of traffic is important, and charging by service providers based on the DSCP values assigned is a reasonable way to control the choice of PHB requested for each packet.

DiffServ is most meaningful when all nodes in the domain support PHB functions, although it is not unreasonable to have some nodes simply apply best-effort forwarding of all traffic while others fully utilize the DSCPs (but note that this may result in different behaviors on different paths through the network). More important is the need to keep PHB consistent through the network—that is, to maintain a common interpretation of DSCPs on each node in the network.

There are some concerns with scalability issues when DiffServ is applied in large service provider networks because of the sheer number of flows that traverse the network. Attention to this issue has recently focused on Multiprotocol Label Switching (MPLS) traffic engineering, and two RFCs (*RFC 2430* and *RFC 3270*) provide a framework and implementation details to support DiffServ in MPLS networks.

4.3 INTEGRATED SERVICES

Integrated Services (IntServ) provides a series of standardized ways to classify traffic flows and network resources focused on the capabilities and common structure of IP packet routers. The purpose of this function is to allow applications to choose between multiple well-characterized delivery levels so that they can quantify and predict the level of service their traffic will receive. This is particularly useful to facilitate delivery of real-time services such as voice and video over the Internet. For these services, it is not enough to simply prioritize or color traffic as in Differentiated Services. It is necessary to make quality of service guarantees, and to support these pledges it is necessary for routers to reserve buffers and queuing space to ensure timely forwarding of packets.

To allow routers to prepare themselves to support the traffic at the required level of service, data flow requirements must be characterized and exchanged. The end points of a data flow need a way to describe the data they will send and a way to represent the performance they need from the network. Transit nodes can then reserve resources (buffers, queue space, etc.) to guarantee that the data delivery will be timely and smooth.

IntServ provides a way to describe and encode parameters that describe data flows and quality of service requirements. It does not provide any means of exchanging these encodings between routers—the Resource Reservation Protocol described in Section 4.4 is a special protocol developed to facilitate resource reservation using IntServ parameters to describe data flows.

4.3.1 Describing Traffic Flows

IntServ uses a model described in *RFC 1633*. The internals of the router shown in Figure 4.1 are enhanced to include an *admission control* component which is responsible for determining whether a new data flow can be supported by a router, and for allocating or assigning the resources necessary to support the flow. Admission control uses an algorithm at each node on the data path to map a description of the flow and QoS requirements to actual resources within the node—it is clearly important that the interpretation of the parameters that describe those requirements are interpreted in the same way on all nodes in the network.

Admission control should not be confused with the closely related concepts of traffic policing (which is done at the edge of the network to ensure that the data flow conforms to the description that was originally given) and policy control (which polices whether a particular application on a given node is allowed to request reservations of a certain type to support its data flows, and validates whether the application is who it says it is). The admission control component on each node is linked by the signaling protocol, which is used to exchange the parameters that describe the data flow. But what information needs to be exchanged?

A lot of research has gone into the best ways to classify flows and their requirements. Some balance must be reached between the following constraints:

- The availability of network resources (bandwidth, buffers, etc.)
- The imperfections in the network (delays, corruption, packet loss, etc.)
- The amount, type, and rate of data generated by the sending application
- The tolerance of the receiving application to glitches in the transmitted data

The most popular solution, used by IntServ, is the *token bucket.* A token bucket is quantified by a data dispersal rate (r) and a data storage capacity—the bucket size (b). A token bucket can be viewed as a bucket with a hole in the bottom, as shown in Figure 4.3. The size of the hole governs the rate at which data can leave the bucket, and the bucket size says how much data can be stored. If the bucket becomes overfull because the rate of arrival of data is greater than the rate of dispersal for a prolonged period of time, then data will be lost. A very small bucket would not handle the case in which bursts of data arrive faster than they can be dispersed even when the average arrival rate is lower than the dispersal rate.

A flow's level of service is characterized at each node in a network by a bandwidth (or data rate) R and a buffer size B. R represents the share of the link's bandwidth to which the flow is entitled, and B represents the buffer space within the node that the flow may use.

Other parameters that are useful to characterize the flow include the peak data rate (p), the minimum policed unit (m), and the maximum packet size (M). The

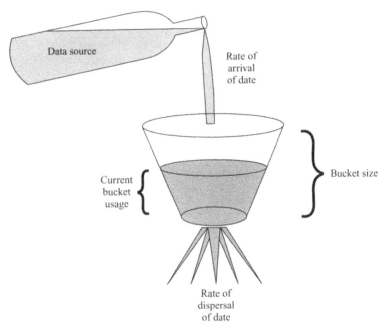

FIGURE 4.3

Token bucket characterization of a data flow.

peak rate is the maximum rate at which the source may inject traffic into the network—this is the upper bound for the rate of arrival of data shown in Figure 4.3. Over a time period (T), the maximum amount of data sent approximates to pT and is always bounded by $M + pT$. Although it may at first seem perverse, the token-bucket rate for a flow and the peak data rate are governed by the rule $p > r$; there is no point in having a dispersal rate greater than the maximum arrival rate.

The maximum packet size must be smaller than or equal to the maximum transmission unit (MTU) size of the links over which the flow is routed. The minimum policed unit is used to indicate the degree of rounding that will be applied when the rate of arrival of data is policed for conformance to other parameters. All packets of size less than m will be counted as being of size m, but packets of size greater than or equal to m will have their full size counted. m must be less than or equal to M.

4.3.2 Controlled Load

The controlled load service is defined using the definitions of a token bucket and the other basic flow parameters described in the preceding section. The controlled load service provides the client data flow with a quality of service

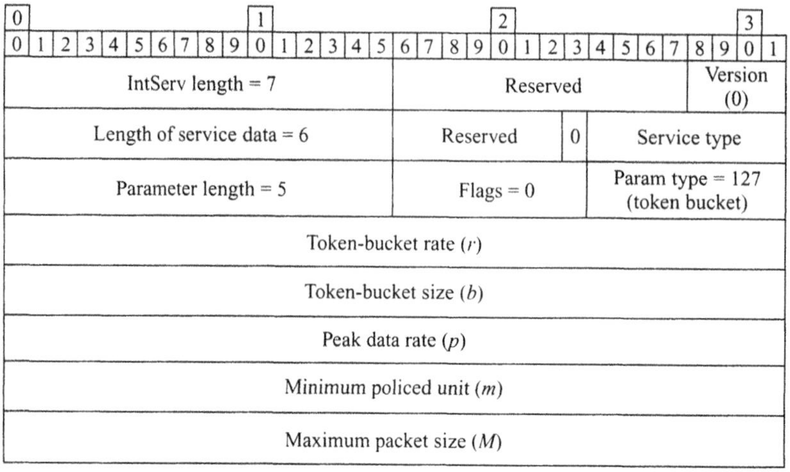

0										1										2										3	
0	1	2	3	4	5	6	7	8	9	0	1	2	3	4	5	6	7	8	9	0	1	2	3	4	5	6	7	8	9	0	1

IntServ length = 7	Reserved	Version (0)
Length of service data = 6	Reserved · 0	Service type
Parameter length = 5	Flags = 0	Param type = 127 (token bucket)
Token-bucket rate (r)		
Token-bucket size (b)		
Peak data rate (p)		
Minimum policed unit (m)		
Maximum packet size (M)		

FIGURE 4.4

Encoding of the IntServ-controlled load parameters as used by RSVP.

closely approximating that which the same flow would receive from an otherwise unloaded network. It uses admission control to ensure that this service is delivered even when the network element is overloaded—in other words, it reserves the resources required to maintain the service.

To provide the controlled load service, the flow must be characterized to the network and the network must be requested to make whatever reservations it needs to make to ensure that the service is delivered. Figure 4.4 shows how the service parameters are encoded in RSVP. When the flow is characterized (on a Path message) the service type field is set to 1, and when the reservation is requested (on a Resv message) the service type field is set to 5 to indicate controlled load. The data rates are presented in bytes per second using IEEE floating point numbers. The byte counts are 32-bit integers.

4.3.3 Guaranteed Service

The guaranteed service sets a time limit for the delivery of all datagrams in the flow and guarantees that datagrams will arrive within this time period and will not be discarded owing to queue overflows on any transit node. This guarantee is made provided that the flow's traffic stays within its specified traffic parameters. This level of service is designed for use by applications that need firm guarantees of service delivery and is particularly useful for applications that have hard real-time requirements.

The guaranteed service controls the maximal queuing delay, but does not attempt to reduce the jitter (i.e., the difference between the minimal and maximal datagram delays). Since the delay bound takes the form of a guarantee, it must be large enough to cover cases of long queuing delays even if they are extremely rare. It would be usual to find that the actual delay for most datagrams in a flow is much lower than the guaranteed delay.

The definition of the guaranteed service relies on the result that the fluid delay of a flow obeying a token bucket (with rate r and bucket size b) and being served by a line with bandwidth R is bounded by b/R as long as R is no less than r. Guaranteed service with a service rate R, where now R is a share of the available bandwidth rather than the full bandwidth of a dedicated line, approximates to this behavior and is useful for managing multiple services on a single link. To guarantee the service level across the network, each node must ensure that the delay imposed on a packet is no more than $b/R + C/R + D$ where C and D are small, per-node error terms defined in Section 4.3.4.

Figure 4.5 shows how the flow parameters are encoded for the use of the guaranteed service when reservations are requested in RSVP. A token bucket is encoded to describe the flow and two additional parameters are used to enable the guaranteed service. The guaranteed service rate (R) increases the token-bucket rate (r) to reduce queuing delays such that $r \le R \le p$. Effectively, it makes the hole in the bottom of the bucket a bit larger so that the build-up of data in the bucket is reduced. The slack (S) signifies the difference between the desired delay for the

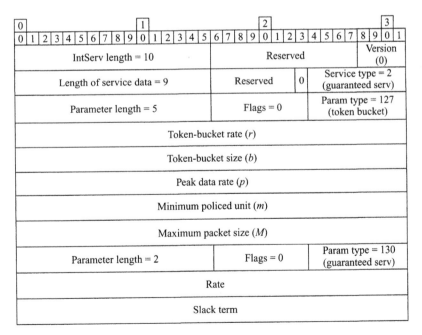

0										1										2										3	
0	1	2	3	4	5	6	7	8	9	0	1	2	3	4	5	6	7	8	9	0	1	2	3	4	5	6	7	8	9	0	1
IntServ length = 10																Reserved												Version (0)			
Length of service data = 9																Reserved							0	Service type = 2 (guaranteed serv)							
Parameter length = 5																Flags = 0								Param type = 127 (token bucket)							
Token-bucket rate (r)																															
Token-bucket size (b)																															
Peak data rate (p)																															
Minimum policed unit (m)																															
Maximum packet size (M)																															
Parameter length = 2																Flags = 0								Param type = 130 (guaranteed serv)							
Rate																															
Slack term																															

FIGURE 4.5

Encoding IntServ guaranteed service parameters as used by RSVP.

flow (s) and the delay obtained by using the rate R, so $S > 0$ indicates the comfort margin. This slack term can be utilized by a router to reduce its resource reservation for this flow if it feels confident that it can always meet the requirements—that is, it can make a smaller reservation and eat into the slack.

4.3.4 Reporting Capabilities

To ensure that Integrated Services functions correctly, it is useful for end nodes to be able to collect information about the capabilities and available resources on the path between them. What bandwidth is available? What is the maximum MTU size supported? What IntServ capabilities are supported?

In RSVP, this information is built up in an Adspec object (shown in Figure 4.6), which is initiated by the data sender and updated by each RSVP-capable node along the path. The Adspec object is originally built to contain the global parameters (type 1). Then, if the sender supports the guaranteed service, there is a set of service parameters of type 2. Finally, if the sender supports the controlled load service there is a set of service parameters of type 5. The IntServ length encompasses the full sequence of service parameters.

As the object progresses through the network, the reported parameters are updated, giving the *composed* parameters for the path. This serves to reduce the capabilities reported as the object progresses. For example, if one node has lower bandwidth capabilities on a link it will reduce the advertised bandwidth in the object it forwards. In this way, when the Adspec object reaches the far end of the path, it reports the best available capabilities along the path.

If some node recognizes but cannot support either the guaranteed service or the controlled load service and the service parameters are present in an Adspec, it sets the Break Bit (shown as B in Figure 4.6) and does not update the parameters for the service type.

The global parameters recorded are straightforward. They report the number of IntServ-capable hops traversed, the greatest bandwidth available (as an IEEE floating point number of bytes per second), the minimum end-to-end path latency (measured in microseconds), and the greatest supported MTU (in bytes). To support the guaranteed service, it is necessary to collect more information than just the global parameters. Two error terms are defined:

- The error term C is rate-dependent and represents the delay a datagram in the flow might experience due to the rate parameters of the flow—for example, time taken serializing a datagram broken up into ATM cells.

- The error term D is rate-independent and represents the worst case non-rate-based transit time variation. The D term is generally determined or set for an individual node at boot or configuration time. For example, in a device or transport mechanism where processing or bandwidth is allocated to a specific time-slot, some part of the per-flow delay may be determined by the maximum amount of time a flow's data might have to wait for a slot.

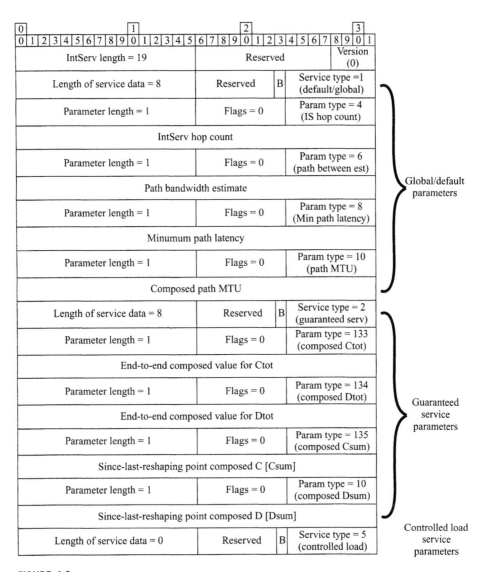

FIGURE 4.6

Encoding of the IntServ parameters as used to collect capabilities information by RSVP.

The terms C and D are accumulated across the path and expressed as totals *(Ctot* and *Dtot)* in bytes and microseconds, respectively. Further, because traffic may be reshaped within the network, partial sums *(Csum* and *Dsum)* of the error terms C and D along the path since the last point at which the traffic was reshaped are also reported. Knowing these four delay terms, a node may calculate how much bufferage is needed to ensure that no bytes will be lost.

Support of the controlled load service does not require any additional information, but it is still useful to know whether any nodes on the path do not support the service. For this reason, a "null" service parameter is inserted in the Adspec object so that the Break Bit may be recorded.

4.3.5 Choosing to Use IntServ

IntServ is sometimes described as an "all or nothing" model. To guarantee a particular quality of service across the network, all nodes on the data path must support IntServ and whichever signaling protocol is used to distribute the requirements. It may be determined, however, that this level of guarantee is not absolutely necessary and that the improvement in service generated by using resource reservations on some nodes within the network may be helpful. Protocols such as RSVP recognize this and allow for data paths that traverse both RSVP-capable and RSVP-incapable nodes.

The focus of IntServ is real-time data traffic. It is not a requirement for data exchanges that are not time-dependent, and such flows are better handled by DiffServ where there is no overhead of another signaling protocol and no need for complex resource reservations at each node. However, if real-time quality of service is required, IntServ provides a formal and simple mechanism to describe the flows and requirements.

Some people, especially those with an ATM background, consider the simplicity of IntServ's description of quality of service to be a significant drawback. Compared with the detailed qualification of flows and behavior available in ATM, IntServ appears to offer a crude way of characterizing traffic. However, IntServ (which is specifically designed for packet routers, not cell switches) has proved useful in the Internet where it is used in conjunction with RSVP to support voice over IP, and its very simplicity has brought it as many supporters as detractors. For the ATM purists, *RFC 2381* addresses how IntServ parameters may be mapped to ATM QoS parameters.

The alternative to using IntServ is to not use it. There are some strong alternative viewpoints:

■ Limitations on bandwidth are likely to apply most significantly at the edges of the Internet. This implies that if an application is able to find a local link of sufficient bandwidth to support its functions, there will always be sufficient bandwidth within the Internet to transfer its data. Although this may be an ideal toward which service providers strive within their own networks, it is rarely the case that end-to-end data transfer across the Internet is limited only by the capacity of the first and last links. With the development of bandwidth-greedy applications, there is a continual conflict between bandwidth demand and availability. Besides, quality of service for real-time applications is not simply an issue of the availability of unlimited bandwidth, but is a function of the delays and variations introduced within the network.

- Simple priority schemes such as DiffServ provide sufficient grading of service to facilitate real-time applications. This may be true when only a proportion of the traffic within the network requires real-time quality of service, in which case simply giving higher priority to real-time traffic can ensure that it is handled promptly and gets the resources it needs. However, as the percentage of high-priority traffic increases, the priority scheme becomes unable to handle the requirements adequately and all high-priority data flows are equally degraded. There is no way to announce that links are over their capacity or to prevent new flows.

- It is the responsibility of the application and its IP transport protocol to handle the vagaries of the network. Adaptive real-time protocols for distributing data have been developed (e.g., the Real-Time Transport Protocol) and provide mechanisms to smooth and buffer delayed or interrupted data. But although these approaches may "heal" the data flows, they can still provide interruptions that the human user is unwilling or unable to accept—readers who have tried to have meaningful conversations over a satellite telephone will know how even a predictable delay of one or two seconds can disrupt dialog.

4.3.6 Choosing a Service Type

Having decided to use IntServ, an application must choose which service to utilize. The controlled load is the simplest service, defining and adhering to a simple token bucket, and should be used wherever the greater control of the guaranteed service is not required. The guaranteed service is less than trivial to use, but provides firm guarantees of service delivery and is particularly useful for applications that have hard real-time requirements and require guaranteed service.

Note that some applications reduce the controlled load token bucket to its simplest form by setting the bucket rate and peak data rate to be equal at the bandwidth required for the service, setting the minimum policed unit to be equal to the maximum packet size, and setting the bucket size to an arbitrarily large multiple of the maximum packet size. Generalized Multiprotocol Label Switching (GMPLS) formalizes this by making bandwidth-only reservations using the controlled load service fields but ignoring all fields except the peak data rate, which identifies the bandwidth required.

Over time, other IntServ services have been defined for specific uses. The *null service* has been defined to allow the use of RSVP and RSVP-TE in MPLS by applications that are unable or unwilling to specify the resources they require from the network. This is particularly useful for mixing DiffServ and IntServ within a single network.

4.3.7 Choosing between IntServ and DiffServ

DiffServ is intrinsically more scalable than IntServ because it has a limited number of classifications—each flow must be assigned to one of 64 DiffServ PHBs, whereas in IntServ each individual flow has its own reservations and characteristics. On the other hand, DiffServ is less precise and requires coordinated configuration of all participating routers—IntServ may be combined with a signaling protocol such as RSVP to allow the PHB for a flow to be dynamically selected and set through the network. Furthermore, IntServ gives finer control of the real-time qualities of traffic delivery.

Some consideration should be given to implementing both IntServ and DiffServ within the same network. This can be done "side-by-side," with all IntServ traffic assigned to a single DSCP or by running IntServ over DiffServ. In the latter case, all traffic is classified and assigned a DSCP, and then whole DSCP classes or individual flows within a DSCP value can have their resources managed using IntServ.

4.4 RESERVING RESOURCES USING RSVP

RFC 2205 defines the Resource Reservation Protocol with the rather improbable acronym RSVP. This protocol is a signaling protocol for use in networks that support IntServ flow descriptions. The protocol is designed to allow data sources to characterize to the network the traffic they will generate, and to allow the data sinks to request that the nodes along the data path make provisions to ensure that the traffic can be delivered smoothly and without packets being dropped because of lack of queuing resources.

RSVP is intrinsically a simple signaling protocol but is complicated by its flexible support of merged and multicast flows. Complexity is also introduced by the fact that the protocol is intended to allocate resources along the path followed by the data within the network (i.e., the forwarding path selected by the routers in the network) and that this path can change over time as the connectivity of the network changes.

RSVP bears close examination not simply for its value for making resource reservations in an IntServ-enabled IP packet forwarding network. The protocol also forms the basis of the signaling protocol used both for MPLS and GMPLS, and so is very important in the next-generation networks that are now being built.

In addition to developing RSVP as a protocol, the IETF also worked on a common application programming interface (API) to allow implementations to make use of RSVP in a standardized way. This meant that application programmers wanting to use RSVP from their applications could be independent of the implementation of RSVP and make use of a well-known API that provided a set of standard services. The IETF, however, "does not do" interfaces and work on the RSVP API (RAPI) was offloaded in 1998 to The Open Group, an implementers' consortium, from where it was used more as a guide than as a rigid standard.

4.4.1 Choosing to Reserve Resources

As described in Section 4.3, IntServ can be used to describe a traffic flow, and to indicate the behavior of network nodes if they are to guarantee the provision of services to carry the flow across the network. This behavior can be met only if the nodes reserve some of their resources for the flow.

The precise nature of resource reservation depends on the implementation of the packet forwarding engine within the routers. Some may make dedicated reservations of buffers to individual microflows. Others may use statistical assignment to make sure that resources will not be over-stretched, provided that all data sources conform to the parameters of the flows they have described. Whatever the implementation, the fact that the network nodes have agreed to make reservations is a guarantee that the required QoS will be met and that traffic will be delivered in the way necessary for the proper functioning of the applications within the constraints of the network.

Several well-known applications, such as Microsoft's NetMeeting, include the ability to use RSVP to improve the quality of voice and video services they deliver. In general, voice over IP for IP telephony or for simple point-to-point exchanges is a prime user of RSVP since the human ear can tolerate only a small amount of distortion or short gaps in the transmitted signal.

4.4.2 RSVP Message Flows for Resource Reservation

The steps to resource reservation in RSVP are *path establishment* and *resource allocation*. RSVP uses the Path message to establish a path from the source to the destination, and a Resv message to reserve the resources along the path. The source of the RSVP flow (the *ingress*) sends a Path message targeted at the destination of the flow (the *egress*), and this message is passed from node to node through the network until it reaches the egress. The Path message is routed in the same way that IP traffic would be routed—the IP traffic would be addressed to the egress node, and by addressing the Path message in the same way, RSVP ensures that the reservations will be made using the same path and hops that will be used by the IP traffic.

The Path message carries a specification of the traffic that will constitute the flow (the traffic specification or *TSpec*). It should be noted, however, that the traffic may already be flowing before the Path message is sent. That is, an RSVP-capable network also supports best effort traffic delivery and resource reservation may be applied at any stage to improve the likelihood of traffic delivery meeting required quality standards.

Each node that processes the Path message establishes control state for the message, verifies that it is happy to attempt to deliver the requested service (e.g., checking the authenticity of the message sender), and builds a Path message to send on toward the egress. The Path messages can collect information about the availability of resources along the path they traverse. The ingress advertises (in the *Adspec*) its capabilities, and each node along the way can modify the reported capabilities to a subset of the original Adspec so that by the time the Path reaches the egress the message contains a common subset of the capabilities of all routers on the path.

The egress computes what resources will need to be reserved in the network. These resources must satisfy the demands of the traffic that will be sent, as described by the TSpec, and must fit within the available resources reported by the Adspec. The egress responds to the Path message with an Resv message that requests the reservation of the computed resources by including an *RSpec*. The Resv is passed hop-by-hop back along the path traversed by the Path message and at each hop resources are reserved as requested. When the Resv reaches the ingress and has completed its resource allocations, the RSVP flow is fully provisioned.

In general, RSVP implementations follow the model described in *RFC 2205*. Control state is maintained separately for Path and Resv flows with only a loose coupling between them. This is not necessarily intuitive but it allows for advanced functions (described in Sections 4.4.6 and 4.4.7) where there may not be a one-to-one correspondence between Path messages and resource reservations, or where the Path may be rerouted while the reservation on the old path is still in place.

Figure 4.7 shows the basic RSVP message flows. At step 1 the application at the ingress quantifies the traffic flow that it is going to send to an application of

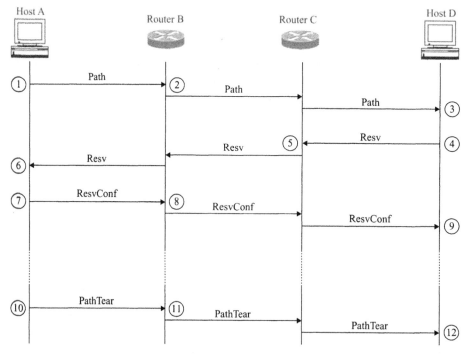

FIGURE 4.7

Basic RSVP message flows.

Host D and requests reservations from the network. Host A builds and sends a PATH message addressed to Host D and this is routed to Router B. Router B (step 2) creates Path state and sends its own Path message toward Host D. When the Path message reaches Host D (step 3), it also creates its Path state, but recognizes that it is the destination of the flow and so delivers the resource request to the target application identified by a destination port ID contained in the Path message.

The target application converts the Path message, with its description of the traffic and the capabilities of the routers along the path, into a request for resource reservation. This request is passed to the RSVP component, which creates Resv state, reserves the requested resources on the local node, and sends an Resv message (step 4). The Resv message is not addressed to the ingress node, but is addressed hop-by-hop back along the path the Path message traversed. This ensures that the resources are reserved along the path that traffic will follow (i.e., along the path the Path message traversed) rather than along the shortest return path. Thus, at Router C (step 5), once the Resv state has been created and the resources reserved, a new Resv is sent out to Router B even if there is a direct route from Router C to Host A. When the Resv reaches Host A (step 6), the resources are reserved and an indication is delivered to the application to let it know that the reservations are in place.

Figure 4.7 also shows the ResvConf message sent by the ingress to the egress to confirm that the resources have been reserved. The ResvConf is sent hop-by-hop along the path of flow (steps 7 and 8) to the egress if, and only if, the egress requested confirmation when it sent the Resv (step 4). When the ResvConf reaches the egress (step 9) it knows that the reservation was successful; this may simplify processing at the egress, which can wait for a ResvConf or a ResvErr (see Section 4.4.5) to confirm or deny successful flow establishment.

When the ingress application no longer needs the reservations in place because it is stopping its transmission of traffic, it tears them down by sending a PathTear message. The PathTear is a one-shot message that traverses the path hop-by-hop (it is not addressed and routed to the egress) and lets each router know that it can release its Path and Resv state as well as any reserved resources. This is shown in Figure 4.7 at steps 10, 11, and 12.

Alternatively, the egress may determine that it can no longer support the reservations that are in place and can ask for them to be torn down. It may send a ResvTear message back toward the ingress along the path of the flow. Each router that receives a ResvTear releases the resources it has reserved for the flow and cleans up its Resv state before sending a ResvTear on toward the ingress. The Path state is, however still left in place since that refers to the request from the ingress. When the ResvTear reaches the ingress it may decide that the flow can no longer be supported with resource reservations and will send a PathTear, as shown in Figure 4.8.

Another alternative is for the ingress to modify the description of the traffic and send a new Path message to which the egress may respond with a new Resv.

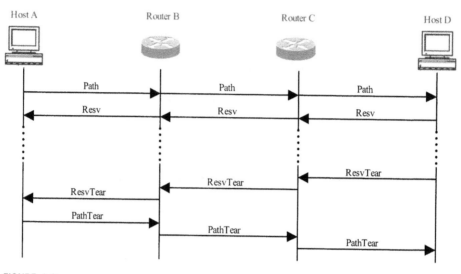

FIGURE 4.8

RSVP ResvTear message flow.

Finally, the ingress may decide to do nothing, leaving its current request in place and hoping that the egress will have a change of heart and will assign new resources. In any event, after a ResvTear the traffic may continue to flow and be delivered in a best-effort manner.

4.4.3 Sessions and Flows

The concepts of *sessions* and *flows* are important in RSVP, but are often confused. A session is defined by the triplet {destination address, destination port, payload protocol}. This information provides the basic categorization of packets that are going to the same destination application and can be handled within the network in the same way. Sessions are identified in RSVP by the Session Object carried on Path and Resv messages, but note that the IP packet that carries a Path message is also addressed to the destination IP address (i.e., the egress end of the session).

A session, however, does not identify the data flow since this depends on the source. A flow is characterized by the pair {source address, source port} in conjunction with the session identifier. This construct allows multiple flows within a single session. This facility can be used for multiple flows from a single source or for merging flows from multiple sources (see Section 4.4.7). Flows are identified on Path messages by the Sender Template Object and on Resv messages by Filter-Spec Objects.

Both the destination and the source ports may be assigned the value zero. This is most useful when the payload protocol does not use ports to distinguish flows. Note that it is considered an error to have two sessions with the same destination address and payload protocol, one with a zero destination port and one with a nonzero destination port. If the destination port is zero, the source port for all the flows on the session must also be zero, providing a consistency check for payload protocols that do not support the use of ports. It is also considered an error to have one flow on a session with source port zero and another with a nonzero source port.

4.4.4 **Requesting, Discovering, and Reserving Resources**

Each Path message carries a Sender TSpec, which defines the traffic characteristics of the data flow the sender will generate. The TSpec may be used by a *traffic control* component at transit routers to prevent propagation of Path messages that would lead to reservation requests that would be doomed to fail. A transit router may decide to fail a Path by sending a PathErr (see Section 4.4.5); may use the TSpec as input to the routing process, especially where equal cost paths exist; or may note the problem but still forward the Path message, hoping that the issue will have been resolved by the time the Resv is processed. The contents of the Sender TSpec are described in Section 4.3. They characterize the flow as a token bucket with peak data rate, maximum packet size, and minimum policed unit.

As the Path message progresses across the network it may also collect information about the available resources on the nodes and links traversed and the IntServ capabilities of the transit nodes. The Adspec object is optional, but if present is updated by each node so that by the time the Path message reaches the egress node it contains a view of the delays and constraints that will be applied to data as it traverses the path. This helps the egress node decide what resources the network will need to reserve to support the flow described in the TSpec. Of course, by the time the Resv message is processed within the network the reported Adspec may be out of date, but subsequent Path messages for the same flow may be used to update the Adspec, causing modifications to the reservation request on further Resv messages.

The Resv message makes a request to the network to reserve resources for the flow. The FlowSpec object describes the token bucket that must be implemented by nodes within the network to support the flow described by the TSpec given the capabilities reported by the TSpec.

The format of the contents of the TSpec, Adspec, and FlowSpec for RSVP are described in Section 4.3.

4.4.5 **Error Handling**

RSVP has two messages for reporting errors. The PathErr message flows from downstream to upstream (the reverse direction from the Path message), and reports issues related to Path state. The ResvErr message reports issues with Resv state or resource reservation and flows from upstream to downstream. So the PathErr is sent back to the sender of a Path message, and the ResvErr is sent back to the sender of a Resv message.

Error messages carry session and flow identifiers reflected from the Path or Resv message and also include an Error Spec Object. The error is specified using an error code to categorize the problem and an error value to identify the exact issue within the category.

The PathErr message flow is shown in Figure 4.9. There are relatively few reasons why Router C might decide to reject the Path request (step 2), but the router might apply policy to the request, might not be able to support the requested flow, or might find that the session clashes with an existing session (one has destination port zero and the other nonzero). It is also possible that Router C does not recognize one of the objects on the Path message and needs to reject the message—this allows for forward compatibility with new message objects introduced in the future. The PathErr message is returned hop-by-hop toward the ingress. Router B (step 3) examines the error code and value and determines whether it can resolve the issue by modifying the Path message it sends. If it cannot, it forwards the PathErr on toward the ingress and does not remove its own Path state.

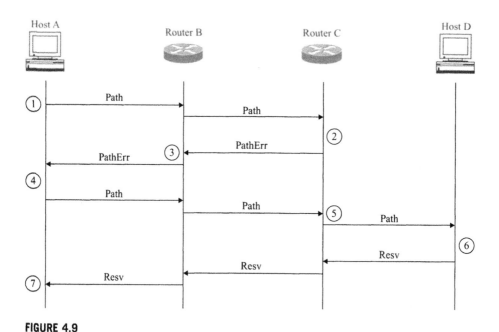

FIGURE 4.9

Example message flow showing the RSVP PathErr message.

When the PathErr reaches the ingress node (step 4) it has three options. It may give up on the whole idea and send a PathTear to remove the state from the network, it may resend the Path message as it is in the hope that the issue in the network will resolve itself (possibly through management intervention), or it may modify the Path message to address the problem. When the new Path reaches Router C (step 5) it will either reject it again with a PathErr or it will accept the message and forward it, leading to the establishment of the RSVP reservation.

PathErr may also be used after a Resource Reservation Protocol flow has been established. The most common use is to report that a reservation has been administratively preempted.

The ResvErr message is used to reject a Resv message or to indicate that there is a problem with resources that have already been reserved. The flow of a ResvErr does not affect Path state, but it does cause the removal of Resv state and frees up any resources that have been reserved. Figure 4.10 shows an example message flow including a ResvErr message.

When the Resv reaches Router B it determines that it cannot accept the message (step 3). The reason may be policy or formatting of the message, as with the Path/PathErr message, or the rejection may happen because the Resv asks for resources that are not available—note that Router B's resources may have been

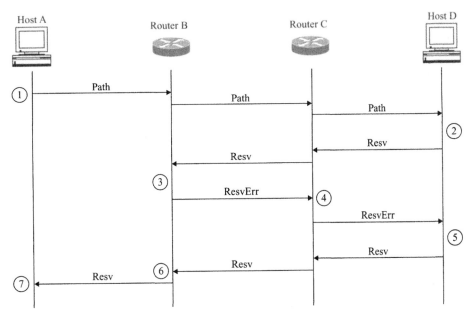

FIGURE 4.10

Example message flow showing the RSVP ResvErr message.

allocated to other RSVP flows after the Adspec was added to the Path message. Some errors can be handled by transit nodes (Router C at step 4), which might issue a new Resv, but usually ResvErr messages are propagated all the way to the egress, removing Resv state and freeing resources as they go.

When an egress (Host D at step 5) receives a ResvErr it has four options. It may reissue the original Resv in the hope that the problem in the network will be resolved, or it may give up and send a PathErr back to the ingress to let it know that all is not well. However, two options exist for making constructive changes to the resource request on the Resv message that may allow the RSVP flow to be established. First, the egress may simply modify the resource request in the light of the error received—this is shown in Figure 4.10 where the new Resv reaches Router B (step 6) and is accepted and forwarded to the ingress. The second constructive change can arise if the Path message is retried by the ingress—as it traverses the network it will pick up new Adspec values that reflect the currently available resources and this will allow the egress to make a better choice of resource request for the Resv.

In practice, there may be some overlap in the procedures for handling a ResvErr at the egress. The egress will usually send a PathErr and retry the old Resv with any updates it can determine and modify its behavior if it receives a new Path message.

4.4.6 Adapting to Changes in the Network

As suggested in the preceding section, RSVP handles problems during the establishment of an RSVP flow by resending its Path and Resv messages periodically. This feature is even more important in the context of changes to the topology and routes of a network.

The initial Path message is propagated through the network according to the forwarding tables installed at the ingress and transit nodes. At each RSVP router, the Path is packaged into an IP header, addressed to the egress/destination host, and forwarded to the next router. The Resv is returned hop-by-hop along the path of the Path without any routing between nodes. The reservations are, therefore, made along the path that the Path message followed, which will be the path that IP data also traverses.

But what would happen if there were a change in the network so that IP data followed a new route? The reservations would remain on the old path, but the data would flow through other routers where no reservations had been made. This serious issue is resolved by having each node retransmit *(refresh)* its Path message periodically—each message is subject to the routing process and will be passed to the new next hop and so onward to the same egress. The Resv is now sent back hop-by-hop along the new path, and reservations are made along the new path to support the data flow that is using it.

Of course, the process described would leave unused resources allocated on the old path, which is not good because those resources could not be used to support other flows. This problem is countered by having the nodes on the old path timeout when they do not receive a Path after a period (generally $5\frac{1}{4}$ times the retransmission period to allow for occasional packet loss). When a node times out, it knows that there is some problem with the upstream node—maybe the link from the upstream node is broken, or perhaps the ingress has simply lost interest in the reservation, or the Path could have been routed another way. When a node stops receiving Path messages it stops forwarding Path and Resv messages and removes the Path state associated with the flow.

Resv messages are similarly refreshed. This provides for survival of packet loss and guarantees cleanup of the Resv state and the allocated resources in the event of a network failure or a change in the Path.

Message refresh processing and rerouting is illustrated in Figure 4.11. Step 1 shows normal Path and Resv exchange from Host A to Host F through Routers C and E (the shortest path). Step 2 indicates refresh processing as Path and Resv messages are resent between the routers, but Host A now routes the Path message to Router B and so through Router D to Router E. Router E (step 4) is a *merge point* for the old and new flows and sends the new Path message on to the egress (Host F) resulting in a new Resv from Host F (steps 5 and 6). Note that the merge point (Router E) may decide to handle the merging of the flows itself by sending an Resv back to Router D without sending a Path on to the destination, Host F.

Router E can now make a reservation on the interface from Router D and send an Resv to Router D. The Resv follows its new path back to Host A through Router B (step 7) and all reservations are now in place on the new path. Note that data is already flowing along the new path and was as soon as the change in the routing table took effect—this was before the Path refresh was sent on the new route. This means that for a while the data was flowing down a path for which it had no specific reservation, highlighting the fact that RSVP is a best-effort reservation process.

Step 8 indicates the refresh process on the new path and on the fragments of the old path that are still in place. Each node sends a Path and an Resv to its neighbor, with the exception that Host A sends a Path only to Router B.

After a while, Router C notices that it has not seen a Path message from Host A (step 9). It may simply remove state and allow the state to timeout downstream or, as in this case, it may send a PathTear to clean up. When the merge point, Router E, receives the PathTear (step 10) it must not propagate it to the egress as this would remove the reservation for the whole flow. Instead, it removes the reservation on the interface (from Router C) on which the PathTear was received and notices that it still has an incoming flow (from router D) so does not forward the message.

At step 11, Host A notices that it hasn't received a Resv from Router C and cleans up any remaining resources.

Because the state messages (Path and Resv) must be periodically resent to keep the RSVP state active, RSVP is known as a *soft state* protocol. The protocol over-

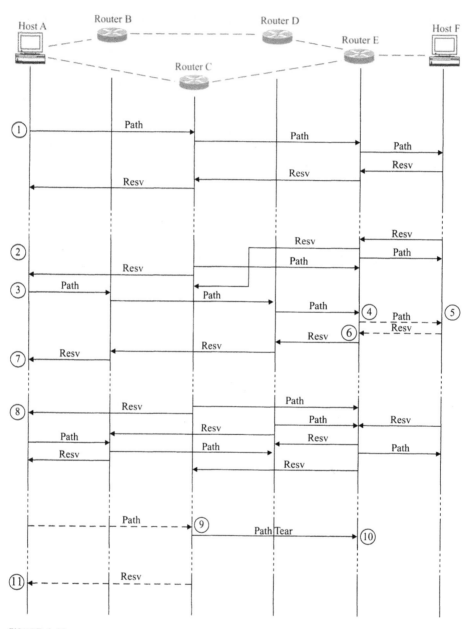

FIGURE 4.11

Message refresh processing and rerouting in an RSVP network.

heads of a soft state have been the cause of many heated debates within the IETF. The concern is that the number of flows in a network may reach a point at which all of the bandwidth on a link, or all of the processing power of a router, will be used up sending Path and Resv refresh messages, leaving no capacity for data forwarding. Several solutions to reduce the impact of refresh processing have been developed and are covered in a separate RFC (*RFC 2961*). They are described in Section 4.4.12.

Even when RSVP messages are being refreshed, there is some risk that during network overload RSVP packets will be dropped too often, resulting in the soft state timing out. For this reason, routers are recommended to give priority to IP packets that indicate that they are carrying RSVP messages.

4.4.7 **Merging Flows**

The preceding sections have alluded to merging flows in two contexts. First, when distinguishing between sessions and flows, the use of RSVP to reserve resources for multipoint-to-point flows was mentioned. Second, the discussion of adapting to changes in the network introduced the concept of a merge point where the old and new paths combined.

RSVP is structured to handle merging of flows within a session so that resources are not double allocated. Figure 4.12 illustrates flow merging in a very simple network to support a multipoint-to-point session from Hosts A and B to Host D. There are two flows: A to D and B to D, with a single session carrying one payload protocol for both flows and terminating at the same port on Host D.

In the example, Host A starts with the usual Path/Resv exchange (step 1). A ResvConf is sent to confirm that the reservation has been installed. Some time later (step 2) Host B wants to join in and sends its own Path message. When this second Path reaches Router C (step 3) it sees that although the flows are different (distinct source addresses) the session is the same (identical destination address, destination port, and payload protocol), so it is acceptable to merge the flows. However, merging the reservations for the flows is the responsibility of the egress host and not the merge point, so Router C forwards a Path message for the new flow.

When the new Path message reaches the egress (Host D at step 4) it may choose to merge the reservations on the shared links—in this case, for the link between Router C and Host D. It looks at the Sender TSpec from the two Path messages and computes the reservations that must be made to accommodate both flows. The reservation requests are made on a single Resv that applies to the whole session, and may be expressed as a single reservation for both flows or as a reservation for each flow.

When the Resv message reaches Router C (step 5) it splits the reservation for the two separate upstream branches. In this simple case the existing branch from Host A does not need to be modified and Router C simply sends a Resv to Host B indicating the reservation that applies to the link from Host B to Router C. This

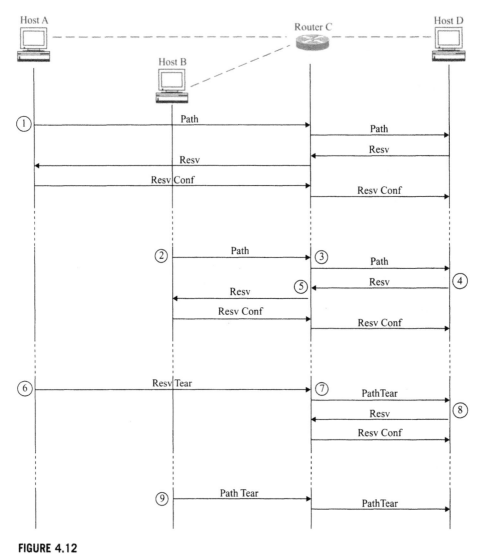

FIGURE 4.12

Simple example of flow merging in an RSVP network.

process may be as simple as removing the reference to the flow from Host A and forwarding the Resv, but more likely it involves some recomputation.

The computation of shared resources may be nontrivial since the requirements may not lead to a simple summation of the resources for the two flows. In particular, some applications such as voice over IP conference calling do not call for each flow to be active at the same time, in which case the reservation for merged flows is no different from that for a single flow.

		Resource sharing	
		No sharing	Sharing allowed
Sender specification	Explicit	Fixed filter style (FF)	Shared explicit style (SE)
	Wildcard	Not defined	Wildcard filter style (WF)

FIGURE 4.13

RSVP styles are defined by the type of resource sharing and how the flows are identified.

Figure 4.12 also shows the removal of flows from a merged situation. At step 6, Host A withdraws from the multipoint-to-point flow and sends PathTear. Router C (step 7) forwards the PathTear, but it must be careful to remove only the state associated with the flow that is removed—in this case, it does not remove any Resv state nor release any resources because they are still associated with the active Path state from Host B. When the egress (Host D at step 8) gets the PathTear it can recompute the reservation requirements; it may do this from its records of Path state or it may wait until it sees a Path refresh for the active flow. In any case, the result is a new Resv with potentially reduced resource requirements. In the simple case, this Resv is not forwarded by Router C since it simply reduces the resource requirements to those needed (and already in place) on the link from Host B to Router C. Finally (step 9), when Host B sends PathTear, all of the remaining state and resources are released.

RSVP defines three *styles* for resource reservation. These are used by the egress to indicate how resources may be shared between flows (i.e., data on the same session from different senders). Two qualities are defined: the ability to share resources and the precision of specification of flow (i.e., the sender). The correlation of these qualities defines three styles, as shown in Figure 4.13. A Style Object is included in a Resv to let the upstream nodes know how to interpret the list of FlowSpec Objects and FilterSpec Objects it carries (indicating resource requests and associated flows—annoyingly, the FlowSpec describes the aggregate data flow resources and not the individual flows which are found in FilterSpecs). This becomes more obvious in conjunction with the message formats shown in Section 4.4.9.

4.4.8 Multicast Resource Sharing

The resource sharing considered in the previous section handles the case of multipoint-to-point flows in which the flows share downstream legs and optimize resource allocations on the legs with the knowledge that the data sources are in some way synchronized and will not flood downstream legs. RSVP also supports

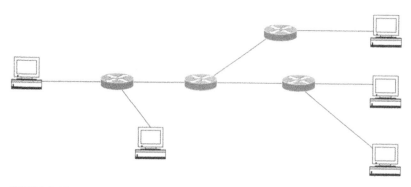

FIGURE 4.14

An RSVP multicast session.

multicast flows (i.e., point-to-multipoint) in which a flow has a single upstream leg that branches as it proceeds downstream as shown in Figure 4.14.

Resource sharing in the multicast case is more intuitive since there is only one traffic source and the resources required to support the traffic are independent of the branches that may occur downstream. However, as the Path message is forwarded from node to node it is copied and sent out on many different legs. Each time it is forked, we can expect to see a distinct Resv message flow in the opposite direction. Each Resv flows back upstream to the ingress and carries a request to reserve resources. Clearly, we do not want to reserve resources for each Resv, and some form of merging of Resv messages must be achieved. On the other hand, some of the egress nodes may require different reservations, so the merging of reservations at upstream nodes may not be trivial.

RSVP uses the same mechanisms for resource sharing in multicast sessions. That is, Resv messages use styles to indicate how they apply to one or more flows or sessions. Beyond this, it is the responsibility of *split points* to merge the requirements received on Resv messages from downstream and to send a single, unified Resv upstream. It is possible that the first Resv received and propagated will ask for sufficient resources, in which case the split point does not need to send any subsequent Resv messages upstream. On the other hand, if a Resv received from downstream after the first Resv has been propagated upstream demands increased resources, the split point must send a new, modified Resv upstream.

Note that a split point must not wait to receive a Resv from all downstream end points before sending one upstream because it cannot know how many to expect and which end points will respond.

A split point that is responsible for merging Resvs must also manage the distribution of ResvConf messages to downstream nodes that have asked for them since these messages will not be generated by the ingress after the first reservation has been installed.

4.4.9 **RSVP Messages and Formats**

Formal definitions of the messages in RSVP can be found in *RFC 2205*. The notation used is called *Backus-Naur Form* (BNF). It is a list of mandatory and optional objects. Each object is denoted by angle brackets "< object >" and optional objects or sequences are contained in square brackets "[< optional object >]." Sequences of objects are sometimes displayed as a single composite object which is defined later. Choices between objects are denoted by a vertical bar "< object one > | < object 2 >."

Note that the ordering of objects within a message is strongly recommended, but is not mandatory (except that the members of composite objects must be kept together) and an implementation should be prepared to receive objects in any order while generating them in the order listed here.

Figure 4.15 shows the formal definition of the Path message. The sequence of objects, Sender Template, Sender TSpec, and Adspec is referred to as the *sender descriptor*. This becomes relevant in the context of Resv messages which may carry information relevant to more than one sender descriptor.

Figure 4.16 shows the formal definition of an Resv message. The *flow descriptor list* (expanded in Figures 4.17 through 4.19) is a composite sequence of objects that allows a single Resv message to describe reservations for multiple sender descriptors requested on Path messages. The type of flow descriptor list that is used depends on the Style Object, which indicates the style of resource sharing. As described in Section 4.4.7, there are three styles: *wildcard-filter* (WF), which applies to all flows on the session; *fixed-filter* (FF), which applies a single reservation to a specific list of flows; and *shared-explicit* (SE), which applies different reservations to different lists of flows on the same session.

The FF flow descriptor is, itself, a composite object containing the FilterSpec and Label objects and optionally a *Record Route* object. Notice that this definition of FF flow descriptor aligns with the definition of the sender descriptor.

```
< Path Message > ::=        < Common Header >
                            [< INTEGRITY >]
                            < SESSION >
                            < RSVP_HOP >
                            < TIME_VALUES >
                            [<POLICY_DATA >]
                            < sender descriptor >
< sender descriptor > ::=   < SENDER_TEMPLATE >
                            < SENDER_TSPEC >
                            [< ADSPEC >]
```

FIGURE 4.15

Formal definition of the RSVP Path message.

```
< Resv Message > ::=        < Common Header >
                            [ < INTEGRITY > ]
                            < SESSION >
                            < RSVP_HOP >
                            < TIME_VALUES >
                            [ < RESV_CONFIRM >]
                            [ < SCOPE >]
                            [ < POLICY_DATA > ]
                            < STYLE >
                            < flow descriptor list >
```

FIGURE 4.16

Formal definition of the RSVP Resv message.

```
< flow descriptor list > ::=        < WF flow descriptor >
< WF flow descriptor > ::=          < FLOWSPEC >
```

FIGURE 4.17

Formal definition of the RSVP WF flow descriptor list used on RSVP Resv messages.

```
< flow descriptor list > ::=    < FF flow descriptor >
                                [ < flow descriptor list > ]
< FF flow descriptor > ::=      < FLOWSPEC >
                                < filter spec list >
< filter spec list > ::=        < FILTER_SPEC >
                                [ < filter spec list > ]
```

FIGURE 4.18

Formal definition of the RSVP FF flow descriptor list used on RSVP Resv messages.

```
< flow descriptor list > ::=        < SE flow descriptor >
< SE flow descriptor > ::=          < FLOWSPEC >
                                    < filter spec list >
< filter spec list > ::=            < FILTER_SPEC >
                                    [ < filter spec list > ]
```

FIGURE 4.19

Formal definition of the RSVP SE flow descriptor list used on RSVP Resv messages.

```
< PathTear Message > ::=          < Common Header >
                                  [ < INTEGRITY > ]
                                  < SESSION >
                                  < RSVP_HOP >
                                  [ < sender descriptor > ]
```

FIGURE 4.20

Formal definition of the RSVP PathTear message.

The last element of the FF flow descriptor is recursive, allowing a list of sub-lists where each sublist starts with a FlowSpec. It also allows the sublist to be just an FF flow descriptor—in this case the FlowSpec is assumed to be identical to the most recent one seen in the message.

This rather complex notation facilitates a rather complex real-world situation in which merged flows or parallel flows share resources. Note that the notation used in the preceding figures differs slightly from that presented in *RFC 2205* in an attempt at greater clarity.

Compound objects are also used for the *shared explicit* case, as shown in Figure 4.19, but note that here only one FlowSpec object may be present. The subsequent SE filter specifications match sender descriptors and all use the one FlowSpec. Again, a variation on the notation of *RFC 2205* is used here for clarity.

Figure 4.20 shows the message format for a PathTear message. The PathTear is modeled on the Path message. The sender descriptor is, however, optional since it is not always necessary to identify the sender when tearing down a flow; the RSVP Hop Object identifies the upstream node, and this is usually enough to clarify the Path state that is being removed. In cases of shared resources in which only one flow from a session is being removed, the sender descriptor must be present to disambiguate the flows.

The ResvTear message shown in Figure 4.21 is modeled on the Resv. Unlike the Path/PathTear relationship, the flow descriptor is mandatory and identifies exactly which resource reservations are being torn.

The PathErr and ResvErr messages shown in Figures 4.22 and 4.23 are based, respectively, on the Path and Resv messages to which they respond. That is, even though a PathErr message flows from downstream to upstream, it is still modeled to look like a Path message. As with PathTear and ResvTear, the sender descriptor is optional on a PathErr but the flow descriptor is mandatory on a ResvErr. Both messages carry the Error Spec Object to indicate the reported problem.

There has been some contention about the presence, or rather absence, of an RSVP Hop Object on a PathErr message. Its presence would certainly have been possible since the message is generated in response to a Path message, and including it would have made implementation easier, but it is not strictly necessary since

```
< ResvTear Message > ::=        < Common Header >
                                [ < INTEGRITY > ]
                                < SESSION >
                                < RSVP_HOP >
                                [ < SCOPE >]
                                < STYLE >
                                < flow descriptor list >
```

FIGURE 4.21

Formal definition of the RSVP ResvTear message.

```
< PathErr Message > ::=        < Common Header >
                               [ < INTEGRITY > ]
                               < SESSION >
                               < ERROR_SPEC >
                               [ < POLICY_DATA > ]
                               [ < sender descriptor > ]
```

FIGURE 4.22

Formal definition of the RSVP PathErr message.

```
< ResvErr Message > ::=        < Common Header >
                               [ < INTEGRITY > ]
                               < SESSION >
                               < RSVP_HOP >
                               < ERROR_SPEC >
                               [ < SCOPE >]
                               [ < POLICY_DATA >]
                               < STYLE >
                               < flow descriptor >
```

FIGURE 4.23

Formal definition of the RSVP ResvErr message.

the PathErr should be received through the interface out of which the Path was originally sent. This debate becomes interesting when a Path is sent out of one interface and then (after a change to the routing table) out of another interface—when a PathErr is received it is important to work out whether it applies to the old or the new path.

```
< ResvConf Message > ::=        < Common Header >
                                [ < INTEGRITY > ]
                                < SESSION >
                                < ERROR_SPEC >
                                < RESV_CONFIRM >
                                < STYLE >
                                < flow descriptor list >
```

FIGURE 4.24

Formal definition of the RSVP ResvConf message.

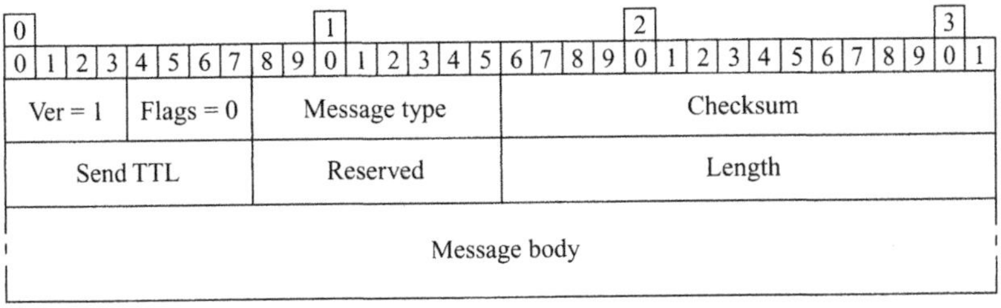

0										1										2										3	
0	1	2	3	4	5	6	7	8	9	0	1	2	3	4	5	6	7	8	9	0	1	2	3	4	5	6	7	8	9	0	1

Ver = 1	Flags = 0	Message type	Checksum
Send TTL		Reserved	Length
Message body			

FIGURE 4.25

Each RSVP message has a common message header.

The ResvConf message shown in Figure 4.24 confirms a specific reservation and so is modeled on the Resv message. The message contains an Error Spec Object, not to report errors, but to report the source of the ResvConf, which might not be the ingress node in the case of merged flows.

As can be seen from Figures 4.15 through 4.24, all RSVP messages begin with a common header—this is shown in Figure 4.25. The header identifies the version of RSVP (currently one) and has a flags field for future use. The message type field identifies the RSVP message using values from Table 4.3. The checksum and length fields are applied to the whole message, including all fields of the header, with the length specified in bytes. The checksum is computed as a standard one's complement of the one's complement sum of the message, with the checksum field replaced by zero for the purpose of computing the checksum. If the checksum field is transmitted containing a zero value, no checksum was transmitted.

The Send TTL field in the message header is used to restrict the number of RSVP hops on a path. Since RSVP messages are intercepted at each RSVP-capable router, the normal IP TTL mechanism can be used only to restrict the number of IP hops between RSVP capable routers. To restrict the absolute length of the RSVP path and to provide some protection against looping, there is a TTL field in the RSVP header. The RSVP and IP TTL fields can also be used to detect the presence

Table 4.3 RSVP Message Types

Message Type	Value Message
1	Path
2	Resv
3	PathErr
4	ResvErr
5	PathTear
6	ResvTear
7	ResvConf

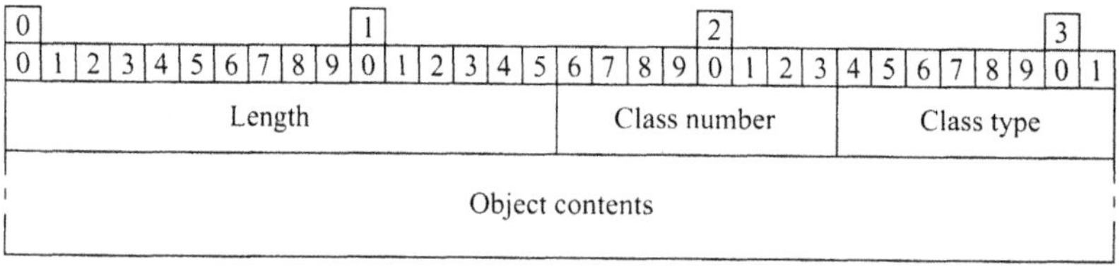

FIGURE 4.26

All RSVP message objects have a common format.

of non-RSVP hops since the two fields will remain in step only if each hop processes both fields.

4.4.10 RSVP Objects and Formats

As already described, RSVP messages are constructed from a common header followed by a series of message objects. All message objects have a common format, shown in Figure 4.26. The objects can be described as length-type-value (LTV) constructs since they begin with a length field that gives the size in bytes of the entire object, followed by indicators of the type of object. The type indicator divides the objects into classes (primary types) indicated by the class number (C-Num) and subtypes indicated by the class type (C-Type). For example, the Session Object has a C-Num of 1, but since it contains an IP address that may be an IPv4 or an IPv6 address, two C-Types are defined.

Although the C-Num value can be treated as a unique integer identifying the class of object, the top 2 bits are overloaded to tell a message recipient how to handle the message if it does not recognize or support an object carried on the message. If the most significant bit is clear, the object must be handled or the

Table 4.4 Top Bits of RSVP Object Class Numbers Direct Processing If Object Is Unrecognized or Unsupported by the Message's Receiver

C-Num Bit Setting	Processing of Unrecognized or Unsupported Object
0bbbbbbb	Reject entire message
10bbbbbb	Ignore object and do not propagate
11bbbbbb	Ignore object, but propagate unchanged

entire message must be rejected. If the top bit is set, unrecognized objects may be ignored and must be propagated or removed from derivative messages according to the setting of the next most significant bit. These bit settings are shown in Table 4.4. Since this is the first version of RSVP, all objects are mandatory and have the top bit of their C-Num clear. Future extensions, such as those for RSVP-TE, may set the top bit to differentiate function when interoperating with older implementations of the base RSVP specification. Note that it is not valid to consider a Session Object with a C-Num that has the top bit set (i.e., with C-Num $129 = 0\times81$). That would be an entirely different C-Num and so would indicate a different object.

All RSVP objects are a multiple of 4 bytes in length. Where necessary, this is achieved using explicit padding. This means that during message parsing each object starts on a 4-byte boundary.

The Session Object shown in Figure 4.27 is used to define the session to which the flow belongs. A session is defined by the destination address (IPv4 or IPv6), the destination port, and the payload protocol, so all these are carried in this object. The C-Type is used to identify whether an IPv4 or IPv6 address is used. The port number may be set to zero to indicate a session that encompasses flows to all ports on the destination node. The protocol identifier is the IP protocol identifier value that indicates the protocol carried by the IP data flow.

The other field, the flags field, has one defined bit for use on Path messages only; if the value 0×01 is set, then the originator of the Path is unable to provide edge-based policing that the actual traffic flow falls within the parameters set in the sender TSpec. The flag is propagated through the network until some node is able to take responsibility for policing the traffic.

The Class Number 3 is used to identify the RSVP Hop Object shown in Figure 4.28. (Note, C-Num 2 is mysteriously undefined!) The object identifies the interface through which this message was sent using an IPv4 or IPv6 address. That is, on a Path message, the address identifies the downstream interface of the upstream node, while on a Resv the address indicates the upstream interface of the downstream node. The RSVP Hop Object is sometimes referred to as the previous hop (PHOP) when it is carried on a message that flows from upstream to downstream (as a Path) and as the next hop (NHOP) when it is on a message that flows from downstream to upstream (as a Resv).

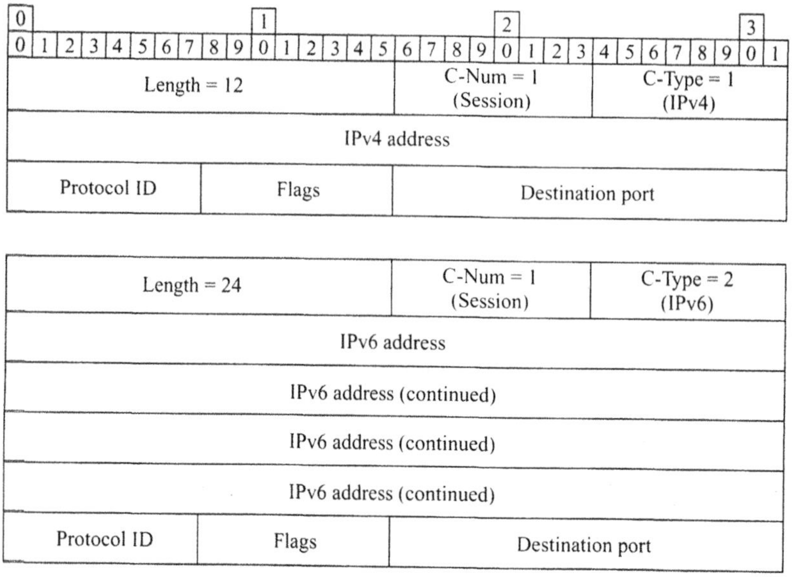

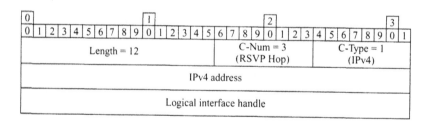

FIGURE 4.27

RSVP Session Object has an IPv4 and an IPv6 type.

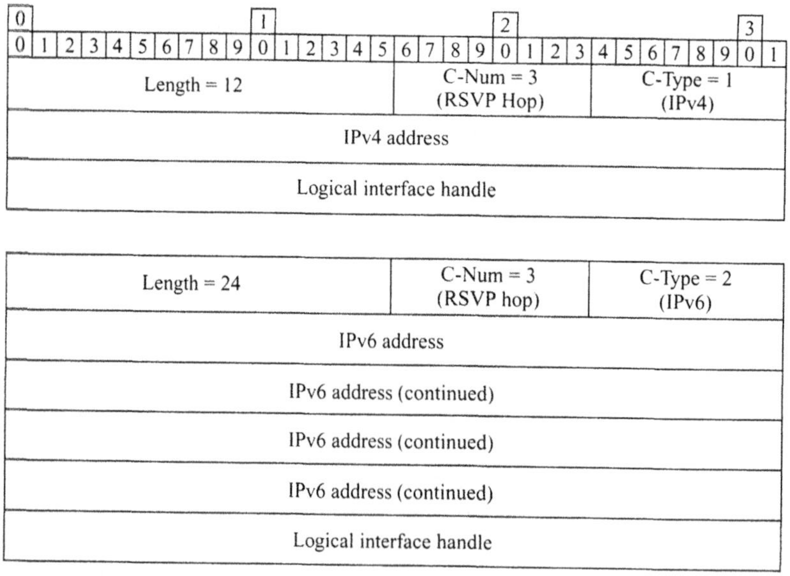

FIGURE 4.28

The RSVP Hop Object has an IPv4 and an IPv6 type.

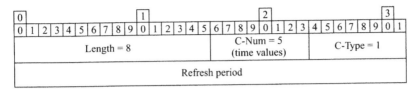

FIGURE 4.29

RSVP Time Values Object.

The RSVP Hop Object also contains a *logical interface handle* (LIH). This value is supplied by the upstream node on the Path message and is reflected back unchanged on the Resv. It can be used by the upstream node as a quick index to the interface without the need to look up any IP addresses (perhaps containing an interface index, or even a pointer to a control block). The fact that the IP address in the RSVP Hop Object changes but the LIH is returned unchanged, has led to innumerable implementation bugs.

The Time Values Object shown in Figure 4.29 has C-Num 5. It carries just one piece of information: the interval between refresh messages sent to refresh state, measured in milliseconds. This object is included in all Path messages and indicates how frequently the Path message will be refreshed. Similarly, the object is present on Resv messages and indicates how often the Resv will be refreshed.

In fact, refreshes are not sent precisely according to the refresh interval. It is a curious fact that messages sent periodically by independent nodes in a network can tend to become synchronized or clustered. If there are very many RSVP flows, this clustering of refresh messages may lead to contention for processing or network resources with a consequent disruption to control or even data traffic. RSVP disrupts this synchronization effect by randomly *jittering* the refresh intervals—*RFC 2205* recommends that the actual refresh interval between refresh messages be picked randomly for each retransmission from the range half to one-and-a-half times the signaled refresh period. Note that the signaled refresh period is not updated for each refresh.

The refresh period is signaled to allow the recipient of the message to know when to expect to receive a refresh. This is important in determining when the soft-state should timeout if no refresh is received. Clearly, the largest interval between two consecutive refreshes will be one-and-a-half times the signaled refresh period. If there is some possibility of losing packets but still continuing to support the flow, this number must be multiplied by the number of refreshes that will actually be sent. This gives a formula for a state timeout (T) as follows:

$$T = K \times 1.5 \times R$$

where R is the signaled refresh period and K is the number of retransmissions (i.e., we are prepared to lose $K - 1$ refresh attempts). To this, add a little time for processing at the send and receive ends and for network propagation (say half of the maximum refresh interval) and the formula becomes:

$$(K + 0.5) \times 1.5 \times R$$

For general use, the value $K = 3$ is suggested in *RFC 2205*, although this might need to be varied for very unreliable networks. Turning the handle on this gives the state timeout period of $5\frac{1}{4} R$ mentioned in Section 4.4.6.

Class Number 6 is used for the Error Spec Object carried on PathErr, ResvErr, and ResvConf messages and shown in Figure 4.30. Two C-Types are defined to indicate IPv4 or IPv6 addressing. The object reports the address of the node on which the error was first detected (or in the case of a ResvConf, the node that originated the message), an error code to describe or classify the error, and an error value to precisely specify the error—values for the error code and error value are listed in Table 4.5.

The Error Spec Object also carries a flags field. Currently just one flag value is defined for use on the wire and this is valid only on ResvErr messages. 0×01 indicates that a reservation is still in place at the failure point.

Malformed messages are not generally reported to end systems in a PathErr or ResvErr and are simply logged locally, or reported through network management mechanisms. The only message formatting errors that are reported to end systems are those that may reflect version mismatches such as unknown object C-Nums

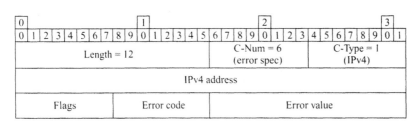

FIGURE 4.30

The RSVP Error Spec Object has an IPv4 and an IPv6 type.

Table 4.5 RSVP Error Codes and Values

Code	Value	Meaning
0	0	Confirmation (used on ResvConf messages only)
1		Admission control failure reported on ResvErr messages when the requested resources are unavailable. The first 4 bits of the error value are *ssur* where: ■ ss = 00: the remaining 12 bits contain an error value listed below ■ ss = 10: the remaining 12 bits contain an organization-specific value unknown to RSVP ■ ss = 11: the remaining 12 bits contain a value specific to a service, unknown to RSVP ■ $u = 0$ means that RSVP must remove local Resv state and forward the message ■ $u = 1$ means that the message is information and that RSVP may forward the message without removing local Resv state ■ The *r* bit is reserved and should be zero.
	1	Delay bound cannot be met.
	2	Requested bandwidth unavailable.
	3	MTU in FlowSpec larger than interface MTU.
2		Policy control failures (defined in *RFC 2750*) appear on PathErr or ResvErr messages to show that the corresponding Path or Resv was rejected for administrative reasons such as authentication or permissions to request the reservation.
3	0	A Resv message was received but the receiver could not correlate it to any Path state for the corresponding session. This is used only on a ResvErr.
4	0	A Resv message was received and, although the receiver has Path state for the corresponding session, it cannot correlate some flow descriptor on the Resv to a sender template on a Path that it has previously sent. This is used only on a ResvErr.
5		The reservation style conflicts with style(s) of existing reservation state on the session. The error value holds the low-order 16 bits of the *option vector* of the existing style (i.e., from the style object of a previous Resv). This is used only on a ResvErr.
	0	The reservation style on a Resv is unknown. This is used only on a ResvErr.
	0	Messages for the same destination address and protocol have appeared, one with a zero destination port and one with a nonzero destination port. This error would normally be used on a PathErr to reflect a problem with Path messages.
8	0	Path messages for the same session have the sender port set to zero and nonzero.

Continued

Table 4.5 RSVP Error Codes and Values *Continued*

Code	Value	Meaning
12		A previous reservation has been administratively preempted. The top 4 bits of the error value are as defined for error code 1. No RSVP-specific error values are defined.
13		An unknown object was received in a Path or Resv message and the high-order bits of the C-Num indicate that such an event should cause the entire message to be rejected. The error value shows the C-Num and C-Type of the unknown object. This error code may appear in a PathErr or ResvErr message.
14		An object with a known C-Num but an unknown C-Type was received in a Path or Resv message. The error value shows the C-Num and C-Type of the unknown object. This error code may appear in a PathErr or ResvErr message.
20		Reserved for use on the API between applications and RSVP.
21		The format or contents of the traffic parameters (TSpec, Adspec, or FlowSpec) could not be processed. The top 4 bits of the error value are broken up as *ssrr* where ss is as defined as for error code one and *rr* is reserved and set to zero. The remaining bits have the values set out below when ss = 00.
	1	Cannot merge two incompatible service requests.
	2	Can provide neither the requested service nor an acceptable replacement.
	3	The FlowSpec contains a malformed or unreasonable request.
	4	The TSpec contains a malformed or unreasonable request.
	5	The Adspec contains a malformed or unreasonable request.
22		A system error occurred while processing the traffic parameters (TSpec, Adspec, and FlowSpec). The error value is system specific and unknown to RSVP.
23		A system error occurred in the RSVP implementation. The error value is system specific and unknown to RSVP.

or C-Types. This choice is made because the report of a formatting error cannot be dynamically corrected by the node that caused the error, but a node that sends an unsupported object may be able to fall back to a mode of operation that does not require the object.

The RSVP Scope Object shown in Figure 4.31 is carried on Resv, ResvErr, and ResvTear messages. It contains a list of addresses of senders (i.e., flow sources) to which the message applies. This is useful to prevent message loops in multicast networks using the Wildcard Filter reservation style, but is otherwise not used. All addresses carried in a single Scope Object are of the same type. The type is

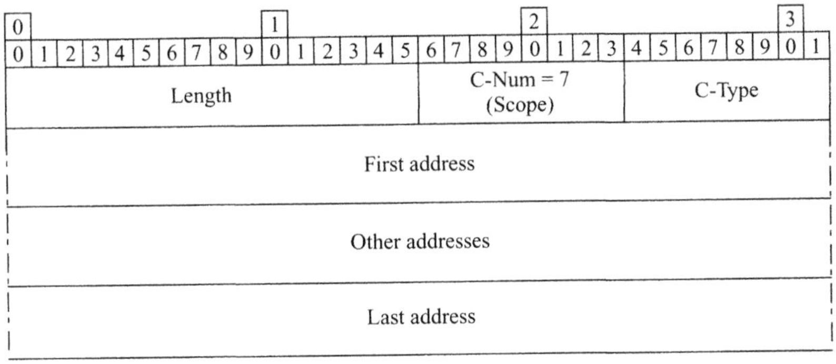

FIGURE 4.31

RSVP Scope Object is a list of addresses of the same type.

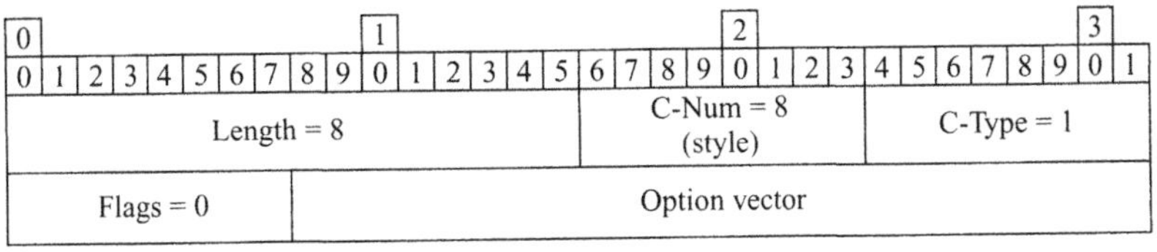

FIGURE 4.32

The RSVP Style Object.

indicated by the C-Type field (set to 1 for IPv4 and 2 for IPv6). Since only one Scope Object may be present on a Resv, scoped Resv messages can apply to sources with one address type only.

The Style Object encodes the reservation style discussed in Section 4.4.7. As shown in Figure 4.32, the object contains a flags field (currently no flags are defined) and an option vector. The option vector encodes the two style components (type of resource sharing, and flows identification) shown in Figure 4.13. Only the least significant 5 bits of the vector are used, as shown in Table 4.6.

The Style Object is mandatory on Resv, ResvTear, and ResvErr messages but not included on Path, PathTear, PathErr, or ResvConf messages (causing Frank Sinatra, Bing Crosby, and Dean Martin to sing, "You either have or you haven't got style").

Figure 4.33 shows the FilterSpec Object carried on Resv, ResvTear, ResvErr, and ResvConf messages to identify senders (flow sources). FilterSpecs with C-Num 10 are identical to Sender Template Objects with C-Num 11 that are present on Path, PathTear, and PathErr messages, where they serve the same purpose. The objects carry one of three C-Types according to the address formats in use, and in addition to the address of the source node, they contain a source port or an IPv6 flow label to indicate the port of flow label used by the application that is sending data. If the

Table 4.6 Bit Settings in Options Vector of RSVP Style Object

Bottom Five Bits	Meaning
00bbb	Reserved
01bbb	Distinct reservations
10bbb	Shared reservations
11bbb	Reserved
bb000	Reserved
bb001	Wildcard
bb010	Explicit
bb011–bb111	Reserved
10001	Wildcard Filter (WF)
01010	Fixed Filter (FF)
10010	Shared Explicit (SE)

source port is zero, the Path message and corresponding reservation request apply to all flows on the session (i.e., to the same destination and destination port, carrying the same payload protocol) from the indicated address.

The Resv Confirm Object shown in Figure 4.34 is included on Resv messages to request that a ResvConf is returned to confirm the reservations. The address specified may be IPv4 or IPv6 according to the C-Type, and indicates the destination to which the ResvConf should be sent. This targeting of a ResvConf is apparently in contradiction to the statement made in Section 4.4.2 that ResvConf messages are forwarded hop by hop along the RSVP path, but it simply allows a node that is not the egress to request a ResvConf from the ingress and know when the message is received that it should not forward it further downstream. The Resv Confirm Object is returned unchanged in the ResvConf message to provide correlation.

The FlowSpec (C-Num 9), Sender TSpec (C-Num 12), and Adspec (C-Num 13) objects use C-Type 2 to indicate that they carry IntServ information describing the traffic flow. The format of the contents of these objects is described in Section 4.3 and defined in *RFC 2210*.

The Integrity Object (C-Num 4) is used to protect against message spoofing that could lead to theft of resources or denial of service to legitimate users. The use and contents of the Integrity Object are described in *RFC 2747* to include a 48-bit key, a sequence number, and a message digest (such as one produced using

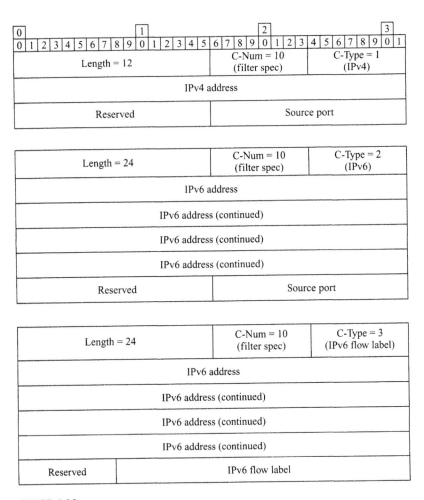

FIGURE 4.33

The RSVP FilterSpec Object has three types.

the MD5 algorithm). Note that IPsec was considered as an alternative to embedding integrity information within RSVP messages, but was rejected because IPsec relies on a clear indication of source and destination points, which is obscured by the addressing model used in RSVP. In addition, RSVP neighbors may be separated by multiple routers which are not RSVP capable and this may confuse the application of IPsec. On the other hand, if the network is simple, IPsec may be used following the rules of *RFC 2207* so that the source and destination port fields are replaced by IPsec Security Parameter Indexes. *RFC 2747* also defines Integrity Challenge and Integrity Response messages to help a node verify that its peer is legitimate.

0										1										2										3	
0	1	2	3	4	5	6	7	8	9	0	1	2	3	4	5	6	7	8	9	0	1	2	3	4	5	6	7	8	9	0	1

Length = 8	C-Num = 15 (resv confirm)	C-Type = 1 (IPv4)
IPv4 receiver address		

Length = 20	C-Num = 15 (resv confirm)	C-Type = 2 (IPv6)
IPv6 receiver address		
IPv6 receiver address (continued)		
IPv6 receiver address (continued)		
IPv6 receiver address (continued)		

FIGURE 4.34

The RSVP Resv Confirm Object has two types.

A final RSVP object, the Policy Object (C-Num 14), is described in *RFC 2205* as "for further study." A slew of RFCs provide input to the problem of managing admission control policy—that is, the question of administering which nodes are allowed to request what reservations under what circumstances. This feature first requires that applications and users are properly identified using the integrity procedures just discussed, and then needs the exchange of policy information between the applications and policy control elements that police reservation requests within the network. RSVP passes the contents of Policy Objects from node to node transparently and simply delivers them to policy control components on the routers.

RFC 2750 proposes a format for the Policy Object to contain a list of RSVP-like objects relating to the reservation request and a series of policy elements to identify the permissions possessed by the application requesting the service and including the identity of the application.

4.4.11 Choosing a Transport Protocol

RSVP is designed to operate over raw IP. The protocol includes sufficient mechanisms to tolerate lost packets and to detect corruption—it needs none of the services provided by an IP transport protocol. RSVP messages are encapsulated in IP packets using the protocol field value 46 (0×2E). Because Path messages are subject to normal routing and may be forwarded through parts of the network that are not RSVP capable, the IP packets that carry them use the source IP address of the node that is the source of the RSVP flow, and the destination IP address of the node that is the destination of the RSVP flow. This creates an issue because intervening RSVP-capable routers need to act on RSVP messages and would not normally see them since the messages would be forwarded according to the destination IP address. To circumvent this problem, the Router Alert IP option is used. This process is also applied to PathTear messages, but all other messages are addressed hop-by-hop (i.e., they carry the IP addresses of adjacent RSVP-capable routers).

Since some host systems (especially older ones) do not provide access to raw IP, RSVP is also specified to operate over the User Datagram Protocol (UDP). UDP is a lightweight transport protocol that is commonly available on host systems. A source host that does not have access to raw IP may send its RSVP messages encapsulated in UDP addresses to the next-hop RSVP-capable router using port 1698. The first router that is RSVP-capable and has access to raw IP (likely to be the first router) is required to convert the RSVP exchange to raw IP for forwarding into the network.

At the egress from the network, a router may need to convert back to UDP encapsulation before it delivers RSVP messages to a host. *RFC 2205* suggests that a router will learn when this is necessary by the receipt of UDP encapsulated messages from that host, but this has an obvious flaw since someone has to receive the first Path message. The net result is that routers must be configured with the capabilities of their adjacent hosts. Most hosts these days provide access to raw IP so that RSVP implementations do not need to use UDP.

4.4.12 RSVP Refresh Reduction

As mentioned earlier, one of the consequences of RSVP being a soft-state protocol is that messages must be periodically exchanged to keep the state active and the reservations in place. One concern with this is that considerable bandwidth and processing capabilities may be used up in simply keeping state active, reducing the capability to establish new state promptly and even, perhaps, affecting the ability to forward data. Refresh reduction is based not on removing the requirement to refresh RSVP state, nor on changing the interval between refreshes. Instead, the focus is on reducing the amount of processing required by both the sender and the receiver of a state refresh message and minimizing the number of bytes that must be sent between the nodes.

RFC 2961 describes a small set of extensions to RSVP to facilitate refresh reduction. These extensions arise from heated debates within the IETF, both about the need for any changes and about the best way to address the issue. In the end, three procedures were standardized: the first and second are independent (although they may be used together), but the third builds on the second.

All three extensions are treated as a single functional block and are used between a pair of RSVP routers only if both support them. This support is signaled in a new flag setting in the flags field in the Session Object. 0×01 is used to indicate support of all the refresh reduction extensions. Indicating support of the extensions does not mean that an RSVP router needs to use all or any of them in messages that it sends, but it must be able to process all of them if it receives them.

The first extension allows multiple RSVP messages to be packaged together as a *bundle* within a single IP message. A new RSVP message type, 12, indicates a Bundle message. A Bundle message is built of an RSVP message header followed by one or more RSVP messages. The number of bundled RSVP messages is not indicated, but the length of the Bundle message itself indicates whether there is more data, and hence another message, when processing of one bundled message has completed. The main advantages of message bundling are a small reduction in the number of bytes transmitted between RSVP routers, and a reduction in processing, especially through the IP stack—a clutch of refresh messages may be collected together into a single bundle and sent at the same time. The format of a Bundle message is shown in Figure 4.35.

When an RSVP node receives a Path or a Resv message it needs to distinguish three cases. The message may be for a new flow, it may be a change to an existing flow (e.g., modifying the bandwidth required for a flow), or it may be a refresh. New flows are easily distinguished because there is no matching stored Path or Resv state. Modification requests can be distinguished from state refresh messages because they contain changes in one or more of the parameters when compared with the previous message received. This means that each time a refresh message is received, an RSVP router must compare it fully with the previous message; since the order of objects in a message may vary without affecting the meaning, the receiver cannot simply compare the whole message as a block of memory, but must compare the objects one by one. This introduces a considerable overhead in processing, which is addressed in the refresh reduction extensions by placing a message identifier on each message. The Message Identifier Object, shown in Figure 4.36, includes a monotonic increasing message identifier number and an *epoch* that is used to disambiguate different instances of an adjacent node so that there is no confusion about the reuse of message ID values if a

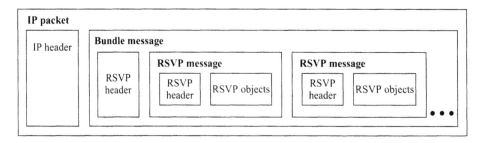

FIGURE 4.35

The Bundle message encapsulates one or more RSVP messages in a single IP message using an additional RSVP message header.

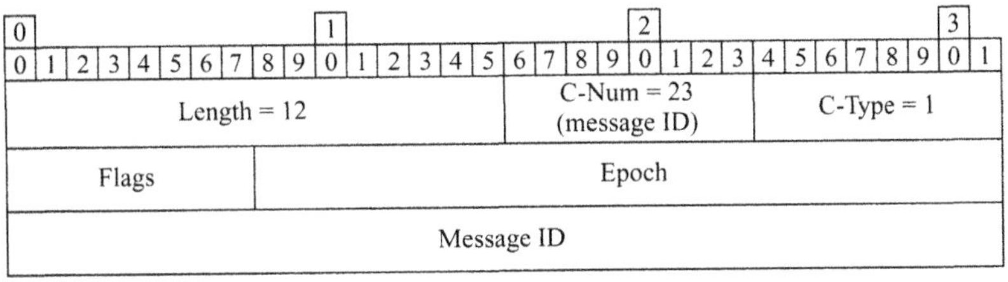

0										1										2										3	
0	1	2	3	4	5	6	7	8	9	0	1	2	3	4	5	6	7	8	9	0	1	2	3	4	5	6	7	8	9	0	1
Length = 12																C-Num = 23 (message ID)										C-Type = 1					
Flags										Epoch																					
Message ID																															

FIGURE 4.36

RSVP Message Identifier Object.

```
< Path Message > ::=        < Common Header >
                            [< INTEGRITY >]
                            [[ < MESSAGE_ID_ACK > < MESSAGE_ID_NACK > ]...]
                            [ < MESSAGE_ID > ]
                            < SESSION >
                            < RSVP_HOP >
                            < TIME_VALUES >
                            [ < POLICY_DATA > ]
                            < sender descriptor >
```

FIGURE 4.37

Formal definition of the RSVP Path message for refresh reduction showing the optional inclusion of Message ID and Message ID Acknowledgment Objects.

node is restarted. The epoch can be a random number or a function of real time.

If the message identifier on a message is identical to that previously received, no further checking is required: the message is a refresh. If the message identifier is lower than that previously received, the message is an old message that has been delayed in the network and can be ignored. If the message number is greater than that previously received, the message must be examined more closely and may be a refresh or a modification. The Message Identifier Object may be carried on every RSVP message. It serves both the purpose of ensuring acknowledged delivery of messages and of flagging Path and Resv messages as refreshes, as shown in Figures 4.37 and 4.38.

Message identifiers uniquely identify individual messages and make it possible to formally acknowledge the receipt of a message. The Message Identifier Object contains a flag (0x01) that requests the receiver to acknowledge receipt. This acknowledgment is carried in a Message Ack Object, as shown in Figure 4.39. The object contains the message identifier of the acknowledged message and may be carried one at a time or as a series in any message that flows in the opposite direction, as indicated for Path and Resv messages in Figures 4.37 and 4.38.

```
< Resv Message > ::=              < Common Header >
                                  [< INTEGRITY >]
                                  [[ < MESSAGE_ID_ACK > < MESSAGE_ID_NACK > ]...]
                                  [ < MESSAGE_ID > ]
                                  < SESSION >
                                  < RSVP_HOP >
                                  < TIME_VALUES >
                                  [ < RESV_CONFIRM > ]
                                  [ < SCOPE > ]
                                  [ < POLICY_DATA > ]
                                  < STYLE >
                                  < flow descriptor list >
```

FIGURE 4.38

Formal definition of the RSVP Resv message for refresh reduction showing the optional inclusion of Message ID and Message ID Acknowledgment Objects.

0										1										2										3	
0	1	2	3	4	5	6	7	8	9	0	1	2	3	4	5	6	7	8	9	0	1	2	3	4	5	6	7	8	9	0	1

Length = 12	C-Num = 24 (Message Ack)	C-Type = 1 (Ack)
Flags = 0	Epoch	
Message ID		

FIGURE 4.39

The RSVP Message Ack Object.

```
< Ack Message > ::=               < Common Header >
                                  [< INTEGRITY >]
                                  < MESSAGE_ID_ACK > < MESSAGE_ID_NACK >
                                  [[ < MESSAGE_ID_ACK > < MESSAGE_ID_NACK > ]...]
```

FIGURE 4.40

Formal definition of the RSVP Ack message.

If there is no message being sent in the opposite direction, the receiver must still acknowledge the received message identifier as soon as possible. It can do this by sending an Acknowledgment message that simply carries the acknowledged message identifiers, as shown in Figure 4.40.

The sender of a message carrying a message identifier that has requested acknowledgment retransmits the message periodically until it is acknowledged or

< Srefresh Message > ::=	< Common Header >
	[< INTEGRITY >]
	[[< MESSAGE_ID_ACK > | < MESSAGE_ID_NACK >]…]
	[< MESSAGE_ID >]
	< srefresh list > | < source srefresh list >
<srefresh list > ::=	< MESSAGE_ID_LIST > | < MESSAGE_ID MCAST_LIST >
	[< srefresh list >]
< source srefresh list > ::=	< MESSAGE_ID SRC_LIST >
	[< source srefresh list >]

FIGURE 4.41

Formal definition of the RSVP Srefresh message.

until it decides that there is a problem with the link or with the receiving node. Retransmission is relatively frequent (roughly every half a second), so it is important not to swamp the system with retransmissions. *RFC 2961* suggests that the sender should apply an exponential back-off, doubling the time between retransmissions at each attempt. It also suggests that a message should be transmitted a maximum of three times even if it is not acknowledged (i.e., one transmission and two retransmissions).

The third extension for refresh reduction recognizes that once a message identifier has been assigned to a state message, it is not necessary to retransmit the whole message—only the message identifier needs to be sent to keep the state alive. The Summary Refresh (Srefresh) message shown in Figure 4.41 is used to send a list of message identifiers in this fashion. The Srefresh message itself does not carry a message identifier in its own right, but each of the identifiers that it does carry can be accepted or rejected, although usually no specific acknowledgement is requested, so only rejections are sent. A rejection uses the Message Nack object, which has C-Type of 2 but is otherwise identical to a Message Ack object. The Message Nack allows some message identifiers out of the set on the Srefresh to be rejected without rejecting all of them. The rejection is necessary if the receiver does not match the message identifier against a stored value—it cannot use the Srefresh to establish new state since the message does not carry the full Path or Resv information.

Message Nack Objects can be carried within the other messages such as the Path and Resv messages shown in Figures 4.37 and 4.38. Alternatively, the Acknowledgment message shown in Figure 4.40 may be used. If the Srefresh is received and accepted, a single Message Ack carrying the message ID of the Srefresh message acknowledges all of the message IDs carried in the Srefresh list. If one or more message IDs in the Srefresh list is rejected, the message itself must still be acknowledged and Message Nacks must be used to reject each unacceptable message ID. There is no need to acknowledge individual message IDs from within the Srefresh list.

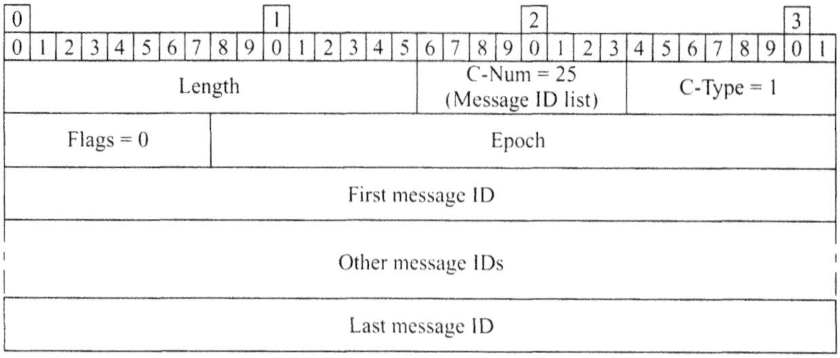

FIGURE 4.42

RSVP Message ID List Object used in the Srefresh message.

The basic Srefresh contains a Message ID List Object, as shown in Figure 4.42. The object lists a series of message IDs for state that is being refreshed, but recognizes that the epoch value does not need to be repeated for each message ID.

The Srefresh message is complicated considerably by multicast issues. It is possible that a downstream node will receive a refresh of Path state from multiple upstream interfaces and care must be taken to send the acknowledgments to the right place and only as frequently as is actually required. The Source Message List Object and Message ID Multicast List Object shown in Figure 4.43 allow a single Srefresh message to refresh state with reference to source and destination addresses—the addresses shown may be IPv4 or IPv6 depending on the object's C-Type (2 or 3 for Source Message List, 4 or 5 for Message ID Multicast List). Note that this format is considerably suboptimal since the addresses must be reproduced for each message ID.

All three refresh reduction procedures can be combined with Acknowledgement and Srefresh messages being bundled along with other messages.

4.4.13 Choosing to Use Refresh Reduction

The choice to use RSVP refresh reduction is not straightforward. Before it can be used at all, the protocol extensions must be supported by the RSVP nodes at each end of a link and flagged in the common message header (flag value 0×01) of all messages, and this may restrict the choice since not all implementations include support for refresh reduction.

Consideration should then be given to the value of each of the three refresh mechanisms. Although, strictly speaking, the setting of the refresh reduction-capable flag in the common message header means that a node fully supports all the mechanisms, it does not actually need to actively use them. The only requirements are that it should be able to receive and correctly process refresh reduction

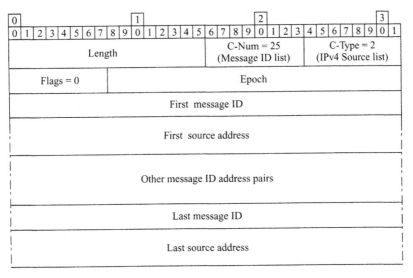

FIGURE 4.43

RSVP Source Message ID List Object and Message ID Multicast List Object.

messages and objects that it receives. This means that in implementations that are suitably configurable the precise refresh reduction operations can be selected individually. Further, in networks that will be made up of only a single vendor's routers, a choice can be made to partially implement refresh reduction.

The basic requirement for two of the options is that message IDs are supported, that is that Path and Resv messages and their refreshes carry message IDs. A sender may choose whether to use a new message ID on each refresh message, a receiver may choose whether to take advantage of the message ID to expedite refresh processing, and a sender may opt to use the Summary Refresh message or to simply retransmit full refresh messages. These choices depend on backward compatibility (existing implementations will check for refreshes by examining each field of a received object), implementation complexity (some implementations find it hard to know whether they are sending a refresh message or one that modifies the previous request, and the Srefresh processing is a considerable amount of new code), and the number of flows between a pair of RSVP neighbors (it may not be necessary to use Srefresh if there are only a few tens of flows).

The value of Bundle messages remains debatable. On an ordinary Ethernet link carrying IPv4 packets, the saving from bundling two RSVP messages together is just 26 bytes (Ethernet header 14 bytes plus IP header 20 bytes, less 8 bytes for the RSVP Bundle message header). When RSVP messages are of the order of 100 bytes each, this saving is only around 10 percent. On the other hand, when small messages such as Acknowledgements and ResvConfs are being sent the savings may be better.

But message bundling requires that the sender has two messages ready to be sent at the same time. The implementation of this may be hard to achieve since it is not advisable to hold on to one message in the hope that another will need to be sent soon. Similarly, it may damage the randomization of state refresh periods to deliberately bunch refreshes into a single Bundle message. Bundling may, however, be of advantage in systems that are able to recognize that there is a queue of messages waiting to be sent and can then collect those messages into a single bundle, and on routers where there is a considerable overhead associated with sending or receiving an IP packet.

4.4.14 Aggregation of RSVP Flows

Aggregation of traffic flows improves scalability within the network since individual nodes need to maintain a smaller number of queues and distinct resources to manage the same amount of traffic. RSVP and IntServ in general maintain reservations for separate micro-flows through the network, and this gives rise to concerns about scalability not just during refresh processing but also on the data path.

Some research has been done into combining DiffServ and IntServ reservations to aggregate traffic and to allow multiple flows of a similar type to be managed together with a single reservation. For example, all flows with the same DiffServ DSCP could be grouped together and handled using the same IntServ reservation (managed though RSVP) with the resources allocated being the sum of the component parts. These ideas are developed further in *RFC 3175*.

4.5 FURTHER READING

Durham, David, and Raj Yavatkar, *Inside the Internet's Reservation Protocol: Foundations for Quality of Service*. John Wiley & Sons, 1999. This book was written by two Intel engineers with in-depth experience of developing the RSVP standards and one of the first RSVP implementations.

Morrow, Monique, and Kateel Vijayananda, *Developing IP-Based Services*. Morgan Kaufmann, 2003. This source provides a brief overview of IP quality of service from the perspective of service providers and equipment vendors.

Wang, Zheng, *Internet QoS: Architectures and Mechanisms for Quality of Service*. Morgan Kaufmann, 2001. This provides excellent coverage of all the important, implementable models for providing service differentiation in the Internet.

Differentiated Services was first proposed as an architecture and then developed by the definition of specific uses. Some key RFCs for Differentiated Services are:

RFC 2430—A Provider Architecture for Differentiated Services and Traffic Engineering
RFC 2597—Assured Forwarding PHB Group
RFC 3246—An Expedited Forwarding PHB
RFC 3270—Multiprotocol Label Switching (MPLS) Support of Differentiated Services

Integrated Services was developed as a framework by the IETF and has since been worked on by many working groups as they have seen the need to incorporate the features into their work. Some key RFCs for Integrated Services are:

RFC 1633—Integrated Services in the Internet Architecture: An Overview
RFC 2210—The Use of RSVP with IETF Integrated Services
RFC 2211—Specification of the Controlled-Load Network Element Service
RFC 2212—Specification of Guaranteed Quality of Service
RFC 2215—General Characterization Parameters for Integrated Service Network Elements
RFC 2381—Interoperation of Controlled-Load and Guaranteed Service with ATM
RFC 2688—Integrated Services Mappings for Low Speed Networks
RFC 2815—Integrated Service Mappings on IEEE 802 Networks
RFC 2997—Specification of the Null Service Type
RFC 2998—A Framework for Integrated Services Operation over DiffServ Networks

RSVP was developed within the IETF by the RSVP working group. The RSVP working group has been closed down because all development work has been completed. However, the new uses of RSVP for MPLS and GMPLS can be seen in the MPLS and CCAMP working groups. Some key RFCs for RSVP are:

RFC 2205—Resource ReSerVation Protocol (RSVP)—Version 1 Functional Specification
RFC 2207—RSVP Extensions for IPsec Data Flows
RFC 2210—The Use of RSVP with IETF Integrated Services
RFC 2747—RSVP Cryptographic Authentication
RFC 2750—RSVP Extensions for Policy Control
RFC 2961—RSVP Refresh Overhead Reduction Extensions
RFC 3175—Aggregation of RSVP for IPv4 and IPv6 Reservations

The RSVP API is published by The Open Group as *The Resource Reservation Setup Protocol API (RAPI)*, document number c809. It can be seen at the group's website in HTML or PDF format at *www.opengroup.org/products/publications/catalog/c809.htm*.

The Service Management Research Group of the Internet Research Task Force (IRTF) has published its findings on the use of quality of service in IP networks in *RFC 3387*—Considerations from the Service Management Research Group (SMRG) on Quality of Service (QoS) in the IP Network.

Quality of Service Routing

5

Quality of service (QoS) is an important issue in any communication network; typically, this can be viewed from the perception of service quality. Eventually any service perception needs to be mapped to network routing, especially since QoS guarantee is required for a particular service class.

In this chapter, taken from Chapter 17 of *Network Routing* by Deep Medhi and Karthik Ramasamy, we discuss what QoS routing means and how different routing algorithms may be extended to fit the QoS routing framework. We also present a representative set of numerical studies with which we can understand the implications of different routing schemes and roles played by different network controls.

5.1 BACKGROUND

We start with some brief background on QoS and QoS routing.

5.1.1 Quality of Service

To discuss *quality of service routing*, we first need to understand what *quality of service* means. Consider a generic request arrival to a network; if this request has certain resource requirements that it explicitly announces to the network at the time of arrival, then QoS refers to the network's ability to meet the resource guarantees for this request.

To understand QoS, we will first consider a network link; no routing is considered at this point. Assume that a request arrives at this network link for a 1-Mbps constant data rate. If the network link has bandwidth available that is more than 1 Mbps, then it can certainly accommodate this request. Thus, the arriving request received the specified QoS. Implicit in this is that the QoS will be continually met as long as this request is active; in other words, for the *duration* of the request, the QoS is met.

Suppose that the network link at the instant of the request arrival has less available bandwidth than the requested bandwidth. In this case, the request cannot be served. When there are many arriving requests requiring resource guarantees and the network link cannot accommodate them, another aspect related to QoS emerges. This aspect of QoS considers that arriving requests usually receive the service guarantee requested with an acceptable probability of not being turned away; in other words, blocking should not be high. That is, the blocking probability of arriving requests is another important consideration in regard to QoS. When we consider from this viewpoint, it is easy to see that traffic engineering and capacity expansion also play crucial parts in regard to QoS since if the network is not engineered with a reasonable capacity level, the likelihood of a request facing blocking would be high. Thus, blocking probability is an important factor in the perception of QoS and is traditionally known as *grade of service* (GoS).

In general, the term QoS is used much more broadly than its use in this chapter in the context of QoS routing. For example, "a network meets QoS" can be interpreted as meeting delay requirements through a network, not necessarily for a specific request.

5.1.2 QoS Routing

Consider now a network instead of just a link. Then for an arriving request that requires guaranteed resources, the network would need to decide what resources it has in its *different* links and paths so that the request can be accommodated. Thus, *QoS routing* refers to a network's ability to accommodate a QoS request by determining a *path* through the network that meets the QoS guarantee. Furthermore, an implicit understanding is that the network's performance is also optimized. In this sense, QoS routing cannot be completely decoupled from traffic engineering.

5.1.3 QoS Routing Classification

What are the types of resource guarantees an arriving request might be interested in? Typically, they are bandwidth guarantee, delay bound, delay jitter bound, and acceptable packet loss. We have already described a bandwidth guarantee. *Delay bound* refers to end-to-end delay being bounded. Jitter requires a bit of explanation. In a packet-based network, packets that are generated at equal spacing from one end may not arrive at the destination with the same spacing; this is because of factors such as delay due to scheduling and packet processing at intermediate routers, interaction of many flows, and so on. In real-time interactive applications such as voice or video, the interpacket arrival times for a call are equally spaced when generated, but may arrive at the destination at uneven time spacing; thus, inter-packet delay is known as *jitter*. *Packet loss* refers to the probability of a packet being lost along the path from origin to destination.

Consideration of these four factors would, however, depend on whether the network is a circuit-based network or a packet-based network. To discuss this aspect and the critical elements related to QoS routing, we also need to consider time granularity in regard to an arriving request. By considering three time-related

Table 5.1 Service Request Type Classification

Type	Average Arrival Frequency	Lead Time for Setup	Duration of Session
Type A	Sub-second/seconds time frame	A few seconds	Minutes
Type B	Day/week time frame	Weeks	Months to years
Type C	Multiple times a day	Minutes	Minutes to hours

factors—arrival frequency, lead time for setup, and the duration of a session/connection—we broadly classify requests into three types as listed in Table 5.1. There are very specific outcomes of these classifications.

In Type A, the network technology is either packet-switched or circuit-switched where circuit-switched networks require bandwidth guarantee while packet-switched networks may have one or all of the requirements: bandwidth guarantee, delay bound, jitter bound, and acceptable packet loss. However, Type B is generally circuit-oriented where a permanent or semi-permanent bandwidth guarantee is the primary requirement; there is very little about on-demand switching. Routing for the Type B classification is traditionally referred to as *circuit routing*; in recent literature, circuit routing is commonly known as *transport network routing*. Between Type A and Type B, there is another form of routing where some overlap of time granularity is possible. We classify this type that has overlapping regions as Type C; for example, routing for this type of service can be accomplished in Multiprotocol Label Switching (MPLS) networks.

Of these classifications, QoS routing arises for a Type A classification. It is thus helpful to consider a taxonomy for QoS routing to understand the relationship between networking paradigms and QoS factors (see Figure 5.1). In the figure, we have included an identifier in parentheses for ease of illustration. First note that classification Q.1.a refers to routing in the current circuit-switched telephone network. An important point to note is that *both* hierarchical and all variations of dynamic call routing fall under Q.1.a in terms of meeting QoS. It may be noted that old hierarchical call routing meets the bandwidth guarantee of a new request if admitted; however, hierarchical call routing is not as flexible as dynamic call routing schemes and requires more bandwidth to provide the same level of service. This then helps in seeing that traffic engineering efficiency is an implicit requirement of QoS routing, a primary reason why dynamic call routing was pursued in the telephone network.

A broader point is that QoS routing can be accomplished by different routing *schemes*—the drivers for QoS routing are developing routing schemes that address issues such as performance benefit, cost, routing stability, management, and so on. Thus, in general, dynamic or adaptive routing is preferred over fixed routing. Classification Q.1.a is a very important area in network routing. Besides

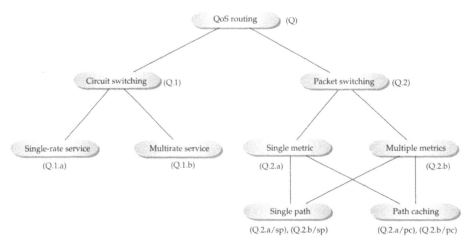

FIGURE 5.1

QoS routing taxonomy.

circuit-switched voice, many problems in optical routing also fall under classification Q.1.a.

Classification Q.1.b is an extension of Q.1.a. Multirate, multiservice circuit-switched QoS routing refers to the case in which there is more than one service class and an arriving request for each service class has a different bandwidth requirement as opposed to Q.1.a, where all arriving requests have the same bandwidth requirement—for example, the current wired telephone network where per-request bandwidth is 64 Kbps. In case of Q.1.b, service classes are rigid and the bandwidth requirement of a request in each class is an integral multiple of the *base bandwidth rate*. If the base bandwidth rate in the circuit-switched voice network is 64 Kbps, then a switched video service can be defined as, say, 384 Kbps, which is then six times the base bandwidth rate. It may be noted that among the dynamic call routing schemes, real-time network routing (RTNR) has been deployed to handle multiple classes of services.

For the packet-switched branch of QoS routing, there are two aspects to consider: single attribute or multiple attributes. By single attribute, we mean only a single criterion, such as the bandwidth requirement, is used as a metric for a request that is considered for QoS routing. By multiple attributes, we mean that more than one factor, such as bandwidth and delay, is being considered for QoS routing.

Note that we do not distinguish here by rates as we have done with Q.1.a and Q.1.b, although theoretically it is possible to discuss single rate and multiple rate. The reason this is grouped together is that packet-switched networks are usually not designed with a single bandwidth rate in mind—any arbitrary bandwidth rate is generally usable due to the packet switching nature. It is, however, indeed possible to deploy a private packet network, for example, a private voice over IP (VoIP) packet network, where all voice calls have the same data rate. Thus, Q.2.a has some aspects of Q.1.b, with the additional flexibility of arbitrary data rate of a request. For classification Q.2.b, multiple criteria are required to handle the decision-making process for an arriving request. This will be discussed in detail later in this chapter.

For both Q.2.a and Q.2.b, there are two possibilities in terms of path consideration: either a single path is considered, or paths are cached for alternate paths consideration. Note that for Q.1.a and Q.1.b, it has been common to consider path caching; in fact, a single path is rarely considered and is not shown in this classification.

5.1.4 Defining a Request and Its Requirement

You may note that so far we have not defined a *request*. Typically, in a circuit-switching context, a request is labeled as a *call*; in a packet-switching context, especially in IP networking, a QoS request is labeled as a *flow*, while terms such as *SIP call* or *VoIP call* are also often used. (There is yet another terminology in the networking literature: *call flows*. This term refers to the flow or sequence diagram of messages in regard to establishing or tearing down a call over an SS7 network or in an SIP environment or when translation is required at a gateway going from SS7 to SIP, or vice versa.) Note that the usage of the term *flow* here is not to be confused with *network flow* or *link flow*.

When a call request arrives, there is a call setup phase that can typically perform functions such as route determination, signaling along the path to the destination, and QoS checking before the call is set up; in essence, a call request must always face a call setup time delay before it can be connected—this is also known as post-dial delay; certainly, this should be minimized. For the services that require a QoS guarantee, the call setup phase needs to ensure that the QoS guarantee can be provided for the entire duration of the call; otherwise, the call request is denied by the network.

5.1.5 General Observations

It is quite possible that a network may not have the *functionality* to guarantee that it can meet QoS for an arriving request, but yet has the resources to meet the request. An IP network without integrated services functionality falls into this category. For example, a VoIP call can receive QoS in an IP network without the network explicitly having the ability to provide a guarantee at the time of request arrival. This can be possible, for example, if the network is engineered properly, or overprovisioned. In general, overprovisioning is not desirable since, after all, a network does cost real money in terms of capacity cost, switching cost, and so on.

Finally, much like best-effort traffic services, QoS routing can also have two components: intra-domain and inter-domain. Most of this chapter is focused on *intra-domain* QoS routing. We will briefly discuss inter-domain QoS routing at the end.

5.2 QOS ATTRIBUTES

In the previous section, we mentioned the following factors in terms of attributes: *residual* bandwidth, delay, jitter, and packet loss. Note that any of these attributes are applicable under classification Q.2, while bandwidth is the only one applicable for classification Q.1. We will now discuss how to classify these attributes in terms of metrics.

Suppose that an arriving request has requirements for bandwidth, delay, jitter, and packet loss identified by b, τ, ζ, and L, respectively. The important question is: How are measures for these factors accumulated along a path in terms of satisfying the guaranteed requirement of an arriving call? To understand this, we will consider a path that is made up of three links numbered 1, 2, and 3, and current residual bandwidth, delay, jitter, and packet loss measures for link i as b_i, τ_i, ζ_i, and $L_i (i = 1, 2, 3)$, respectively. We can then list the path measures as shown in Table 5.2.

You can see that the packet loss measure is a nonadditive multiplicative one; however, it can be looked at from another angle. If L_i ($i = 1, 2, 3$) is very close to zero, which is typically the case for packet loss, again due to traffic engineering requirements, the expression for path measure can be approximated as follows:

$$1 - (1 - L_1)(1 - L_2)(1 - L_3) \approx L_1 + L_2 + L_3$$

Thus, the packet loss measure becomes an additive measure. We can then classify the different attributes into two groups in terms of metric properties:

- *Additive*: Delay, jitter, packet loss
- *Nonadditive (concave)*: Bandwidth

Broadly, this means that from a routing computation point of view, delay, jitter, and packet loss metrics can be classified under shortest path routing while the

Type	Path Measure	Requirement
Bandwidth	$\min\{b_1, b_2, b_3\}$	$\geq b$
Delay	$\tau_1 + \tau_2 + \tau_3$	$\leq \tau$
Jitter	$\zeta_1 + \zeta_2 + \zeta_3$	$\leq \zeta$
Packet loss	$1 - (1 - L_1)(1 - L_2)(1 - L_3)$	$\leq L$

Table 5.2 Path Measures

bandwidth requirement metric falls under widest path routing. It may be noted that a buffer requirement at routers along a path for an arriving request requiring a QoS guarantee is another possible metric that falls under the nonadditive concave property; however, unlike the rest of the metrics discussed so far, a buffer requirement is checked as the call setup signaling message is propagated along the path chosen, rather than being communicated through a link state advertisement.

To summarize, for classification Q.2, both additive and nonadditive concave metrics are possible, while for classification Q.1 only nonadditive concave is appropriate. In the next section, we will discuss adaptations of shortest path routing and widest path routing for a request requiring a QoS guarantee.

5.3 ADAPTING SHORTEST PATH AND WIDEST PATH ROUTING: A BASIC FRAMEWORK

Out of different attributes classified into two categories, we will use one metric each from additive and nonadditive (concave) metric properties for our discussion here. Specifically, we will use delay for the additive property and bandwidth requirement for the nonadditive property. We assume the reader is familiar with shortest path routing and widest path routing. You may note that the discussion in this section is applicable only to classification Q.2.

The applicability of a particular routing algorithm for a packet-switched network depends on whether the network is running a distance vector protocol or a link state protocol. While the basic idea of shortest path or widest path routing would work under both these protocol concepts, we will assume that a link state protocol framework is used since most well-known intra-domain routing protocol frameworks are link state based.

5.3.1 Single Attribute

We first consider that requests have a single additive metric requirement in terms of delay attribute. A simple way to adapt the shortest-path routing algorithm paradigm here is by using delay as the link cost metric. Suppose a request arrives with the delay requirement no greater than $\bar{\tau}$.

> For an arriving request requiring a guaranteed delay requirement of $\bar{\tau}$, do the following: Compute the shortest delay using the shortest path first algorithm; if the result is less than $\bar{\tau}$, then admit the request; otherwise, deny the request.

Note that the request arrives for a particular destination. Thus, unlike the standard shortest path first (SPF) algorithm, here the shortest path computation must be computed only for the specific destination of a request. Consider the shortest path first algorithm discussed in Chapter 2 of *Network Routing* by Deep Medhi and Karthik Ramasamy. Once a new node k is identified with the minimum cost path, it can be checked whether this k is the destination of the request; if so, the algorithm can stop. At this point, this delay cost is then compared against the arriving request's delay requirement; if met, the request is accepted, otherwise it is denied.

What if the single metric is in terms of the bandwidth requirement of a request? This scenario is similar to the delay-based one. Suppose that an arriving request has a bandwidth requirement of $\bar{b}$. Then, we can use the following rule:

> For an arriving request with a guaranteed bandwidth requirement of $\bar{b}$, do the following: Compute the widest path using for the specific destination; if this value is higher than $\bar{b}$, then admit the request; otherwise, deny the request.

In many instances, it is desirable to obtain the widest path with the least number of hops for the path. Although this is sometimes referred to as the *shortest-widest* path, it is not a good name since shortest does not indicate the context in which this is meant. Thus, we will refer to it as the *least-hop-widest* path. How do we find the widest path with the least number of hops? Consider again the widest path first algorithm. In this algorithm, k in S_i with the maximum residual bandwidth is determined. Instead of storing just one k, the list of nodes where the maximum residual bandwidth is attained is determined. If this list happens to have more than one element, then k is chosen so that it is the least number of hops from source node i. In essence, this means that if there are multiple paths with maximum residual bandwidth, choose the one with the least number of hops; if there are still such multiple paths, one is randomly selected. In the same manner, a *least-hop-minimum delay* path can be determined when a delay metric is used.

5.3.2 Multiple Attributes

In this case, consider an arriving request specifying that both the delay and the bandwidth requirement must be satisfied. This can be addressed from the point of view of which factor is to be considered the dominant one: delay or bandwidth. This, however, depends on which is found: a bandwidth feasible path while the delay is minimized, or a delay feasible path while maximizing available bandwidth.

Again, we can adapt the widest path and shortest path routing framework. To determine the minimum delay path that satisfies the bandwidth requirement of a request, we can initialize any link that does not meet the bandwidth requirement temporarily as a link with infinite delay; this method of considering a nonadditive metric requirement with an additive shortest path computation is generally known as *constrained shortest path routing*. Instead, if we were to determine a maximum residual bandwidth—the widest path while meeting the delay requirement—we can initialize any link that does not meet the delay requirement by temporarily setting the residual link bandwidth to zero; this form can be classified as *constrained widest path routing*. Note that for a constrained shortest path, the constraint is on bandwidth, while for a constrained widest path, the constraint is on delay. For source node i and destination node v, we present both routing algorithms in Algorithm 5.1 and Algorithm 5.2 for completeness. The notations are summarized in Table 5.3.

Table 5.3 Notation for QoS Routing

Notation	Remark
i	Source node
v	Destination node
N	List of all nodes
N_k	List of neighboring nodes of k
S	List of nodes considered so far
S'	List of nodes yet to be considered
τ_{ij}	Link delay on link i-j (set to ∞ if the link does exist, or not to be considered)
T_{ij}	Delay from node i to node j
b_{ij}	Residual bandwidth on link i-j (set to 0 if link does exist, or not to be considered)
B_{ij}	Bandwidth available from node i to node j

Algorithm 5.1 QoS minimum delay path with bandwidth feasibility

```
S = {i}    // permanent list; start with source node i
S' = N \ {i}    // tentative list (of the rest of the nodes)
for ( j in S' ) do
    // check if i-j directly connected and link has required bandwidth b̄
    if ( τᵢⱼ <∞ and bᵢⱼ ≥ b̄ ) then
        Tᵢⱼ = τᵢⱼ    // note the delay cost
    else
        τᵢⱼ = ∞; Tᵢⱼ = ∞    // mark temporarily as unavailable
    endif
endfor
while (S' is not empty) do    // while tentative list is not empty
    T_temp = ∞    // find minimum-delay neighbor k
    for ( m in S' ) do
        if ( Tᵢₘ < T_temp ) then
            T_temp = Tᵢₘ; k = m
        endif
    endfor
    if ( Tᵢₖ > τ̄ ) then    // if minimum delay is higher than delay
                                    tolerance
        'No feasible path exists; request denied'
        exit
    endif
    if ( k == v ) then exit    // destination v found, done
    S = S ∪ {k}    // add to permanent list
    S' = S'\{k}    // delete from tentative list
    for ( j in Nₖ ∩ S') do
        if ( Tᵢⱼ > Tᵢₖ + τₖⱼ and b̄ₖⱼ > b ) then    // if delay is less via k
            Tᵢⱼ = Tᵢₖ + τₖⱼ
```

```
      endif
    endfor
  endwhile
  if ( T_{iv} ≤ τ̄ ) then     // final check, if the path meets delay
  requirement
      'Request accepted'
  else
      'No feasible path exists; Request denied'
  endif
```

Algorithm 5.2 QoS widest path with delay feasibility

```
  S = {i}    // permanent list; start with source node i
  S' = N \ {i}    // tentative list (of the rest of the nodes)
  for ( j in S' ) do
    // if i-j directly connected and link has required bandwidth b
    if ( b_{ij} > b̄ and τ_{ij} < ∞) then
        B_{ij} = b_{ij}; T_{ij} = τ_{ij}
    else
        b_{ij} = 0; B_{ij} = 0; τ_{ij} = ∞; T_. = ∞    // mark temporarily as
                                                          unavailable
    endif
  endfor
  while (S' is not empty) do    // while tentative list is not empty
    B_{temp} = 0    // find neighbor k with maximum bandwidth
    for ( m in S' ) do
      if ( B_{im} > B_{temp} ) then
          B_{temp} = B_{im}; k = m
      endif
    endfor
    if ( B_{ik} < b̄ ) then     // bandwidth is higher than the request
                                   tolerance
        No feasible bandwidth path exists; request denied
        exit
    endif
    if ( k == v ) then exit    // destination v is found; done
    S = S ∪ {k}    // add to permanent list
    S' = S'\{k}    // drop from tentative list
    for ( j in N_k ∩ S' ) do    // path has higher bandwidth
      if ( B_{ij} < min{B_{ik}, b_{kj}} ) then
          B_{ij} = min{B_{ik}, b_{kj}}
          T_{ij} = T_{ik} + τ_{kj}
      endif
    endfor
  endwhile
  if ( B_{iv} ≥ b ) then     // final check; if path meets bandwidth
                                 requirement
      'Request accepted'
  else
      'No feasible path exists; Request denied'
  endif
  end procedure
```

5.3.3 **Additional Consideration**

We next consider a general question: can we provide QoS routing in a packet environment where buffer guarantee at routers is also required? For this, assume that the packet network is an integrated services environment. For a request requiring bandwidth guarantee on demand, we also need to consider whether the router's scheduling algorithm can guarantee requests in terms of buffering, in addition to bandwidth guarantee on links. This brings up the issue of scheduling with routing. It has been shown that this combined problem can be addressed with a polynomial time algorithm that factors in capacity and constrained shortest path.

5.4 **UPDATE FREQUENCY, INFORMATION INACCURACY, AND IMPACT ON ROUTING**

In the previous section, we provided the computational framework for QoS routing for classification Q.2 by considering single or multiple attributes. What is missing is how often attribute information is obtained and/or when the computation is performed. To discuss these important aspects, we will again assume a link state framework is used.

Ideally, it appears that if a node knows the state of each link in terms of the applicable attributes (either single or multiple) *instantaneously*, it can then invoke routing computation. There are, however, practical limitations on this utopian view:

- An instantaneous update is almost impossible in a real network; very frequent updates can lead to excessive information exchange, which can overload a network. In fact, it has now become a common practice in many routing protocols to include a hold-down time to assert that no updating of information is allowed that is more frequent than the hold-down time. Also note that if a particular link state is advertised too frequently due to a legitimate change in the link state status, some form of dampening is still applied by a receiving node to avoid having an undesirable performance consequence, and before flooding to its neighboring node.

- There are two possibilities in regard to routing computation: (1) perform the computation periodically, or (2) perform it on demand for every arriving request. The second option is usually avoided since an important requirement in QoS routing services is that the call setup time, also known as post-dial delay, for an arriving request is as small as possible. There is an important lesson to be learned here from RTNR. In an almost fully mesh network environment with a separate signaling (SS7) network for link state message exchanges, RTNR was initially intended to be deployed with per call computation in mind; in actuality, the computation is based on the information queried for the *previous* call in order to avoid increasing post-dial delay to an undesirable level. For a general packet network, performing routing computation on demand for each arriving request can be taxing on the CPU load of the node—thus, this is also not desirable.

■ It is not difficult to realize that if the link state information obtained at a node is delayed due to periodic/asynchronous update or dampening, the link state information will be somewhat stale or inaccurate. Due to such inaccurate information, it is questionable whether it is worth doing a per-call routing computation.

To summarize, for QoS routing, it is more appropriate to perform a routing computation periodically than on a per-call basis and to build a routing table. Taking this entire scenario into account, the arrival of link state information and the timing of the routing computation are depicted in Figure 5.2. It may be noted that due to the periodic computation framework, instead of executing a constrained shortest path or constrained widest path on a per-pair basis, it can be performed on a source to all destination basis, albeit with the option that for a specific pair computation can be triggered if needed. In any case, it is important to note that if there is a network link failure, usually link state flooding and routing computation are triggered immediately so that changes can be accommodated by each node.

There is, however, an important consequence of periodic/update and periodic routing table computation. Suppose that the routing is hop-by-hop and each node has only one entry for each destination identified by the next hop. When an actual request arrives, there may not be enough resources along the path (dictated by the routing table) to establish the call. Thus, this request is denied entry, which then affects the overall call-blocking probability. Note that just being locked into one path during two consecutive routing computations does not necessarily mean that all arrivals will be blocked during this window; it is important to note that

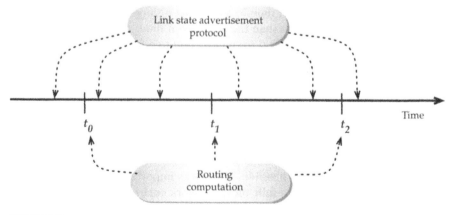

FIGURE 5.2

Time of link state advertisement and routing computing for QoS routing.

during this time window, some exiting calls might be over-releasing resources that can be used by newly arrived calls. In any case, to maintain the GoS aspect of QoS, there are two possibilities: (1) updates must be done frequently enough so that the newly obtained path does not block too many calls, or (2) the network is engineered with enough capacity/resources so that the overall blocking effect is maintained at an acceptable level. The first option belongs to traffic engineering while the second option belongs to capacity expansion. Note that it is also important to maintain the GoS aspect of QoS to avoid excessive user-level retry in case calls are blocked.

Since an important goal of QoS routing is to provide good traffic engineering, we may ask the following question: can we consider more than one path from a source to a destination? This will partly depend on whether the network is capable of providing hop-by-hop routing and/or source routing. In the case of hop-by-hop routing, the only option for multiple paths is if there are two paths of equal cost, also known as equal-cost multipath (ECMP). It is difficult to find multiple equal-cost paths in a constrained-based routing environment. In a source routing environment, multiple paths can be cached ahead of time, which then leads to the possibility of *alternate routing* options.

5.5 LESSONS FROM DYNAMIC CALL ROUTING IN THE TELEPHONE NETWORK

There has been extensive experience with alternate routing for dynamic call routing for the telephone network. First, we summarize the typical network environment for dynamic call routing in telephone networks:

- The network is fully mesh, or nearly fully mesh.
- Calls attempt a direct link path first (if available); then an alternate path is attempted; alternate paths are made of at most two links.
- The path cost is nonadditive, concave.
- The alternate paths to be considered and the number of such paths to be cached depend on specific routing schemes.
- Call setup can be based on progress call control or originating call control.
- In the presence of originating call control, a call crankback can be performed to try another path, if such a path is listed in the routing table.
- Routing schemes use a link state framework.
- Link state update, setup messages, and crankback messages are carried through out-of-band signaling, for example, using an SS7 network.
- The main performance measure is minimization of call-blocking probability, which can dictate the choice of a routing scheme. However, factors such as messages generated due to call setup, crankback, and link state updates can also be deciding factors.

There are key lessons learned from such a dynamic call routing environment:

- In general, a dynamic call routing scheme increases throughput, but has a meta-stability problem beyond a certain load-to-capacity ratio in the network.

- A trunk reservation feature is used to protect a direct link from being excessively used by alternate routed calls to avoid metastable behavior. In essence, trunk reservation works as a link-level admission control. An important consequence that sounds counterintuitive is that a network may not accept a call even if it has capacity under certain conditions.

- For effective traffic engineering, especially under overload conditions, several control measures such as dynamic overload control, call gapping, and hard to reach may need to be invoked.

To reiterate, dynamic call routing in a telephone network is operating for *single-rate* homogeneous service—all are voice calls requiring the same amount of bandwidth for the duration of the call. The first question then is what changes in regard to a heterogeneous service environment where arriving calls require *differing* bandwidth. This is discussed in the next section.

5.6 HETEROGENEOUS SERVICE, SINGLE-LINK CASE

To understand an important difference going from a single-rate service case to a multiple-rate service case, we illustrate a performance scenario that has important implications for QoS routing. Note that this analysis requires some understanding of offered load in Erlangs (Erls) and call blocking, using just a single link without the presence of routing. The results discussed this section are summarized in Table 5.4.

Table 5.4 Call Blocking for Different Services under Various Scenarios

Link Capacity (Mbps)	a_{low} (Erls)	a_{high} (Erls)	m_{low} (Mbps)	m_{high} (Mbps)	Reservation (Yes/No)	B_{low}	B_{high}	$W_{composite}$
50	38.0	—	1	—		1.03%	—	1.03%
50	19.0	1.9	1	10	No	0.21%	25.11%	12.66%
85	19.0	1.9	1	10	No	0.05%	0.98%	0.52%
85	22.8	1.9	1	10	No	0.08%	1.56%	0.75%
85	22.8	1.9	1	10	Yes	1.41%	0.94%	1.20%
85	22.8	1.9	1	10	Yes, *Prob* = 0.27	1.11%	1.10%	1.11%

Consider a service that requires 1 Mbps of bandwidth during the duration of the call. Assume that the link capacity is 50 Mbps; thus, this link can accommodate at most 50 such calls simultaneously, that is, the effective capacity of the link is 50. Assume that the call arrival pattern is Poisson with an average call arrival rate at 0.38 per second, and that the average duration of a call is 100 seconds. Using Equation 11.2.2 from *Network Routing* by Deep Medhi and Karthik Ramasamy, we can determine that the offered load is $0.38 \times 100 = 38$ Erls.

Furthermore, using the Erlang-B loss formula Equation 11.2.3, we can find that 38 Erls offered to a link with 50 units of capacity results in a call-blocking probability of 1 percent. Since most networking environments would like to maintain a QoS performance requirement for call blocking below 1 percent probability, we can see that users will receive acceptable QoS in this case. Note that to meet QoS, there are two issues that need to be addressed: (1) each call must receive a bandwidth guarantee of 1 Mbps, if admitted, and (2) the call acceptance probability is below 1 percent so that users perceive that they are almost always going to get a connection whenever they try.

Next, consider the situation where we allow a new 10-Mbps traffic stream on the *same* 50-Mbps link to be shared with the basic 1-Mbps traffic stream. We start by splitting the 38 Erls of offered load equally (i.e., 19 Erls to the 1-Mbps traffic class and 19 Erls to the 10-Mbps traffic class). However, note that each 10-Mbps call requires 10 times the bandwidth of a 1-Mbps call. Thus, a more appropriate equitable load for a 10-Mbps traffic stream would be 1.9 Erls (= 19/10) when we consider traffic load level by accounting for per-call bandwidth impact. The calculation of blocking with different traffic streams and different bandwidth requirements is much more complicated than the Erlang-B loss formula; this is because the Erlang-B formula is for traffic streams where all requests have the *same* bandwidth requirement. The method to calculate blocking in the presence of two streams with differing bandwidth is known as the Kaufman–Roberts formula. Using this formula, we can find that the blocking probability for a 1-Mbps traffic class will be 0.21 percent, while for a 10-Mbps traffic class it is 25.11 percent.

We can see that for the same amount of load exerted, the higher-bandwidth traffic class suffers much higher call blocking than the lower-bandwidth service in a *shared* environment; not only that, the lower-bandwidth service in fact has much lower blocking than the acceptable 1 percent blocking. If we still want to keep the blocking below 1 percent, then there is no other option than to increase the capacity of the link to a higher capacity (unless the network is completely partitioned for each different service). After some testing with different numbers, we find that if the link capacity is 85 Mbps, then with 19 Erls load of 1-Mbps traffic class and 1.9 Erls load of 10-Mbps traffic class, the call blocking would be 0.05 percent and 0.98 percent, respectively. The important point to note here is that with the introduction of the higher-bandwidth traffic class, to maintain a 1 percent call-blocking probability for each class, the link capacity is required to be 70 percent (= (85 − 50)/50) more than the base capacity.

Now, consider a sudden overload scenario for the 1-Mbps traffic class in the shared environment while keeping the overall capacity at the new value: 85 Mbps. Increasing the 1-Mbps traffic class by a 20 percent load while keeping the higher bandwidth (10 Mbps) traffic class at the same offered load of 1.9 Erls, we find that the blocking changes to 0.08 percent and 1.56 percent, respectively. What is interesting to note is that although the traffic for the lower-bandwidth call has increased, its overall blocking is still below 1 percent, while that of the higher-bandwidth call has increased beyond the acceptable threshold level; yet there has been *no* increase in traffic load for this class. These are sometimes known as *mice and elephants* phenomena. Here mice are the lower-bandwidth service calls, while elephants are the higher-bandwidth service calls. However, unlike IP-based TCP flows, the situation is quite different in a QoS-based environment—it is the mice that get through while elephants get unfair treatment.

This suggests that some form of admission control is needed so that higher-bandwidth services are not treated unfairly. One possibility is to extend the idea of trunk reservation to *service class* reservation so that some amount of the link bandwidth is logically reserved for the higher-bandwidth service class. Taking this into account, assume that out of 85 Mbps of capacity, 10 Mbps of capacity is reserved for the elephant (10 Mbps) service class; this means that any time the available bandwidth drops below 10 Mbps, no mice (1 Mbps) traffic calls are allowed to enter. With this change in policy, with 20 percent overload for mice traffic from 19 Erls, while elephant traffic class remains at 1.9 Erls, we find that the call blocking for mice traffic would be 1.41 percent and 0.94 percent, respectively—that is, the elephant traffic class is not affected much; this is then good news since through such a service class–based reservation concept, certain traffic classes may be protected from not getting their share of the resources.

Now, if an equitable blocking is still desirable for both service classes, even though only the low bandwidth stream is overloaded, then some mechanisms are needed to increase the blocking for the elephant service class. A way to accomplish this is to consider a probabilistic admission control; this rule can be expressed as follows:

> An amount of bandwidth threshold may be reserved for higher-bandwidth calls, which is activated when the available bandwidth of the link falls below this threshold. As a broad mechanism, even when this threshold is invoked, lower-bandwidth calls may be admitted based on meeting the acceptable probabilistic admission value.

To compute blocking for each traffic class with differing bandwidth *and* a probabilistic admission control and reservation. In Table 5.4, we list the probabilistic admission control case along with reservation and no reservation for the higher-bandwidth traffic class; you can see that equity in call blocking can be achieved when, with reservation, 27 percent of the time low-bandwidth calls are still permitted to be admitted.

We now consider the other extreme when only high-bandwidth 10-Mbps calls, still with 38 Erls of traffic, are offered. To keep call-blocking probability at 1 percent, with 38 Erls of offered load, a link would still need 50 units of *high-bandwidth* call-carrying capacity; this then translates to a raw bandwidth of 50 × 10 Mbps = 500 Mbps. Thus, we can see that depending on whether a network link faces low-bandwidth calls, or a mixture of low- and high-bandwidth calls, or just (or mostly) high-bandwidth calls, for the same offered load exerted, the link requires vastly different raw link bandwidth to maintain a QoS performance guarantee.

Finally, while we discuss call blocking for each individual traffic class, it is also good to have a network-wide performance objective in terms of bandwidth measure. Suppose that a_{low} is the offered load for the low-bandwidth traffic class that requires m_{low} bandwidth per call; similarly, a_{high} is the offered load for high-bandwidth traffic, and m_{high} is the bandwidth requirement per call of high-bandwidth calls, then a bandwidth blocking measure is given by:

$$W_{composite} = \frac{m_{low}a_{low}B_{high} + m_{high}a_{high}B_{high}}{m_{low}a_{low} + m_{high}a_{high}}$$

These composite performance measure values for the cases that were considered earlier are also listed in Table 5.4. While this composite measure is a good overall indicator, it can miss unfair treatment to high-bandwidth calls.

Generalizing from two service classes to the environment where *each* arriving call i has an arbitrary bandwidth requirement mi, the composite bandwidth blocking measure, known as bandwidth denial ratio (BDR), is given by

$$W_{composite} = \frac{\sum\limits_{i \in BlockedCalls} m_i}{\sum\limits_{i \in AttemptedCalls} m_i}$$

However, we have learned an important point from our illustration of low- and high-bandwidth traffic classes: that higher-bandwidth classes may suffer higher blocking. We can still consider a simple generalization to determine whether a similar occurrence is noticed when *each* call has a differing bandwidth. Based on profiles of calls received, they may be classified into two or more groups/buckets in terms of their per-call bandwidth requirements, and then have the above measure applied to each such group. For example, suppose that a network receives calls varying from a 64-Kbps requirement to a 10-Mbps requirement; calls may be put into, say, three buckets: 0 to 3 Mbps, 3 Mbps to 7 Mbps, and higher than 7 Mbps. If higher-bandwidth groups have a significantly higher-bandwidth blocking rate than the average bandwidth blocking rate for all calls, then this is an indicator that some form of admission control policy is needed so that the higher-bandwidth call groups do not necessarily have a significantly higher-bandwidth blocking rate.

5.7 A GENERAL FRAMEWORK FOR SOURCE-BASED QOS ROUTING WITH PATH CACHING

We now consider a general alternate call-routing framework where calls are heterogeneous. To consider a general framework, we first summarize several goals of QoS routing:

- Reduce the impact on the call setup time by keeping it as low as possible.

- Minimize user-level retry attempts (i.e., it is preferable to do retry *internally* to the network as long as the call setup time is not drastically affected). It is important to note that user level retry attempts cannot be completely avoided, at least in a heavily loaded network—a network where the ratio of traffic to network bandwidth is at a level beyond the normally acceptable tolerance for service guarantee.

- Allow the capability for the source node to select a path from a number of possible routes very quickly for each arriving request. Also, allow *crankback* capability as an optional feature.

- Allow a call admission control feature that can be invoked.

To keep call setup time minimal and the need to minimize user-level retry along with the recognition that on-demand route determination can be taxing suggests that having multiple path choices can be beneficial in a QoS routing environment; this is often referred to as *alternate path routing*. Since path caching is necessary to be able to do alternate path routing, we refer to it as the *path caching option*. Where these are multiple path choices, but where inaccurate/stale information means that blocking on a selected path cannot be completely ruled out, crankback is a nice optional feature that can be used to quickly try another path and so avoid user-level retry.

Finally, a framework should allow the ability to incorporate a number of routing schemes so that network providers can choose the appropriate one depending on their performance and systems configuration goal.

5.7.1 Routing Computation Framework

The basic idea behind this framework addresses the following: how is the selection of paths done, when are they selected, and how are they used by newly arrived requests? For calls requiring bandwidth guarantees, another important component that can complicate the matter is the definition of the cost of a path based on possibly both additive and nonadditive properties. Later, we will consider our framework using an extended link state protocol concept. Before we discuss this aspect, we describe a three-phase framework: (1) Preliminary Path Caching (PPC) phase, (2) Updated Path Ordering (UPO) phase, and (3) Actual Route Attempt (ARA). Each of these phases operates at different time scales.

The first phase, PPC, does a preliminary determination of a set of possible paths from a source to destination node, and their storage (caching). A simple case for this phase is to determine this set at the time of major topological changes. PPC, in the simplest form, can be thought of as topology dependent (i.e., if there is a change in the major topological connectivity), then the PPC phase may be invoked. This can be accomplished by a topology update message sent across the network in a periodic manner. This process can be somewhat intelligent: If a link availability is expected to be less than a certain threshold for a prolonged duration or if the link is scheduled for some maintenance work, then PPC can also be used for pruning the link and a new topology update, thus letting nodes determine a new set of cached paths.

Essentially, PPC uses a coarse-grained view of the network and determines a set of candidate paths to be cached. A simple mechanism to determine the set of paths for each source node to each destination node may be based on hop count or some administrative weight as the cost metric using the k-shortest paths algorithm. Thus, for this phase, we assume the link cost metric for determining a set of candidate paths to be additive.

The second phase, UPO, narrows the number of QoS acceptable paths; this module uses the most recent status of all links as available to each source node. Since the PPC phase has already cached a set of possible paths, this operation is more of a compare or filter to provide a set of QoS acceptable paths. Furthermore, for a specific service type or class, this phase may also *order* the routes from most acceptable to least acceptable (e.g., based on path residual bandwidth), and will, in general, have a subset of the routes "active" from the list obtained from the PPC phase. In this phase, the cost metric can be either additive (e.g., delay requirement) or nonadditive (i.e., bandwidth requirement), or a combination, where one is more dominant than the other. Another important factor to note about the UPO phase is that the value of the link state update interval may vary, with each node being able to select the interval value; for simplicity, we will refer to this as the routing link state update interval (RUI). This phase should be more traffic dependent (rather than on-demand per call) with a minimum and maximum time window on the frequency of invocation.

The third phase is ARA. From the UPO phase, we already have a reasonably good set of paths. The ARA phase selects a specific route on which to attempt a newly arrived flow. The exact rule for selecting the route is dependent on a specific route selection procedure. The main goal in this phase is to select the actual route as quickly as possible based on the pruned available paths from the UPO phase.

There are several advantages of the three-phase framework:

- Different routing schemes can be cast in this framework.

- It avoids on-demand routing computation; this reduces the impact on the call setup time significantly since paths are readily available; that is no "cost" is incurred from needing to compute routes from scratch *after* a new flow arrives.

- The framework can be implemented using a link state routing protocol with some extension. For the PPC phase, some topology information, for example, needs to be exchanged at coarse-grain time windows. During the UPO phase, periodic update on the status of link usage is needed at a finer grain time window. Since different information about links is needed at different time granularity for use by the PPC and the UPO phase, we refer to this as the *extended* link state protocol concept.

■ Each of the three phases can operate independently without affecting the other ones. For example, in the PPC phase, the *k*-shortest paths can be computed either based on pure hop count or other costs such as link speed–based interface cost. In some schemes the UPO phase may not be necessary.

A possible drawback of the framework is that path caching will typically require more memory at the routers to store multiple paths; this will certainly also depend on how many paths are stored. However, with the decreased cost for memory, a path caching concept is more viable than ever before. Additionally, there is some computational overhead due to *k*-shortest path computation on a coarse-scale time window. Our experience has been that *k*-shortest path computation takes only a few seconds to generate 5 to 10 paths in a 50-node network on an off-the-shelf computer. Thus, this overhead is not remarkable since it is done in the PPC phase. If needed, a router architecture can be designed to include a separate processor to do this type of computational work periodically.

5.7.2 Routing Computation

Consider the source destination node pair $[i,j]$. The set of cached paths for this pair determined at time t (the PPC phase time window) is denoted by $P_{|i,j|}(t)$ and the total number of paths given by $\#(P_{|i,j|}(t))$. For path $p \in P_{|i,j|}(t)$, let $L^p_{i,j}(t)$ denote the set of links used by this path.

Let $b_l(t)$ be the available capacity of link l at time t (obtained using the link state protocol for the UPO phase). Then, from a bandwidth availability perspective, the cost of path p for $[i,j]$ is determined by the nonadditive concave property of the available capacity on the bottleneck link along the path:

$$z^p_{|i,j|}(t) = \min\{b_l(t)\}$$
$$1 \in L^p_{|i,j|}(t)$$

Since the path is known from the PPC phase, this filter operation is quite simple. If the index p is now renumbered in order of the most available bandwidth to the least available bandwidth at time t, that is, from the widest path, the next widest path, and so on, then we have:

$$z^1_{|i,j|}(t) \geq z^2_{|i,j|}(t) \geq \cdots \geq z^{\#(P|i,j|(t))}_{|i,j|}(t)$$

Similar to node i, all other source nodes can use the same principle to determine their own ordered path sets.

How is the available capacity of various links known to nodes i? This can be determined by receiving used capacity of various links through a link state protocol, either in a periodic or an asynchronous manner. Note the availability of the bandwidth on a link is dependent on whether trunk reservation is activated. Suppose the capacity of link l is C_l, and the currently occupied bandwidth as known at time t (based on link state update) is $u_l(t)$. In the absence of trunk reservation, the available bandwidth on link l is given by:

$$b_l(t) = C_l - u_l(t)$$

If, however, a part of the link bandwidth $r_l(t)$ for link l is kept for trunk reservation at time t, then:

$$a_l(t) = C_l - u_l(t) - r_l(t)$$

The former is sometimes also referred to as the residual bandwidth and the second as the available or allowable bandwidth.

There are two important observations to note. First, if the last update value of $u_l(t)$ changes dramatically, it can affect the decision process. Thus, in practice, an exponential weighted moving average value $u_l(t)$ is more appropriate to use than the exact value from the most recently obtained measurement. Second, the reservation allocation for different service classes may be different; thus, it may be beneficial to keep different sets of alternate paths to consider for different service classes. This means that each service class is essentially sliced into a virtual topology.

5.7.3 Routing Schemes

The computation just described can be used in a number of ways. An obvious one is the maximum available capacity-based scheme (widest path); furthermore, the availability can be proportioned to different paths to select a weighted path, similar to dynamically controlled routing (DCR).

The decision on computation routes may depend on whether the information is periodically updated. Finally, the crankback feature availability is a factor to consider; here we will assume that the crankback is activated only at the source node. This means that during the call setup phase, an intermediate node does not try to seek an alternate path; instead, it returns the call control to the originating node when the call does not find enough resources on the outgoing link for its destination.

Recall that a fundamental component of the QoS routing framework used here is path caching. With this, in the PPC phase, a k-shortest paths algorithm is used to generate a set of paths, which is cached. At this phase, the cost metric used is additive. For the routing schemes, an extended link state protocol is used to disseminate the status of the link (different information) at the PPC phase and the UPO phase. Since paths are already cached, the UPO phase can use a simple filtering mechanism to order paths based on available bandwidth (for services that require bandwidth guarantee for QoS). If there are services that have other QoS requirements such as path delay, these requirements can be easily incorporated in the UPO phase as additional filters.

Also recall that an important goal of reducing the impact on flow setup time is addressed by the framework through the notion of path caching. Due to the three-phase framework, the newly arrived flow attempts one of the paths already pruned by the UPO phase—so there is no on-demand route computation delay in this phase. Depending on the periodicity of the UPO phase and the arrival of the link state advertisement, the pruned path set can have outdated information. Thus, some newly arrived flows can be assigned to a path that may not have any available bandwidth at this instant. This cannot be completely avoided unless the frequency of the update interval is reduced; if this is done, then more frequent link state advertisement would be necessary, which leads to an increase in network traffic.

5.7.4 **Results**

For performance studies, we consider maximum available capacity routing with periodic update and crankback (MACRPC), as well as for no crankback (MACRPNC). Note that MACRPC uses the shortest widest path on residual bandwidth but with trunk reservation turned on, and the computation is periodic. For comparison, the utopian scheme, maximum available capacity routing with instantaneous computation (MACRIC), is also considered. This is possible since we have used a simulation environment where the instantaneous feature can be invoked. Also, we consider a sticky random routing scheme that extends the dynamic alternate routing scheme to the multiservice case, which is labeled as cached sticky random adaptive routing (CaSRAR). Results presented here are based on call-by-call routing simulation for randomly arriving calls that follow the Poisson process.

Revisit Homogeneous Traffic Case

We first start with results on call blocking for the homogeneous service case as the number of cached paths K changes from 2 to 15 (for a 10-node fully connected network); this is reported in Figure 5.3 for both the case of no reservation and with trunk reservation set at 40 percent; while a very high trunk reservation value such as 40 percent is rarely used in an operational network, the intent here is to show how results are influenced, with and without trunk reservation. It is interesting to note that for the no reservation case, the increase of cached paths does not necessarily result in improvement in performance for *all* routing schemes. We see improvement only for MACRPNC. However, with trunk reservation activated, performance can improve with the increase in K for *all* routing schemes. This substantiates the claim on performance degradation in the absence of trunk reservation as reported elsewhere.

Furthermore, our result shows that this behavior is not necessarily consistent for *all* routing schemes. For the utopian scheme, MACRIC, the performance degrades drastically as K increases when there is no trunk reservation. Although this may sound surprising, this is possibly caused by overuse of multiple-link paths through instantaneous checking, which leads to local optimization and

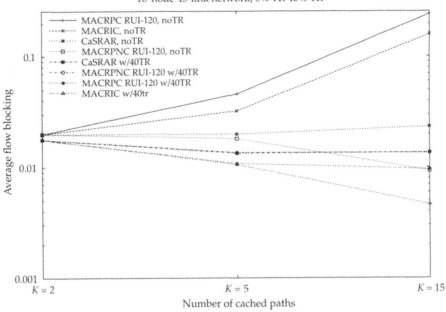

FIGURE 5.3

Homogeneous service fully connected network (with and without trunk reservation).

bistability. We observe the same problem with MACRPC when there is no trunk reservation. Overall, CaSRAR and MACRPNC are more robust in the absence of trunk reservation. However, in the presence of high trunk reservation, as K increases we found that MACRIC and MACRPC had better performances than CaSRAR and MACRPNC. Overall, these results show that path caching is indeed helpful; however, the actual routing schemes and factors such as trunk reservation do matter.

Service Class Performance

Next we discuss the case of heterogeneous services where three different service classes with differing bandwidth requirements for each service class are offered. We consider two cases: the network capacity in the first one is dimensioned for low BDR (less than 1 percent) while the second one is dimensioned for moderately high BDR (over 5 percent). (Dimensioning or sizing refers to determining the capacity needed in a network to carry a given traffic offered load at a prespecified level of performance guarantee.) From the scenario where the network is dimensioned for low BDR (Figure 5.4(a)), we found that in the presence of trunk reservation, as K increases, the BDR decreases for all schemes (similar to the homogeneous case). However, this is not true when the network is dimensioned

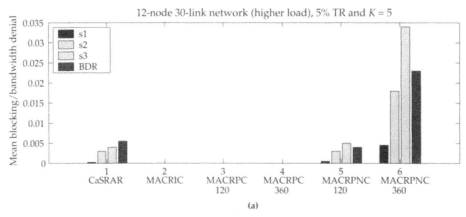

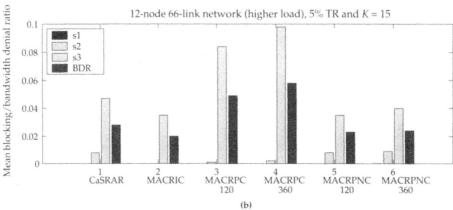

FIGURE 5.4

Performance of different routing schemes (and update periods): (a) low-load, sparsely connected case, (b) higher-load case.

for moderate BDR (Figure 5.4(b)), even in the presence of moderate trunk reservation. The pattern is somewhat closer to the homogeneous case with no trunk reservation. What we can infer is that even in the presence of trunk reservation, the ability to hunt over multiple paths through crankback is beneficial in a network designed for low BDR, but crankback can be detrimental when the network is designed for moderately high BDR as it impacts network performance (and can also lead to higher flow setup time due to frequent path hunting).

Now we discuss briefly the role of the UPO phase. Recall that different routing update interval (RUI) parameter values can be used for the UPO phase. As one would guess, with more frequent updates (i.e., for a smaller value of RUI), the inaccuracy in link state information decreases. It is observed that both schemes MACRPC and MACRPNC give better performance with more frequent updates as would be intuitively guessed. However, it appears that inaccuracy in link state information can be well compensated by the availability of crankback in a network designed for low BDR. Specifically, we note that MACRPC with an RUI of 360 seconds has much lower BDR than MACRPNC with an RUI of 120 seconds (Figure 5.4(a)). However, the reverse relation holds when the load is moderately high (Figure 5.4(b)). We also saw in an earlier example (through MACRIC) that instantaneous information update is not always beneficial in terms of network performance (as well as negatively affecting flow setup time considerably). Overall, we can infer that inaccuracy in link state information is not necessarily bad, and in fact, can be well compensated through path caching; in any case, the specifics of the routing scheme do play a role here.

So far we have discussed performance using the network-wide indicator bandwidth blocking rate. We are next interested in understanding the effect on each service class. For this, we have considered three service classes in increasing order of bandwidth requirement; that is, the first service (s1) class has the lowest bandwidth requirement per flow, while the third service class (s3) has the highest bandwidth requirement per flow.

For a network dimensioned for low BDR, we found that with a moderate to large number of path caching, CaSRAR and MACRPNC tend to give poorer performances to the higher bandwidth service class (s3), whether the network is fully or sparsely connected (Figure 5.4(a) is shown here for the sparsely connected case). Furthermore, the inaccuracy of routing information due to the update interval of the UPO phase does not seem to affect MACRPC for different service classes but can noticeably affect MACRPNC (Figure 5.4(a)). To check whether the same behavior holds, we increased the load uniformly for all service classes. We made some interesting observations (Figure 5.4(b)): The lowest-bandwidth service (s1) has uniformly low flow blocking for *all* routing schemes; however, the highest-bandwidth service class (s3) is affected worst under MACRPC at the expense of the lower-bandwidth classes, therefore MACRPC is more unfair to higher-bandwidth services as the network load uniformly increases. In general, we found that CaSRAR works better than the other schemes in providing smaller variation in performance differences seen by different service classes.

Call Admission Control

While it is known that higher-bandwidth, reservation-based services experience worse performance than lower-bandwidth, reservation-based services in a single-link system, these results indicate that this behavior holds as well in a network *with* dynamic routing and trunk reservation. In other words, routing and trunk reservation *cannot* completely eliminate this unfairness. Thus, in a network, if fairness in terms of GoS to different service classes is desirable, then additional mechanisms are needed. In this context, a concept called *service reservation* beyond traditional trunk reservation has been proposed. This concept can be manifested, for example, through source-based admission control at the time of flow arrival.

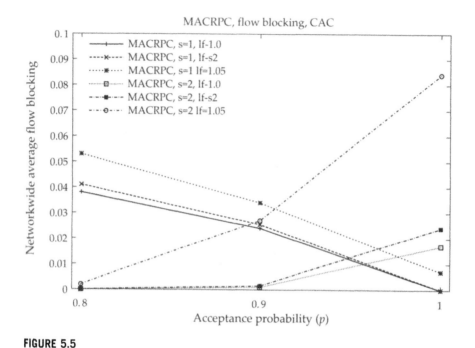

FIGURE 5.5

Performance impact in the presence of source-based admission control.

While a good source-based admission control scheme for a general topology network in the *presence* of QoS routing operating in a link state protocol environment and trunk reservation remains a research problem, a probabilistic source-based admission control scheme for fully connected networks in the presence of routing and for two service classes has been presented. The ability to provide service fairness in terms of fair GoS using this source-based admission control scheme in the presence of routing and trunk reservation is shown in Figure 5.5. This is shown for three different values of network load with two service class scenarios (shown for normal load "lf-1.0," 5 percent s2 overload "lf-s2," and 5 percent network-wide overload "lf-1.05," all for MACRPC). The right-most entries (corresponding to $p = 1$) denote the *no* source-based admission control case. As we can see, with the increase in load, the higher-bandwidth service suffers the most in the absence of source-based admission control. As the admission control parameter is tuned (by changing p toward 0.8) to invoke different levels of source-based admission control, it can be seen that service-level fairness in terms of GoS can be achieved.

Dynamic Traffic

Finally, we discuss network performance impact due to network traffic dynamics. To show this we consider a homogeneous service, fully connected network where one source-destination node pair has dynamic traffic while the rest of the traffic pairs have stationary traffic (no source-based admission control is included here). For our study, the dynamic traffic has been represented through a time-dependent, stationary process that follows a sinusoidal traffic pattern. For the case with no trunk reservation, we have found that MACRPC has much worse performance than both CaSRAR and MACRIC as traffic changes for the dynamic traffic class (pair); CaSRAR adapts very well with traffic changes, although it has no UPO phase. It is interesting to note that just the presence of dynamic traffic between a source-destination node pair can cause the rest of the (stationary) traffic to show dynamic performance behavior (Figure 5.6).

We also considered the case in which trunk reservation is imposed; purposefully, we set the reservation at an unusually high value of 40 percent to understand the performance implication—the result is shown in Figure 5.7; from this figure, we note two phenomena: (a) MACRPC performs better than CaSRAR for dynamic traffic, and (b) the imposition of dynamic performance on the stationary traffic (from the dynamic traffic class) is no longer there. Also, we found that the overall performance improves in the presence of trunk reservation in a dynamic traffic

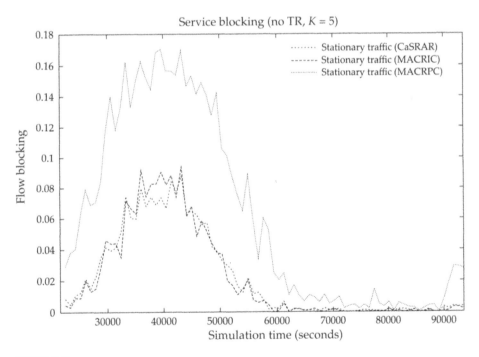

FIGURE 5.6

Dynamic performance behavior of *stationary* traffic due to the influence of dynamic traffic (no trunk reservation).

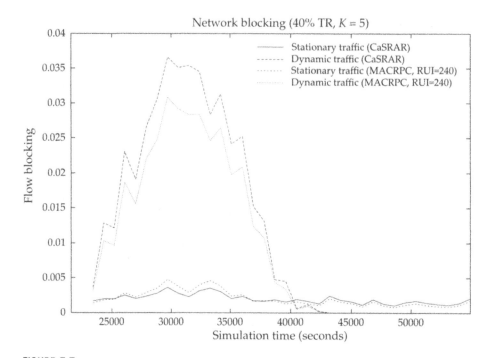

FIGURE 5.7

Performance of dynamic and stationary traffic (with trunk reservation).

scenario (similar to the stationary traffic case). From these results an important question, although not directly within the purview of routing, arises: Should a network allow a dynamic traffic stream/class to impose its behavior on a stationary traffic stream? In other words, should a stationary traffic stream suffer higher flow-blocking just because the load for the dynamic traffic stream is increasing? This cannot be addressed alone through the three-phase QoS routing framework or any other QoS routing framework. However, the impact can be controlled through the use of trunk reservation and under controls; this is where lessons on controls may be taken into consideration.

5.8 ROUTING PROTOCOLS FOR QOS ROUTING

The following subsections discuss protocols employed in QoS routing.

5.8.1 QOSPF: Extension to OSPF for QoS Routing

The OSPF extension for QoS routing mechanisms, described in *RFC 2676*, is commonly referred to as QOSPF. You may note that every OSPF hello, database description, and link state advertisements (LSA) contain an options field that is 1 byte long. One of the bits in the options field, originally known as the T-bit to indicate if an originating router is capable of supporting type of service (ToS), was later removed. Instead, the QOSPF specification proposed to reclaim this bit and renamed it as the Q-bit to indicate that the originating router is QoS routing capable. When this bit is set, two attributes are announced with a link state: bandwidth and delay.

An important aspect about the QOSPF protocol is that it specifies the path computation mechanism, which is divided into the pre-computed option and the on-demand option. For the pre-computed path option, a widest path version of the Bellman–Ford approach based on bandwidth was proposed. For the on-demand computation, a widest shortest path version of Dijkstra's algorithm that considered bandwidth and hop count was proposed; this is essentially least-hop-widest path routing discussed earlier in this chapter.

Note that in QOSPF, as part of the protocol, both the path computation algorithm and the attributes to be exchanged were specified. It is important to distinguish this approach from traffic engineering extensions of OSPF in which the extension on exchange of information has been standardized, while the actual path computation mechanism is left for the provider to decide.

5.8.2 ATM PNNI

Asynchronous transfer mode (ATM) technology is a packet-mode networking technology with its own protocol stack architecture and addressing. In ATM, all packets are of fixed 53-byte size, known as *cells*. The Private Network–Network Interface (PNNI) protocol, originally defined around the mid 1990s, is the standard for QoS routing in ATM networks. PNNI is based on a link state routing protocol framework; it has the basic elements of a link state routing protocol such as the hello protocol, database synchronization, and flooding. However, PNNI is a *topology state* protocol since besides the status of links, the status of nodes can also be flooded; accordingly, the PNNI topology state element (PTSE) is equivalent of the link state advertisement.

Parameters associated with a topology state are divided into two categories: metrics and attributes; the main distinction is whether information is considered on an entire path basis ("metric"), or an individual node or link basis ("attribute"). Examples of metrics are cell delay variation and maximum cell transfer delay. Attributes are either performance-related such as the cell loss ratio, the maximum cell rate, and the available cell rate, or policy-related such as the restricted transit. Since packet sizes are fixed, cells as units are used instead of the raw bandwidth rate; thus, effectively, the maximum cell rate refers to the total bandwidth of a link, and the available cell rate refers to the available bandwidth, both counted in cells as units. Although all information required for computing paths is provided, PNNI did not prescribe any specific way to do path computation; in this sense, PNNI is a visionary protocol and is one of the early routing protocols to decouple the routing information exchange part from the routing algorithm computation.

PNNI allows crankback and alternate routing, much like dynamic nonhierarchical routing (DNHR) and RTNR for dynamic call routing in the telephone network. Crankback can be local; that is, the control for a connection need not be sent back to the ingress switch for performing crankback. By using addressing hierarchy, PNNI also handles scalability on information dissemination and storage. That is, through addressing hierarchy, aggregation of information about a group of nodes and links that are at the same hierarchy is performed—such a group is identified as a *peer group*; the aggregated information about a peer group is disseminated, instead of announcing the PTSE for each element within the group. Thus, a peer group can be thought of as a domain; in this sense, PNNI has both intra- and inter-domain flavors in the same protocol. Although PNNI routing is considered to be source-routing based, this is true only within a peer group; to reach an address that is in a different group, a *designated transit list* is created that identifies the peer groups the connection control message is to visit during the connection setup; once such a request reaches a group identified in the designated transit list, the group is responsible for actual source route within its group to the appropriate egress node, which, then, hands off to the next peer group for further processing.

5.9 SUMMARY

In this chapter, we have discussed QoS routing. We started by discussing what QoS means, and the scope of QoS routing and its inherent relation to traffic engineering. Based on arrival and service frequency, we have also identified how different services may be classified into three types of classifications; this was summarized in Table 5.1. We have indicated that QoS routing falls under the Type A classification.

We then presented a taxonomy for QoS routing and showed how QoS routing can be divided based on different types of networks, and whether one or more attributes are to be considered in the QoS routing decision, especially for packet-switched networks. Next we discussed extendibility of widest and shortest path routing to QoS routing. An important issue to consider here is that periodic updating of information induces inaccuracy on link state information—thus, to properly address service performance, a path caching mechanism that allows alternate path routing can be helpful; this is presented as a three-phase framework. Performance results are presented to understand the interrelation in the presence of heterogeneous guaranteed services, update frequency, traffic dynamism, and so on.

The importance of QoS routing goes beyond the telephone network. It is also applicable to MPLS, optical, and wavelength routing when service requests with guaranteed resource requirements are to be connected on demand and quickly.

Before we conclude, we briefly comment on QoS guarantee in a generic best-effort network such as the Internet. This QoS guarantee issue should not be confused with QoS routing. In an intra-domain environment running a best-effort model, QoS guarantee for services are quite possible if the network is engineered to meet QoS guarantee—this might require overprovisioning. A better environment is a differentiated services environment, where priority to certain packets can be given by using a router's scheduling algorithm for services that require certain guarantee—in this case, the overprovisioning can be moderate since the routers have mechanisms to discriminate packets that require guarantee and those that do not. MPLS is also a mechanism to enable QoS guarantee. In an inter-domain environment, it is much more difficult since each provider on a path for a request that requires QoS guarantee would need to have the proper mechanisms—this is difficult in practice since it might not be possible to enforce every provider to provide the same QoS guarantee. However, instead of stringent QoS guarantee, it is possible to provide certain quality through broad service level agreements (SLAs). SLAs are possible to implement among different providers through which traffic may flow. Thus, meeting SLA agreements can be thought of as meeting "soft" QoS guarantee.

Quality of Service in IP-Based Services

6

Although there are many IP technologies that are very helpful in building basic IP-based services and networks, those technologies may not be able to meet the requirements of all customers who make use of the Internet Protocol (IP) network. Some customers may have additional quality-of-service (QoS) requirements (other than just connectivity), such as guaranteed bandwidth, guaranteed minimized end-to-end delay and jitter, security, data privacy, and so on. With the rapid emergence of modern applications—B2B, e-commerce, video-on-demand, and voice over IP—the requirements listed are important, so there is more demand on IP-based networks to deliver the QoS requirements of the various applications.

Applications like voice over IP and video are sensitive to delay and jitter. *Delay* is the amount of time taken by the IP network to deliver a packet from the source to the destination. *Jitter* is the variation in the delay. Unlike traditional IP-based applications that depended on best-effort services, voice over IP applications have strict delay and jitter requirements. Packets from these applications must be delivered to the destinations with a finite delay (about 150 milliseconds). Video applications, such as videoconferencing and video on demand, have bandwidth requirements in addition to delay and jitter requirements. They require *guaranteed end-to-end bandwidth,* meaning that at any given time the IP network can guarantee a minimum throughput (measured in kilobits per second) from source to destination.

Privacy and security of data are of special concern to customers like banks and insurance companies. Privacy means that this data should not be accessible to others, and security means that even if the network is insecure and the IP packets transporting the data are accessible, contents of the packets must still be secure and not be compromised. These customers deal with sensitive data and are very concerned about the safety of that data. Since the traffic from these customers traverses the same IP backbone of the service provider, it is necessary to ensure that data privacy is maintained at any given time.

This chapter, excerpted from Chapter 7 of *Developing IP-Based Services* by Monique Morrow and Kateel Vijayananda, examines the techniques and protocols used to meet the quality of service expectations of the users of IP networks. The mechanisms discussed can help service providers to enhance and add new IP-based services to their portfolios in order to meet the additional requirements of their customers. The demand for QoS in an IP network is increasing every day. With the rapid emergence of applications like voice over IP and video-on-demand, the expectations of customers are also increasing. QoS and applications like voice over IP are discussed in separate sections.

6.1 QUALITY OF SERVICE

The term *quality of service,* or *QoS,* can be used in a broad sense and, depending on context, can have several meanings. QoS is normally understood to indicate a set of service requirements that have to be met by a network. QoS functions are intended to deliver the service requirements that have been guaranteed by the network. This is achieved by giving the network operator control over the usage of network resources, including bandwidth, memory to store and forward packets, and CPUs. Some of the techniques that can be used to satisfy QoS requirements are the following:

Resource reservation at each node in the network. Reservation is done according to policies implemented by the service provider based on customer requirements. The reservation mechanism depends on routing tables/routing protocols to find the path with sufficient resources. This gives the operator control over the resources that are allocated to customers.

Scheduling mechanisms to effectively allocate resources based on demand. The scheduling mechanisms have to be implemented by the service provider based on customer requirements.

A combination of resource reservation and scheduling mechanisms to manage the network resources and meet the QoS requirements of the customers.

Scheduling mechanisms are local to a network device. However, in order to ensure the end-to-end QoS requirements (meaning that QoS is guaranteed along all the links and nodes, from the source node to the destination node), it is important that all of the nodes in the network have a common agreement on how to implement the scheduling mechanisms. Resource reservation also requires cooperation among all of the nodes in a network. All of the nodes that are in the path from the source to the destination must implement the reservation policy. Resource reservation depends on routing to find out the path from the source to the destination and reserve resources on all of the nodes.

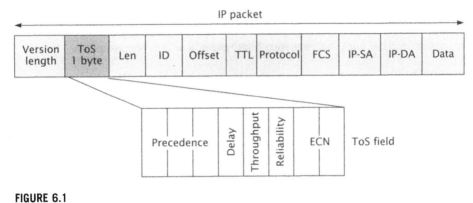

FIGURE 6.1

ToS field of an IP packet.

QoS in an IP network is not an afterthought. Founders of IP had envisioned the need for QoS and have provided for a field called *type of service* (ToS) in the IP header (see Figure 6.1) to facilitate QoS in IP networks. Traditionally, IP networks offered best-effort services, meaning that the only QoS offered was that packets might be eventually delivered to the destination. Since the Internet was mostly used by applications like Telnet and file transfer, best-effort service was enough to meet the QoS requirements of these applications. The QoS requirements of the applications that use the Internet today are much higher.

Internet QoS development has undergone a lot of standardization to provide end-to-end QoS over the Internet. These standardization efforts are concentrated in two areas:

Integrated services: Based on reserving the resources on all network devices for each *flow*, or *connection*, before data from the connection is transported across the network. This requires a reservation protocol like RSVP to be understood by all network devices. (Section 6.1.2 provides more details about this activity.)

Differentiated services: Based on managing the resources on all network devices for each flow (based on some information, e.g., IP address, ToS field, or tags) as the data packets are transported through the network. This requires implementing QoS functions like packet classification, policing, traffic shaping, and the queuing mechanism on each network device. (More details about differentiated services can be found in Section 6.1.3.)

6.1.1 QoS Parameters

The QoS guarantees provided by the network are measured using the performance of the network. Bandwidth, packet delay and jitter, and packet loss are some common measures used to characterize a network's performance. The QoS requirements vary depending on the requirements of the applications: for voice over IP or IP telephony, delay, packet loss, and jitter are important; for applications that involve bulk data transfer, bandwidth is a QoS requirement.

Bandwidth

The term *bandwidth* is used to describe the throughput of a given medium, protocol, or connection. It describes the size of the pipe that is required for the application to communicate over the network. An application requiring guaranteed bandwidth wants the network to allocate a minimum bandwidth specifically for it on all the links through which the data is transferred through the network. Depending on the type of network, the bandwidth guarantee can be provided at either the IP layer or the data-link layer. Guaranteed bandwidth at the IP layer depends on the type of data-link network. Not all data-link network support guarantees bandwidth when several IP connections share the same network—for example, it is not possible to reserve bandwidth in an Ethernet network with several hosts.

Packet Delay and Jitter

Packet delay, or latency, at each hop consists of serialization or transmission delay, propagation delay, and switching delay.

Serialization or transmission delay: The time it takes for a device to send the packet at the output rate. This depends on the size of the packet and the link bandwidth. A 64-byte packet on a 4 Mbps line takes 128 µs to be transmitted. The same 64-byte packet on a 128 Kbps line takes 4 ms to be transmitted.

Propagation delay: The time taken for a bit to be transmitted by the transmitter and to be received by the receiver. This is a function of the media and the distance, and is independent of bandwidth.

Switching delay: The time taken for a device to start transmitting a packet after receiving it. This depends on the status of the network and the number of packets in transit at this hop.

End-to-end delay for a packet belonging to a flow is the sum of all of the preceding types of delays experienced at each hop. All packets in a flow need not experience the same delay—it depends on the transient delay in each hop in the network. If the network is congested, queues will be built at each hop, and this increases the end-to-end delay. This variation in the delay is called *jitter*. Queuing mechanisms at each node can be used to ensure that the delay of certain flows is minimized and also that the jitter has an upper bound. (This is described in Section 6.1.4.)

Packet Loss

Packet loss specifies the number of packets lost in the network during transmission. The loss can be due to corruption in the transmission media, or packets can be dropped at congestion points due to lack of buffer space in the incoming or outgoing interface. Packet loss due to drops should be rare for a well-designed network that is correctly subscribed or undersubscribed. Packet loss due to faulty transmission media can also be avoided by building good physical networks.

QoS at Layer 2

Depending on the QoS requirements, QoS functions are available at the data-link layer (Layer 2) and network layer (Layer 3) of the Open Systems Interconnection (OSI) model. Guaranteed bandwidth as a QoS requirement can be provided by several Layer-2 technologies, such as Frame Relay or asynchronous transfer mode (ATM), when the physical medium is shared by several Layer-3 connections simultaneously. ATM can also meet other QoS requirements such as minimizing delay and jitter.

6.1.2 Integrated Services Model

The *integrated services* (IntServ) model is based on the concept of requesting resources along all the links in a network from the source to the destination. This reservation is done using protocols such as the *Resource Reservation Protocol* (RSVP)—a network-control protocol that enables Internet applications to obtain special QoSs for their data flows. The RSVP is not a routing protocol; instead, it works in conjunction with routing protocols and installs the equivalent of dynamic access lists along the routes that routing protocols calculate. RSVP occupies the place of a transport protocol in the OSI model seven-layer protocol stack.

Researchers at the University of Southern California Information Sciences Institute (ISI) and Xerox Palo Alto Research Center originally conceived RSVP. The Internet Engineering Task Force (IETF) is now working toward standardization through an RSVP working group. RSVP operational topics discussed later in this chapter include data flows, QoS, session start-up, reservation style, and soft-state implementation.

How Does It Work?

IntServ using RSVP works in the following manner:

1. Applications signal their QoS requirements via RSVP to the network.
2. Every network node along the path must check to see if the reservation request can be met.
3. Resources are reserved if the service constraints can be met.
4. An error message is sent back to the receiver if the constraints cannot be met.
5. Network nodes make sure there are no violations of the traffic contract.
6. Nonconforming packets are either marked down or dropped.

The following are some of the main drawbacks of the IntServ model:

- It is an "all-or-nothing" model, meaning that it cannot be partially deployed—every node in the network must implement it in order for it to work.
- The network needs to maintain each reservation for each flow.
- It is oriented for real-time traffic.
- *Scalability:* The number of RSVP reservations is directly proportional to the number of IP streams that require resource reservation. This issue is addressed by aggregating multiple RSVP reservations into one reservation. Work is currently ongoing to provide aggregated RSVP.

An example of an application that uses the IntServ model is voice over IP, which makes use of RSVP to make path reservations before transporting voice traffic over a data network. For more details, see Section 6.2.3.

6.1.3 Differentiated Services Model

The *differentiated services* (DiffServ) approach to providing QoS in a network is based on employing a well-defined set of blocks with which one can build a variety of services. It is based on the *differentiated services code point* (DSCP) byte and ToS byte of the IP packet. The DiffServ architecture provides a framework within which service providers can offer a wide range of services to customers, each service being differentiated based on the DSCP field in the IP packet. This value specifies the *per-hop behavior* (PHB) of the packet as it traverses the service provider network.

Differentiated Services Code Point

To allow traffic to have different policies applied to it, some method of differentiation of packets is required. Within the IP header is an eight-bit field known as *type of service* (ToS), within which three bits are used as precedence, allowing for eight classes to be used. This field has recently been redefined by the IETF as the differentiated services code point (DSCP) and uses six bits of the field, allowing for 64 different classes. Figure 6.2 shows the details of the DSCP field (and also the precedence field) of the IP header. In the case of DSCP, the currently unused bits are not used and are reserved for future implementation.

Multiprotocol Label Switching (MPLS) has only three bits in the experimental (EXP) field of the MPLS (shim) header. The IP precedence bits (three left-most bits of the ToS field of the IP header) are copied to the EXP field of the MPLS header when the MPLS header is appended to the packet. This effectively means that full use of DSCP can only be made in links where MPLS is not enabled. All other links in the network run MPLS, but only the first three higher-order bits of DSCP can be used to classify traffic.

The limited number of bits in the MPLS header is not necessarily a drawback of MPLS. MPLS is used in the core network. The DSCP field of the IP header is

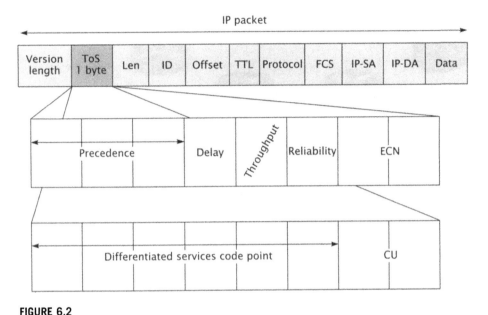

FIGURE 6.2

Description of the ToS field of the IP header.

used to classify the customer traffic. In the core network, traffic from several customers can be aggregated into a single class. Typically, there are up to four classes in the core network: voice, priority, guaranteed bandwidth, and best-effort. Since the MPLS packet encapsulates the IP packet with the MPLS header, the DSCP field in the IP is not lost and can be recovered at the edge of the network when the MPLS header is stripped and the IP packet is forwarded to the customer.

DiffServ Architecture

All the nodes that follow the DiffServ model are in a *DiffServ domain*. All the nodes on a DiffServ domain observe the PHB of a packet based on the DSCP value. Figure 6.3 shows the DiffServ architecture and the two functional building blocks, traffic conditioners and PHB.

Traffic conditioners are used to classify the IP packets by marking the ToS or DSCP field of the IP packet or the EXP bit of the MPLS packet. Traffic conditioners are applied when the traffic enters the DiffServ domain. These functions are implemented on the edge nodes of the DiffServ domain. Packets are policed and marked based on the traffic profile. The DSCP field of the packets is also marked based on the traffic profile. The traffic conditioner used to police the packet may drop the packets if they do not match the profile or may shape the traffic when it does not meet the requirements of the profile.

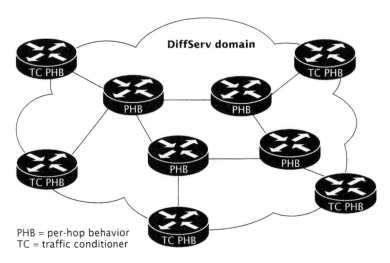

FIGURE 6.3

DiffServ architecture.

PHB functions must be implemented on all of the nodes in the DiffServ domain. They allocate resources for the packets to be scheduled and transmitted out of each node and implement the drop policy when there is congestion.

DiffServ versus IntServ

The DiffServ model is more scalable than the IntServ model and has fewer flows than the IntServ model. However, this model requires that the traffic conditioners and PHB be implemented in the DiffServ domain. Provisioning the services using the DiffServ model can be challenging because the traffic conditioners and PHB have to be correctly implemented on every interface of all the nodes in the Diff-Serv domain. It can be a tedious task to implement and verify the implementation on all of the nodes. The IntServ model on top of the DiffServ model is an interesting concept that can be used to take advantage of both models. While the DiffServ model will make it scalable, the IntServ model will assure that resources are made available to each flow for which the IntServ model is used.

6.1.4 IP QoS Implementation

IP QoS implementation can be divided into the following categories:

Classification: This involves marking the IP packet (setting DSCP or the IP precedence value) based on customer requirements. Once the packets are correctly classified, they can be properly handled by the other QoS mechanisms like congestion management and policing to implement end-to-end QoS requirements. Packet classification is typically done on the edge of the network. Some-times the service provider reclassifies packets in the core network by re-marking certain fields in the packet. This reclassification is required when traffic is aggre-gated, however, the service provider must ensure that the original value of the IP precedence (DSCP) field in the IP packet is restored at the edge of the service provider network when the packet is delivered to the customer. This can be done in an MPLS network because two fields are available. The IP precedence field can be used to classify customer packets, and the MPLS EXP field can be used by the service provider to reclassify packets in the core network.

Congestion management: This involves the creation of queues, assignment of packets to the proper queues, and scheduling of queues and the packets within the queues. The number of queues depends on the customer requirements and the number of CoSs offered by the service provider. Assignment of packets to queues and the scheduling policies are determined by the service provider depending on the type of QoS offered to the customer. For example, high-priority traffic such as voice over IP requires preemptive queue mechanisms that will ensure that the packets are scheduled and transmitted before other packets.

Congestion avoidance techniques: Congestion avoidance is a preemptive mecha-nism that monitors the network load and ensures that there is no congestion in the network. Congestion avoidance is achieved by dropping the packets; the packets that have to be dropped are determined based on the drop policy. This depends on the CoSs offered by the service provider. For example, during network congestion, traffic from the best-effort class should be dropped first. Traffic from the guaranteed bandwidth class should not be dropped before the minimum bandwidth has been guaranteed to that class.

Policing and shaping mechanisms: These ensure that each CoS (based on the marked IP packet) adheres to the service contract. The service contract can include several issues, such as bandwidth, burst size, and delay.

QoS signaling: This is used between nodes in the network to signal the QoS requirements of each class and to reserve resources. RSVP is a QoS signaling protocol that can be used to reserve resources like bandwidth. QoS signaling mechanisms also depend on routing protocols to determine the best path between the source and the destination.

Implementing QoS in an IP network is a challenging task. It requires a good understanding of queuing theory and the requirements of customers in order to determine the parameters for the queuing policies. One challenge is the commu-nication between the signaling plane (QoS signaling protocols like RSVP) and the data-forwarding plane (congestion in the network) to ensure that the resource reservation for an application can be done in the correct manner. For example, RSVP uses bandwidth as the resource in order to do reservations. In addition to bandwidth, other network resources like queue buffers on the network devices are also important resources that are required to guarantee QoS. Congestion in the network device due to lack of queue buffers must be communicated to RSVP so that RSVP can use alternate paths (between the source and the destination) that have enough network resources (e.g., bandwidth, queue buffers) to meet the QoS requirements of the application making the RSVP request.

6.1.5 Creating New Services Using QoS

Applications like voice over IP have strict QoS requirements regarding delay, jitter, and bandwidth. Real-time applications like video-on-demand also have QoS requirements that cannot be met by the best-effort services offered by a traditional IP network. By enabling QoS in the IP network (either by using the DiffServ model, the IntServ model, or both), service providers can offer differentiated services or guaranteed services (or both) to their customers. This will also enable them to offer new services like voice over IP and use the last mile, or local loop, to implement telephony services.

Differentiated services (offered using the DiffServ model) can help the service provider to distinguish between business customers (who pay more money for the services) and customers who are satisfied with best-effort services. By offering better QoS to the business customers—by allocating sufficient bandwidth and ensuring that the traffic from the business customer gets forwarded preferentially over the best-effort customer in case of congestion—the service provider can have oversubscription in their network and still meet the QoS requirements of all of their customers.

A QoS-enabled network will also help the service provider to offer additional services such as guaranteed bandwidth to a customer. Applications like video-on-demand and videoconferencing have bandwidth requirements. By ensuring guaranteed bandwidth to customers, the service provider assures customers that their network is capable of meeting the bandwidth requirements of the customers' applications.

QoS implementation helps the service provider to offer bundled services, like voice, video, and data, on a single physical link. This requires QoS implementation on a link between the customer premises and the service provider POP to differentiate between the voice, video, and data traffic. Cable, ADSL, Frame Relay, ATM, and Ethernet are examples of access technologies with which the service provider can offer bundled services.

6.2 VOICE OVER IP

Of the key emerging technologies for data, voice, and video integration, voice over IP (VoIP) is arguably one of the most important. The most QoS-sensitive of all traffic, voice is the true test of the engineering and quality of a network.

Demand for voice over IP is leading the movement for QoS in IP environments, and will ultimately lead to use of the Internet for fax, voice telephony, and video telephony services. Voice over IP will ultimately be a key component of the migration of telephony to the LAN infrastructure.

6.2.1 Requirements

Voice traffic is sensitive to delay and delay variations. Communication between gateways must be reliable and be delivered on time. In an IP network, reliable packet delivery can be assured by using robust transport and session protocols. However, routers and specifically IP networks offer some unique challenges in controlling delay and delay variation (see Section 6.1.4 for more details).

Traditionally, IP traffic has been treated as best-effort, meaning that incoming IP traffic is transmitted on a first-come, first-served basis. Packets have been variable in nature, allowing large file transfers to take advantage of the efficiency associated with larger packet sizes. These characteristics have contributed to large delays and large delay variations in packet delivery. The second part of supporting delay-sensitive voice traffic is to provide a means of prioritizing the traffic within the router network in order to minimize the delay and delay variation. Section 6.1 provides details about assuring QoS in an IP network.

6.2.2 Components

In this section, we briefly introduce the components that are involved in delivering voice traffic over a data network:

Packet voice network: Responsible for converting the voice traffic into data packets and delivering the voice traffic over a data network

Protocols such as H.323 and session initiation (SIP): Help to provide multimedia communication (voice, video, and data) over a data network and operate with the traditional voice networks

Packet Voice Network

All packet voice systems follow a common model, as shown in Figure 6.4. The packet voice transport network, which may be IP-based, Frame Relay, or ATM, forms the traditional cloud. At the edges of this network are devices, or components, called *voice agents* or *gateways.* It is the mission of these devices to change the voice information from its traditional telephony form to a form suitable for packet transmission. The network then forwards the packet data to a gateway serving as the destination, or the called party. This voice-agent connection model demonstrates the two issues in packet voice networking that must be explored to ensure that packet voice services meet user needs.

The first issue is voice coding: how voice information is transformed into packets and how the packets are used to recreate the voice. Voice has to be

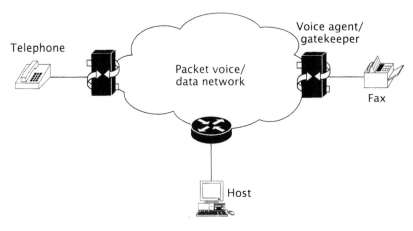

FIGURE 6.4

Packet voice network.

transformed into digital signals before it can be transported over a packet network. At the other end of the packet network, the digital signal has to be reconverted into voice signals. Special devices are used to convert voice to a digital signal and then back to voice. These devices are called coder-decoders (CODECs).

The second issue is the signaling associated with identifying the calling party and ascertaining where the called party is in the network. Two signaling protocols, H.323 and SIP, are discussed in Section 6.3.

Voice Coding

Analog communication is ideal for human communication. However, analog transmission is neither robust nor efficient at recovering from line noise. Analog signals have to be digitized before they can be transported over a packet voice network. Digital samples are composed of one and zero bits, and it is much easier for them to be separated from line noise. Therefore, when signals are regenerated, a clean sound can be maintained.

When the benefits of this digital representation became evident, the telephony network migrated to *pulse code modulation* (PCM). PCM converts analog sound into digital form by sampling the analog sound 8000 times per second and converting each sample into a numeric code. After the waveform is sampled, it is converted into a discrete digital form. This sample is represented by a code that indicates the amplitude of the waveform at the instant the sample was taken. The telephony form of PCM uses 8 bits for the code and a logarithm compression method that assigns more bits to lower-amplitude signals. The transmission rate is obtained by multiplying 8000 samples per second by 8 bits per sample, giving 64,000 bits per second, the standard transmission rate for one channel of telephone digital communications.

Two basic variations of 64 Kbps PCM are commonly used: MU-law and A-law. The methods are similar in that they both use logarithmic compression to achieve 12 to 13 bits of linear PCM quality in 8 bits, but are different in relatively minor compression details (e.g., MU-law has a slight advantage in low-level signal-to-noise ratio performance). Usage has historically been along country and regional boundaries, with North America using MU-law and Europe using A-law modulation. It is important to note that when making a long-distance call, any required MU-law to A-law conversion is the responsibility of the MU-law country.

Another compression method often used is *adaptive differential pulse code modulation* (ADPCM). A commonly used instance of ADPCM, ITU-T G.726 encodes using 4-bit samples, giving a transmission rate of 32 Kbps. Unlike PCM, the four bits in ADPCM do not directly encode the amplitude of speech but the differences in amplitude as well as the rate of change of that amplitude, employing some very rudimentary linear predictions.

The most popular voice-coding standards for telephony and packet voice include the following:

G.711: Describes the 64 Kbps PCM voice-coding technique outlined earlier. G.711-encoded voice is already in the correct format for digital voice delivery in a public phone network or through PBXs.

G.726: Describes ADPCM coding at 40, 32, 24, and 16 Kbps; ADPCM voice may also be interchanged between packet voice and public phone or PBX networks, provided that the latter has ADPCM capability.

G.728: Describes a 16 Kbps low-delay variation of *code-excited linear prediction* (CELP) voice compression. CELP voice coding must be transcoded to a public telephony format for delivery to or through telephone networks.

G.729: Describes CELP compression that enables voice to be coded into 8 Kbps streams. Two variations of this standard (G.729 and G.729 Annex A) differ largely in computational complexity, and both generally provide speech quality as good as that of 32 Kb/sec ADPCM.

G.723.1: Describes a technique that can be used for compressing speech or other audio signal components of multimedia service at a very low bit rate.

6.3 OPERATING VOICE OVER IP

The following subsections discuss various VoIP standards.

6.3.1 H.323

H.323 is the standard that has been developed for multimedia communication over a LAN or network that does not provide guaranteed QoS. The accepted model for internal signaling for IP packet voice networks is the H.323 standard. While H.323 is popularly viewed as a packet video standard, it actually defines a set of multimedia communications standards between users. In fact, only voice services are required for H.323 participation; video and data support are optional.

H.323 defines a complete multimedia network, from devices to protocols. Linking all of the entities within H.323 is H.245, which is defined to negotiate facilities among participants and H.323 network elements. A scaled-down version of ISDN's Q.931 call protocol is used to provide for connection setup.

Figure 6.5 shows the components of H.323. In H.323 terms, the voice agents are *terminals,* although the common usage of this concept suggests a single user. H.323 also defines a *gatekeeper* function that performs the address translation and also mapping between a telephone number and the IP address of the remote gateways. If the network in a packet voice application is actually made up of several different kinds of transport networks, H.323 defines a *gateway* function between networks that performs the packet data format translation and signaling translation required for proper communications across the network boundary. The most common use of this gateway is the conversion of videoconferencing from H.320 to H.323 format, permitting packet video users to communicate with traditional room- or cart-based video systems that rely on the circuit-switched form of video.

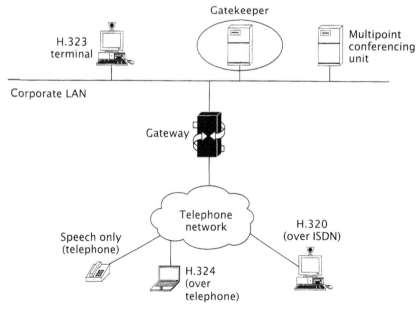

FIGURE 6.5

Components of H.323.

6.3.2 Session Initiation Protocol

The session initiation protocol (SIP) is an application-layer control protocol that can establish, modify, and terminate multimedia sessions or calls. These multimedia sessions include multimedia conferences, distance learning, Internet telephony, and similar applications. SIP is defined in *RFC 2543*.

SIP is a peer-to-peer protocol where end devices *(user agents,* or *UAs)* initiate sessions. The two components of an SIP system are UAs and network servers. Calling and called parties are identified by an SIP address. (Figure 6.6 shows the SIP components.) UAs are client end-system applications that contain both the *user-agent client* (UAC) and a *user-agent server* (UAS), otherwise known as a *client* and *server.* The client initiates the SIP request and acts as the calling party. The server receives the request and returns the response on behalf of the user and acts as the called party. Examples of UAs include SIP phones, gateways, PDAs, and robots.

Network servers are optional components in the context of SIP. There are three types of servers: proxy server, redirect server, and location server.

Proxy server: Acts on behalf of the UA and forwards the SIP messages to the other UAs after modifying the header. Rewriting the header identifies the proxy server as the initiator of the request and ensures that the response follows the same path back to the proxy server.

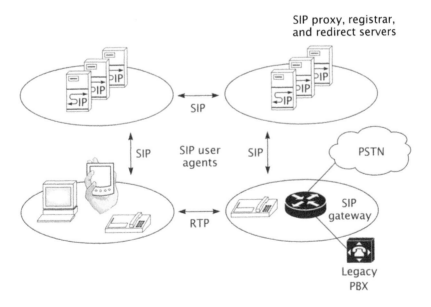

FIGURE 6.6

Components of SIP.

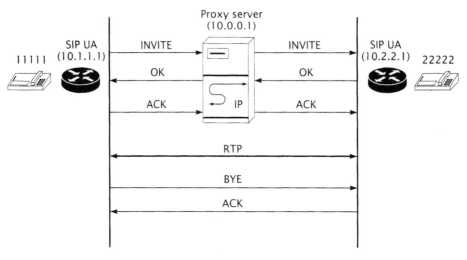

FIGURE 6.7

Call setup using an SIP proxy server.

Redirect server: Accepts SIP requests from the UA and sends a redirect response back to the UA with the address of the next server or the calling party. Redirect servers do not accept calls, nor do they forward or process SIP requests.

Location server: Maintains the SIP address of UA devices. The redirect server and the proxy server use the location server to locate the called UA.

SIP addresses, also called SIP *universal resource locators* (URLs), exist in the form of *user@host.* The *user* portion can be a name or telephone number, and the *host* portion can be a domain name or network address. The following examples depict two possible SIP URLs:

- *sip:vijay@vijay.com*
- *sip:0012012012222@10.10.10.10*

Figure 6.7 shows a call setup using a proxy server. A UA can send an SIP request directly to the local proxy server or to the IP address and port corresponding to the called party (e.g., *vijay@10.10.10.10*). Sending it to a proxy server is relatively easy because the calling UA does not have to know the exact URL of the called user agent.

6.3.3 How Does Voice over IP Work?

The general steps to connect a packet voice telephone call through a voice over IP router are described in the example that follows. This example is not a specific call flow, but it gives a high-level view of what happens when you make a phone call work over a packet voice network. The general flow of a two-party voice call is the same in all cases:

1. The user picks up the handset, signaling an off-hook condition to whatever the local loop is connected to (e.g., PBX, PSTN central office switch, signaling application in the router).

2. The session application issues a dial tone and waits for the user to dial a phone number.

3. The user dials the number, which is accumulated by the session application.

4. The number is mapped via the dial plan mapper to an IP host (by sending a request to the gatekeeper), which talks either to the destination phone directly or to a PBX, which finishes completing the call.

5. The session applications run a session protocol (e.g., H.323) to establish a transmission and a reception channel for each direction over the IP network. Meanwhile, if there is a PBX involved at the called end, it finishes completing the call to the destination phone.

6. If using RSVP, the RSVP reservations are put in place to achieve the desired QoS over the IP network.

7. The voice CODECs/compressors/decompressors are turned on for both ends, and the conversation proceeds using IP as the protocol stack.

8. Any call progress indications and other signals that can be carried in band (e.g., remote phone ringing, line busy) are cut through the voice path as soon as an end-to-end audio channel is up.

9. When either end hangs up, the RSVP reservations are torn down (if RSVP is used), and the session ends, with each end going idle waiting for another off-hook.

When the dial plan mapper determines the necessary IP address to reach the destination telephone number, a session is invoked. H.323 is the current session application. Figure 6.8 shows a breakdown of the steps taken to form the H.323 session. The initial TCP connection is usually made on port 1720 to negotiate the H.225 portion of the H.323 session. During this portion, the TCP port number for the H.245 portion of the H.323 session is passed back to the calling unit.

During the H.245 portion of the H.323 session, the RTP and RTCP addresses are passed between the calling unit and the called unit. The RTP address used is in the range of 16,384 plus four times the amount of channels available on the calling device. After all portions of the H.225 and H.245 sessions are complete, the audio is then streamed over RTP/UDP/IP. (RTP stands for *real-time protocol.*)

6.3.4 Services Using Voice over IP

This section presents a discussion on how voice over IP can help a service provider in creating new services and reducing operational costs. By offering voice

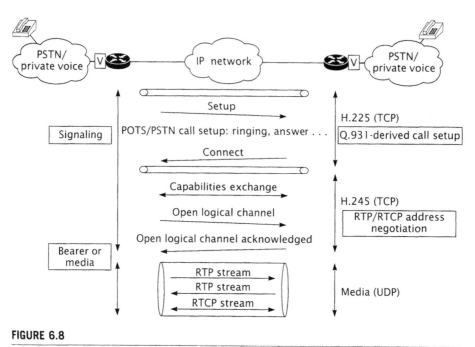

FIGURE 6.8

Call setup in a voice over IP environment.

and data services over a single network, service providers can reduce the costs of managing two networks. Voice over IP can also help service providers to augment their portfolio with add-on services that will provide customers with single network connectivity for both voice and data services.

Merging Voice and Data Networks

Voice over a packet network uses less transmission bandwidth than conventional voice because the digitized signal is compressed before it is transmitted. This allows more traffic to be carried on a given connection in a packet network as compared to a conventional voice network. Where telephony requires as many as 64,000 bits per second, packet voice often needs fewer than 10,000. For many companies, there is sufficient reserve capacity on national and international data networks to transport considerable voice traffic, making voice essentially "free." A packet/data network can deliver voice traffic using less bandwidth. Given a certain amount of bandwidth, more voice traffic can be transported using an IP network compared to a voice network.

Voice over IP is an excellent solution that can help to carry both voice and data traffic using the same IP network (see Figure 6.9). An IP network connects two remote sites, Site A and Site B. Voice (telephone) and data applications are connected to the router at each site. The router is also the gateway for the voice over IP application. X1234 and X5678 are the telephone numbers of Site A and

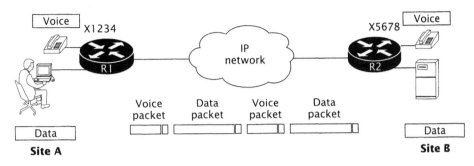

FIGURE 6.9

Merging voice and data networks using voice over IP.

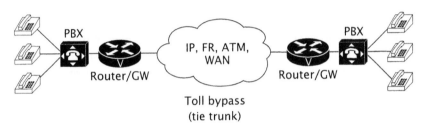

FIGURE 6.10

Toll bypass using voice over IP.

Site B, respectively. The IP network transports both voice and data packets. The same network connection between Site A and Site B is used to transport both voice and data traffic. Merging voice and data onto one network can help reduce the cost of maintaining two networks both in terms of infrastructure and the staffing required to maintain the networks. The challenge lies in ensuring that the IP network can guarantee the quality required for delivering voice traffic. (Section 6.1 provided details about how to overcome some of these challenges.)

Toll Bypass

Toll bypass will be the most common application that corporations will look toward for deploying voice over IP networks. It allows corporations to replace the tie lines that currently hook up their PBX-to-PBX networks and route voice calls across their existing data infrastructures (see Figure 6.10). Corporations will also use voice over IP to replace smaller key systems at remote offices while maintaining larger-density W voice over IP equipment at the sites with larger voice needs. Another benefit to using voice over IP is that real-time fax relay can be used on an interoffice basis, an advantage since a large portion of long-distance minutes is fax traffic.

6.4 IP SECURITY

IP security (known as *IPsec*) provides interoperable, high-quality, cryptographically based security for IPv4 and IPv6. The security services offered by IPsec include:

- Access controls (connectionless integrity ensuring data is transmitted without alteration)
- Data origin authentication (knowing received data is the same as sent data and who sent the data)
- Protection against replays and partial sequence integrity
- Confidentiality (encryption)
- Limited traffic flow confidentiality

One of the most common ways of breaching the security of a network is to capture some genuine data and then play it back to gain access. Therefore, IPsec provides a means of securing against this data capture and replay. While it is good to know whether data has been tampered with, a priority for most customers is that they do not want their data read by unwanted parties. The most common way of preventing the wrong people from reading data is encryption. This not only protects data but also provides limited traffic flow confidentiality, as it can hide the identities of the sender and receiver.

The IPsec protocol suite comprises a set of standards that are used to provide privacy and authentication services at the IP layer. The current IPsec standards include three algorithm-independent base specifications that are currently standards-track RFCs. These three RFCs, listed next, are in the process of being revised, and the revisions will account for numerous security issues with current specifications.

RFC 2401, the IP security architecture: Defines the overall architecture and specifies elements common to both the IP authentication header and the IP encapsulating security payload.

RFC 2402, the IP authentication header (AH): Defines an algorithm-independent mechanism for providing exportable cryptographic authentication without encryption to IPv4 and IPv6 packets.

RFC 2406, the IP encapsulated security payload (ESP): Defines an algorithm-independent mechanism for providing encryption to IPv4 and IPv6 packets.

RFC 2408, the Internet security association and key management protocol (ISAKMP): Defines the procedures for authenticating a communicating peer, creation and management of security associations, key-generation techniques, and threat mitigation (e.g., denial of service and replay attacks). All of these are necessary to establish and maintain secure communications (via IP Security Service or any other security protocol) in an Internet environment.

RFC 2409, the Internet key exchange (IKE): Describes a protocol using part of the Oakley key-determination protocol and part of the secure key-exchange mechanism (SKEME) in conjunction with ISAKMP to obtain authenticated keying material for use with ISAKMP and for other security associations, such as AH and ESP.

6.4.1 Concepts and Terminologies

This section introduces the concepts and terminologies related to IPsec. The fundamental concepts are authentication, encryption, key management, and security association.

Authentication

Authentication, in IPsec terms, is knowing that we trust the "person" that has sent us the data, that the data has not been altered in transit, and also, but to a lesser extent, being able to prove that the data was sent. This can be achieved by using a hashing algorithm: The sender takes the data and a key (a password of sorts) and hashes these together. The answer, which is always the same length for that particular key and hashing algorithm, is known as a *message authentication code.* IPsec refers to the message authentication code as the *integrity check value* (ICV). The message authentication code and the data are sent to the receiver. The receiver takes the data, the key, and the hashing algorithm and performs the same calculation as the sender. The receiver compares his or her answer, that is, the message authentication code, with that sent by the user. If the answers match, the receiver knows that the data has not been altered (or the answer would be different) and knows who sent the data (the person who knows the same key).

Encryption

Encryption is the transformation of a clear text message into an unreadable form to hide its meaning. The opposite transformation, retrieving the clear text message, is decryption. The keys are often symmetric—that is, the same key is used for encryption and decryption. The most common encryption algorithm is the *data encryption standard* (DES). DES is a block encryption algorithm: it takes the data and encrypts it in blocks of bits. The blocks of data are 64 bits and the most common key lengths are 56 or 168 *(triple DES, or 3DES).* With DES, the 56-bit key is often expressed as a 64-bit number, with every eighth bit used for parity. From the key, 16 subkeys are derived that are used in 16 rounds of the algorithm. The cipher text is always the same length as the clear text.

Key Exchange

Both authentication and encryption are based on the use of keys. A key is a bit pattern that is used to encrypt messages. The length of the key depends on the encryption technique. The key is used by the sender, who encrypts the message with it, and by the receiver, who decrypts the message with it. Therefore, the key has to be exchanged between the sender and the receiver.

The IPsec protocol suite also includes cryptographic techniques to support the key management requirements of the network-layer security. ISAKMP provides the framework for Internet key management and the specific protocol support for negotiation of security attributes. By itself, it does not establish session keys; however, it can be used with various session key establishment protocols, such as Oakley, to provide a complete solution to Internet key management.

The Oakley key-determination protocol provides the important security property of *perfect forward secrecy* and is based on cryptographic techniques that have survived substantial public scrutiny. Perfect forward secrecy ensures that if any single key is compromised, only the data encrypted with that particular key will be compromised; it will not compromise any data encrypted with subsequent session keys.

The ISAKMP and Oakley protocols have been combined into a hybrid protocol. The resolution of ISAKMP with Oakley uses the framework of ISAKMP to support a subset of Oakley key-exchange modes. This new key-exchange protocol provides optional perfect forward secrecy and full security association attribute negotiation, as well as authentication methods that provide both repudiation and nonrepudiation. Implementations of this protocol can be used, for example, to establish virtual private networks (VPNs) and also to allow users from remote sites (who may have a dynamically allocated IP address) access to a secure network.

Authentication Header

An authentication header (AH) provides an authentication and integrity mechanism for IP traffic. Figure 6.11 shows the fields of the AH. The preceding IP header will contain a protocol value of 51. The next header field identifies the type of the next payload. The value specified is one of the IP protocol numbers, as defined in the most recent assigned numbers (currently *RFC 1700*).

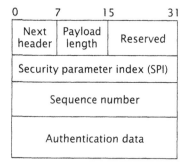

FIGURE 6.11

Fields of the authentication header.

Original IP datagram

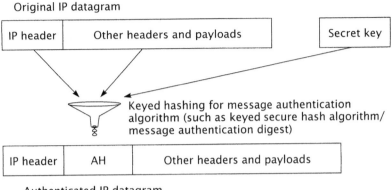

Authenticated IP datagram

FIGURE 6.12

Generating an authentication header for an IP packet.

The payload length is the length of the header in 32-bit words minus 2. The reserved field is always set to zero. The security parameter index (SPI) is 32 bits long, and the value is determined when the *security association* (SA) is established. The sequence number is also 32 bits long and is always present, even if anti-replay is not enabled. The sequence number is set to zero when the SA is established and will never cycle if anti-replay is enabled. The size of the authentication data field contains the message authentication code—which in IPsec terminology is the ICV. It must be a multiple of 32 bits, and padding can be added if needed.

An extra authentication header is inserted onto the IP header (see Figure 6.12). HMAC (keyed hashing for message authentication) algorithms, such as secure hash algorithm (SHA) or MD5, are used to generate the AH. This header is generated using the entire IP packet and a secret key. Fields of the IP packet that get modified in transit (TTL, ToS, header checksum, flags) are not used in generating the AH. This header is used to verify that the content of the IP packet has not been modified.

Although IPsec is connectionless, it uses a sequence number to detect duplicate packets in order to provide protection against *denial-of-service* (DoS) attack. This mechanism is referred to as *anti-replay* because it prevents packets from being duplicated and retransmitted by hackers as part of a DoS attack. The sequence number in the AH is used to detect duplicate packets. AH does not ensure the confidentiality of the payload of the IP packet. This means that AH does not encrypt the payload.

Encapsulated Security Payload
The encapsulated security payload (ESP) encrypts the entire payload of the IP packet using DES or 3DES in order to provide confidentiality for the payload of

the IP packet. As shown in Figure 6.13, the ESP header is inserted between the IP header and the encrypted payload to generate the encrypted IP packet. It also provides for an optional authentication/integrity mechanism for the payload. ESP can be used by itself or in conjunction with AH. ESP is defined in *RFC 2406*.

Figure 6.14 shows the details of the ESP header. The IP header contains a protocol value equal to S0 to indicate that the IP packet has an ESP header. (The SPI and sequence numbers have been discussed in the preceding section.)

There are three different reasons why padding may be added: The first is that the encryption algorithm may require the data to be multiples of numbers of bytes.

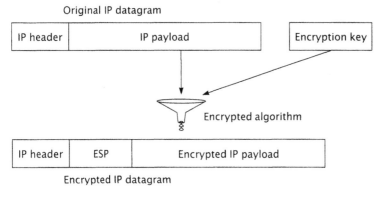

FIGURE 6.13

Encryption using ESP.

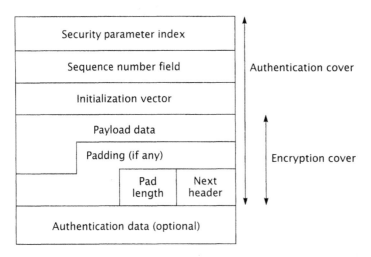

FIGURE 6.14

ESP header.

The second is that the pad length and next header fields must be right-aligned within the 4-byte words. The last, and sometimes surprising reason, is to hide the size of the packet. The standard defines that a user may add between 0 and 255 bytes of padding. The pad length is the number of bytes of padding preceding this field. This field is always present, so if no padding is added, the field will be zero. The authentication data field is present if the security association demands authentication, and its length is dependent on the authentication algorithm used.

Security Association

The concept of security associations (SAs) is fundamental to IPsec. An SA is a connection that provides security to the traffic it carries. The security is either AH or ESP, but not both. An SA applies in one direction only, so for security for both inbound and outbound traffic, two SAs will be established. If both AH and ESP are required for a particular connection, an SA bundle will be established. An SA is identified by three parameters: a destination IP address, the security protocol (AH or ESP), and the SPI. The SPI is a 32-bit number that is used to uniquely identify the particular SA. Numbers 1 to 255 are currently reserved by the Internet Assigned Numbers Authority (IANA) for future expansion.

There are two main types of SAs: transport mode and tunnel mode (see Figure 6.15). In a transport mode SA, the source and destination of the IP packet also do the IPsec processing. In this case, each end station would have a stack that was IPsec capable and the traffic would be secured end to end. If one or more of the devices is a security gateway—for example, a router—the SA is in tunnel mode. In this scenario, the IPsec processing is not done by either the source or the destination of the IP packet.

In Figure 6.15, the IP packets would only be secured between the two routers. Sometimes people refer to the routers as "acting as a proxy"—they are providing

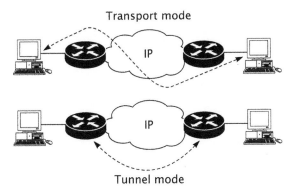

FIGURE 6.15

Two modes of SAs.

security for clients who are unable to provide security for themselves, or providing security in addition to that provided by the clients. It is important to realize that a particular IP packet may experience both types of SAs in the path between source and destination. For example, the sending station may use ESP to encrypt the packet. The sending station would establish an security association in transport mode. The forwarding router may then apply authentication header security to that packet using an SA that is in tunnel mode.

So what is the difference between tunnel and transport mode, other than the device that performs the IPsec processing? The main difference is that in transport mode, the security is applied to upper protocol levels, whereas in tunnel mode, the security is applied to the entire IP packet. Figures 6.16 and 6.17 show the difference in the packets generated by tunnel mode and transport mode.

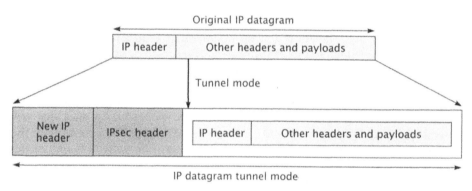

FIGURE 6.16

Tunnel mode packets.

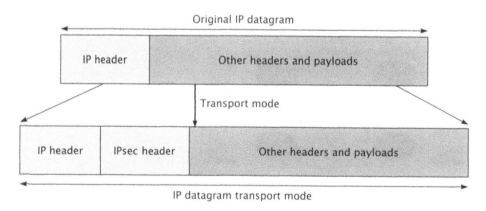

FIGURE 6.17

Transport mode packets.

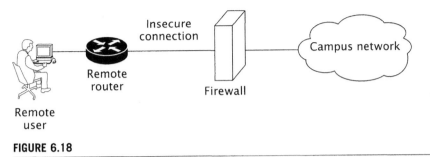

FIGURE 6.18

Router to firewall security.

6.4.2 **How Does IPsec Work?**

The IPsec standard will enable interoperable, secure, and authenticated data flow at the IP level for interchangeable devices, including hosts, firewall products, and routers. The following example illustrates how IPsec is used to provide for authenticated, confidential data communication between the remote router and campus firewall, shown in Figure 6.18. All traffic from the remote router destined to the campus firewall must be authenticated before passing traffic through. The router and firewall must first agree on a security association, which is an agreement between the two on a security policy. The SA includes:

- Encryption algorithm
- Authentication algorithm
- Shared session key
- Key lifetime

A security association is unidirectional, so for two-way communication, two SAs must be established, one for each direction. Generally, the policy is the same, but this leaves room for asymmetrical policies in either direction. These SAs are negotiated via ISAKMP, or they can be defined manually. After the SA is negotiated, it is then determined whether to use authentication, confidentiality, and integrity or simply authentication. If only authentication is desired, the current standard specifies the use of a hashing function. Specifically, implementations must use at least the MD5 algorithm with 128-bit keys. The packet header and data are run through the hashing function, and the results of the hash computation are inserted into the specified field in the authentication header. Note that for IPv4, the following fields are set to zero:

- Type of service (ToS)
- Time to live (TTL)
- Header checksum
- Offset
- Flags

The new packet, with the authentication header between the IP header and data, is now sent through the router to the campus destination. When the firewall receives the packet, it verifies the authenticity of the packet by recomputing the hash with the hashing function specified in the SA. The hashing function must be the same on both sides. As shown in Figure 6.18, the firewall then compares its computed hash with the parameter found in the field in the AH, and if they match, it is assured of authentication and integrity (i.e., that the packet came from the remote router and no bits have been modified). Note that since the original packet is expanded because of the insertion of the AH, fragmentation may be required. Fragmentation occurs after the AH for outgoing packets and before the AH for incoming packets.

If there is also a requirement for confidentiality, then the SA specifies that all traffic from the remote router destined to the campus firewall must be authenticated and encrypted before passing traffic through. The ESP provides authentication, integrity, and confidentiality. Note that since the original packet is expanded because of the insertion of the AH, fragmentation may be required. Fragmentation occurs after ESP for outgoing packets and before ESP for incoming packets.

6.4.3 IPsec Advantages

The advantages of IPsec network-layer security include the following:

- It can support completely unmodified end systems, though in this case, encryption is no longer strictly end to end.
- It is particularly suitable for building VPNs across nontrusted networks.
- It can support transport protocols other than TCP (e.g., UDP).
- It hides the transport-layer headers from eavesdropping, providing somewhat greater protection against traffic analysis.
- With AH and replay detection, it protects against certain DoS attacks based on swamping (e.g., TCP synchronization attacks).

6.4.4 IPsec versus MPLS-VPN

After reading this section on IPsec, some questions may arise:

- How do the VPNs created using IPsec differ from the MPLS-VPNs?
- Is there any need for MPLS-VPNs if VPNs can be created using IPsec?
- What additional benefits does IPsec bring to the table?

The VPNs created by IPsec and MPLS-VPNs are quite different. MPLS-VPN creates VPNs at the network layer by using special routing protocols that help to distinguish between different networks and by using packet-forwarding mechanisms based on labels to forward packets only within the VPN. The mechanisms used by MPLS-VPNs are scalable and can be used to create and maintain several VPNs. The MPLS-VPN solution is scalable because there is no need to build and maintain point-to-point tunnels between the different sites of the VPN. The number of labels required to build a VPN is directly proportional to the number of sites (or the total number of network addresses within a VPN).

IPsec forms VPNs by creating associations between hosts and other network entities that belong to the same VPN and ensuring that communication is possible only between network elements that are part of the association. The solution provided by IPsec is not scalable for a large number of VPNs because one needs to form associations between the different entities belonging to a VPN and the complexity of the number of associations is $O(N^2)$, where N is the number of hosts belonging to a VPN. The advantage of IPsec lies in the additional security mechanisms. IPsec can supplement the security by means of authentication and encryption.

IPsec and MPLS-VPN are not two competing technologies, but they supplement each other so as to overcome the disadvantages of each other. IPsec on top of an MPLS-VPN provides a solution that is more secure (with the additional security provided by IPsec) and also scalable (by using MPLS-VPN). IPsec can be used to strengthen the security of the network and also to protect the integrity and confidentiality of the data that is transported across the IP network.

6.5 SUMMARY

This chapter has provided an overview on some advanced topics related to IP-based services. These topics supplement the features supported by IP and enhance the services that can be offered by the IP network. For readers who are interested in more details about the topics covered in this chapter, the section that follows provides suggestions for further reading.

Today, the requirements of applications using the IP network are more than just "best-effort." In order to meet requirements like guaranteed bandwidth; minimized delay, jitter, and packet loss; and security, it is necessary to implement the QoS functions in the network. Transporting voice over an IP network helps to merge the voice and data networks. This helps customers to reduce the cost of maintaining two networks and also to make effective use of the IP networks. Voice over IP has QoS requirements such as minimizing delay and jitter and ensuring bandwidth. By enhancing the QoS functions of an IP network, it can support applications like voice over IP.

6.6 FURTHER READING

Davidson, J., and J. Peters, *Voice Over IP Fundamentals*. Cisco Press, 2000: A detailed source for information about voice-coding techniques and standards, and also about H.323.
RFC 2205, "Resource Reservation Protocol (RSVP)—Version 1: Functional Specification." Braden, R., et al., IETF, 1997.

RFC 2210, "The Use of RSVP with IETF Integrated Services." Wroclawski, J., IETF, 1997.

RFC 2474, "Definition of the Differentiated Services Field (DS Field) in the IPv4 and IPv6 Headers." Nichols, K., et al., IETF, 1998.

RFC 2475, "An Architecture for Differentiated Services." Blake, S., et al., IETF, 1998.

RFC 2597, "Assured Forwarding PHB Group." Heinanen, J., et al., IETF, 1999.

RFC 2598, "An Expedited Forwarding PHB." Jacobsen, V., et al., IETF, 1999.

RFC 3175, "Aggregation of RSVP for IPv4 and IPv6 Reservations." Baker, F., et al., IETF, 2001: Provides detailed techniques for aggregating traffic flow reservations using RSVP control.

Vegesna, S., *IP Quality of Service*. Cisco Press, 2001: Gives more details about QoS implementations in an IP network.

The Foundation of Policy Management

7

Management is critical to the delivery of quality of service. The network resources must be marshaled to meet the customer requirements, and the traffic flows must be suitably arranged with a view across the whole network. This means that it is not enough to manage each link or node in isolation, and the traffic demands created by the customer cannot be handled individually. Instead, a series of network-wide policies must be implemented and applied to each provisioning request. This gives rise to the concept of policy-based management.

This chapter, from *Policy-Based Network Management* by John Strassner, provides a brief retrospective of how policy-based network management (PBNM) has been conceived in the past. This will be used to point out two fundamental problems of previous solutions—the lack of use of an information model, and the inability to use business rules to drive configuration of devices, services, and networks. A path forward, and benefits resulting from this improved approach, are described.

7.1 INTRODUCTION—A RETROSPECTIVE

Policy management means many things to many people. As Michael Jude writes,

> When first conceived in the late 1990s, PBNM promised enterprise information technology shops the ability to control the quality of service (QoS) experienced by networked applications and users. . . . In fact, the hype went further than that: Vendors promised that CIOs or CEOs would soon be able to control policies through a simple graphical interface on their desk. Behind the scenes, those instructions would translate into specific traffic management adjustments, bypassing traditional network operations.

QoS means many things to many people. Contrary to popular belief, QoS does not mean "just" an increase or decrease in bandwidth speed. Rather, it means differentiated treatment of one or more metrics. These metrics are completely dependent on the type of application(s) that the QoS is being designed for. Thus, QoS for a voice application is usually different than QoS for a mission-critical data application, because the characteristics of each application are different. This causes the specific QoS mechanisms to be made different.

My favorite definition of QoS is "managed unfairness." This describes the differences in how network elements are programmed to provide different QoS mechanisms to treat various application traffic streams differently. Clearly, this is complex to perform for the same type of devices; the complexity of this configuration increases dramatically if different devices with different capabilities and commands are used in the same network.

Differentiated QoS, which is the ability to provide different configurations of QoS for different types of applications, is the key to opening up new avenues of revenue. Because providing QoS is currently very difficult, the application of policy to provide differentiated QoS is one of the primary drivers for implementing PBNM solutions.

The emphasis on managing and implementing QoS describes some of the buildup and excitement that followed the dawn of PBNM. The reason, of course, is because networks are complex, and running different services, each of which has different requirements on the same network, is very difficult. People who were looking for a "quick fix" to their network problems were disappointed; PBNM was found to be a time intensive, complex, and expensive. There were several reasons for this:

- Most early PBNM solutions were single-vendor approaches and could only manage some of the devices on the network. As a result, multiple incompatible PBNM solutions had to be introduced to manage the entire network, which caused hard-to-solve integration problems.

- PBNM solutions were focused on particular technologies and devices. For example, a QoS policy server might be able to control most (but probably not all) of the QoS functions of a particular vendor's device or device families. However, it probably could not control other types of technologies, such as security and Internet Protocol (IP) address management.

- PBNM solutions focused on the IP world. This caused disruption in organizations that have different technologies present in their networks.

- PBNM solutions were misunderstood.

- PBNM solutions rushed forth without a solid set of standards in place.

Although the first three problems are important, the last two are fundamental problems that prevented the first wave of PBNM solutions from realizing their goals.

In addition, two other problems prevented wide adoption. First, the solutions initially available were not very scalable, and hence could not easily be used in large service provider networks despite the fact that they provided some attractive technology (e.g., configuring QoS functions). Second, network monitoring technology lagged behind the new provisioning technology promoted by PBNM solutions to control the network. As a result, there was no easy way to monitor whether the PBNM solutions were actually working.

7.1.1 Early PBNM Solutions Missed the Point

In its early days, PBNM was characterized (and unfortunately, this characterization continues somewhat today) as a sophisticated way to manipulate different types of QoS. The motivation for this was to avoid overprovisioning the network, (i.e., enough resources are present for the network to respond to any anticipated need). The problem with this approach is that it is static and cannot adjust to the changing environment. Thus, if the network is provisioned according to the maximum expected load, resources will be wasted most of the time. Furthermore, if that load is exceeded for some reason (e.g., a heavy day of stock trading), then the network will still be unable to perform.

PBNM was used to set the QoS levels based on inspecting different fields in the header of traffic that was being sent. People then reasoned that PBNM could also be used for other applications (such as ensuring that high-priority traffic was delivered ahead of less important traffic and that different services received the level of service that they were contracted for) and for different types of security applications (such as refusing traffic from an unknown source to enter the network or starting an accounting application when a connection was completed).

The common theme to each of these (and other) applications is the desire to link the way the business runs to the services that the network provides. Regardless of application, PBNM was defined as reacting to a particular condition and then taking an appropriate action. The missing point is that some centralized authority has to decide which users and applications get priority over other users and applications.

Business rules are defined as the set of rules, regulations, and practices for operating a business. They often define and sometimes constrain business processes. Business processes are defined as the means by which one or more activities are accomplished in operating business practices. They take the form of an interconnected set of business functions (perhaps constrained by various business rules) to obtain a specific set of business goals.

Recently, the focus has turned to integrating business rules and processes with PBNM solutions. This focus makes intuitive sense, as it is certainly natural to want the network to provide services according to business contracts. However, the relationship can be, and should be, deeper than that. Business rules and processes govern how a system is run. They are responsible for the many decisions that must be made for every action performed by the system.

If policies are the reasons for doing something and business rules and processes are the means for doing it, why not connect them together? Although this seems obvious in retrospect, precious few information models have been constructed with this direction and capability. An important corollary of this decision is as follows:

PBNM solutions require information models that contain business and system entities that can be easily implemented.

This chapter describes a unique object-oriented information model, Directory Enabled Networks-new generation (DEN-ng). It is being developed in the Tele-Management Forum (TMF). The development is led by this author, and many different companies are involved. The author's company, Intelliden, is also actively involved in implementing DEN-ng and has incorporated it into the latest release of its product. Other companies, such as British Telecom, Telecom Italia, Telstra, MetaSolv, Hewlett Packard, and Agilent, have participated in reviews of DEN-ng.

An object-oriented information model is a means to represent various entities in a managed environment. An entity can be a person, a computer, a router, or even a protocol message—anything that needs a uniform and consistent representation for configuration and management is a possibility for definition and representation in DEN-ng.

An object-oriented information model provides a common language in which different types of management entities can be represented. This common language is of the utmost importance. Operational support systems (OSSs) are large, complex sets of applications that are composed of best-of-breed applications. This tendency to use best-of-breed applications encourages the use of "stovepipe" applications, which are applications that maintain their own definition of data. Much of the data used by each stovepipe application should be shared with other stovepipe applications. Unfortunately, this simply cannot be accomplished unless a common language exists to represent these common data.

One difficulty in building an OSS lies in the large variety of different management objects that must be harmonized and shared among the different management applications being used. Further exacerbating this problem is the fact that different types of management data have different characteristics. For example, very volatile data, such as statistical interface measurements, changes much too fast to be placed in a directory. Other data are very appropriate to put into a directory. Thus, an OSS needs to use multiple repositories to accommodate the different characteristics and uses of different management information.

An object-oriented information model, such as DEN-ng, is independent of any specific type of repository, software usage, or access protocol. Therefore, DEN-ng can be used as a single authoritative means for describing how different management information are related to each other.

To put this into perspective, Figure 7.1 shows five exemplary management applications that comprise an OSS. Notice that for two of these applications, the same data appears. For the username attribute, two different names are given. This makes it very difficult for applications to realize that these two different names actually refer to the same attribute of the same object. Furthermore, both applications define the same employee attribute. However, the data types are different.

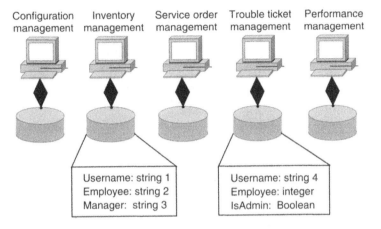

Configuration management   Inventory management   Service order management   Trouble ticket management   Performance management

Username: string 1
Employee: string 2
Manager: string 3

Username: string 4
Employee: integer
IsAdmin: Boolean

FIGURE 7.1

Problems in not using a single information model.

This can cause problems in trying to write a single query to gather data based on this and other attributes across these two repositories.

Thus, unless there is a way to relate different information that are implemented using different data models to each other, it will be impossible to share and reuse management information. This raises the cost of the OSS and increases the probability that errors (resulting from the inability to share and reuse management data) will be embedded in the system. Furthermore, it means that entire processes will be repeated to derive and/or retrieve the same data (because the data cannot be shared). Instead, what is desired is a single, unified information model that relates the differences in data model implementations to each other.

DEN-ng is unique because it contains business and system entities that can be used to build management representations and solutions. In fact, in the Intelliden implementation, the DEN-ng information models are translated to two types of data models (Java and directory models). Specifically, business and system entities are represented in generic form in the information model and are then translated to platform-specific implementations. The Intelliden product uses these models to define business rules to activate network services. Other companies, such as MetaSolv (in their case, primarily a database), are using different repositories to implement DEN-ng and the shared information and data (SID).

7.1.2 Early PBNM Solutions Were Ahead of the Standards

The Internet Engineering Task Force (IETF) took the DEN policy model and, in August of 1998, formed a working group to start modeling policy. This working group was originally co-chaired by myself and was based on using the DEN policy model. This model concentrated on the generic representation of policy and chose QoS as a representative application that would be modeled as a

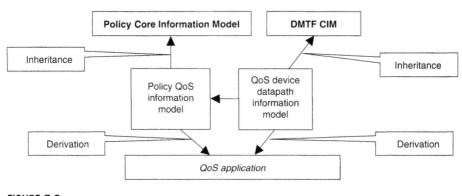

FIGURE 7.2

Structure of the IETF information models.

separate set of extensions of the generic representation of policy. This is shown in Figure 7.2.

The policy core information model defined a framework of classes and relationships that could represent the *structure* of policy of any discipline. This is an important point. The use case in 1998 is still the same as it is now—to build a single PBNM solution that can be used to manage different types of policies required by different applications. For example, QoS for voice applications is fundamentally different than QoS for data applications. As such, the target of the Policy Core Information Model (PCIM) was to be able to represent how a policy was defined—it was not targeted at defining the *content* of the policy.

The policy QoS information model refined this framework and added semantics to represent policies that could be used to control QoS mechanisms. The QoS device data-path information model was derived from the Distributed Management Task Force's (DMTF) common information model and represented much of the original DEN network model. The QoS device data-path information model was used to represent the various mechanisms that the policy QoS information model would be used to manage. Both information models were designed to provide *content* within a common overall *representational structure*.

The DMTF's Common Information Model (CIM) was proposed as a way to provide a high-level representation of network elements. Thus, the policies could be "grounded" and applied to a network device. For example, a policy could describe a change in a function of a device; the content of this change could be represented by the policy QoS information model, and the structure of the policy could be represented in PCIM.

Unfortunately, the CIM model was too high-level and confused many people in how policy would be applied. For example, the CIM had no representation of either a physical port or a logical device interface (and this is true even today). This made it very difficult for people to picture how policies were going to be applied and built. Furthermore, the DMTF CIM was not really an information model—it was more of a data model. An information model is supposed to be independent of platform and technology. The DMTF CIM is based on the use of "keys"—special attributes that are used to name and uniquely identify a particular object. Keys are really a database construct, and their use must be carefully considered or else mapping to other types of data models that do not use keys (or have different keys than those of a database) will be much harder. This is why specific constructs used in one type of data model should not be part of a more general information model.

In contrast, DEN-ng is a true information model in that it does not contain keys or other technology-specific concepts and terms. It instead concentrates on defining managed objects and their interrelationships. This is also true of the TMF's SID, of which the DEN-ng information model is one component.

The approach shown in Figure 7.2 was good. It took a very long time, however, to get the participants in the IETF to agree to these models. The PCIM was not published as an RFC until February 2001. Although the policy QoS information model was ready, it was not published as *RFC 3644* until November 2003. The QoS device data-path information model is further behind.

There were many reasons for the holdup. This was the first time that the IETF was working with information models. Second, policy models of this depth had not been done before in the industry. The main holdup was the fact that the IETF is composed of many different people; each of whom are there primarily to represent the companies that they work for. Each network vendor had by then launched its own set of policy applications. No one wanted a standard to come out that would brand their products as noncompliant! Thus, the standards were worked on, and watered down, and watered down some more, until they represented something that everyone could agree on.

The delay in issuing standards is due to these reasons plus the delay in getting different companies (through their IETF members) to announce consensus. Members are always fearful that a last-minute change in the standard will adversely impact their companies' products, and so consensus building is a relatively long process.

However, there was another, more serious, problem. The above models focused "just" on network devices. Although the PCIM was generic in nature, it was also limited. For example, there was no model of how a policy rule would be evaluated. More importantly, there were no business entities in these models and very few non-network entities. Thus, there was no formal way to define how business rules could use policy to control network services. The primary motivation for building the DEN-ng model was to address these problems.

7.2 WHERE WE ARE TODAY

Today, work has proceeded in various standards bodies and forums to rectify these problems. Prominent among these is the work of the TMF. Two examples of this work are in the new generation operational systems and software (NGOSS) architecture and the TMF's shared information and data (SID) model.

7.2.1 The NGOSS Architecture

The NGOSS Architecture is characterized by the separation of the expression and execution of business processes and services from the software that implements these business processes and services. Fundamentally, NGOSS is concerned with defining an architecture that automates business processes.

For example, policies can be used to choose which set of processes are used to perform a function. Feedback from executing processes can then be used to change which policies are in force (or even applicable) at any given time. Thus, although either policy management or process management can be used by itself to manage an NGOSS system, to do so is to fail to realize the greater potential afforded by using both to manage the same system.

The NGOSS behavior and control specification defines in high-level terms the architectural ramifications of using policy management. The NGOSS policy specification, defines in high-level terms the definition of a policy model that includes business, system and implementation viewpoints. This is based on work from the International Organization for Standardization (ISO) on a Unified Modeling Language (UML).

Although these are evolving specifications, credit should be given to the TMF for having the vision to try and specify these important concepts and also to develop them for all to use. A good example of this is the Catalyst programs of the TMF. These team demonstrations are usually led by a service provider or independent software vendor (ISV) and are designed to demonstrate one or more concepts of the NGOSS architecture. This work is important because it defines architectural and implementation ramifications of using PBNM solutions. This is one of the few forums in the world where this is being studied in depth by commercial, academic, and industrial players.

One of the prominent differences between the design of DEN-ng and the design of other information models is that DEN-ng was built to support the needs of the NGOSS architecture. All other information models that the author is familiar with were *not* built to support any particular architecture.

The TMF approach is inherently better suited to produce useful standards faster. First, it is centered on real-world work that is proven to be implementable through its Catalyst programs. Second, the TMF has as one of its goals the production of a shared information model. While the IETF emphasizes protocol development, the TMF emphasizes architecture and information modeling. Finally, because the different vendors are all united in achieving common goals (architecture and information modeling), it is easier for them to come to agreement than in the IETF.

7.2.2 The TMF Shared Information and Data Model

The TMF's shared information and data (SID) model is a federated model, which means that it is composed of different "sub-models," which have either been contributed by companies, mined from other standards, or developed within the TMF.

The communications industry is seeking technological advances that will improve time to market for new products and services. Service providers and enterprises like to use best-of-breed software. However, this software is hard to integrate with other software products constructed in a similar manner. Furthermore, each software product that is produced in a "vacuum" more than likely redefines concepts that are used by other applications.

To achieve true interoperability (where data from different components can be shared and reused), a common language needs to be developed and agreed on. This goal is even more important in an NGOSS system, because one of its key architectural principles is to use component-based software, interacting through contracts. Therefore, the TMF embarked on building a shared information model that could be used as a single source for defining common data.

The SID consists of inputs from Intelliden, MetaSolv, British Telecom, Telstra, Vodaphone, Motorola, Agilent, AT&T, and others. Material donated includes DEN-ng and several models and model snippets from many of these companies. The objective of the SID is to provide the industry with a common language, defined using UML, for common shared data. By agreeing on a common set of information/data definitions and relationships, the team sets forth a common language used in the definition of NGOSS architectures.

Another important feature of the SID is that it contains multiple models that concentrate on different disciplines. Most other information models concentrate on a single subject, such as networking. In contrast, the charter of the SID is to define business and system concepts for a variety of different domains. These domains characterize how network elements and services are represented, used, and managed in business and system environments.

7.2.3 The Ingredients in a Compelling PBNM Solution

The industry is now starting to appreciate the complexity of PBNM solutions. PBNM is more than writing a policy rule and more than building elaborate UML models; it is about a paradigm shift.

Historically, network management has focused on setting parameters of individual interfaces of a device one at a time. Recent innovations of policy management, ranging from new protocols to the use of information models to represent policy rules, have helped simplify this daunting task. However, in and of themselves these are insufficient to develop PBNM solutions that will solve network configuration problems and help make network services profitable once again.

We need a more extensible, more robust solution. The key to implementing this solution is to think more holistically about policy management. Most people consider policy to be a set of rules that express a set of conditions to be monitored and, if those conditions are met, one or more actions will be executed. This definition fails to take into account two key issues: users and process.

First, different types of people use policy. Business people do not want to express their policies in networking terminology, and networking people do not want policies written using business concepts. However, business and network personnel must work together to ensure that network services are managed according to the business goals of the organization. A new form of policy is needed that can translate business needs into device configuration.

However, this by itself is not enough. The second missing feature is process. No matter how simple or how sophisticated, every configuration change has an underlying set of business rules that govern its deployment. Business procedures will define who checks the change for correctness (sometimes from a technical and a business point of view). They identify who must approve the change and who must implement the change. They also describe how to verify that the change has been properly implemented and what to do if a problem is discovered.

Policies define how the shared resources of the organization are accessed and allocated. Different users and services have different needs, and policy is the tool that enables the appropriate process to be applied as a function of business priority. This enables network services to be adjusted in response to the changing environment (e.g., new users logging on, different application usage, and so forth) by providing dynamic and automatic (re)configuration of the appropriate network devices according to the business rules of the organization.

The realization that business rules and processes, device configuration, and service activation are all tightly bound together provides the clue to our answer. We need a robust, extensible information model that can represent the managed environment as a set of entities. If policies are also entities that exist in this information model, then we can be assured that policies are represented using the same tools, and therefore can be applied to users, applications, device interfaces, services, and other managed objects. The information model provides a set of formalisms through which we can build a robust system.

7.3 DEFINITION OF POLICY MANAGEMENT

Policy is typically defined as a set of rules. Each policy rule consists of a condition clause and an action clause. If the condition clause is TRUE, then the actions in the action clause are allowed to execute. Therefore, our first definition of policy management is:

Policy management is the usage of rules to accomplish decisions.

Policy is usually represented as a set of classes and relationships that define the semantics of the building blocks of representing policy. These building blocks usually consist of a minimum of a policy rule, a policy condition, and a policy action and are represented as shown in Figure 7.3. This simple UML model shows the relationships between these three classes. Attributes and methods have not been shown to keep the discussion simple. The figure shows that a PolicyRule

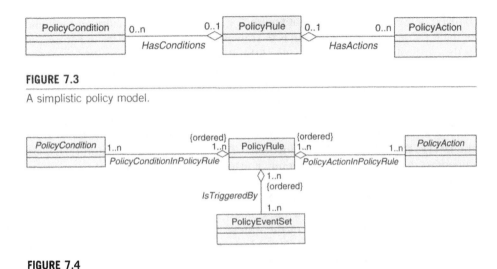

FIGURE 7.3

A simplistic policy model.

FIGURE 7.4

A simplistic view of the DEN-ng policy model.

contains a set of conditions and a set of actions. These are represented by the *hasConditions* and *hasActions* aggregations, respectively (an aggregation is a special type of relationship that is used to represent whole–part dependencies).

PBNM solutions usually use an information model to represent policy. Some of the better ones also use an information model to represent the subject and target of the policy. DEN-ng is unique, in that it does this for business, system, and implementation viewpoints. By representing what you want the policy to do and how you want it to act, you can use the power of an information model to represent how different entities relate to each other. For example, two different users can be logged on to the same system but receive different classes of service, which dictate how the applications that each operate are handled in the network.

An information model is a means for defining common representation of information. This enables management data to be shared, reused, and altered by multiple applications. The DEN-ng policy model is different to other policy models in the industry. However, three differences are important to discuss now.

The first difference is the use of an event model to trigger the evaluation of the policy condition clause. This changes Figure 7.3 to Figure 7.4, which can be read as follows:

> On receipt of an Event, evaluate the PolicyCondition of a PolicyRule. If it evaluates to TRUE, then execute the set of PolicyActions that are associated with this PolicyRule.

The second difference is the use of constraints to better define (through restriction and more granular specification) what the model represents. For example, it makes no sense to define a PolicyRule that does not have any conditions. This is allowed in the simplistic model of Figure 7.3, because the cardinality on each end of the *hasConditions* aggregation is 0. However, this is not the case in Figure 7.4, as the cardinality is 1..n on each side of the *PolicyConditionInPolicyRule* aggregation. Another example is the Object Constraint Language (OCL) expression "{ordered}." This expression requires that the PolicyEvents, PolicyConditions, and PolicyActions are each ordered when aggregated in the PolicyRule.

The third difference is that DEN-ng uses a finite state machine to represent the state of a managed entity. Most current information models, such as those from the DMTF, the IETF, and the International Telecommunications Union (ITU), are *current-state* models, (i.e., they define a managed entity to represent a state of an object). Although important, that does not make a closed-loop system. In particular, it does not enable the life cycle of the managed object to be represented.

Therefore, DEN-ng defines a finite state machine and instantiates multiple current state models to represent the different states that a managed object can take. This enables behavior of an individual or a group of managed objects to be represented. More importantly, the behavior of an object or set of objects can be related to the value of one or more attributes that are used to represent the current state of the attribute. This helps simplify the design of closed-loop PBNM solutions. For example, suppose that a particular state transition sets the attribute of an entity to a particular value and that this represents a bad or failed state. The changing of this attribute value is in fact an *event*, which can be used to trigger the evaluation of a PolicyRule. The PolicyRule can cause a state transition back to a valid state, which is checked by ensuring that the value of the attribute is changed to an acceptable value.

> Without events or a state machine, such closed-loop control is not possible. More important, policy is represented as a means to control when a managed object transitions to a new state.

This notion is simple, yet powerful. It succinctly captures the connotation of "control" that policy has and shows how policy can be used to govern the behavior of a managed object throughout its life cycle. Furthermore, it provides a means to control the behavior of a managed system in a predictable and consistent fashion. Events represent external stimuli that correspond to changes in state. If policies are used to control state transitions, then policies can be defined that govern each state of the managed object—from creation to deployment to destruction. This guarantees that the correct state of the managed object is achieved in response to a given event, in a simple and consistent manner.

7.4 INTRODUCTION AND MOTIVATION FOR POLICY MANAGEMENT

The promises of policy management are varied, powerful, and are often conceptualized as a single, simple means to control the network, as illustrated in Figure 7.5.

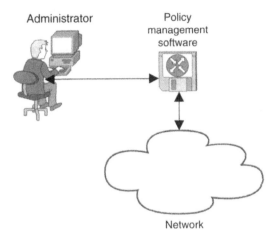

FIGURE 7.5

Promise of policy management.

The simplicity of the components shown in Figure 7.5 is part of the appeal of policy management. In particular, the ability to hide vendor-specific interfaces behind a uniform information model is very important. Without this ability, a common interface to programming the same function in different network devices cannot be accomplished. This is one of the toughest problems a network manager needs to deal with—how to string a network of multivendor equipment together to provide a seamless set of customer-facing services. Furthermore, the growth of large ISP networks that seek to provide multiple specialized services exacerbates this problem.

This drive for simplicity has led to six commonly heard value propositions for policy management that position policy management as a means of:

- Providing better-than-best-effort service to certain users
- Simplifying device, network, and service management
- Requiring fewer engineers to configure the network
- Defining the behavior of a network or distributed system
- Managing the increasing complexity of programming devices
- Using business requirements and procedures to drive the configuration of the network

These six points are discussed in more detail in the following subsections.

7.4.1 Providing Different Services to Different Users

The Internet was built to handle traffic on a best-effort basis. Clearly, people will not be satisfied with best-effort service. People want *predictable* services— services that they can rely on for providing information and functionality that they desire (whether the Internet is being used or not). This is the fundamental motivation for QoS.

When I worked at Cisco, we used to describe QoS as "managed unfairness." This complements the above desire for information and functionality that meet a specific set of needs. QoS is not just about providing faster downloads or more bandwidth. Rather, it is about providing the right set of functionality to provide a user with the service(s) that the user is requesting. Although this may mean faster downloads or more bandwidth, the point is that such metrics in and of themselves are not a good definition of QoS.

QoS is more difficult to provision and manage than it may first appear because of two main factors:

1. Its complexity of implemention.
2. The variety of services that can use it.

The complexity of implementing QoS is caused by two main factors: (1) network vendors continue to add additional types of mechanisms that can be used (by themselves or with other mechanisms) to implement QoS and (2) different devices have different QoS mechanisms. This makes it hard to ensure that the same relative levels of service are implemented by different devices that use different mechanisms.

Another problem is the lack of specificity in standards. For example, the IETF has completed a set of RFCs that specify different approaches for implementing differentiated services (e.g., the Differentiated Services RFCs). However, these RFCs by themselves are not sufficient to build an interoperable network because they concentrate on specifying behavior without specifying how to implement that behavior. For example, none of the RFCs specify what type of queuing and drop algorithms to use to implement a particular type of behavior. This is in recognition of the IETF—this is in fact in recognition of the fact that network vendors have designed a vast arsenal of different mechanisms to condition traffic as well as recognizing that different services uses different QoS mechanisms.

Thus, we have the first motivation for policy management—the promise of using a set of standard declarations for managing the different QoS mechanisms required to implement a service. This desire is amplified by the fact that multiple users want different services. Clearly, a service provider or enterprise cannot provide tens or hundreds of different services because of the complexity of managing these different services coupled with the fact that most approaches (such as DiffServ) define far less than these. DiffServ, for example, provides a set of 64 total code points, but these are divided into 32 standard and 32 experimental code points. Most service providers offer between three and ten different services. This provides the second motivation for policy management—the promise of providing a small set of standard rules that can be used to manage the set of services provided to multiple customers.

7.4.2 Simplifying Device, Network, and Service Management

PBNM was conceptualized as a set of mechanisms that can be used to "fine-tune" different network services. Similarly to how a stereo equalizer gives the user control over the response of the stereo to different frequencies, a PBNM-based system provides a set of mechanisms that can be used to condition traffic flowing through the network. PBNM systems also have the ability to define a complex set of mechanisms that can be used to implement a predefined service. This is a particularly attractive characteristic—choosing a single command to implement what previously consisted of a set of commands.

In addition, the real power of PBNM systems is through abstraction. Imagine a network where a switch feeds a router. The switch uses the IEEE 802.1q specification for delivering QoS, while the router uses DiffServ. This causes a problem, because there is not a defined set of standards for relating an 802.1q marking to a DiffServ code point (DSCP). Now, assume that the switch is programmed using simple network management protocol (SNMP) set commands, while the router is programmed using command-line interface (CLI) commands. The network administrator is now forced to learn two different ways to program a single network connection.

The motivation for PBNM is one of simplification through abstraction. By providing an intermediate layer of policy rules, PBNM users can concentrate on the task at hand, rather than the myriad programming models and traffic conditioning mechanisms used to program a device.

However, an equally powerful motivation exists—recovery from changes and failures. Networks present an ever-changing infrastructure for providing services. The day-to-day management of this infrastructure includes making subtle changes to how different components are configured. Sometimes, these changes can adversely affect network services. These changes are hard to find, because most of the time, the change being made is not obviously related to the service that was being changed. In addition, networks can develop faults that impair the ability of the network to provide services that people and applications depend on. When this happens, administrators tend to fix the fault by changing the configuration of the device.

These and other factors culminate in a set of changes that, over time, impact the ability of the device to support one or more of its services. When this happens, PBNM systems can be used to restore the configurations of devices to their original state. Thus, PBNM provides a means to fix the fault and to also keep track of the state of various network devices. This requirement for tracking state is one of the reasons why DEN as well as DEN-ng both use finite state machine models.

7.4.3 Requiring Fewer Engineers to Configure the Network

There is an acute shortage of engineers that understand new technologies and mechanisms implemented by network vendors. There are even less engineers that understand these technologies and are able to deploy and manage them on a network. In addition, the cost of using an emerging technology is very high, interactions with other legacy technologies are not completely known, and management costs associated with initially deploying the technology often outweigh the advantage provided by that technology.

For example, many network operators choose to overengineer their networks to address any performance concerns rather than deploy QoS techniques. This is because the cost associated with learning the new technologies (and the tools used to deploy them) and managing them is much higher than the savings in bandwidth-related costs that would result from deploying these technologies. Another factor is the previous lack of specificity mentioned—if different technologies are being used, then they can only interoperate if their functionality is specified at a sufficiently detailed level. For example, there is no standard that defines how to map ATM's concept of QoS to the different DSCP values that are present in an IP network.

The theory behind being able to use fewer personnel to run a network is based on distributing intelligence to managed devices and applications that manage devices so that dynamically changing environments can be more easily managed and controlled. Although the number of skilled individuals may be reduced, it is wrong to think that PBNM applications will eliminate the need for specialized network engineers. Skilled personnel will always be needed to build and operate systems.

However, PBNM systems provide two important benefits. First, the majority of network configuration tasks are simple in nature and do not require a specialist. Many of these are also repetitive. If the PBNM system can be programmed to deal with these mundane changes, then they enable more highly skilled engineers to be used on other, more strategic, problems. Second, PBNM systems enforce process. Figure 7.6 illustrates this.

PBNM can be used to define processes, such as:

- Which personnel are qualified to build a configuration change
- Which personnel must approve a configuration change

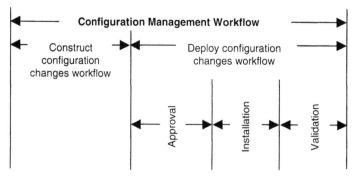

FIGURE 7.6

Processes used in configuration management.

- Which personnel must install a configuration change
- Which personnel must validate a configuration change

These four processes are meant to be exemplary in nature and should not be construed as being the "only" processes involved in device configuration.

The strength of PBNM is that these four processes (and others) can be enforced by a PBNM system independent of whether the PBNM system is used to implement a configuration change or not. For some reason, this message has not been emphasized by most vendors. Even some researchers tend to ignore it, concentrating instead on the representation of policy. Two counterexamples to this trend are Intelliden and Metasolv, both of which are building software to help in this area.

PBNM systems also offer the ability to ensure that the same approved processes are used to consistently implement specific types of configuration changes. The Intelliden product is a good example of offering these benefits.

7.4.4 Defining the Behavior of a Network or Distributed System

Networks are growing in complexity because of several factors, including an increasing number of people using networks, a growing number of different applications used, and an increase in the number of different services required by network users.

These factors all help to create an ever-growing overhead of operating and administrating networks. As a result, it is very difficult to build management systems that can cope with growing network size, complexity, and multiservice operation requirements. There is also a need to be able to dynamically change the behavior of the system to support modified or additional functionality after it has been deployed.

A single network device can have thousands of interfaces or subinterfaces. Clearly, if an administrator has to manually configure each of these, the network cannot scale. For example, assume each device interface takes 10 minutes to configure and that there are 10,000 total interfaces. This works out to requiring 69.44 days, or 9.92 weeks, to program this set of interfaces. Without software, this is simply not possible. In addition, the chances of making an error without automation software are enormous.

PBNM software can help in several ways. First, it can be used to define policy rules once and mass deploy them. For example, the Intelliden product has a concept called "command sets" that enable sets of configuration changes (which are controlled by policy) to be deployed to multiple devices concurrently. Second, policy rules can be used in either an ad hoc or reusable fashion. Although ad hoc policy rules are intended to be used once, reusable policy rules (or even policy components) are designed to be used multiple times by different applications. This concept can be used to help simplify the arduous process of configuring different interfaces. For example, an access control list can be defined that filters on certain fields in the IP header and then performs a set of actions if those fields matched or not. This is a fundamental building block that can be used for many different types of policies. Third, large systems will execute many different policies. PBNM systems should enable different sets of policies to be analyzed to ensure that they do not result in conflicting actions.

However, and most important, PBNM software can be used to capture business logic that is associated with certain conditions that occur in the network. Although centralizing the development and management of this business logic is important, coordinating its proper application is mandatory for large systems. This last point raises four important questions that the reader should ask when evaluating PBNM systems:

- How many physical devices is the PBNM software capable of managing?
- How many logical components (e.g., subinterfaces) is the PBNM software capable of managing?
- How many changes per time period (e.g., minute or hour) can the PBNM software execute?
- How does the PBNM solution handle errors?

Each of these points is important. The third point is especially important, because most organizations operate using a "time window" in which changes must occur. The point, then, is how many changes can your PBNM software physically perform during that time window? The reader will find that this is often the limiting factor in choosing a PBNM system. The fourth point is also critical, because one of the reasons for deploying a PBNM solution is to automate complex tasks. The form of this question is different than a simple "can it scale" question. Vendors will all claim that their solutions scale. Thus, a much easier way to be sure of what you are buying is if it can provide a common error handling methodology for large deployments. This is a simpler and better test of what you are buying.

7.4.5 Managing the Increasing Complexity of Programming Devices

Present-day IP networks are large, complex systems that consist of many different types of devices. Different devices are chosen for cost and functionality. However, from the end-user's point of view, it is imperative that the end-user not have to be explicitly aware of these differences. In other words, the network should appear as a single homogenous entity that provides services for the end-user.

Therefore, when most services are defined, they are characterized as having a set of properties that exist from one end of the network to the other. For example, think of a service level agreement that specifies availability (which in this example is defined as remote access accessibility without busy signals). While the service provider is likely to specify different times for different networks (e.g., a connection to a U.S. network versus a connection to a European network), it certainly will not specify availability between different parts of the network. Not only is this too hard to do (and very costly for the service provider), it doesn't really matter, because the service is specified as an end-to-end service. The end-user does not care what devices or QoS mechanisms are used or what the latency or drop rate is along an intermediate path in the network as long as the service that was contracted for is successfully delivered.

Network engineers do not have this luxury. In fact, ensuring that all of the different devices that comprise a network interoperate smoothly is far from a trivial task. This is because different devices have different functionality, represented as different commands that are available to the network developer. The problem is that these different network devices are each responsible for doing their best in providing *consistent* treatment of the traffic. Clearly, if the two devices have different commands, then this is harder to achieve, because a mapping needs to be defined to map the different commands to each other.

For example, consider two Cisco devices, one running a pre-12.x release of IOS (a common operating system used by Cisco routers and other types of devices) and another running a 12.x release of IOS. Suppose that the task is to provide QoS for traffic that contains voice, video, and data. Both devices can do this. However, the actual commands that are used are very different. As an example, the design for the 12.x device is likely to use low latency queuing, which is not available in pre-12.x IOS releases. Thus, someone (or something) has to provide a mapping between the set of commands used in each version of an operating system. Clearly, if different devices are using different operating systems, this mapping becomes both harder and more important. Mapping the commands is a good start, but even that is not sufficient. Other factors must also be taken into account. Two important ones are side effects and dependencies in executing each command.

Sometimes, when a command is executed, effects occur that cause other entities to be affected besides the ones that are targeted by the command. These are called side effects, because though these changes were not intended, they nevertheless happened. If these commands have any side effects, then they must be noted, and if the side effects affect the traffic, then they must be emulated for each device.

Exacerbating this situation is the notion of hardware and software dependencies. For example, a device that uses an older processor may be unable to perform the same functions as a device that uses a newer processor past a certain line rate. This is a hardware dependency and must be accounted for to ensure that each device performs traffic conditioning in a consistent manner. Similarly, software dependencies exist; if they affect the flow of the traffic, then their effect must be emulated in devices that do not have these same software dependencies.

If that is not bad enough, new technologies have emerged or will continue to emerge to either address current limitations or to perform a task better. Thus, the PBNM system must be capable of addressing new commands and features of the devices that it supports. This is best done using an information model to abstract the different functionality that is present in multiple devices. For example, Figure 7.7 shows a simplified approximation of the DEN-ng QoS model, which is an information model designed to represent QoS. (Remember that a line with an

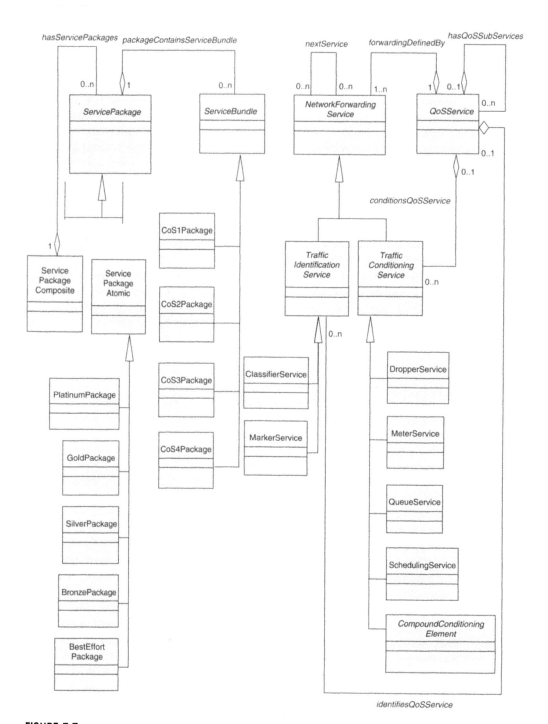

FIGURE 7.7

Simplified DEN-ng QoS model.

arrowhead denotes inheritance in UML. Thus, GoldPackage is a subclass of ServiceBundle, which is a subclass of CustomerFacingService, which is a subclass of Service.)

In DEN-ng, there are two types of services: CustomerFacingServices and ResourceFacingServices. This is modeled as two separate subclasses that inherit from the Service superclass.

CustomerFacingServices are services that a customer is directly aware of. For example, a virtual private network (VPN) is a service that a customer can purchase. ResourceFacingServices are network services that are required to support the functionality of a CustomerFacingService, but which the customer cannot (and should not!) know about. For example, a service provider doesn't sell Border Gateway Protocol (BGP, a means of advertising routes between networks) services to a customer. Yet, BGP is required for different types of CustomerFacingServices to operate correctly. Thus, BGP is an example of a ResourceFacingService.

A ServicePackage is an abstraction that enables different CustomerFacing Services to be packaged together as a group. Thus, a GoldService user may access high-quality voice, video, and data, whereas a SilverService user may be unable to use voice.

Several types of ResourceFacingServices are shown in Figure 7.7. QoSService is an abstraction that relates the particular networking architecture to its ability to provide QoS. For example, ToSService uses the three-bit Type of Service bits in IPv4 to define the QoS that can be given, whereas DiffServService uses the six-bit code point to define much more granular QoS for IPv4. Because a given network may have both DiffServ-compliant and DiffServ-unaware devices, the information model provides a formal way to synchronize their configurations, so that a given ToS setting provides the same QoS as a particular DiffServ setting.

Finally, NetworkForwardingService defines how traffic is conditioned. This consists of two types of "sub-services": the ability to identify traffic and the ability to affect the order in which packets are transmitted from the device. Again, because these are two distinct concepts, two distinct subclasses (TrafficIdentificationService and TrafficConditioningService, respectively) are used to represent these concepts. With respect to TrafficIdentificationServices, ClassifierService performs the separation of traffic into distinct flows that each receive their own QoS, whereas MarkerService represents the ability of a device to mark or re-mark the ToS or DiffServ bits. This marking tells the other devices what type of QoS that flow should receive. With respect to TrafficConditioningServices:

- DropperService drops packets according to a particular algorithm, which has the effect of telling certain types of sending applications to slow their transmission.
- MeterService limits the transmission of packets.
- QueueService delays the transmission of packets.
- SchedulingService defines which queue (of multiple output queues) should send packets.

- CompoundConditioningService models advanced features, which are combinations of the preceding basic services.

The objective in such a model is to describe a particular feature (such as metering) and how that feature relates to other features (e.g., classification and dropping) in a particular function (e.g., traffic conditioning) using classes and relationships. The idea is that if the abstractions are defined properly they can be used to model the types of functions that are present in different vendor devices and accommodate new functionality.

Put another way, the model can be used as a design template for constructing commands that are to be applied to a device or set of devices. The advantage of such a model is that the model can be used to represent the functionality desired and can hide the intricacies of translating to different implementations from the user. In fact, this is one of the principles on which the Intelliden R-Series was founded.

Sometimes, such models are all that is needed, and enable vendor-specific programs that are derived directly from these models to be used. Often, however, additional information is required. In the DEN-ng information model, this will take the form of subclasses that are used to model vendor-specific differences from the model.

7.4.6 Using Business Rules to Drive Network Configuration

The thesis of *A New Paradigm for Network Management* is that existing network management architectures prevent business processes from being used to drive the configuration and management of the network. In essence, this paper states that businesses must define and implement network services according to their own business processes and policies. Although this is true for all businesses, it is even more true for the so-called "next generation network" initiatives and corporations that are striving to become more profitable by changing the network services that they provide.

Business driven device management (BDDM) is one example of using business rules to drive network configuration. As defined by the author, BDDM is a new paradigm that enables business rules to be used to manage the construction and deployment of network configuration changes. The difference is that BDDM controls both the construction and the deployment of configuration changes using a combination of policies and processes.

Most of the current research in PBNM systems revolves around the definition of policy class hierarchies that can be used to represent functionality of a network device. BDDM leverages this work, but combines it with policies and processes that define how configuration changes are created, deployed, and modified in a scalable and consistent manner. Part of the desire to use business rules to drive the configuration of a device is because business rules provide a higher-level view of what needs to be accomplished. This is necessary to ensure that those changes will not disrupt the operation of the device or the network. This, in turn, requires other entities besides devices and services (such as users and their various different roles) to be modeled.

Although abstractions that are used to represent business entities can still be modeled in UML, their content and detail is significantly different than that used for device and service entities. The administrator does not have to understand the low-level details of the technology used to support a particular business need to direct its usage. For example, suppose that a network operator needs to define three levels (gold, silver, and bronze) of customers. An administrator can easily assign each customer to a particular level based on their contract. A variety of techniques can be used to implement these three services in the network; one such example is to use DiffServ.

However, there is a difference between the business person (whose job is to assign a particular service level to a customer) and a network administrator, (who is responsible for implementing commands that will enable the network to recognize and enforce these three network service levels). Both the business person and the network administrator can use policies. For example, a business person may need to write policies for handling service outages or interruptions, whereas a network administrator will be more interested in writing policies that control how the configuration of a device is changed. This difference is fundamental to how policies for each are used and expressed and mandates that different representations of policy should be used for the business person and the network administrator.

If business rules and processes are not used to manage changes made to the configuration of network devices, the device's configuration is reduced to changing lines in a file. This doesn't reflect how the business operates! Even worse, this means that the network is probably not reflecting the proper set of services that the organization needs to run its business. The semantics of what to change, when to change it, and who can change it are all captured using business rules and processes. These semantics must be used to drive how the configuration is constructed and deployed.

However, the problem is more complex than "just" modeling QoS commands or defining which user can make a configuration change. Fundamentally, different types of people—having different responsibilities and different functions in the organization—use policy for a variety of reasons. Network terminology is not appropriate for expressing business policies. Similarly, business terminology is not usually precise enough to be used for device management and programming. However, it is essential that the network is operated in line with the business goals of the organization, and this means that business and network personnel must work together to ensure that they have a common understanding of their objectives. A set of policies that supports the translation between one type of policy and another is therefore needed.

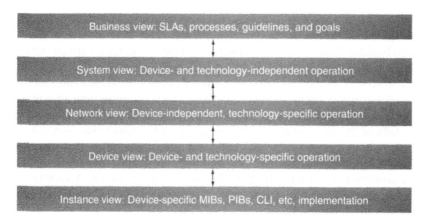

FIGURE 7.8

Policy continuum as defined in DEN-ng.

This translation between different types of policies is called the *policy continuum* (see Figure 7.8). Each level in the policy continuum addresses a specific type of user that has a very specific understanding of the managed entities operating at that particular level of abstraction. The PBNM system must translate these entities and concepts between layers of the policy continuum. The DEN-ng model is the only information model that uses the concept of a policy continuum.

This chapter uses the new DEN-ng information model to represent managed entities, people, and applications that use those managed entities and policy entities. The advantage of using a single information model that has multiple domains is that it is easier to relate different elements in each domain to other elements in other domains.

7.4.7 Summary of the Benefits of PBNM

The traditional promise of PBNM is that people will be able to deploy more complex services across a wider array of devices with fewer highly skilled individuals. This will in turn simplify network and service management. This is augmented by newer promises, such as those envisioned by BDDM, which use business requirements to drive the configuration of the network. This forms a tight closed-loop system, in which decisions governing the behavior of the network and the services that it provides are driven by business rules.

The results of these promises are compelling: increased revenue, faster time to activate services, and decreased expenses.

The next two sections will focus on two key themes: (1) the need for and use of a shared information model and (2) the benefits of using PBNM.

7.5 THE NEED FOR A NEW SHARED INFORMATION MODEL

The two big issues that face us today concerning network devices and network management are:

- Lack of a consistent product model prevents predictable behavior
- No standard for shared data

7.5.1 Lack of a Consistent Product Model

The lack of a consistent product model means that, despite all the standards that you hear about, different vendors build devices with different hardware and software. One router can have vastly different characteristics and functionality than another router. This situation is exacerbated when mergers, acquisitions, and divestitures occur, as the customer ends up buying completely different devices that happen to have the same logo and vendor name on them. Therefore, when different devices are used in the same network, predictable behavior cannot be obtained. Standards help define invariant parts of the programming model. However, they are usually not explicit enough to guarantee interoperability. For example, *RFC 2474* defines the structure of a differentiated services code point (DSCP), which is used to indicate how to condition traffic. The invariant portion of this RFC includes the fact that a DSCP is six bits long, and certain bit patterns are already defined. However, this RFC does not define which dropping and queuing algorithms to use for different bit patterns. Thus, multiple vendors can be compliant with the differentiated service standard (of which this RFC is one element) without being able to interoperate.

This is also true, but to a lesser degree, of the emerging policy information model standards. *RFC 3060* and *RFC 3460* define a class hierarchy and relationships for representing generic policy elements, while further work in the IETF extends these to QoS models. There is even a Lightweight Directory Access Protocol (LDAP) mapping, and the beginnings of one for policy core extension LDAP schema. These classes and relationships help define how policy is used to control various QoS mechanisms. However, these models have very limited semantics and are subject to interpretation by different applications. For example, these networking concepts are not linked closely enough to network device and service entities to specify how policy could be used to program device features (let alone commands). As a simple example, because these models do not specify the concept of a device interface they cannot be used to specify how to program a device interface.

More importantly, these models do not contain any associations to business entities, such as Product and Customer. Thus, they cannot be used to define which Services from which Products are assigned to which Customers. This also contributes to the complexity of building a management system, because now additional components must be used if business rules and processes are used to drive the configuration of the network.

A networking model that is associated with other models that represent users and targets of networking services and a policy model that controls how networking services are implemented and provided to users are needed. This requires a layered, integrated information model.

7.5.2 Lack of a Standard for Representing Shared Data

Until the TMF launched its SID model effort, no standard existed for sharing and reusing data for network devices and services. The common information model (CIM) of the DMTF is rooted in instrumentation of desktop applications. Although the model has reached out over the last few years to encompass additional concepts, it still lacks many telecommunications concepts that enterprise and service provider networks need. For example, its physical device model has no physical port, and its logical model has no device interface. Without these, the model cannot be used in telecommunications applications. The CIM is not a bad model; it is simply not a self-contained model that can be used for telecommunications applications.

This is precisely why the DEN-ng and the SID efforts were started. The DEN-ng effort was designed to extend and enhance the original DEN effort to tie it more closely to the NGOSS effort of the TMF. The design of the DEN-ng model is unique, because one of its use cases is to support the NGOSS architecture specification.

The DEN-ng effort focuses on modeling network elements and services. However, it provides a business, system, and implementation viewpoint of these models. The focus of the SID is on the entire NGOSS environment. The SID uses many models, including DEN-ng, to provide comprehensive coverage of entities and concepts present in an NGOSS environment.

DEN-ng is being developed in the TMF because the TMF Catalyst programs can be used to validate and spread the model across different service providers, vendors, and independent software vendors (ISVs). This distribution vehicle (which also provides detailed feedback) is lacking in other standards bodies and forums and is one of the main reasons why DEN-ng was developed in the TMF.

The DEN-ng policy model was developed using an iterative top-down, bottom-up approach. Business concerns were first considered, which provided a high-level structure for and helped define key concepts of the overall policy information model. This model was then augmented by adding detail necessary to build a system. This is currently where the public part of the DEN-ng set of specifications exists.

Intelliden's vision is to take this a step further in its product line. Once these business and system views are defined, a set of tools will be produced that will focus on translating the information model to two different data models: a directory data model and a Java model. This will enable the information model to be implemented in software. A second set of tools will be developed, which will focus on ease of implementation (Figure 7.9).

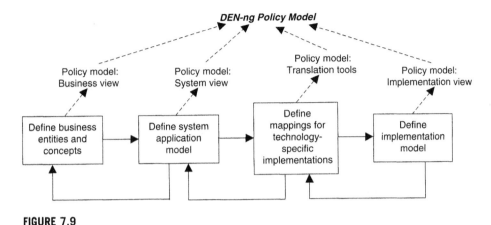

FIGURE 7.9

Design approach for building the DEN-ng policy model.

This brief description is meant to show the reader that information models can and should be used to drive software implementations. By embedding the information model in a product, that product is better able to adjust to changing features and functions. For example, in the Intelliden R-Series, the different functions of IOS are modeled using extensions of the DEN-ng logical model. When a new IOS train is released, Intelliden only has to update the model. Code is then generated that understands these features, and these features are updated as part of that release's product catalog. These features are assigned as capabilities to that particular IOS version.

This is a great example of building to accommodate the future. The information model provides a formal structure to represent different device capabilities. Software can then be written that uses this formal structure to represent these capabilities in the R-Series product. This enables the structure of the R-Series to be fixed; when new IOS releases are produced by Cisco, Intelliden updates the information model, new Java code is generated, and the *rest of the interface and APIs of the product stay the same*.

As another example, in the Intelliden implementation, the information model is used for the following tasks:

- Representing different functions that can be programmed using the IOS software
  - Routing and forwarding functions
  - Peering with other hosts and devices
  - Traffic classification and conditioning functions

- Representing different commands and their structure as a function of a particular software release

- Representing different hardware and software capabilities of a given device

- Defining business policies that control
  - Who can perform what changes on which devices
  - Who must approve a certain change (or category of changes)
  - When a change is deployed

- Defining system policies that control when certain actions happen (e.g., when a device is examined for changes to its configuration and/or to its physical composition)

- Defining implementation policies that control how changes are made and how services are activated

The information model serves as the centralized authority that links different parts of the managed environment to each other. As shown in the preceding example, the information model is used to define different types of policies used to control various types of behavior. Business, system, and implementation parts of the product are all seamlessly integrated using the DEN-ng information model.

7.5.3 Why an Information Model Is Important

An information model is more than just a representation of a set of objects. The most important feature of an information model is its ability to describe relationships between managed objects. From this, other types of models and diagrams, such as defining how data flows within the system, can be defined.

The information model serves as a normalization layer. By concentrating on invariant aspects of an object (e.g., a device has physical ports over which information flows), a framework can be defined that can represent the different features and functions of heterogeneous devices. Device-specific differences can then be modeled by extending the common framework to accommodate the features and functions of these different devices.

Without a common framework, different device features and functions cannot be easily accommodated because there is no common set of objects that can be used to build them from. In other words, to accommodate ten new features, a system that does not have a common information modeling framework must define ten new sets of objects (and more if interactions between these objects are to be modeled). If it is desired to interoperate between these ten new features, then in the worst case, all of the permutations of each new object operating with not just the other objects, but existing objects, must be defined.

Compare this to a system that uses a common framework. Adding ten new features means that the framework itself will be expanded to accommodate as many of these as extensions (i.e., subclasses) as possible. Furthermore, by developing these new features as extensions, interoperability with existing concepts and information is guaranteed.

It is not feasible to have a single information model that can represent the full diversity of management information that is needed. This is because the characteristics of managed data are very different and require many different subject

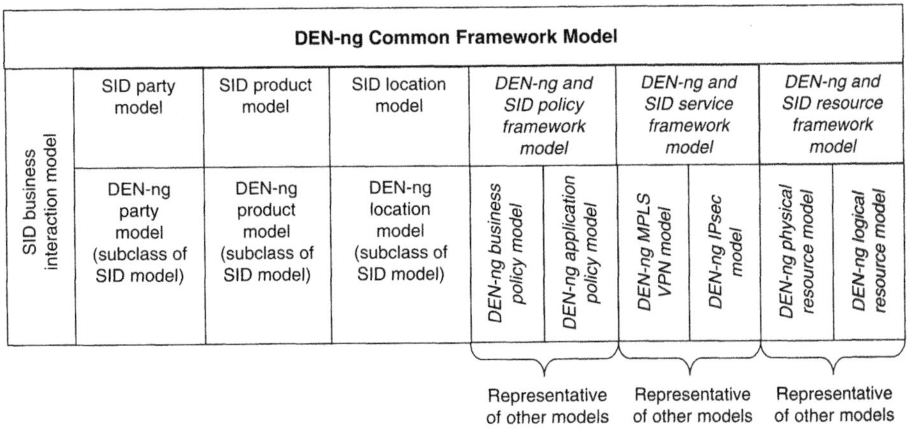

DEN-ng Common Framework Model									
SID party model	SID product model	SID location model	DEN-ng and SID policy framework model		DEN-ng and SID service framework model		DEN-ng and SID resource framework model		
DEN-ng party model (subclass of SID model)	DEN-ng product model (subclass of SID model)	DEN-ng location model (subclass of SID model)	DEN-ng business policy model	DEN-ng application policy model	DEN-ng MPLS VPN model	DEN-ng IPsec model	DEN-ng physical resource model	DEN-ng logical resource model

(left side vertical label: SID business interaction model)

Representative of other models   Representative of other models   Representative of other models

FIGURE 7.10

Simplified view of the DEN-ng layered information model.

matter experts. DEN-ng solved this problem by defining a layered information model that used patterns and roles.

A layered information model is one in which a common framework is built that supports different domain models. A simplified view of the DEN-ng layered information model is shown in Figure 7.10.

The DEN-ng common framework model consists of a set of classes and relationships that enable the different lower-level models to be associated with each other. Because DEN-ng and SID are complementary, the DEN-ng model takes the work of the SID team and either uses it in an unaltered state (as shown by the business interaction model) or makes minor modifications to it (as is done in the party, product, and location models). Note that for the Party, Product, and Location models, DEN-ng takes the SID models and defines new subclasses wherever possible. This means that the DEN-ng versions are more granular versions of the SID models. If DEN-ng needs to change something in the SID, then it is submitted as a change for review by the SID team. In addition, many parts of the DEN-ng model are in the process of being contributed to the SID team, as is shown in the policy, service and resource models. Each of these is in reality another framework model, which additional sub-models "plug into." For example, the DEN-ng policy model provides a generalized framework that business policy, application use of policy, and other policy models can each plug into.

To provide as extensible a framework as possible, DEN-ng uses patterns and roles to model common concepts in as generic a way as possible. This differentiates DEN-ng from most other models (e.g., DMTF, IETF, and ITU), as they do not use roles and patterns.

Modeling objects describes entities in a system, their inter-relationships and behavior, and how data flows within the system. This provides the ability to represent and understand the programming model of the device. Three examples are CLI, SNMP, and Transaction Language One (TL1). TL1 is a set of ASCII instructions that an OSS uses to manage a network element—usually an optical device. More importantly, it provides the ability to understand dependencies between hardware and software. For example, a router may have a line card that has a main CPU and memory that are dedicated to performing traffic conditioning functions. This may work fine at low speeds (e.g., a fractionalized T1). However, at high speeds, such as OC-48, suppose that this particular type of CPU cannot keep up. Or even if it could, suppose that there was not enough memory.

This is an example of a dependency that most current PBNM systems will not catch. That is, the card has the correct operating system version, and the operating system says that it can perform this type of function. However, the physical media is simply too fast for this card to perform this type of function. The reason that most PBNM systems will not catch this dependency is because there is no convenient way to represent it. In contrast, any PBNM system that uses an information model, such as DEN-ng, will be able to model this and other dependencies naturally.

Information modeling provides a common language to represent the features and functions of different devices. DEN-ng uses the concepts of *capabilities* to represent functions of an entity and *constraints* as restrictions on those functions. Think of the information model as defining a common language that enables the different capabilities of each device to be represented in a common way. This enables them to be programmed together to deliver a common service. But sometimes, a particular environment might restrict the use of certain commands. For example, export control laws might restrict different encryption or other features from being used. These are modeled as constraints. *The combination of capabilities and constraints form a set of powerful abstractions that can be used to model current and future devices and services.*

7.5.4 Linking Business, System, and Implementation Views

Most information models have focused on policy as a domain that is isolated from the rest of the managed environment. Here, domain is used to signify a set of related information and concepts. In contrast, the main use case for the DEN-ng policy model is to define a policy model that is closely integrated with the rest of the managed environment. The DEN-ng policy model is best thought of as an information model that defines how policy interacts with the rest of the managed environment (which is also represented as an information model). This has three important consequences, discussed in the following subsections.

Isolation

It was apparent that building a policy information model in isolation of other information models was not going to work. The original DEN specification, as well as CIM, each had many different domains in addition to policy. However, little effort was made to associate policy in detail with these other domains. In addition, the original DEN and CIM models did not specify in enough detail how policy could be applied to a managed object. The DEN-ng model takes a different approach. It builds out the policy model as one of the last domain models and then concentrates on associating appropriate parts of the policy model with appropriate parts of other domain models.

Concentration on Policy

The existing models concentrated on representing policy. They either did not address or addressed in a very superficial way how policy affected other managed entities. The difference here is subtle but important. Current policy models concentrate on defining the structure of a policy rule, what its condition terms are, and so forth. Although there was a lot of talk about policy changing a value in a device configuration file, the details of *how* that was accomplished were left unspecified. For example, the IETF and DMTF models do not specify the concept of a device interface or physical port. If the device uses CLI to change its configuration, how then can policy be used if these fundamental concepts are not modeled? The DEN-ng policy model fixes this unfortunate situation by developing other domain models alongside the policy model and ensuring that appropriate elements in the policy model can be associated with appropriate elements in other models. The goal of DEN-ng is the ability to translate policy expressions *directly* to running code—something that cannot be done with existing models.

Static View of Policy

The original models (and almost all current additions to those models) are still thinking of policy in a very static way (i.e., they use policies to express the static configuration of target devices). Most models concentrate solely on the network layer and do not provide an information model for representing business entities and how they affect target devices. In fact, there is very little literature on detailed information models that are designed with business views in mind, and even less literature describing how business information models can be linked to information models of other domains.

For example, how does a changed Service Level Agreement (SLA) affect device configuration files? Clearly, the SLA defines how traffic should be treated, but when it is changed, the policy of treating that traffic is changed—how is that accomplished? Or how does a customer, who has just bought a new product with a higher class of service, get that service installed and running? These are two simple examples of linking the business world, with its set of entities and concepts, to the system and networking worlds, which have different expressions for those concepts. Although policy is required, unless the representations are equated, the business, system, and networking domains will always remain disconnected. This adversely affects service activation and deployment.

Business Systems in NGOSS

Both the IETF and the DMTF approaches make no attempt to represent business entities and objectives. Although a few other approaches do, none has addressed

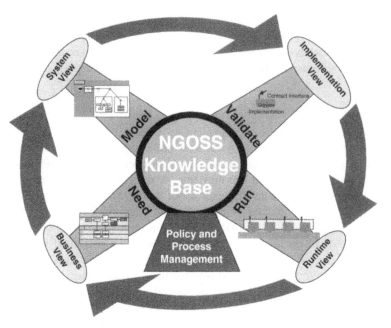

FIGURE 7.11

TMF NGOSS architecture.

building a set of models that are designed to support business, system, implementation, and run-time views that are closely tied to an overall architecture.

This concept is shown in Figure 7.11, which is a conceptual view of the NGOSS architecture. The NGOSS knowledge base is a collection of information and data models, specifications, contracts, code, and supporting documentation that collectively and cooperatively describe how to build an NGOSS system. The four quadrants represent the business, system, implementation, and runtime views. The overall behavior of the system is driven by the holistic combination of policy and process management functions.

The TMF has developed a set of principles and procedures to coordinate each of these four processes. This takes the form of the various architectural specifications (e.g., TMF053 series), the TMF documents, the contract work, and other elements, which together form the NGOSS knowledge base. Each of the DEN-ng domain models were built to fit into this approach.

A key objective of the NGOSS methodology is the development of models that focus on particular characteristics and procedures in an NGOSS system. These are characterized by the four viewpoints shown in Figure 7.11. The viewpoints are in turn tied together through the use of common shared information and a common means to exchange that information—contracts. The combination of the SID and contracts allow interoperability to be realized.

The SID (as well as DEN-ng) was built to provide a set of entities that model business, system, implementation, and run-time concepts. Put another way, the SID (and DEN-ng) were built to help realize the NGOSS architecture shown in Figure 7.11 by providing a common language to represent the transition of a concept from the business through the run-time views.

One main goal of the DEN-ng policy model was to accommodate the NGOSS architecture as shown in Figure 7.11. The DEN-ng policy model accomplishes this goal in two ways. First, it uses the different layers of the policy continuum to define different abstractions that must be modeled. This enables the different users of policy to work with and express concepts in their own terminology, rather than having the terminology and concepts of a static model given to them, never to be changed. Second, the different viewpoints are each supported by different views of the DEN-ng information model. This is realized by focusing on different entities for each of the DEN-ng domain models.

7.6 THE BENEFITS OF PBNM

There are many benefits to PBNM solutions. Some of the original drivers were listed at the beginning of this chapter. This section describes some of the more popular current benefits.

7.6.1 An Intelligent Alternative to Overprovisioning the Network

The economic downturn has forced companies to stop overprovisioning their networks and instead look to more intelligent means of delivering needed network services.

Overprovisioning may be done for several reasons. An organization may be running several mission-critical applications that must run in a timely, non-interrupted fashion. Or, it may use overprovisioning to achieve the desired levels of application delivery, such as quality of service, which its users require. However, the real reason that most networks have been overprovisioned is that it is supposedly easier and cheaper than its alternative—classifying, prioritizing, and conditioning the different types of traffic that exist in the network.

In truth, although overprovisioning can deliver on some of its promises, it cannot really solve QoS, and it is very expensive. With respect to QoS, overprovisioning attempts to solve the problem by making it go away. That is, its approach is to provide more resources than will be needed. However, QoS is all about *levels*. For example, although the following mechanisms all take a different approach to QoS, they all use a particular level on which to act:

- Congestion management methods, which essentially are different ways to sort and schedule traffic
- Congestion avoidance methods, which use various techniques to avoid congestion from occurring

- Policing and shaping enable the input and output rates of traffic to be controlled

Part of managing different types of traffic is planning on which types of traffic need which resources and trying to ensure that those resources exist. The problem with overprovisioning is that it never establishes a minimum level of performance. In addition, you must be careful what you overprovision. For example, providing extra bandwidth for certain types of applications, such as SNA and voice, does nothing; these applications need strict requirements on jitter, latency, and delay.

Of course, other problems exist with overprovisioning. The most important of these is that your network is being severely underutilized most of the time. Overprovisioning means that you will provision the network for a particular capacity. The longer you run at less than that capacity, the less your valuable (and expensive!) equipment is used.

PBNM solutions can be used to intelligently allocate resources. There is no free lunch here, however. A lot of work must be done, and the amount of work is arguably more than simply throwing equipment at the problem, as is done in overprovisioning. This is because what is important is ensuring that different applications having different needs of the network can peacefully coexist. This is more difficult than simply "throwing bandwidth" at the problem. However, the benefits are a more efficient, cost-effective, streamlined operation. Plus, as PBNM is implemented to classify traffic, it can also be used for a variety of other tasks (such as providing better security) at the same time.

7.6.2 Providing Better Security

As the number of users and applications proliferate, networks get more complex, and with complexity, comes risk. One important form of risk is resource abuse.

The benign form of resource abuse is when authorized users misuse their network privileges (e.g., downloading large music or video files when the network is congested, playing network games, and other acts). Users often do not realize what an adverse effect such acts can have on a network. PBNM solutions can help by simplifying the enforcement of policies that clamp down on these abuses and prevent them from happening.

The worrisome form of resource abuse is when unauthorized users attempt to gain access to corporate information. A variant of this is when malicious users attempt to disrupt the operation of the network by either a denial of service attack or by sending a worm or virus into the network. PBNM can help categorize traffic into expected and unexpected types and assign rules to deal with each. For example, if a web-based virus is detected, a PBNM product can easily shut down the ability for routers to forward web traffic. This helps contain the problem while it is being diagnosed.

The dangerous form of resource abuse is when an employee or similarly trusted user decides to willfully misuse his or her privileges and violate a company's intellectual property rights. Studies show that the greatest threats to intellectual property come from within a company. PBNM lets administrators restrict users to only those applications and information sources that they need during their current session.

Any one of these forms can stop unauthorized applications from using shared resources that they should not have access to. For example, if the goal is to meet a particular SLA that has availability levels specified, the seemingly innocent use of the network to download research information may cause periods of congestion that cause the SLA to fail. An SLA is a business concept. Therefore, it makes sense to let the business and IT personnel define which users can use which shared resources. This allows the company to define its network utilization based on the real requirements of the business contract.

PBNM solutions are a good match for business policies that seek to optimize the performance of the network—the PBNM tools can be used to catch such unwanted occurrences and help ensure that the SLA is met. PBNM solutions can also be used to reveal traffic usage patterns, so that policies can be fine-tuned on an ongoing basis.

The common thread in all of these examples is that PBNM tools operate by first classifying traffic. Just as classification is used to decide what type of traffic conditioning to give to a particular flow, it can also be used to determine whether a particular user can access a resource or not. Depending on the capabilities of the PBNM tool, it may be able to do even more. For example, some PBNM tools can perform "deep packet inspection" and examine the contents of URLs. Security improvements can be done if the PBNM tool enables administrators to write policies to perform these checks and actions.

7.6.3 Managing Device Complexity

Network devices can be classified along several different dimensions. Some of the more important ways of classifying network devices are:

- What is the role of this device? For example, will it be on the edge or in the core? Is it a border router?
- What is the physical capacity of this device? For example, how much of a particular resource (e.g., number of ports) does a device have?
- What is the logical capacity of this device? For example, how many VPNs can a particular device support?
- What is the programming model (e.g., CLI, SNMP, TL1, etc.) used to program the device?
- What is the programming model used to monitor the device?
- Which version of the operating system is this device going to use?
- What are the critical features (i.e., commands) that this device must support?
- Which types of cards are available for this device?
- Is the configuration small enough to fit in flash memory, or does it require RAM?
- Which types of services are planned to be activated on this device?

This is a very short list of many of the different factors that need to be considered. An information model is well-suited for managing this complexity, as it is able to represent these different device characteristics, and relate them to each other. For example, the simplified DEN-ng model shown in Figure 7.10 provides separate physical and logical resource models. Associations and constraints can be defined that relate different logical features to different physical features, thereby building up a more complete picture of the device. Similarly, policy can be applied to control which combinations of features can be used in a given situation. Separating the different domain models (e.g., physical resource from logical resource in the preceding example) enables each domain model to change without adversely impacting the other domain models. All that needs to be updated are the relationships between the different domain models. Furthermore, the ability to work on each domain model in parallel enables the information model to be more rapidly updated to accommodate new devices.

The benefit of using an information model to model device features and functionality is that this method is robust enough to justify the investment in understanding the capabilities of the information model. It provides a robust starting point for managing device and service complexity and offers an extensible and scalable platform to accommodate the future requirements of new devices and services.

7.6.4 Managing Complex Traffic and Services

The world has changed. Today, more types of applications are available that generate more types of traffic than ever before. Some sophisticated applications generate several types of traffic of different types (e.g., H.323 traffic, which generates both UDP and TCP flows). Other applications provide unpredictable behavior (e.g., they open random ports for communication).

In addition, networks have increased in complexity. Security is more important than ever, because a network can carry many different types of traffic. Many of the individual flows representing this traffic load have different requirements. In the typical converged network (i.e., a network that carries data, voice, and video application traffic), some of the flows are sensitive to delay and jitter, whereas others are not. Thus, different flows require different types of traffic conditioning. For example, using any of the weighted fair queuing approaches will adversely affect voice traffic. Instead, voice traffic demands priority queuing so that jitter, latency, and delay can be controlled. However, if priority queuing is used for data traffic, relatively unimportant flows can swamp the priority queue and effectively starve other types of traffic. As another example, some traffic is classified as mission critical. If this traffic is to share the same network resources, then it demands completely different treatment to avoid compromising its usage.

Therefore, simply throwing bandwidth at network traffic is no longer the answer (not that it ever was for certain types of flows, such as SNA traffic, but people keep stubbornly associating PBNM with bandwidth). The real problem that network administrators face today is how to enable multiple applications that each demand slightly different resources from the network to not just peacefully coexist, but to work and consume shared resources according to their importance.

PBNM solutions are natural choices for these types of applications. PBNM solutions are predicated on analyzing traffic and classifying it into one of several predefined categories. Each category will correspond to preprovisioned traffic conditioning that is suited to the type of traffic that is being carried by that application. Advanced network technologies, such as MPLS or DiffServ (or even both), can be used to mark this traffic so that appropriate traffic conditioning is applied.

7.6.5 Handling Traffic More Intelligently

Because PBNM solutions rely on classification, they provide the opportunity to make other more intelligent decisions regarding how to handle all types of traffic. In addition to deciding how the flow is to be conditioned, the classification decision itself can be used to help direct different types of traffic. For example:

- Nonauthorized users, as well as other forms of unwanted traffic, can be denied access to network resources. This is not to say that firewalls or VPNs are no longer needed; rather, it means that an additional measure of security is present and available.
- Business-critical applications can be identified immediately and transported using special mechanisms, such as policy-based routing (i.e., based on a classification decision, traffic can be instructed to use a special path that normal traffic is not allowed to use).

Many more examples could be given. PBNM solutions provide the inherent intelligence to be used to accomplish more tasks than those that were originally intended.

7.6.6 Performing Time-Critical Functions

PBNM solutions can simplify and better implement two basic types of time-critical network functions.

1. Changing device configurations within a specific time-window
2. Performing scheduled provisioning functions

The first point reflects the need to address common maintenance functions. Most organizations perform maintenance operations on their network at night or during other nonbusiness hours to avoid any inadvertent adverse effects on the operation of network services. The second point addresses small, simple changes for a specific customer or set of customers. This is the "network equivalent" of setting up a conference call.

Part of the allure of PBNM solutions is that they can address both of these functions.

7.7 SUMMARY

This chapter provided a quick retrospective on how PBNM was designed. Despite many of its early limitations, such as being a single-vendor approach and being focused on a particular technology, great promise was envisioned for PBNM solutions. Accordingly, vendors poured resources into making various types of policy solutions, and the press hyped these new solutions.

Unfortunately, these early solutions were misunderstood and were quickly developed without supporting technology and, most importantly, standards. Interoperability was destroyed, and PBNM started to get a bad reputation.

Fortunately, the TMF rejuvenated this effort. It brought a completely different approach—one predicated on tying policy to an architecture that used a shared information model—to the forefront. The TMF's NGOSS architecture emphasized the importance of business rules and processes, something that was lacking in previous efforts. Furthermore, it resurrected early work done using viewpoints to help provide an integrated, multifaceted approach for defining policy. This was picked up by the TMF's SID effort. The SID is a federated approach that incorporates DEN-ng and other models and information definitions. *The result is that policy has reemerged as a new approach that is tightly integrated with other domain models.*

The DEN-ng effort was based on this premise. It added additional insight, such as the use of a policy continuum and a finite state machine, to transform it to a *collected set of models, each of which represented a state of a managed object. Policy, then, was redefined as the means to control when a managed object transitioned to a new state.*

With this introduction in place, the motivation for PBNM was examined in more detail. Part of the allure of PBNM was its simplicity. Other benefits were also its ability to provide different services to different users, its promise of simplifying device, network, and service management, and its promise of requiring less engineers to do the work. Newer promises, such as helping to define the behavior of a system and managing the ever-increasing complexity of devices and services, were added.

However, the true breakthrough was when PBNM was defined as a means for business rules to drive the configuration of the network. This brought forth the promise of changing the network from a cost center to a profit center. Although the other benefits are very important, they only incrementally affect profitability. Transforming the network into a profit center is very compelling, as it affects the bottom line of the entire organization.

To complete this transformation, two key ingredients were needed. The first was the establishment of a shared information model. This was needed for many reasons, but one of the most important ones was interoperability. Modern-day OSSs are not purchased from a single vendor, as they are too complex. Instead, they are built from best-of-breed applications. For these applications to scale, they should be constructed as components. For the components to share and reuse data, they need to use the same data, defined in a "universal language" that any OSS component that needs to share data can use. This universal language takes the form of a layered information model. DEN-ng and the SID are part of that solution.

The second ingredient is a revolution in how management applications are built. Management applications should be constructed using models to define their data and architecture. This revolutionary idea is epitomized by the NGOSS architecture. Its design process uses four viewpoints—business, system, implementation, and runtime—to define the functionality and processes of the architecture. Interoperability is achieved using the SID and contracts, which define how data are communicated using XML.

Finally, five new benefits of PBNM solutions were provided. Two focused on providing more intelligence to routing and managing traffic. Instead of over-provisioning the network and wasting valuable resources, policy-based network management can be used to intelligently assign different traffic to preprovisioned paths that already have the appropriate traffic conditioning in place. In addition, managing complex traffic and services, where different types of traffic having different needs compete for the same shared resources, can be efficiently managed using PBNM solutions.

Additional benefits were provided by realizing that the classification portion of PBNM solutions can be used for providing better security, accommodating the needs of confidential and mission-critical traffic, and others.

Finally, PBNM can be used to manage device complexity. Combined with an information model, a system can be built that can accommodate new types of devices that have new types of functionality by changing the information model and ensuring that software can be used to translate changes in the information model to code. In other words, the structure, GUI, and APIs of the application remain constant; only the internals (which are governed by the information model) change. An example of this new avant-garde application is the Intelliden R-Series.

7.8 RESOURCES

Alhir S., *UML in a Nutshell—A Desktop Quick Reference*. O'Reilly, 1998.

Faurer, C., J. Fleck, D. Raymer, J. Reilly, A. Smith, and J. Strassner, "NGOSS: Reducing the Interoperability Tax." TMW University Presentation, October 2002.

"GB921: eTOM—the Business Process Framework, version 2.6." *TeleManagement Forum*, March 2002 (TMF member document).

"GB922: Shared Information/Data (SID) Model: Concepts, Principles, and Business Entities and Model Addenda v1.5." *TeleManagement Forum*, May 2002 (TMF member document).

"GB922: Common Business Entity Definitions Addenda 1P." *TeleManagement Forum*, May 2002 (TMF member document).

ISO, "RM-ODP Part 1. Overview and Rationale." ISO/IEC 10746-1:1998(E).

Jude, M., "Policy-Based Management: Beyond the Hype." *Business Communications Review*, March:52–56, 2001.

Moore, B., D. Durham, J. Strassner, A. Westerinen, and W. Weiss, "Information Model for Describing Network Device QoS Datapath Mechanisms." Draft-ietf-policy-qos-device-info-model-08.txt, May 2002.

Moore, B., L. Rafalow, Y. Ramberg, Y. Snir, A. Westerinen, R. Chadha, M. Brunner, R. Cohen, and J. Strassner, "Policy Core Information Model Extensions." Draft-ietf-policy-pcim-ext-06.txt, November 2001.

"The NGOSS™ Technology Neutral Architecture Specification, Annex C: Behavior and Control Specification." *TeleManagement Forum*, TMF 053, version 0.4, November 2002.

"The NGOSS™ Technology Neutral Architecture Specification, Annex P: Policy Specification." *The TeleManagement Forum*, TMF 05, version 0.3, work in progress.

"The NGOSS™ Technology Neutral Architecture Specification." *TeleManagement Forum*, TMF 053, version 3.0, April 2003.

Reyes, A., A. Barba, D. Moron, M. Brunner, and M. Pana, "Policy Core Extension LDAP Schema." Draft-reyes-policy-core-ext-schema-02.txt, June 2003.

RFC 2474, "Definition of the Differentiated Services Field (DS Field) in the IPv4 and IPv6 Headers." Nichols, K., S. Blake, F. Baker, and D. Black, December 1998.

RFC 3060, "Policy Core Information Model—Version 1 Specification." Moore, B., E. Ellesson, J. Strassner, and A. Westerinen, February 2001.

Rumbaugh, J., I. Jacobson, and G. Booch, *The Unified Modeling Language Reference Manual*. Addison-Wesley, 1999.

Snir, Y., Y. Ramberg, J. Strassner, R. Cohen, and B. Moore, "Policy QoS Information Model." Draft-ietf-policy-qos-info-model-04.txt, November 2001.

Strassner, J., *Directory Enabled Networks*, Chapter 10. Macmillan Technical Publishing, 1999.

Strassner, J., "A New Paradigm for Network Management: Business Driven Network Management." Presented at the SSGRR Summer Conference, L'Aquila, Italy, July 2002.

Strassner, J., "NGOSS Technology Overview." TMW Asia-Pacific Conference, August 2002.

Strassner, J., B. Moore, R. Moats, and E. Ellesson, "Policy Core LDAP Schema." Draft-ietf-policy-core-ldap-schema16.txt, October 2002.

The UML 1.4 specification is downloadable (see *www.ibm.com/software/rational/*).

The home page of the definition of the Differentiated Services working group of the IETF is *www.ietf.org/html.charters/OLD/diffserv-charter.html*.

Low-latency queuing combines strict priority queuing with class-based weighted fair queuing; see *www.cisco.com/en/US/products/sw/iosswrel/ps1830/products_feature_guide09186a0080087b13.html*.

An innovation policy-driven configuration management and activation product can be seen at *www.intelliden.com*.

QoS Policy Usage Examples in Policy-Based Network Management

8

This chapter, using extracts from Chapter 10 of *Policy-Based Network Management* by John Strassner, provides several examples of how policy is used in a system. The policy continuum figures prominently in the recommended approach for building Policy-Based Network Management (PBNM) systems because it enables the business, system, and implementation views to be seamlessly integrated. In addition, the multiple uses of policy will be emphasized through examples in this chapter.

8.1 INTRODUCTION

The purpose of this chapter is to show how policy is used in different situations in PBNM systems. There are two ways that policy is commonly described. One group of people thinks of policy as a way to change lines in the configuration file of a device. Another group of people thinks of policy as only appropriate for expressing rules in the business world.

Of course, both are right. Unfortunately, neither of these represents the use of the full potential of how policy can be used. The Directory Enabled Networks-new generation (DEN-ng) concept of policy is epitomized through the use of the policy continuum. The policy continuum is the basis for defining how policy is defined and used for different constituencies, ranging from the business analyst to the system designer to the network administrator. These uses, as well as others that are suited for different users of the policy continuum, constitute the potential of PBNM. The holistic use of the policy continuum, and its ability to integrate the needs of the business and system worlds, is key to realizing the potential of PBNM solutions.

This chapter focuses on using policy to manage, as well as control, the configuration of devices. The policy continuum will be used to express policies at different levels of abstraction and integrate them together to form a cohesive set of policies.

8.2 POLICY APPROACHES

There are two fundamentally different approaches that can be used to develop a PBNM system. They can be categorized as static versus dynamic. In either case, it is important to note that this categorization is based on how the policies are *applied*: In both cases the policies remain *constant*—it is the *environment* that is changing. Thus, the approaches differ in how the environment is to be controlled.

8.2.1 Static versus Dynamic

Static approaches are also called pre-provisioned approaches. Here, the idea is to pre-provision the network according to some predefined scheme and plan into that pre-provisioning the ability for different behaviors to take effect when conditions warrant. The classic example of this is to use Differentiated Services (DiffServ) to define traffic conditioning according to different predefined levels (e.g., Gold, Silver, and Bronze) and group traffic into sets whose forwarding behavior (i.e., how the packet is treated within the router between its input and output interfaces) is the same. This is done by applying various rules to classify traffic at the edge and "mark" it (via setting appropriate bit values in the IP header) according to a set of predefined "code points." These code points define a particular type of forwarding behavior (e.g., dropping, metering, policing, shaping, queuing, and scheduling) that should be applied.

Dropping means the selective dropping of packets, whether randomly or algorithmically. This is used to tell TCP-based traffic to slow down the transmission rate. Metering is the act of limiting the amount of incoming traffic to a predefined rate, and is also called "rate limiting." Policing combines metering with dropping and optionally (re-)marking to indicate that further conditioning is necessary to downstream elements. Shaping is similar to policing, except that it is applied on the egress (whereas policing is applied on the ingress) and contains buffering of packets (policing does not provide any buffering). Queuing is the act of delaying the transmission of a packet by storing it and possibly transmitting the packet in a different order than it was received. Scheduling is the act of defining which packet to send from which queue when the interface is free.

The essence of a static approach is to allow changes in the environment to be accommodated by the rules embedded in the network. In other words, policies are used to initially provision the network, and then the network runs on "autopilot" until something significant happens that requires the download of new policies. This works based on the ability to program complex behaviors into the network that "do the right thing" in response to small or medium environmental changes. For example, DiffServ has the notion of "drop probabilities" within a particular class. As traffic rate increases, the probability of dropping a packet increases. When a packet is dropped, and the application sending the packet is a TCP-based application, then the dropping of a packet causes the transmission rate of the application to be slowed. Thus, we have a simple self-regulating mechanism that is appropriate for many types of traffic. (Note that I said "many types of traffic" and not *all* types of traffic.) Clearly, dropping packets in a VoIP application corresponds to dropping parts of a conversation, which is not desirable.

What if "doing the right thing" is too complicated in order to be pre-provisioned? This is where dynamic approaches are used. Note that DiffServ can also be used in a dynamic approach. For example, suppose that the input interface of a DiffServ router is monitored in order to observe the number of input flows, and a policy exists that will change the traffic conditioning based on statistics of this interface, such as number of packets dropped. This has the effect of dynamically adjusting a pre-provisioned mechanism. Note that the policy itself is static—it is the changing statistics that cause the policy to be invoked.

However, the classic example of a dynamic mechanism is of course signaling, such as with the Resoure Reservation Protocol (RSVP). In this approach, a client asks for a new feature from the network, such as additional bandwidth. The client signals its need of this new feature by explicitly asking for new bandwidth. This, of course, requires a decision to be made as to whether this request should be granted or not. Such requests cannot be "pre-provisioned," since they cannot be anticipated beforehand.

8.2.2 A Better Taxonomy: Proactive versus Reactive

Clearly, these approaches can be mixed. One can adjust pre-provisioned features just as easily as one can pre-provision certain additional features that are not invoked until necessary. Thus, a better way to categorize these approaches is by classifying them as proactive versus reactive.

Proactive changes generally take the form of changing the configuration of a device by pushing a new set of commands to it. Proactive changes are usually implemented as an attempt to avoid an undesirable state. For example, there are many different ways to condition traffic. Not only can traffic be rate-limited at the input (often called "policing"), it can also be regulated at the output (often called "shaping"). The network devices can be preprogrammed to perform either of these functions, or the network can be programmed to incorporate these functions at any desired time. Typically, this is done in a closed-loop fashion by observing traffic patterns and comparing them with desired traffic patterns.

Note that this is simply another variation of using a Finite State Machine (FSM)—a device dropping too many packets can be thought of as being in an undesirable state. Thus, we can use one or more policies to develop configuration changes that alter the traffic conditioning functions of the device in such a way as to stop the dropping of too many packets. This set of configuration changes can be thought of as transitioning the state of the network device back to an allowed state.

Reactive mechanisms enable parts of the network to offer high QoS guarantees without having to over-provision those parts of the network that need to offer additional guarantees. Traditionally, specialized protocols, such as RSVP, were used to convey those additional guarantees.

Advantages and Disadvantages of Proactive Mechanisms

One of the important advantages of proactive mechanisms is that sets of them can be easily configured to define how to change device configurations given an event and/ or condition. Once these changes are implemented in the network, the network can then run in a relatively hands-off manner. Another important advantage is scalability. As will be seen, signaling and other reactive mechanisms come with a relatively high price: the maintaining of individual state for each device that is participating in a signaling path. Proactive mechanisms don't require such state because they represent decisions taken to implement a predefined set of behaviors.

The main drawback to proactive mechanisms is that they cannot have any idea of which resources specific applications entering at different points of the network need. This will tend to waste precious shared resources. (i.e., instead of efficiently allocating extra resources exactly where they are needed, proactive systems will configure entire portions of the network to act a particular way).

Advantages and Disadvantages of Reactive Mechanisms

The obvious advantage of reactive mechanisms is that they provide a way to explicitly signal additional needs on demand. As we will see, this enables a more efficient use of the network. However, signaling mechanisms offer several important additional advantages that shouldn't be discounted.

Signaled information is, by definition, additional information that is to be applied to a particular flow or set of flows. The beauty of signaled information is that it can traverse the same network path as the traffic that it is intended to manage. This additional specificity differentiates it from proactive mechanisms, since the latter by definition cannot usually be linked to specific paths. Thus, the advantage of signaling mechanisms is that specific QoS needs for specific paths can be easily communicated. Furthermore, if the needs cannot be met for some reason anywhere along the path, an explicit notification can be provided. This enables an application to pinpoint exactly where it cannot get the QoS that it desires, which enables the application to either search for a different path, accept degraded QoS, or postpone its request.

The most important advantage of reactive mechanisms is the ability to embed additional information into the signaling mechanism. That is, in addition to requesting (for example) additional bandwidth, RSVP can be used to carry additional information, such as user and application information. This is described in many different RFCs. Identity representation can be used to securely identify the owner and the application of the communicating process in RSVP messages in a secure manner. Policy elements can be used to identify different application traffic flows, and a preemption priority policy element can be defined to assign a relative importance, or ranking, within the set of flows competing for preferential treatment.

The importance of signaling here is that without signaling, such information is typically unavailable. For example, user information is not available in standard packet headers. Even if it was, it and other types of information (such as application identification) would typically be hidden by the use of IPsec, which is often used to secure traffic. The ability to signal information can greatly simplify management, because typically, services are allocated in terms of users and applications. This provides us important information to be able to map users and applications to terms that are recognizable to network devices, such as IP addresses and ports.

Of course, nothing in life is free. The advantages of reactive mechanisms such as signaling come with several attendant costs. The first is additional setup and processing time for all devices, hosts, and end systems that are using the mechanism. Thus, the first rule is to not use such mechanisms for short-lived flows, or the flow is likely to be finished before the network is finished being (dynamically) configured.

A second-order effect from this additional setup and processing time is an increase in network traffic due to the increased overhead required so that signaling can be used. Thus, for this method to be effective, flows using signaling should ideally generate much more traffic than is required to set up their traffic conditioning.

However, the main problem with such mechanisms is the need to carry state information for each device participating in the flow. Otherwise, the device has no idea whether it should grant the use of additional resources, how long to grant them for, and other factors.

The Solution: Use Both

Integration of these two approaches is being discussed in several forums. One good example is the IETF ISSLL working group, which was formed to address (in part) how to integrate these two efforts—Integrated and Differentiated Services. There are several important works that form part of the output of this working group that define how this can be done. Integrated Services (IntServ) can be supported over a Differentiated Services network. This in effect provides the best of both worlds. For example, different RSVP flows can be aggregated and tunneled over a common DiffServ network.

There are other important variations of this general theme. For example, a single RSVP reservation could be used to aggregate other RSVP reservations across a common transit routing region.

8.2.3 The Role of Policy

Policies are essential to the use of either proactive or reactive models. Policies enable configuration changes, such as how many resources are to be applied for any given use. For this to be done, however, we need to revisit the notion of policy subjects and policy targets. The definitions of these two terms are as follows:

A policy subject is a set of entities that is the focus of the policy. The subject can make policy decision and information requests, and it can direct policies to be enforced at a set of policy targets.

A policy target is a set of entities that a set of policies will be applied to. The objective of applying policy is to either maintain the current state of the policy target, or to transition the policy target to a new state.

Using these definitions, we see that policy subjects are the controlling entities in the policy equation, with policy targets being the means by which policies can be used to change the behavior of the system. However, applying policy correctly is more complicated than it appears.

Equating Different Views of the Same Policy

The first problem is that different policy subjects have different views of the network. Thus, unless a common unifying factor (such as FSM) is used, the same policy executed by different policy subjects could have markedly different behavior. The most likely cause of this would be because the different policy subjects would make different decisions because they were monitoring different objects. The advantage of using a FSM in this case would be to enable the different contexts to be mapped to the same state.

Capability Mapping

The next and bigger problem is that different devices have different capabilities. This manifests itself in several different ways. For example, two different devices could have different commands and/or different features. This makes it very difficult to use these devices to condition the same flows in concert.

Consider two devices that have slightly different capabilities. The same policy cannot be applied unaltered to both devices, unless the different capabilities have the exact same command. This is highly unlikely if the devices have different end-user capabilities. But the problem is actually more involved than this. Mapping to the same commands assumes that each device is able to process the same events and respond to the same conditions. This means that for each of the three fundamental building blocks of a policy (event, condition, and action clauses), a mapping must be done to define equivalent functions in each device. Furthermore, it also assumes that the end result of executing the policy has the same side effects. This is in general a bad assumption to make in this case. The presence of different capabilities is often a good indication that the devices internally are implemented quite differently. For example, turning on fancy queuing might have different effects due to different implementations.

As another example, consider the subfunction of classification. Suppose the two devices both need to classify traffic, and the policy uses Differentiated Services Code Points (DSCP) to specify how the device is supposed to classify traffic.

If one of the devices is not capable of handling DiffServs, then neither device will be able to read the policy and perform the classification portion of the policy (which may be part of the condition or action clauses). Cases like this can be mitigated somewhat using the policy continuum. Deciding that DSCPs should be used is a technology-specific feature. This means that there are two levels above the continuum (the business and system levels, to be exact) that each contain a higher-level specification of this classification function. Thus, a sophisticated PBNM system could refer to the original policy continuum to retrieve a higher-level specification of the classification function. (Note that in this example, it is important to ensure that the values of the DSCPs map to the, more limited, values of the other mechanism, for example type of service (ToS); otherwise, the devices cannot be guaranteed of performing the same actions.)

Accommodating Device Limitations

While different capabilities make it difficult to ensure that different devices are performing the same function, often devices have a set of restrictions or limitations that must be accounted for when a policy is translated. Two common examples are rule depth and condition complexity.

Rule depth manifests itself by limiting the number of rules that can be loaded or executed at a given time. There may be many reasons for this, such as a lack of memory or processing power. The problem lies in the complexity of the environment that the PBNM system component is operating in. Often, complex environments require many different rules to be executing concurrently. The only real solution to this problem is to try and reformulate or combine rules so that the limitations of the device do not adversely affect the deployment of the policy rules.

Condition complexity refers to how many different condition expressions are in a single condition clause, as well as how many different types of operators are used to combine different expressions into a single clause. Both of these factors can restrict the complexity of the condition that can be implemented by a device. Sometimes, conditions can be simplified by converting to a different representation. For example, in Boolean logic, there are some expressions that are very difficult to implement using conjunctive normal form (i.e., a Boolean expression defined as a logical ANDing of logical ORed terms), yet fairly simple to implement using disjunctive normal form (i.e., a Boolean expression defined as a logical ORing of logical ANDed terms). Options such as these should be used to see if the condition can be translated into a form that the PBNM system component can handle. Otherwise, the only recourse is for the PBNM system component to inform the rest of the system that it is unable to process that condition or rule.

Accommodating Different Programming Models

Different devices can also have different programming models that make controlling them together very difficult. This takes the following two very different forms.

1. Two different devices use completely different programming models, yet both need to participate in implementing or enforcing a particular policy. The most common example is where one device uses a vendor-specific command-line interface (CLI), while the other device uses Simple Network Management Protocol (SNMP). The obvious problem is that there is no common information model that equates the actions of the vendor-specific CLI commands to the actions of the SNMP commands.

2. A device uses one programming model to configure a function and a different programming model to monitor that same function. Without the use of a common information model, it will be very difficult to correlate the same concepts in each programming model.

In either case, the PBNM system must provide a mapping between the commands of these different programming models. It is highly recommended that a single common information model, such as DEN-ng, be used to do this. In fact, DEN-ng has a model wherein CLI, SNMP, TL1, and other management methods can be used as part of the same overall task. These and other problems greatly complicate PBNM system design. This is why policy and information modeling need to be used together to solve these problems.

8.2.4 Abstracting Network Interface Management into Network Service Management

One of the important ideas behind policy management is that policies control services. This means that the programming of network device interfaces is of secondary importance—the main objective is to provision a service. This is a fundamentally different approach than currently used in most management systems. Figure 8.1 shows how current network management systems program network services. In this approach, a set of n management applications are responsible for programming a set of m device interfaces. Note in particular that a given management application may be responsible for programming multiple device interfaces from multiple devices.

The problem with this approach is that network services are not being programmed. Rather, device interfaces are being programmed. This means that the burden of constructing a network service is placed on the administrator. Specifically, the administrator must know which applications can manage which device interfaces, how to build part of a service on a device interface, and what role each device interface plays in the construction of the network's services.

Figure 8.2 shows how current network management systems program network services. In this approach, the objective is for the PBNM system to program the network service directly. Clearly, device interfaces are still programmed. However, they are no longer the primary focus—the service is instead the primary focus.

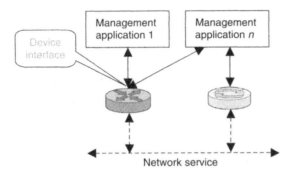

FIGURE 8.1

Current approaches program device interfaces (as shown), not network services.

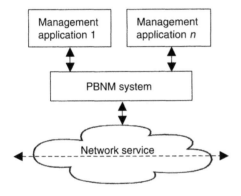

FIGURE 8.2

The PBNM system to program the network service directly.

In the figure, the Element Management Layer (EML) of traditional TMN systems is still there. The point, however, is that in the PBNM approach, the EML is just another way to instruct the device to do something. This is radically different than the purpose of the EML in traditional TMN systems, which is to control and manage the set of devices. This shift reflects the fact that the PBNM approach views the network as a provider of services, and therefore needs to define the service first and then instruct the device what to do to meet the needs of the service.

In the TMN approach, the EML is the focus because the service is present only in the brains of the designers. There is no "service" when the device is being programmed by CLI through a device interface, because there is no view or definition of the service in the CLI! (This also applies to SNMP, TL1, and other programming models.) Rather, there is only a view of what that particular device interface can do.

Thus, in the PBNM approach, the PBNM system as a whole is responsible for programming the network service. It abstracts the task of programming individual device interfaces. Put another way, policy in a PBNM system is used to control a set of policy targets that collectively provide a network service. This means that each policy target must interpret the policy (and the policy rules that make up the policy) in the same way.

This enables a different approach to building a network service to be taken compared to the nonpolicy approach shown in Figure 8.1. Specifically, the PBNM approach can model the semantics of a network service, such as the relationship between the roles played by different objects supplying the network service, directly. This is usually impossible to do using a non-PBNM approach because the methods used (e.g., CLI and SNMP) do not have the concept of a role, or constructs that show directly the dependencies and relationships between different objects that support a service.

8.3 QOS POLICY USAGE EXAMPLES

This section will use the results of the previous section to provide three different examples of how PBNM systems can be used. Each of these three examples will be concerned with using policies to configure and enforce a particular type of QoS.

A common thread that emerges from these three application examples is that policy-based management does not solve the entire problem by itself. Just because a PBNM system is being used does not mean that people no longer have to understand how a network works! Rather, the point of policy-based management is to make life easier for the administrator.

For example, suppose that a network is shared by multiple departments. If it happens to be the end of the month, the finance department may need prioritized use of the network to ensure that its large (and very important) monthly reports are delivered on time. Without a PBNM system, the best that can be hoped for is for the network administrator to either ask other network users to limit usage of the network during these times, or for the network administrator to manually prioritize the traffic corresponding to the finance application. The former is very difficult, not just because human nature seeks empowerment and does not like being told what to do, but more importantly because it is very hard for a given user to understand what impact (if any) the application that they are running will have on the finance application. The latter is manually intensive and therefore error-prone.

PBNM is thus a means for the network administrator to proactively manage the network, as opposed to reacting to how users are using the network.

8.3.1 Providing Differentiated Services for Applications Using a Shared Network

The objective is to enable different applications to get different service levels from a common network, according to some prioritized usage defined by policy. We are interested in providing this preferential access because without predictable response for different types of applications, it is impossible to offer value-added services that people will buy. We therefore have at a minimum two distinct uses of policies:

1. Policy to define which application gets which type of service
2. Policy to define how the traffic belonging to a particular application is conditioned

Conceptually, what we want to do is to classify which applications should get priority treatment. We will define priority treatment as the ability to gain preferred access to shared network resources. Assuming that we have many different applications (say, 20), we decide that we will aggregate traffic into three different classes: Gold, Silver, and Bronze. Our traffic will be assigned to the "Gold" class, meaning that it will always get preferential use of shared resources.

One way of satisfying these goals is to detect the traffic emitted by various applications, and then mark those packets according to a scheme wherein the traffic of each application is placed into a particular class of service (CoS). Traffic from each CoS gets appropriately conditioned so as to provide a level of preferred access to shared resources. This is illustrated in simplified form in Figure 8.3.

Note that all of the different traffic conditioning functions are not shown in Figure 8.3 for the sake of simplicity. The point of this basic approach is that at the edge, we apply complex conditioning functions to classify traffic into different

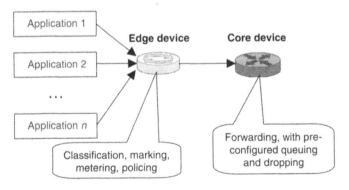

FIGURE 8.3

Basic traffic conditioning functions.

groups, or aggregates. We may do some basic policing and other functions to limit the rate and volume of traffic to conform to the capabilities in the core of our network, but this is done so as to make the job of classification more effective. Once the traffic hits the core of the network, the job of the routers is to forward traffic as fast as possible. They may apply queuing and dropping functions, as specified by the packet markings that they receive, to adjust traffic as necessary so as to satisfy CoS parameters. However, their main goal is to forward traffic. Hence, we can use the simplified representation shown in Figure 8.3.

This idyllic situation is complicated by the fact that some applications generate more than one type of traffic. For example, H.323 traffic generates many types of different TCP and UDP traffic flows. Database applications routinely open ports on demand that do not conform to a predefined set of port numbers. These and other factors make it very difficult to efficiently classify a particular flow as belonging to a given application.

Clearly, it is wasteful to classify all of those flows with the same marking. However, it is important that different flows receive the conditioning that they need in order for the overall application to have the desired end-user experience. Thus, we need some intelligence in the PBNM system that knows that different flows corresponding to a single application can have different markings, as long as the overall traffic conditioning for that particular application meets the objectives of its CoS.

This approach to providing Differentiated Services is what the DiffServ working group set out to accomplish. DiffServ describes a set of QoS capabilities that can be delivered from one end of the network to another.

8.3.2 The DiffServ Approach

DiffServ is an approach that instructs the network to deliver a particular kind of service based on the QoS marking specified by each packet. This specification is made using the 6-bit DSCP setting in IP packets or source and destination addresses. The DSCP is a tag that instructs each device in the network to perform appropriate traffic conditioning functions, such as metering, shaping, dropping and queuing.

DiffServ defines four per-hop behaviors (PHBs). A PHB is defined as the externally observable forwarding behavior applied at a DiffServ-compliant node to a DiffServ behavior aggregate (remember, packets from multiple sources or applications can belong to the same behavior aggregate). The four standard PHBs are:

- Default PHB
- Class-selector PHB
- Assured forwarding (AF) PHB
- Expedited forwarding (EF) PHB

The default PHB specifies that a packet marked with this DSCP will receive the traditional best-effort service from a DiffServ-compliant node. Packets arriving at a DS-compliant node whose DSCP value is not mapped to any other PHB will also get mapped to the default PHB.

The class-selector PHB is a set of DSCPs intended to preserve backward-compatibility with any IP precedence scheme currently in use on the network. These class-selector PHBs retain most of the forwarding behavior as nodes that implement IP precedence-based classification and forwarding. Class-selector PHBs ensure that DS-compliant nodes can coexist with IP precedence-based nodes. This set of PHBs enable routers that are compliant with DiffServ to be used with routers that are not compliant with DiffServ but are compliant with ToS.

Note that from the DEN-ng point of view, this is *not* a complete mapping. While this does identify the basic functionality that needs to be supported by both types of routers, it does not define the complete behavior and semantics of each router. For example, it does not take into account side effects, such as resources consumed, of a router. Often, the functionality of a router is diminished when an advanced type of queuing is being run, due to the increased resources needed to support the advanced queuing function. DEN-ng seeks to model these and other features as *capabilities* that are either available or not available; any dependencies, as well as pre- and postconditions that arise from using that particular capability, are also modeled.

The assured forwarding PHB is nearly equivalent to controlled load service available in the IntServ model and is used to define a method by which different behavior aggregates can be given different forwarding assurances. This is usually done by first defining the type of buffering that will be used and then allocating a percentage of the available bandwidth per class. Since different applications have different characteristics, different buffering and queuing strategies are employed. For example, one would not use class-based weighted fair queuing for voice because it is too fair (meaning that it will not properly discriminate voice traffic and attempt to fairly interleave voice packets with other application packets) and will not be able to deliver the latency and jitter guarantees that voice requires.

As stated previously, the purpose of defining a behavior aggregate is to group different applications together that have the same general characteristics. The AF specification defines three drop precedence values that you can use (within each class) to further differentiate between different types of applications. If the applications are all TCP-based, then dropping a packet tells the application to slow down its transmission rate. In effect, this penalizes traffic flows within a particular behavior aggregate that exceed their assigned bandwidth.

Finally, the EF PHB can be used to provide a guaranteed bandwidth service. Applications such as voice over IP (VoIP), video, and online trading programs require this kind of service. The EF PHB specifies a low loss, low latency, low jitter, and assured bandwidth service.

Figure 8.4 shows a simplified view of the DEN-ng model to represent these concepts.

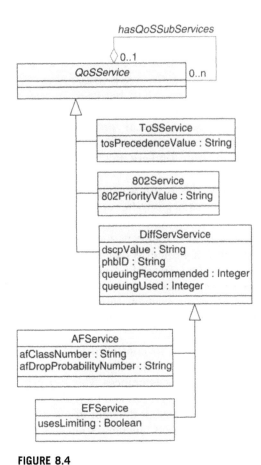

FIGURE 8.4

Simplified DEN-ng DiffServ model.

Using DEN-ng to Help Implement DiffServ

Although the different types of services are specified by DiffServ, the specific implementation (e.g., queuing and dropping algorithms) for each service is *not* specified. The EF and AF specifications "hint" that class-based weighted fair queuing and priority queuing, respectively, should be used, but neither mandates the use of a particular type of algorithm. This is where the information model can help standardize the implementation of these types of services. The idea is to define a template that specifies how a particular PHB will be implemented, and attempt to use this template with every instance of that particular service. If a particular device *foo* cannot support the exact features defined by this template, then the DEN-ng concept of *capabilities* can be used to map between the features that *foo* has and the desired features that are specified in the template.

For example, assume that there are different types of routers available in the network. Some are DiffServ-compliant, while others use different means (e.g., the ToS byte in the IP header) to recognize different types of traffic. Furthermore, assume that these different routers have different capabilities.

In this particular situation, DiffServ gets us part way to a solution, but it cannot specify the complete solution. This is because it only specifies the marking to be used to identify a PHB—it doesn't specify *how to implement* the PHB. Furthermore, it cannot be used to specify the implementation of how different device capabilities are mapped to each other. Finally, as pointed out above, it cannot be used to define what capabilities are no longer available when a given capability is used.

Thus, we arrive at the motivation for using an information model, such as DEN-ng, to represent DiffServ and other capabilities of network devices in a common representation. The DEN-ng information model was developed to facilitate normalization of functions (so that mapping between functions could be more easily accomplished) and to define dependencies and inter-relationships between functions using the notion of capabilities.

DEN-ng provides the ability to normalize different functions, and map them to device-specific implementations. For example, the information model can define "AF" (which is a particular DSCP) as being implemented with class-based weighted fair queuing, along with a particular set of values for weighted random early detection (a type of dropping algorithm). This corresponds to the "template" definition of this DSCP. If a particular device doesn't have class-based weighted fair queuing, but does have other types of queuing mechanisms, then the information model can identify these other types of queuing mechanisms and organize them under a common ontology. The PBNM system could then determine the set of queuing mechanisms that a given device has, and choose the appropriate one to use to implement AF for that device. Clearly, this method can be used for any desired function, not just queuing.

Since DEN-ng has the concept of a capability, it can relate any feature or function of a managed element being modeled to a capability of that managed element. This link enables relationships between one feature and other features to be established, which lets us define dependencies between these features. For example, capabilities can be used to specify the particular type of traffic conditioning that would be performed for a given type of traffic. Note that this doesn't replace DiffServ—rather, it enhances the use of DiffServ.

An example is shown in Figure 8.5, which represents a (very) simplified DEN-ng model for representing the relationships between QoS and other *ResourceFacingServices* and how they may be offered as a *ServiceBundle* to a *Customer*. This example model works as follows.

In DEN-ng, there are two basic types of services. *CustomerFacingServices* are services that customers purchase, whereas *ResourceFacingServices* are services that are not purchased directly by the customer but are still required to support a *CustomerFacingService*. This relationship is shown at the top of the hierarchy in Figure 8.4.

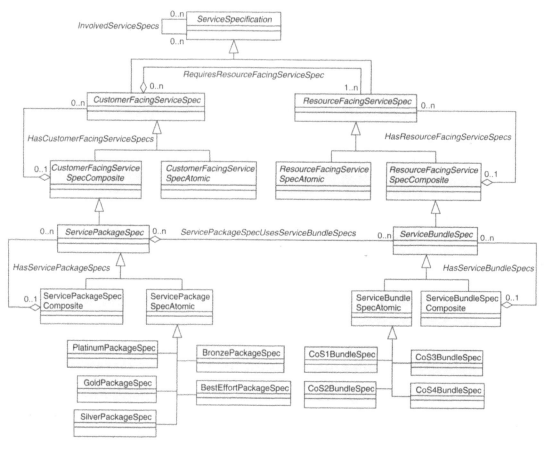

FIGURE 8.5

Information model for QoS service implementation.

For example, consider an MPLS VPN. Customers buy VPNs, so an MPLS VPN is an example of a *CustomerFacingService*. Further assume that this particular type of MPLS VPN is as defined in *RFC 4364*. This type of VPN mandates the use of Border Gateway Protocol (BGP) for route advertisement. However, service providers do not sell BGP. Thus, we also have the concept of a service that is related to the *CustomerFacingService* but is itself not sold. DEN-ng defines this as a *ResourceFacingService*. This enables the various supporting services that are needed to model a particular *CustomerFacingService* to be modeled (and, more importantly, to have their relationships established to the *CustomerFacing-Service*), while keeping the semantics between a *CustomerFacingService* and a *ResourceFacingService* separated.

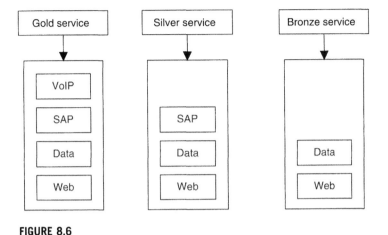

FIGURE 8.6

Bundling of CustomerFacingServices.

In this example, the service provider offers three different service packages—Gold, Silver, and Bronze—which may represent the grouping of services. This is illustrated in Figure 8.6. For instance, by grouping the same services into Bronze, Silver, and Gold, the service provider can represent better performance for the Gold services than the Silver services. Referring to Figure 8.6, we see that all three services are given Data services. The difference is that the quality of data service is best in Gold service and worst in Bronze service.

These different packages may also be used to represent access to a service not available at a lower level. For example, as represented in Figure 8.6, VoIP may be available only if the customer purchases Gold service.

The concept of a *ServiceBundle* enables the service provider to group a set of related services together as a package. Different *ServiceBundles* enable a service provider to model the concept of "upgrading" to a higher performance service bundle, in order to access new or better performing services.

The discussion so far has defined the set of classes necessary to build a class structure to represent different types of *services*. The next part of the discussion will examine how to represent QoS.

The next step in the process is to realize that each service in the *Service-Bundle* needs its own set of *QoSServices*. A set of *QoSServices* is needed because different devices with different capabilities are used as a set to provide a service. In this example, we had two different types of routers—one that used the ToS byte and one that used DSCPs—to indicate how to condition traffic. Therefore, a *service* in a *ServiceBundle* may need both *DiffServServices* as well as *ToSServices* (where *DiffServService* and *ToSService* represent a set of classification, marking, and traffic conditioning services based on using DSCPs and ToS settings, respectively). The job of the PBNM system is to recognize this and provide a means for all of these different services to be represented.

This process is formally defined in the DEN-ng model as follows. A *QoS Service* is a subclass of *ResourceFacingService*, which can be related to a *CustomerFacingService* through the *CFServiceRequiresRFServices* aggregation. This aggregation is used to define the set of *ResourceFacingServices* that are required to support a particular *CustomerFacingService*. Thus, we have the ability to define which set of *QoSServices* are required by any particular *CustomerFacingService*.

This is a powerful concept. For example, it enables a set of *CustomerFacing Services* to all use the same *QoSService*, thereby ensuring that their side effects will be very similar. In this example, the different *CustomerFacingServices* can still be distinguished from each other through the use of classification and marking, and traffic conditioning can similarly be assigned different values and hence different effect. However, the power of the DEN-ng design is that it *masks* these details from the business analyst. Thus, all the business analyst needs to be concerned with is which customer gets which level of QoS, not with how each level of QoS is implemented.

Alternatively, different *CustomerFacingServices* can use different *QoSServices*. The difference in the *CustomerFacingServices* is now explicit. Note, however, that the same fundamental services—classification, marking, and traffic conditioning—are provided in either case. This gives the network designer maximum flexibility in defining the set of network services that a particular customer receives.

We need some way to map between DSCPs and ToS settings. This can be done by using the information model to first define such a mapping and second, to relate instances of the *DiffServService* class to instances of the *ToSService* class. By ensuring that both *DiffServServices* and *ToSServices* are defined as *QoSServices*, they are identical from an abstract point-of-view. This is important because in each case they use a similar set of services that are keyed off of a marking in the IP header of the packet. The mark of a good information model is the ability to represent concepts that occur in the environment being modeled by simple, natural means. This abstraction is the first step in doing this.

We can define a mapping between values of a ToS byte and DSCP values by instantiating these two classes and writing simple OCL expressions to relate the eight different ToS settings to eight corresponding DSCP values. This by itself is important, but we need to define what these values mean. The problem that we face is that there is no standard that defines which specific services are required to implement the desired traffic conditioning. Thus, we represent this as two additional types of *ResourceFacingService—TrafficConditioningService* and *TrafficIdentificationService* classes.

TrafficIdentificationService and *TrafficConditioningService* abstract the fundamental processes of classifying and marking packets and defining how those packets are to be treated internally by the routers. However, we need a way to

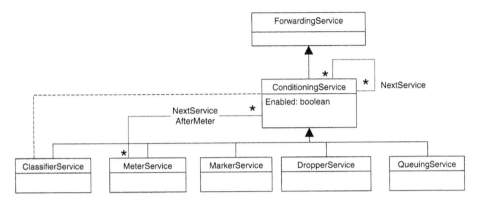

FIGURE 8.7

Simplified CIM representation of traffic conditioning and classification services.

describe the different mechanisms that can be used in implementing *DiffServ Services* and *ToSServices*. Therefore, DEN-ng defined the notion of a *Network ForwardingService*. This is the base class from which all functions that operate on network traffic in the forwarding path of a network device derive.

A previous attempt at modeling these features was built by the IETF and later modified by the DMTF. In simplified form, it looks as shown in Figure 8.7.

There are several problems with this model. First, classification and marking are mistakenly categorized as *ConditioningServices*. These two services have nothing to do with traffic conditioning. Furthermore, it does not differentiate between a metering service (also called a policer), which limits the traffic to a specified maximum rate, versus a shaper service, which delays transmission (by buffering the traffic) so that the total resulting traffic is limited to a particular value. The implementation of a policer versus a shaper has different architectural elements and different commands and therefore should be separated in the model.

In the DEN-ng model, neither the *ClassifierService* nor the *MarkerService* are *TrafficConditioningServices*. Rather, they are generalized services that perform the function of further identifying network traffic, through classification and packet marking. This was the motivation for calling them *TrafficIdentification Services* in the DEN-ng model. Note also that the two associations *NextService AfterMeter* and *NextServiceAfterClassifierElement* technically go to a subclass of *ClassifierService*, but this has been simplified in the figure.

This enables the *TrafficConditioningService* to focus on representing specific mechanisms inside the router that can be programmed by the PBNM system to supply different types of traffic conditioning. The key to specifying which traffic conditioning mechanisms are to be used is by marking the packets appropriately; this is represented by the *MarkerService* in the DEN-ng model of Figure 8.4. In order to mark the packets, the traffic must first be classified into different flows that may in turn be aggregated together, so that the same traffic conditioning can be applied to them. This is the purpose of the *ClassifierService*. A more complete portion of the DEN-ng QoS model, which shows these points, follows.

By defining a *TrafficConditioningService* class and a *TrafficIdentification Service* class as defined in Figure 8.8, we can relate one or more of each of these two types of *services* to a *DiffServService* as well as a *ToSService*. To be exact, we can define a particular set of *TrafficConditioningServices* and *TrafficIdentificationServices* to be used to implement a *DiffServService*, and either the same or a different set of *TrafficConditioningServices* and *TrafficIdentificationServices* to be used to implement a *ToSService* (or any other *QoSService*, for that matter).

Furthermore, the types as well as the values of *TrafficConditioningServices* and *TrafficIdentificationServices* can be different for the *DiffServService* compared to the *ToSService* (or any other *QoSService*, for that matter). For example, the *ToSService* could use a single *MeterService* with two attribute values, whereas

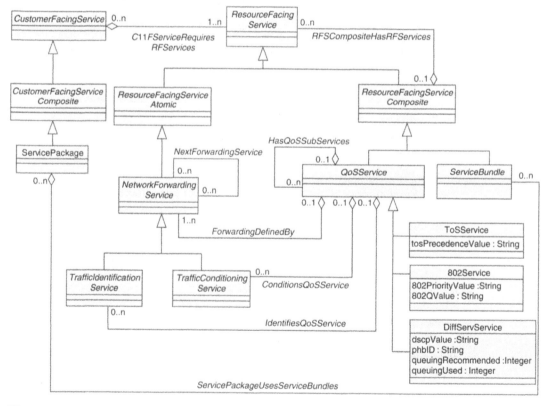

FIGURE 8.8

DEN-ng representation of *QoSServices*.

the *DiffServService* might need two or more cascaded meters to provide multiple metering levels, each with its own set of attribute values that are different than those used for the *ToSService*.

Figure 8.8 shows a simplified view of the DEN-ng top-level quality-of-service model. Attributes and other detail have been suppressed to simplify the figure. There are four important points to make about this figure. First, *CustomerFacing-Services* aggregates *ResourceFacingServices* using the aggregation *CFService-RequiresRFServices*. Second, *ServicePackage* aggregates *ServiceBundle* using the *ServicePackageUsesServiceBundles* aggregation. Third, the (business) attributes for the *QoSService* subclasses are shown to emphasize their different natures. However, despite these differences, they can each define their own set of *NetworkForward-ingServices* using the *ForwardingDefinedBy* aggregation. Finally, a *ServiceBundle* aggregates *QoSServices* using the *RFSCompositeHasRFServices* aggregation.

In spite of these differences, however, the important point about this design is that the *ToSService* and the *DiffServService* are related to each other, since they come from the same definition (*QoSService*). This happens *naturally* through the definition of the DEN-ng model.

The *IdentifiesQoSService* aggregation is used to define the set of *Classifier Services* and *MarkerServices* that are needed to identify a particular *QoSService*. Note that this is an aggregation, because sophisticated traffic classification may require more than one *ClassifierService*.

Consider, for example, Figure 8.9, which shows Gold traffic being split into three types of subtraffic flows—flows that are completely, partially, and noncon-

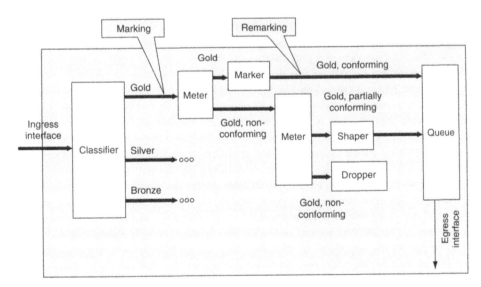

FIGURE 8.9

Complex classification and marking in the forwarding path.

forming to the basic traffic profile defined for Gold service. (Remember, this is a conceptual realization of the different functions provided inside the router). This can be implemented in several ways. The simple method in the figure shows two cascaded meters being used to separate the traffic into three types of flows. We could also have used two sets of classifiers.

Figure 8.9 also shows the close bond between *ClassifierServices* and *Marker Services*. Here, we have used two different *MarkerServices*, at different points in the traffic conditioning process, in order to re-mark packets after some preliminary service (such as metering) has been performed. Note that both are conceptually part of identifying traffic and in so doing often define which particular *Traffic ConditioningService* is required.

The *ConditionsQoSService* is used to specify the set of *TrafficConditioning Services* that are required by a particular *QoSService*. This enables different traffic conditioning services to be specified for a particular *QoSService*. Alternatively, as stated earlier, it is possible that a particular implementation might want the exact same type of *TrafficConditioningServices* for two different *QoSServices*. For example, if the traffic consists of voice and data, then regardless of whether we are using a *DiffServService* or a *ToSService*, we still want to use a form of priority queuing for voice and a form of class-based weighted fair queuing for data (please note that these subclasses exist in the DEN-ng model, but are not shown to make the diagram easier to read). In this particular example, what is important is to specify an appropriate scheduling algorithm, which controls how these different queues are combined and serviced by an output interface of the device. This is present in the DEN-ng QoS model but is not shown for the sake of simplicity.

Note that the model shown in Figure 8.8 enables another form of differentiation. In the last example, specifying advanced traffic conditioning functions using DSCPs is more flexible than it is using a set of ToS markings. This is because there are 64 DSCP values versus 8 ToS values, and also because the DiffServ specification defines dropping as part of the per-hop behavior. This can be easily accommodated in the DEN-ng QoS model by simply relating dropping and queuing services to a DSCP, versus only relating a queuing service to a *ToSService*. However, in the DEN-ng model, this is not done, because ToS-based services will require *DroppingServices* as well.

The DEN-ng model represents these different mechanisms (and others not shown, such as a scheduler) as a set of building blocks that can be combined in different ways, according to the capabilities of the network device. This generic binding of different services is represented by the *NextService* association, which enables any *NetworkForwardingService* to follow any other *NetworkForwardingService*. The DEN-ng model uses OCL to constrain which mechanisms can be first or last in the interface, as well as which can follow which. For example, it would be technically incorrect to make a dropper the first or last element (e.g., the first or last mechanism after the input interface and before the output interface, respectively) in the forwarding path. Similarly, following a dropper by a dropper doesn't make sense, whereas following a meter with another meter does indeed make sense. Note that this level of specificity does not exist in the IETF and CIM models.

Three problems would surface if this and other dependencies were modeled in detail. First, the model would become very complicated and therefore much harder to understand. Second, the more explicit the model becomes at a granular level, the more likely it is that our generic model will conflict with how different vendors are implementing these device-specific mechanisms. Third, if this behavior isn't specified, then the degree of control that can be exerted over the device is less.

If OCL isn't available, the alternative is to either not specify this at all or to build a set of different associations to model individual behavior. If we want the model to be UML compliant, then we must remember that the different associations are not necessarily subclasses. This is because in UML there is a distinct difference between associations and association classes. This is a problem with the DMTF CIM model in general—it is not UML compliant and represents all associations as association classes. The DEN-ng model can represent these subtleties because it is derived from the UML meta-model and is therefore UML compliant.

In summary, the DEN-ng approach is to model a generic capability in a simple, extensible way, and then constrain it appropriately. Thus, the basic DEN-ng QoS model uses the *NextService* association as shown in Figure 8.8 and offers two ways to constrain it. The preferred way is to provide OCL expressions that restrict how the *NextService* association is applied. The DEN-ng specification also discusses how to subclass this model to explicitly model more detailed, and restrictive, combinations of *NetworkForwardingServices*. This latter may be appropriate if the capabilities of specific vendor devices are being modeled.

8.3.3 Putting It All Together

We have had a brief glimpse of DiffServ- and ToS-based services, and now is the time to see how policy is applied to implement them.

The basic approach is to integrate the policy and QoS models into one single information model. This is done using the policy continuum. Throughout Strassner's *Policy-Based Network Management*, five different levels in the policy continuum are defined—business, system, network, device, and instance levels. The (generic) QoS model fits in at the system and network levels, and partially at the device level. The policy model, of course, is applicable to all levels of the policy continuum. The difference is because the policy model is itself a federated model, consisting in reality of five different models. Each of these five models is focused on a particular level of the policy continuum. In contrast, the QoS model is concerned with modeling QoS in a generic fashion, and thus concentrates on a subset of the policy continuum.

The business view is concerned with ensuring that the applicable business rules and processes are used to *direct* how the PBNM system is to be managed.

It does this in terms of business entities, such as *customer*, *service*, and *product*. Thus, the business rule *"John gets Gold service"* can be expressed in terms of a *customer* (John) who has bought a *product* that provides a *service* (Gold service) for one or more applications he is using.

The system view expands on this view, detailing the composition of key objects that are to be managed. For example, if the customer has contracted for VPN-based connectivity, *how* will that connectivity be provided? At the business level, it is a "blob," but at the system level, the "blob" has been transformed into a specific type of VPN (e.g., an MPLS VPN using BGP to advertise routes and OSPF to connect the different provider routers together). Note the importance of the use of a single information model. This enables the same concepts to be shared among the business and system views, even though they are at two different levels of abstraction.

The network view further specifies how to implement the service by defining the set of technologies that will be used to implement the service. However, this is done in a device-independent way: it may define the use of RSVP to reserve bandwidth, but this definition is independent of how any particular vendor implements support for RSVP. Thus, the RSVP model will be limited to representing only those features and functions that are present in the appropriate standards or commonly implemented by multiple vendors.

The device view binds this approach to specific device features. This is the level wherein different devices are chosen to support the VPN service, and so differences in support and implementation of standards like RSVP become important. This level also represents a melding of the standards-based DEN-ng model and extensions to this model that represent how specific vendors implement features defined in the standard. For example, DEN-ng defines a *QueueService* and even defines the basic characteristics of several popular queuing algorithms (e.g., class-based weighted fair queuing). However, it only defines those features that are described in the standards, or are otherwise commonly implemented by multiple vendors. Thus, in order to bind this specification to the specific vendor devices that are implementing class-based weighted fair queuing, it is necessary to extend the DEN-ng model to represent the specific vendor implementation.

(As an aside, note that there are many different implementations of class-based weighted fair queuing, even from the same vendor. This is because in order to perform functions such as class-based weighted fair queuing at line rate, the algorithm must be implemented using application-specific integrated circuits, or ASICs. Different products use different ASICs, even if they are manufactured by the same vendor. For example, this commonly occurs when one company acquires another company. Hence, even a single vendor can have significantly different algorithm implementations for different products.)

Finally, we need to *program* the device. Each device has its own programming model. If the device view can describe extensions to the DEN-ng framework that represent the capabilities of the device that can be used, then the instance view can in turn translate this model into the appropriate vendor-specific CLI commands that are needed. The instance and device views work hand in hand. The instance view models vendor- and device-specific commands, while the device view translates these vendor-specific features into extensions of a common framework. We can therefore represent vendor-specific features as part of a common set of capabilities, which enables us to map different vendor-specific features to each other. *The effect of this is to be able to view the system in a standard way while being able to program the system using different vendor-specific programming models.*

Thus, we see that networking, customer, and other objects come into and go out of focus, according to what view is being used. However, policies are always present, regardless of what view is being used. In order to see this, let's continue the development of our example.

In the example "*John gets Gold service*," several underlying business policies come into play, including:

- Why is John entitled to get Gold service?
- What does Gold service provide John?
- How will the PBNM system ensure that John gets Gold service?
- What will the PBNM system do if John doesn't get Gold service?

Business rules are used to define which users receive which types of services, as well as what applications can be accessed within a particular service offering. Different classes of service are often used to provide better than best-effort service to either a specific set of users and/or a specific set of applications. This answers the first question.

To answer the second question, first recall Figure 8.5, which illustrated the use of classes of service to provide access to special applications. However, it also can be used to designate differences between traffic from the same application. For example, consider two flows from the same application. One belongs to a Gold service, and the other belongs to a Bronze service (perhaps because the two users have different service contracts). Even though this traffic is from the same application, Gold service will ensure that the first user gets "better" service than the second user. Here, "better" can mean many things, depending on the particular application that is being used. For example, it may mean faster download times, or provide an application with less latency and jitter.

The fourth question is also easy to answer. Clearly, a policy needs to be used to define the action(s) taken if the system violates its contractual obligation to provide Gold service. If policy is not used, then each violation will need to be addressed on an individual basis, which cannot scale. The use of policy is preferred to ensure that a consistent and extensible response can be applied to a large number of conditions. (The basic DEN-ng policy model is a triplet consisting of event, condition, and action clauses. This strategy enables policies to be defined that describe what actions to take when, for example, an SLA is violated.) The structure of the event-condition-action policies facilitates associating the "normal" policies with their counterparts that describe "violations."

The third question is related to how the system is being managed. Assume that the PBNM system uses a model to represent the various components of the system that provides Gold service. One way to ensure that business rules are used to implement which users get which services is to translate the *concepts* present in the business view into a set of *objects* that can be managed.

Specifically, if DEN-ng is used, then the management of objects will be done by defining Finite State Machine (FSM). The FSM approach defines how to model the behavior of a managed entity using a set of transitions that identify the current and desired states that a managed entity should be in. The model is used to identify the set of statistics, attributes, and other characteristics of a managed object that define the current state, or characteristics, of that object. For example, we may know that a software object may be in the "installed" state but not in the "deployed" state because the measurement of certain statistics, via the reading of particular object values, confirms that this object is installed but not yet deployed. The object values are, of course, defined in the information model.

This means that a *set* of models needs to be used. This is because, in general, different states in the FSM correspond to different attribute values as well as different sets of objects. In addition, different relationships and constraints may be activated, based on the entity changing states. These changes require different instances of the same model to be used to track the transition between states.

Therefore, a given model may be used by one or more of the five different views in the policy continuum, as shown in Figure 8.10. The DEN-ng approach to PBNM uses an FSM in this fashion. As shown in Figure 8.10, each view can make use of one or more models. Each model can represent one or more managed objects. Thus, *as the view of the managed object is changed in the policy continuum, the model for that managed object changes appropriately.*

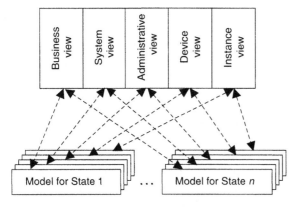

FIGURE 8.10

Use of individual models to represent FSM states in the policy continuum.

This is a key feature of the DEN-ng model and cannot be overemphasized. Put another way, the DEN-ng view states that each of the views in the policy continuum is equally important. Consequently, each view has its own model. The information model serves to unite each of these different views, and relate the different objects that are present in one view to a potentially different set of objects in another view. Note that this feature is unique to DEN-ng and the SID, and is a by-product of the New Generation Operations Systems and Software (NGOSS) effort.

Some managed objects are not present in a particular view because they are not germane to that view. In fact, the appearance of a particular managed object in a given view is indicative of the role played by a particular managed object in that view. The disappearance of a managed object simply means that it is not relevant or that it has been replaced by another object in that view. This is illustrated in Table 8.1.

The business view focuses on a high-level description of how to manage the environment. At this level, the relationship between products, services, and customers is usually of paramount importance. No details of how the service is going to be implemented are provided, because they are not important at this level of abstraction. Rather, the business view supplies a consistent view of common business entities from which network services are derived. Policies are used to describe

Table 8.1 Sample Managed Objects Corresponding to Different Levels of the Policy Continuum

Level in the Policy Continuum	Sample Objects in This Level of the Policy Continuum
BUSINESS VIEW (John gets Gold service)	Customer (with John as an instance); Product; Service; *ServiceOffering*; *CustomerFacingService*; Applications; SLA
SYSTEM VIEW (define multiple classes of service)	Business objects plus *ResourceFacingService*; *DeviceRoles*; *DeviceCapabilities*; *QoSService*
NETWORK VIEW (decide to use DiffServ and ToS; use RSVP for bandwidth guarantee)	System objects plus define all subclasses of *QoSService* and *NetworkForwardingService* needed to build a complete representation of the different QoS services for each CoS
DEVICE VIEW (decide on vendor-specific features; pick specific devices and software releases)	Use models of each vendor-specific device (derived as refinement of above standard model); use *DeviceCapabilities* to map between their functional differences
INSTANCE VIEW (write device-specific CLI)	Use above models to generate CLI for each state in the FSM

the fundamental business relationships (e.g., why does John get Gold service, and what happens if this contract is violated) present at this level.

The system view defines the particular approach that will be used and the supporting concepts and objects needed to implement that approach. In this example, it defines the concept of different service offerings that each use different classes of service. It defines the concept of a *ResourceFacingService*—a service that is not purchased by the customer, but is nevertheless needed to support the *CustomerFacingService*. It defines roles and device capabilities and the notions of QoS. All of these objects add additional detail to the model. They also offer new opportunities for policies to be used to control the objects introduced at this level. It may be viewed as a link between pure business policies and device configurations.

At the administrative level, the particular technologies (DiffServ and ToS markings in this example) that will be used are specified. This in turn defines the various objects necessary to manage the implementation of these technologies. It helps define the mapping between these different technologies, although it does not define their configuration. Policies are used to ensure that the technologies are each managed according to the higher-level business policies that they are supporting.

At the device level, it defines the basic parameters of devices and helps choose which OS release and line cards of which devices should be used through the identification of these basic parameters. However, since it does not model device-specific features, it can not be used to specify the configuration of the network devices being used. Policies are used to manage the intricacies of the specific devices that are being used to support the higher-level policies already defined. The instance level models the CLI that configures each device in each state. Policies are used to manage how device configuration is created and deployed, as well as how different device configuration changes are coordinated with each other.

We can therefore draw a very important conclusion:

> Policies ensure that the semantics of different levels of the policy continuum
> are applied to managed objects at appropriate levels of the policy continuum.

In other words, policies are not just a way to manage a device. Remember that fundamentally, a policy represents goals and a method for achieving those goals. Therefore, they can also be used to ensure that the semantics at different levels of the policy continuum are properly matched up and supported.

More importantly, this approach enables us to define a policy as a way to control the transitioning of a current state to a new state. Here, "control" of a state transition means defining the semantics of the transition—who is in charge of the transition, what the transition is used for, when it occurs, where it occurs, and why it is being done. This uses the DEN-ng concept of archetype—who, what, when, where, and why—to control the state transition. The "what" part of this is typically implemented by using the policy to select one or more processes to implement the state transition. Thus, we have the following important conclusion:

Policies are used to control the state that a managed object is in at any given time; the state itself is modeled using an information model such as DEN-ng.

This leads to one last conclusion:

The policy model is used to control which mechanisms to use, when to apply them, and when to change device configurations. Integrating policy and device management is done by integrating the policy model with appropriate models of the device using a Finite State Machine.

For example, the QoS model can be thought of as specifying the changes needed to a current device configuration in order to provide a desired traffic conditioning; given this, the policy model can be thought of as controlling which processes are used to implement the appropriate device configuration changes.

8.3.4 **Using Signaling**

Signaling can be used with or without the provisioning approaches previously described. In signaling, the idea is that important information is valid at a particular time, or because a particular set of conditions are active. This is fundamentally different than provisioning approaches, which seek to embed rules within a device so that the device knows how to respond when it detects different types of traffic. Nevertheless, there are similarities between signaling and provisioning policies. This section will provide examples to clarify its use.

Requesting High QoS

Both provisioning and signaling can be used to request QoS. However, the way in which each requests QoS is fundamentally different. Provisioning is limited by the extent in which network traffic capabilities can be understood. This understanding takes the form of building into each device's configuration commands the ability to recognize and appropriately condition each type of traffic flow that is received. In other words, network traffic patterns are *anticipated*, and devices are programmed to react to a particular flow, match it against their installed rules, and take action. Clearly, the problem is that if the current traffic patterns do not match what was pre-provisioned (or do not properly accommodate those patterns), then business rules (at least!) will be violated, and the network will not support the desired behavior.

A problem that is potentially far worse is when traffic guarantees are desired. If the network isn't overengineered, then significant variances in its load can cause it to be oversubscribed. Oversubscription does not work well for pre-provisioned networks trying to support traffic guarantees because the guarantees themselves get compromised. However, overengineering is not desirable, because most of the time the resources are wasted. Signaling offers the ability to adjust network resources on a granular basis. In addition, it can provide additional important information on a per-flow basis to supplement the use of pre-provisioned policies, as described in the next section.

Supplying Useful Identification Information

PBNM systems rely on the ability to identify sources and/or users of traffic as part of the classification process. However, there are many difficult problems that are often encountered. For example, applications may dynamically negotiate for port numbers, making it impossible to predefine a classification rule to detect the application based on its port number. Worse, if IPsec is used, ports are encrypted and therefore cannot be used at all in the classification process. Finally, if there are community machines (e.g., a "guest" machine, or one for general usage), how can the PBNM system tell which user is using a particular machine?

Fortunately, most signaling applications have the capability of generating messages that can be used to describe the traffic and/or the users or applications sending or receiving the traffic. For example, the RSVP protocol has the ability to send additional information describing users and applications. This can be used to help identify users and applications so that further processing may be applied. In the case of IPsec traffic, hosts provide an SPI that can be used as classification criteria instead of ports.

Thus, we see that signaling applications can be used to supply critical information in addition to asking for specific requests such as bandwidth. The power of signaling applications is that resources can be requested (as well as information supplied) from particular devices along a path. This enables the network service to be fine-tuned to suit the current needs.

Signaling Example

RSVP is arguably the most popular protocol used for requesting QoS resources from the network. Policy can be used to control whether to admit or reject an RSVP request based on the request's attributes and the specified policy. A signaling policy can be used for several things. Three examples are:

1. To control the admission priority of resources
2. To provide preemption support
3. To provide mapping of services signaled by RSVP (or another suitable protocol, such as COPS) to Differentiated Services in a core network

The first two functions are used to control whether to accept or deny a request, and what to do if there are many different flows competing for the same resource. Admission priority controls what applications can have their resource requests granted, while preemption priority defines a relative ranking among the set of admitted flows that are competing for shared resources. The third enables different technologies, used by different control approaches (signaling vs. provisioning) to be mapped together.

An admission request decision can be based on comparing an RSVP TSpec (specification of the traffic flow) or FlowSpec (the amount of QoS resources requested) against a meter. Metering is the function of monitoring the arrival times of packets of a traffic stream, and determining the level of conformance of each packet with respect to a preestablished traffic profile. This allows basing an admission decision both on the properties of the reservation request itself as well as on the current temporal resource allocation.

For example, consider the following policy:

> Allow resource assignment via RSVP for flows coming from the HR subnet up to a total aggregated rate of 256 Kbps.

The meter is used to track the current state of resource allocated to the HR subnet, and compares any new request for resources against a 256 Kbps traffic profile. In this policy, individual resources will be admitted, so long as their cumulative rate doesn't exceed 256 Kbps.

Policy can be used to control and/or modify RSVP messages. Sample actions include:

- Replace/add DCLASS object in RSVP message
- Replace/add preemption priority object in RSVP message
- Trigger an error/warning RSVP message
- Instruct the RSVP node to proxy RSVP message as if sent by the RSVP end nodes

The first two examples enable explicit control to be exerted over the behavior of the nodes involved in the signaling decision. The third example—triggering warnings and errors—enables end-nodes to be notified that their resource reservation is about to be adversely impacted (e.g., about to expire). The final example is an optimization. For example, if the device is part of the boundary of a DiffServ core network, it may be more efficient to simply map the RSVP request to a specific PHB, rather than forwarding the RSVP Path message.

8.4 **RESOURCES**

ITU-T Recommendation M.3010, "Principles for a Telecommunications Management Network," May 1996.

OMG Unified Modeling Language Specification, Version 1.4, sections 3.41–3.49, September 2001.

RFC 1510, "Classless Inter-Domain Routing (CIDR): An Address Assignment and Aggregation Strategy." Fuller, V., T. Li, J. Yu, and K. Varadhan, September 1993.

RFC 2205, "Resource ReSerVation Protocol (RSVP)—Version 1 Functional Specification." Braden, R. (ed.), L. Zhang, S. Berson, S. Herzog, and S. Jamin, September 1997.

RFC 2207, "RSVP Extensions for IPSEC Data Flow." Berger, L., and T. O'Malley, September 1997.

RFC 2474, "Definition of the Differentiated Services Field (DS Field) in the IPv4 and IPv6 Headers." Nichols, K., S. Blake, F. Baker, and D. Black, December 1998.

RFC 2475, "An Architecture for Differentiated Services." Blake, S., D. Black, M. Carlson, E. Davies, Z. Wang, and W. Weiss, December 1998.

RFC 2597, "Assured Forwarding PHB Group." Heinanen, J., F. Baker, W. Weiss, and J. Wroclawski, June 1999.

RFC 2752, "Identity Representation for RSVP." Yadav, S., R. Yavatkar, R. Pabbati, P. Ford, T. Moore, and S. Herzog, January 2000.

RFC 2872, "Application and Sub-Application Identity Policy Element for Use with RSVP." Bernet, Y., and R. Pabbati, June 2000.

RFC 2998, "A Framework for Integrated Services Operation over DiffServ Networks." Bernet, Y., P. Ford, R. Yavatkar, F. Baker, L. Zhang, M. Speer, R. Braden, B. Davie, J. Wroclawski, and E. Felstaine, November 2000.

RFC 3175, "Aggregation of RSVP for IPv4 and IPv6 Reservations." Baker, F., C. Iturralde, F. Le Faucheur, and B. Davie, September 2001.

RFC 3181, "Signaled Preemption Priority Policy Element." Herzog, S., October 2001.

RFC 3246, "An Expedited Forwarding PHB (Per-Hop Behavior)." Davie, B., A. Charny, J.C.R. Bennett, K. Benson, J. Y. Le Boudec, W Courtney, S. Davari, V. Firoiu, and D. Stiliadis, March 2002.

RFC 3247, "Supplemental Information for the New Definition of the EF PHB (Expedited Forwarding Per-Hop Behavior)." Charny, A., J.C.R. Bennett, K. Benson, J. Y. Le Boudec, A. Chiu, W. Courtney, S. Davari, V. Firoiu, C. Kalmanek, and K. K. Ramakrishnan, March 2002.

RFC 4364, "BGP/MPLS VPNs." Rosen, E., et al., February 2006.

Strassner, J. (ed.), *Mining Information from the DMTF CIM into the TMF SID*. TM Forum GB922, July 2002.

The home page of the Differentiated Services working group of the IETF is *www.ietf.org/html.charters/OLD/diffserv-charter.html*. The home page of the Integrated Services working group of the IETF is *www.ietf.org/proceedings/96dec/charters/intserv-charter.html*. The home page of the ISSLL working group of the IETF is *www.ietf.org/proceedings/96dec/charters/issll-charter.html*.

The TMF Interface Implementation Specification of the Fine Grain NGOSS Catalyst Project is specified in the document TMF839v1.5, and on the members-only website: *www.tmforum.org/sdata/documents/TMFC1379%20TMFC1000%20TMF839v1[1].5.pdf*.

IPv6 Quality of Service

Providing quality of service (QoS) in IP networks has long been an important but elusive goal for IETF working groups. The original IPv4 header specification included a type of service (ToS) field that was rarely if ever implemented: It would have required implementers to make judgments about which of their packets were to be given worse-than-normal treatment. This simplistic approach has been replaced over the years with the Differentiated Services (DiffServ) approach, and the ToS field has been renamed the Differentiated Services (DS) field in *RFC 2474*, "Definition of the Differentiated Services Field (DS Field) in the IPv4 and IPv6 Headers."

DiffServ allows the use of the DS field for data that indicates how a packet should be treated by routers. Rather than assigning a priority, the DS field is used to assign membership in a group that has a set of policies associated with it. These DiffServ *behavior aggregates* (groups of packets that are to be treated in the same way by a router at network boundary) work the same way in both IPv4 and IPv6.

In an effort to remedy the faults of the ToS approach used in IPv4, an early goal of the IPv6 effort was to replace ToS with the concept of *flows*, which were to behave somewhat like behavior aggregates. The Flow Label field in the IPv6 header was first discussed in the early 1990s with *RFC 1809*, "Using the Flow Label Field in IPv6." This specification was published half a year before the original IPv6 specifications in 1995. At that time, the field raised more questions than it answered, including how to determine which packets should be assigned a flow, how routers should handle flows that they didn't have flow routing information for, and even the length of the field itself (before 1995 it was 28 bits long, by 1995 it had shrunk to 24 bits, and by 1998 it had reduced to its currently specified size of 20 bits).

By 1998 and the revised IPv6 specification in *RFC 2460*, the Flow Label field was still considered experimental as the questions regarding its use had yet to be resolved through extensive implementation and experimentation. A new specification that explains appropriate use of the Flow Label in IPv6 was published in 2004 as a proposed standard in *RFC 3697*.

Up to the late 1990s, applications that depended on underlying network protocols relied on Transmission Control Protocol (TCP) to respond to network congestion. However, in January 1999, the experimental *RFC 2481*, "A Proposal to Add Explicit Congestion Notification (ECN) to IP," was published detailing an approach to congestion management that could include the network layer protocol, IP. Updated to proposed standard in September 2001, *RFC 3168*, "The Addition of Explicit Congestion Notification (ECN) to IP," updates some of the mechanisms discussed in this chapter.

In this chapter, taken from Chapter 15 of *IPv6: Theory, Protocol, and Practice* by Pete Loshin, we cover the IPv6 approach to QoS, including the use of the DiffServ field in IPv6, followed by discussion of IPv6 Flow Labels and the use of Explicit Congestion Notification with IPv6.

9.1 QOS BASICS

The IP model is a democratic one: All packets are (in theory) treated equally, getting a "best-effort" delivery service from the systems in the Internet. This has several implications for application performance and in some cases limits applications in a number of ways.

- Packets may be delivered in order or out of order
- Packets may be delivered smoothly or in spurts
- Packets may or may not be delivered

In the case of real-time applications, this can require that receiving hosts buffer data as it comes in, adding delay on top of whatever network delay exists. Instead of passing incoming network data directly to the application, the incoming data is stored temporarily as the host waits for all data, including out-of-order data and data that may be temporarily delayed, to arrive.

The unpredictability of the IP datagram service is due to the way routers handle traffic: Packets come in from various sources, arriving at the router on different interfaces with different networks, and the router processes those packets in the order they are received.

Despite the first pass at the problem through assignment of type of service values, IP as originally defined lacks mechanisms for differentiating between packets that have quality of service requirements and those that don't.

- Transient congestion, such as caused by a surge of packets from one source, can cause unpredictable results. A packet surge may delay other traffic passing through a router. Or it might not.

- All datagrams are created equal, which means that there is no way to give one datagram priority over another.

- Individual routers can be configured to favor packets being sent to or from some particular network interface, but once the packet is routed, it will be treated just like any other packet by other routers. IP lacks a mechanism for flagging packets at their source and indicating that they should be treated differently in some way from source to destination.

■ Even if packets can be flagged for special treatment, IP lacks the mechanisms for tracking packets and monitoring performance and resource use.

QoS protocols are intended to differentiate between packets on an end-to-end basis and adding the mechanisms necessary to allocate resources throughout a path for packets that require them.

9.1.1 **Approaches to Quality**

The two basic approaches to adding QoS to the Internet are the Integrated Services (IntServ) and DiffServ models. Introduced and defined in 1994 in *RFC 1633*, "Integrated Services in the Internet Architecture: an Overview," the IntServ effort grew out of implementation experience with multicast of IETF meetings. According to *RFC 1633* authors, real-time applications work poorly across the global Internet "because of variable queuing delays and congestion losses."

In addition to QoS for real-time applications, the IntServ model would allow network service providers control over how bandwidth is shared. Allowing all the available bandwidth to be allocated among different classes of traffic even when the network is under a heavy load means that applications can count on having a minimum amount of bandwidth to work with even when the network is congested—instead of being summarily cut off when packets are dropped silently and the hosts on the other end drop the connections.

The ability to control which traffic categories are allowed how much of the available bandwidth is called *controlled link sharing*. The IntServ approach defines a service model in which best-effort and *real-time services* (services over which there is some control of end-to-end packet delay) coexist and are facilitated through controlled link sharing.

Whether or not overly influenced by their experiences with multicast, the IntServ working group has agreed that any QoS solution would have to support multicast: Real-time applications such as videoconferencing require the ability to handle multiple recipients of the same packets.

9.1.2 **Reserving Resources**

QoS generally requires network resources—specifically, network bandwidth and reliable routes—to ensure a uniform quality of service. The process of provisioning circuits, as in asynchronous transfer mode (ATM) and other telecommunication-oriented network protocols, is necessary before any communication can occur between a source and a destination. The *Resource ReSerVation Protocol* (RSVP), defined in *RFC 2205*, "Resource ReSerVation Protocol (RSVP)—Version 1 Functional Specification," defines a mechanism by which hosts can, in effect, provision a connection across the connectionless IP Internet. RSVP, a required part of the IntServ model, also requires IntServ-capable routers in the network over which services are to be provided.

This reservation infrastructure can be dispensed with when services are provided to more general categories of packet, rather than the very specific IntServ flows. DiffServ does not specifically require any mechanism on hosts, but vests the responsibility for managing bandwidth with the network itself. DiffServ packets are marked for special treatment by their applications, but the specific way in which those packets are treated is left to routers.

9.1.3 IntServ in a Nutshell

Central to IntServ is the concept of flow: If packets share source and destination IP addresses as well as source and destination ports, then one can assume those packets are all part of an application's stream of data flowing between source and destination, with all that entails.

The IntServ approach requires that routers keep track of all these flows, examining each packet to determine whether it belongs in a flow and then computing whether there is enough available bandwidth to accept the packet. In other words, IntServ requires the following functions:

Admission control: Can the router, or the network at large, provide service to the flow? Can it provide service to the individual packets that comprise the flow? What about other, non-QoS packets?

Packet classification: Every packet admitted must be classified. What flow does it belong to? What level of QoS does it get? The three options are to treat the packet "normally" giving it best-effort; *controlled load* for allocating some portion of an uncongested network; and *guaranteed service* for real-time delivery with delays minimized to within preset levels of service.

Packet scheduling: Once a packet is classified, how is it scheduled? Should some packets jump ahead of others? How are packets within a queue treated when the queue exceeds its limits?

Combined with RSVP, IntServ tends to be cumbersome to implement and it certainly is not scalable to the global Internet. Nevertheless, it is quite good at managing flows of data within smaller networks. Ultimately, however, IntServ has proven inadequate to the task of providing a single solution to the QoS problem: The IntServ mechanisms are not seen as being scalable to the global Internet, and they can be difficult to implement.

The next pass at the problem became known as *DiffServ* to differentiate it from IntServ. Cursory examination of the RFCs may not shed much light on the differences between the two, but there are considerable differences. Where IntServ is focused on ways of sharing available bandwidth among unique *flows* (series of packets with the same source and destination IP and port addresses),

DiffServ approached the problem by suggesting that a less granular classification of packets could provide the desired result.

9.1.4 DiffServ in a Nutshell

There is no way that Internet backbone routers can contend with the demands of tracking individual flows in an IntServ-enabled global Internet, but network customers and service providers both increasingly demand some form of QoS that can scale well in the global Internet. Differentiated Services answers the call by streamlining the process. DiffServ over IP is documented in *RFC 2474*, "Definition of the Differentiated Services Field (DS Field) in the IPv4 and IPv6 Headers."

Rather than building an elaborate infrastructure for emulating a circuit-based network on top of IP, DiffServ allows communicating endpoints to classify their packets into different treatment categories. These categories are identified with a per-hop behavior, or PHB. The PHB is the action that a DiffServ routing node can be observed to take when it receives a packet. When a PHB is defined, DiffServ routers are supposed to treat packets marked with that value in a certain way.

For example, the Expedited Forwarding (EF) PHB (specified in *RFC 2598*, "An Expedited Forwarding PHB") is billed as "premium service" and indicates that the packets in that behavior aggregate (BA) should all be processed as they are received, rather than be queued or dropped. Unlike IntServ with its traffic flows, the DiffServ model calls for the use of BAs at each DiffServ router: These are associated with a PHB that indicates how the router will treat the packet.

Aggregates or aggregated flows may also be referred to as classes of packets; routers are configured to respond to these different classes in different (appropriate) ways. Routers may also be configured to break up these classes into subaggregations to be treated slightly differently. For example, a router might be configured to forward premium-service packets from preferred customers over links that are more reliable than premium-service packets coming from customers subscribing to a "budget-premium" service.

DiffServ brings with it the ability to create network service policies specific to a single router, some part of a network, or an entire DiffServ routing domain. As long as their policies don't affect the ability to provide guaranteed QoS, network providers can fine-tune their DiffServ routers to differentiate how they treat packets.

The DiffServ model distributes the task of allocating resources to the routers within a DiffServ domain, providing greater flexibility as well as more efficient routing. A backbone router could process DiffServ traffic far more easily than it can process IntServ traffic: There is no need to negotiate RSVP reservations with all intermediary routers—and no overhead necessarily associated with failure to maintain an RSVP session with one particular router. With DiffServ, the PHB mandates how the packet is treated, and different routers can provide the same service without having to maintain state for a particular connection, as with IntServ.

9.1.5 **DiffServ versus IntServ**

At first glance, DiffServ and IntServ may seem to be competing with each other. However, the two models are complementary, with IntServ working best within smaller domains, whereas DiffServ provides somewhat less precise handling of packets across much larger networks; the two can even be used together, as documented in *RFC 2998*, "A Framework for Integrated Services Operation over DiffServ Networks."

In this informational document, the authors see IntServ, RSVP, and DiffServ as "complementary technologies," each of which is intended to achieve end-to-end quality of service. "Together," they write, "these mechanisms can facilitate deployment of applications, such as IP-telephony, video-on-demand, and various nonmultimedia mission-critical applications. IntServ enables hosts to request per-flow, quantifiable resources, along end-to-end data paths and to obtain feed-back regarding admissibility of these requests. DiffServ enables scalability across large networks."

9.2 **DIFFERENTIATED SERVICES AND IPV6**

The behavior defined for the Differentiated Services field in both IPv4 and IPv6 is the same, so an understanding of DiffServ for IPv4 should carry over to DiffServ for IPv6. In both protocols, the Differentiated Services field is defined for the six bits following the protocol version number in the IP header. Those bits were originally specified in IPv4 as the type of service (ToS) field in *RFC 791*, and originally specified as the Traffic Class field for IPv6 in *RFC 2460*.

RFC 2474, "Definition of the Differentiated Services Field (DS Field) in the IPv4 and IPv6 Headers," spells out how DiffServ works for both protocols. The following are some other RFCs of interest for DiffServ.

- *RFC 2963*, "A Rate Adaptive Shaper for Differentiated Services"
- *RFC 2998*, "A Framework for Integrated Services Operation over DiffServ Networks"
- *RFC 3086*, "Definition of Differentiated Services Per Domain Behaviors and Rules for their Specification"
- *RFC 3260*, "New Terminology and Clarifications for DiffServ"
- *RFC 3290*, "An Informal Management Model for DiffServ Routers"
- *RFC 2430*, "A Provider Architecture for Differentiated Services and Traffic Engineering (PASTE)"
- *RFC 2474*, "Definition of the Differentiated Services Field (DS Field) in the IPv4 and IPv6 Headers"
- *RFC 2475*, "An Architecture for Differentiated Service"
- *RFC 2638*, "A Two-bit Differentiated Services Architecture for the Internet"
- *RFC 2983*, "Differentiated Services and Tunnels"

Closely related to the issue of differentiated services is the use of flows in IPv6, as will be seen in the next section.

9.3 IPV6 FLOWS

The Flow Label field in the IPv6 header was originally designed as a 28-bit field (see notes in *RFC 1809*), reduced to 24-bits by 1995, and ultimately to 20 bits, as defined in *RFC 2460*. *RFC 2460* states the following.

> The 20-bit Flow Label field in the IPv6 header may be used by a source to label sequences of packets for which it requests special handling by the IPv6 routers, such as non-default quality of service or "real-time" service. . . . Hosts or routers that do not support the functions of the Flow Label field are required to set the field to zero when originating a packet, pass the field on unchanged when forwarding a packet, and ignore the field when receiving a packet.

In an appendix to *RFC 2460*, a *flow* is defined as "a sequence of packets sent from a particular source to a particular (unicast or multicast) destination for which the source desires special handling by the intervening routers." That "special handling" might be specified by a resource reservation protocol or by some data within the flow packet headers such as a hop-by-hop option. As to the specifics of the implementation of flows, however, *RFC 2460* is silent other than to specify the characteristics of the value of the Flow Header field.

- Packets that don't belong to flows must have the Flow Header set to zero.
- Each flow is assigned in a random or pseudo-random manner and (in combination with source address) is uniquely identifiable.
- The Flow Label is assigned by the source of the flow.
- Packets that belong to the same flow must all originate from the same source address, must be addressed to the same destination, and must be sent with the same value in the Flow Label Header field. Flows are traditionally also identified by the transport layer protocol in use, as with TCP.

As of 1998, the Flow Label was considered an experimental portion of the IPv6 specification; five years after, the IETF had not yet published the IPv6 Flow Label specification as a proposed standard RFC. Publication of *RFC 3697* titled, "IPv6 Flow Label Specification," occurred in March 2004.

The definition of a flow, meanwhile, has changed.

> A flow could consist of all packets in a specific transport connection or a media stream. However, a flow is not necessarily 1 : 1 mapped to a transport connection.

One change from *RFC 2460* is that flows can be specified without reference to the destination address or transport layer protocol type. These values may not always be available in the IPv6 header, particularly if the packet is fragmented or encrypted.

The flow label may not be changed from the value assigned by the sender, unlike the DiffServ value, which may be modified to reflect the appropriate behavior aggregate for a particular router or network as it traverses the Internet. Routers that don't offer flow-related handling are required to ignore the Flow Label and treat the packet as any other.

IPv6 nodes that use flow labeling should assign separate flows for different and unrelated transport layer connections as well as for different and unrelated application layer data streams. Thus, a multi-user host with multiple Telnet sessions from different users to the same remote host should assign a separate flow to each of those sessions.

9.4 EXPLICIT CONGESTION NOTIFICATION IN IPV6

Quality of service specifications are largely intended to address the problem of how to guarantee a particular level of service for a particular set of packets. For example, an ISP may want to offer its customers a level of service that uses only their premium, high-performance networks. To achieve that level of service, the ISP would need to be able to differentiate packets coming from subscribers to that service and assign those packets to a behavior aggregate for which the routing policy is to always route on the most expensive link.

Network congestion can occur on any link as a result of high-demand conditions or router malfunctions, and in most cases nodes sending packets that encounter congestion are only able to detect the condition as a result of some timer—usually in the transport or application layer protocols—timing out. Explicit Congestion Notification was first proposed as an experiment for the transport layer in *RFC 2481*, "A Proposal to Add Explicit Congestion Notification (ECN) to IP," in 1999, and quickly moved to the standards track in 2001 when it was published as *RFC 3168*, "The Addition of Explicit Congestion Notification (ECN) to IP."

Using ECN and a Congestion Manager implementation, nodes are able to negotiate the use of ECN. The ECN field in the IPv6 (and IPv4 header, as well), consists of the two bits after the Differentiated Services field. Unlike in earlier proposals, the two bits are used together as *codepoints* rather than as separate flag bits. The four different values possible for these two bits—00, 01, 10, and 11—indicate whether the end-nodes (sender and destination) are using an ECN-Capable Transport as well as whether there is congestion at the sender (though not so much congestion that would cause the node to have dropped the packet). These are the four codepoints and their uses:

- 00—When a node is not using ECN, it puts zeroes in the ECN field.
- 01/10—These two codepoints are treated in the same way and are also called ECT(0) [for the value 01] and ECT(1) [for the value 10]. These

values are set by the sender to indicate that ECN is supported at both ends of the transmission.

■ 11—Routers that are just beginning to experience congestion, or that are experiencing mild congestion, can signal their state by setting the codepoint to 11 in outgoing packets.

The following current RFCs provide more information about Explicit Congestion Notification and congestion control in general.

■ *RFC 2481*, "A Proposal to Add Explicit Congestion Notification (ECN) to IP"
■ *RFC 2914*, "Congestion Control Principles"
■ *RFC 3124*, "The Congestion Manager"
■ *RFC 3168*, "The Addition of Explicit Congestion Notification (ECN) to IP"
■ *RFC 2884*, "Performance Evaluation of Explicit Congestion Notification (ECN) in IP Networks"

9.5 SUMMARY

Quality of service, IPv6 Flows, and Explicit Congestion Notification are all related to the quest for better service over an Internet in which, by definition, all packets are supposed to be treated equally. As we've seen in this chapter, quality of service is designed to offer consumers of Internet connectivity options for guaranteed levels of service, while IPv6 flows and Explicit Congestion Notification are designed to provide improved routing and connectivity for any nodes on the Internet.

Ultimately, the goal of providing improved performance becomes more important as the network grows larger. An important part of network management that can grow unwieldy in larger networks is the task of configuring nodes.

QoS in IP Networks Using SIP

In this chapter, based on Chapter 21 of *Internet Multimedia Communications Using SIP* by Rogelio Martinez, we will introduce the quality-of-service (QoS) topic as applicable to IP communication scenarios. QoS is a complex topic, and we will describe in this chapter just some basic ideas that allow the reader to understand the mechanisms and protocols that exist to provide quality of service.

We will start by looking at some of the available architectures at the IP transport level to provide QoS, such as integrated services and differentiated services. Then we will introduce the framework for policy control, which enables the introduction of more intelligence in the admission control decisions for QoS. Then we will see how these ideas are applied in a SIP-based communication scenario and what the necessary SIP extensions are in order to integrate the SIP/SDP session establishment process with the underlying IP transport-level processes for quality of service.

10.1 QUALITY OF SERVICE IN IP NETWORKS

Many communication scenarios involve the exchange of real-time traffic such as voice or video. In real-time traffic scenarios, it is critical that packets arrive at the destination no later than a certain time after they were transmitted by the source. If they arrive later, playback cannot happen and they have to be discarded. If the amount of packets arriving late increases, the quality of service perceived by the end user suffers, and, eventually, the received media (speech, video) may become unintelligible.

In a congested IP network, routers cannot cope with incoming packets as they come, so the routers are forced to queue the packets. This causes packet delay to increase, which, in turn, may cause real-time traffic packets to be discarded at the receiver. If congestion is severe, then the queue length limits are reached, and routers start to lose packets. In any case, a network congestion situation causes the end users to perceive a degraded quality of service.

In an unloaded IP network, this effect is not produced because packets are forwarded as soon as they are received, and therefore queues do not develop. Hence, an approach to provide quality of service for real-time communications has traditionally been, and still is, to overdimension IP networks. Obviously, one may argue that this is not the most cost-effective solution.

Our experience with the Internet of the twenty-first century tells us that Internet backbones are reasonably well dimensioned so as not to cause a problem for, for instance, voice transmission. Millions of people today around the world make telephone calls over the Internet with reasonably good quality. However, the explosion of high-bandwidth multimedia services, such as video, might pose a challenge in the future.

Even if there seems to be extra bandwidth in Internet backbones, there is still a point in the network where bandwidth is limited: the access. Although xDSL technology has helped to overcome this issue in recent years, the issue still remains for access networks that are inherently limited in bandwidth, such as wireless networks.

There are, and there will be, cases where overdimensioning the network is not an option, and therefore it is critical to implement some kind of mechanism that helps preserve a certain quality of service for particular traffic flows and/or for particular users. If we assume that resources are limited, and that there is no endless extra capacity in the networks, assuring quality of service necessarily implies some way of prioritizing some packets over others. This calls for a different model from the traditionally egalitarian best-effort Internet model.

In general terms, prioritization could be implemented for those types of traffic (such as the real-time traffic) that have very stringent quality of service requirements. In that way, a router might prioritize a packet belonging to a real-time flow (e.g., UDP packet carrying voice) over a packet belonging to non-real-time flow (e.g., TCP packet carrying email). Another key aspect to consider here is charging. A network provider might want to charge for the provision of quality of service.

Even if the techniques to offer quality of service and policy control in an Internet environment have been defined for a long time, their implementation is marginal, as of today, in the public network. However, the concepts of quality of service and policy control are again becoming hot topics with the advent of telecommunication standards such as those produced by the 3rd Generation Partnership Project (3GPP) and ETSI TISPAN. These standards, conceived for telecom operators, define the use of a controlled SIP-based private infrastructure in order to offer multimedia services (the so-called IP Multimedia Subsystem, or IMS). These standards build on the traditional Internet ideas for quality of service, taking them a step beyond, and allowing telecom operators to offer quality of service to their subscribers while at the same time providing the tools to enable charging for the use of QoS.

The fact that, in some cases—for example, in wireless networks—bandwidth is limited, calls for such QoS mechanisms. Moreover, having the control of the access network—and thus, the key to the provision of quality of service—is a tool in the telecom operators' hands in order to compete with Internet multimedia service providers that cannot offer such a quality of service. All in all, it is therefore expected that the techniques for IP quality of service will gain relevance in the short term associated with the deployment of telecom operators' controlled multimedia networks.

Having said this, we will review in this chapter some of the traditional ideas around QoS in IP networks. These ideas will form the foundation that will allow the interested reader to understand the evolved QoS architectures that are now being defined—and, in some cases, deployed—in the remit of controlled 3GPP and ETSI TISPAN multimedia networks.

The approaches to QoS in IP networks are independent of the application layer—they all occur at IP level. This is a key design principle of the Internet, and has the tremendous advantage of allowing the two domains, application layer and transport layer, to evolve separately. Nevertheless, there is a need, at some point, to integrate the SIP application layer with the media transport layer, as we will see during this chapter.

The first sections in this chapter deal with the application-independent Internet approaches for providing quality of service and policy control. The last sections in this chapter will cover how to integrate the SIP layer (i.e., the control plane) with the previous approaches in an IETF-like multimedia network.

10.2 MECHANISMS FOR QOS

The IETF has developed extensions to the IP architecture and the best-effort service model in order to deliver quality of service. More specifically, two additional models have been defined:

- Integrated Services (IntServ)
- Differentiated Services (DiffServ)

10.2.1 Integrated Services

The Integrated Services approach is based on having the IP routers give preferential treatment to some IP flows over others. An IP flow is defined as a distinguishable stream of related datagrams that result from a single user activity and require the same QoS as described in *RFC 1633*. In practice, an IP flow is distinguished by the combination of protocol, source and destination IP address, and source and destination port.

To implement a preferential treatment for some flows, IP routers would need to incorporate a couple of new functions:

The classifier: That is, a component that inspects the incoming packet and marks it as entitled to receive a specific QoS treatment by the router. The classifier passes the packet to the scheduler.

The scheduler: This component looks at the mark set by the classifier, and manages the forwarding of the packets in the different queues. The scheduler might, for instance, based on the mark, decide that a packet pertaining to a particular flow is forwarded before another packet pertaining to a different flow, even if the latter packet arrived earlier to the queue than the former.

The IntServ approach defines two different services:

- The controlled load service defined in *RFC 2211*
- The guaranteed service described in *RFC 2212*

Both of them represent an enhanced quality of service as compared with the basic best-effort service provided by the Internet. The controlled load service provides users with a quality of service that closely resembles the QoS that they would receive from an unloaded network. Even if the network is congested with best-effort traffic, the controlled load service would give preference to packets subject to QoS, hence emulating the behavior of an unloaded network. The controlled load service does not offer a guarantee that the delay will be bounded for a particular flow; it just gives preferential treatment to some packets versus others.

The guaranteed service, on the other hand, provides a specific flow with the assurance of a bounded delay.

To implement integrated services, we need some additional pieces that we did not mention so far. First, clients need to have a mechanism to ask for resources to be reserved in routers so that they can assure a specific quality of service. Second, routers need to have the capability of accepting or rejecting new reservation requests based on their existing available resources. The first functionality is called resource reservation; the second is referred to as admission control.

Figure 10.1 represents the different functionalities in an IP router extended with IntServ functionality.

Resource reservation may be implemented with Resource ReSerVation Protocol (RSVP), defined in *RFC 2205*. Clients can, via the RSVP protocol, signal the routers the identification of the flow (protocol, source and destination IP address, and source and destination UDP/TCP port) and the required quality of service for it. Routers check if they have available resources to honor the request. If they have, then the packet classifier and scheduler are configured accordingly so as to give a specific treatment to the packets in the flow as soon as they arrive.

RSVP reservations are unidirectional; in order to reserve resources in both directions, two reservation processes need to be performed.

The way RSVP works is quite simple. To reserve resources in one direction, a two-step process is followed. First the transmitter sends an RSVP Path message that is destined to the receiver (i.e., destination IP address is the receiver's address). As this message traverses the routers in the path to the recipient, it will store in each RSVP-enabled router the address of the previous RSVP router (conveyed in the RSVP PHOP parameter). When the Path message reaches the

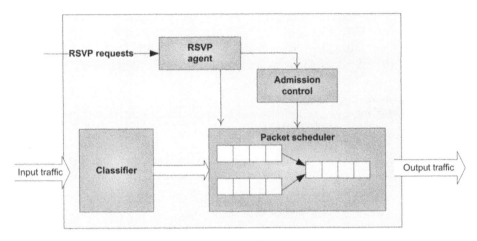

FIGURE 10.1

IP router, including IntServ functionality.

receiver, the receiver will create an Resv message that is used to actually reserve the necessary resources in the routers. The Resv message will backward traverse all the routers previously traversed by the Path message.

Routing of the Resv message is performed in a hop-by-hop way using the state previously stored by the Path message. In that way, it is assured that the resource reservation is done in the very routers that will handle the packets from transmitter to receiver, which will follow the same route taken by the Path message. This is shown in Figure 10.2.

10.2.2 Differentiated Services

The Differentiated Services approach is also based on giving preferential treatment to some packets over others in the routers. However, instead of treating different flows separately, the DiffServ approach relies on border routers marking the incoming packets with a tag called Differentiated Services Code Point (DSCP). Then the internal routers in the network just need to look at the DSCP in the packet and, based on it, apply a specific per-hop behavior (PHB) that is configured in the router. In other words, DiffServ is based on applying specific treatment to aggregations of packets, rather than to specific flows, as in Integrated Services. This fact allows Differentiated Services to scale much better than Integrated Services.

Figure 10.3 shows the DiffServ approach. Differentiated Services are defined in *RFC 2474, RFC 2475, RFC 2597*, and *RFC 3260*.

10.2.3 Integrated Services over DiffServ Networks

The fact that the IntServ approach requires routers to classify different flows (and hence to look to several protocol fields in order to identify the flow) impacts its

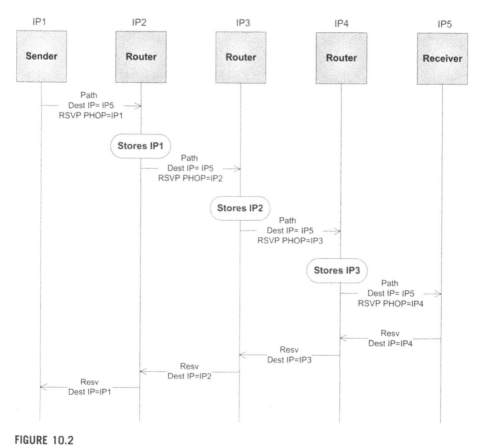

FIGURE 10.2

Basic message exchange in RSVP.

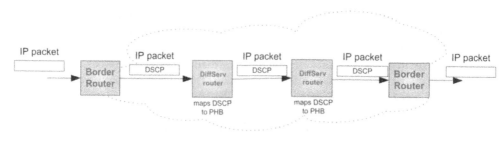

FIGURE 10.3

DiffServ network.

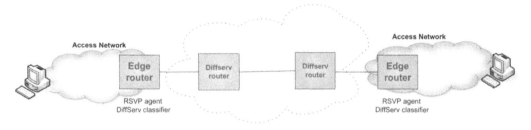

FIGURE 10.4

Use of RSVP with an IntServ access network and DiffServ core network.

scalability. Thus, it is not considered a good approach for the core of the network, though it might be a good fit for the access network. For the core, the DiffServ approach is a better choice. In this way, both mechanisms might prove to be complementary when offering end-to-end quality of service to end users. Moreover, RSVP might be used, not only to reserve resources in the access network, but also to signal to the edge router, between the access (IntServ) and the core (DiffServ) network, how to set the DiffServ mark in packets pertaining to a particular flow. This approach is described in *RFC 2998*. Figure 10.4 shows a possible scenario.

Variants of this approach are proposed for the newest IP-based next generation networks (3GPP IMS, TISPAN NGN), where, instead of RSVP, typically other protocols are used to signal the QoS requirements (e.g., 3GPP Generic Tunneling Protocol, GTP).

10.3 POLICY-BASED ADMISSION CONTROL

We saw in the previous section that resource reservation requests need to undergo an admission control function. This function is typically implemented in the access network's edge router. The admission control component takes the decision to accept or reject the resource reservation request based on two factors:

- The requester's resource reservation request
- The available capacity in the router

Nevertheless, service providers might want to base the admission control decision on additional parameters, such as the requester's identity, his or her user profile, time of day or week, and so forth. For instance, the service provider might want to grant access to quality of service only to those users who have paid an extra amount.

RFC 2753 specifies a framework for policy-based control over admission control decisions. The framework defines two functional entities: the policy

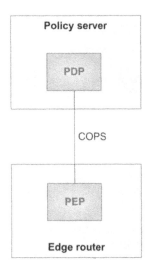

FIGURE 10.5

Policy architecture.

enforcement point (PEP) and the policy decision point (PDP). The architecture is shown in Figure 10.5.

The PEP is a component located in a network node (e.g., router) that receives the resource reservation request. If that request requires a policy decision, the PEP will then formulate a request for a policy decision and send it to the PDP. This request may contain information such as the description of the flow or the amount of requested bandwidth that was present in the original received request, plus additional information.

The PDP, when receiving the request, may look for additional info (e.g., might query a user profile database). Then the PDP makes a policy decision and communicates it back to the PEP.

The PEP receives the decision and enforces it—that is to say, accepts or rejects the original request. This is shown in Figure 10.6, where an incoming resource reservation request is rejected after a policy decision is made.

A possible option for the protocol between PEP and PDP is the Common Open Policy Service (COPS) protocol, *RFC 2748* and *RFC 4261*. COPS employs a simple client-server model where the PEP sends requests, updates, and deletes to the PDP, and the PDP returns decisions back to the PEP. The COPS protocol uses TCP as a transport.

COPS was proposed for the communication between PEP and PDP in the first releases of 3GPP IMS. Since Release 7 (R7), it has been replaced by an application on top of the DIAMETER protocol. The DIAMETER base protocol is defined in *RFC 3588*.

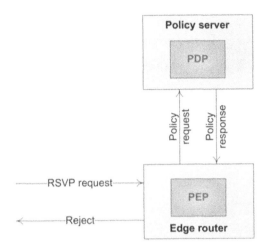

FIGURE 10.6

The PEP applies a PDP decision and rejects an RSVP reservation request.

10.4 SIP INTEGRATION WITH RESOURCE RESERVATION: THE PRECONDITIONS FRAMEWORK

10.4.1 Motivation

Let us imagine that John wants to set up a voice call using SIP, and that he wants to use resource reservation so as to ensure a certain quality of service. The reservation of network resources requires knowing the IP address, port, and session parameters of the called party (so as to identify the flow in the RSVP request). This information is obtained as a result of the Source Description Protocol (SDP) negotiation, in the SDP answer. Therefore, John will send the initial INVITE carrying the SDP offer. The INVITE request will cause Alice's user agent (UA) to ring and respond with a 180 (Ringing) provisional response that includes the SDP answer. At this point, John starts the resource reservation process because he has all the session information to do that. Let us imagine that the resource reservation process fails because there is one router in the path that rejects the resource reservation request. The call would then be dropped, but Alice has already been alerted, therefore resulting in a negative end-user experience. This is shown in Figure 10.7.

To avoid this problem, we need to make sure that the user is alerted only after network resources have been successfully reserved. This implies that SIP session establishment and resource reservation need to be somehow coordinated. The preconditions framework is a SIP extension defined in *RFC 3312* (the main spec) and *RFC 4032* (an update to the previous one) that specifies the way to integrate resource management with SIP and solve these issues. We will describe the usage of the framework for integrating QoS resources; however, the framework is general enough so as to be used for other types of resource management.

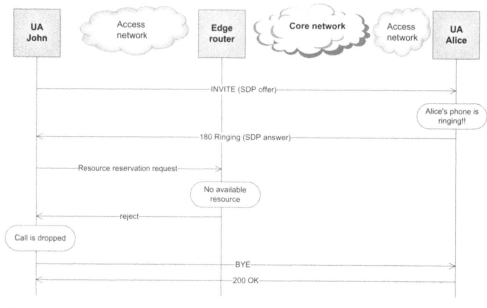

FIGURE 10.7

Example negative end-user experience.

10.4.2 Overview

RFC 3312 introduces the concept of a precondition. A precondition is a set of constraints about the session that need to be fulfilled before the called user can be alerted. The set of constraints is included in the SDP offer. When the called user receives the SDP offer, it generates an answer, but does not alert the user or proceed with session establishment. The recipient waits for the precondition to be met—that is, it waits for the resources to be reserved. As soon as the precondition is met, alerting can occur, and the session establishment can be resumed.

Figure 10.8 shows how this would work for a call between John and Alice. John does not want Alice to be alerted until network resources are reserved in both directions in order to ensure quality of service. So he sends an INVITE request indicating that preconditions are required. This is indicated by:

- Including a SIP Require header field set to the option tag "precondition"
- Including some additional attributes in the SDP offer (see the next section)

When the INVITE reaches Alice's UA, the UA knows that Alice should not be alerted. Alice's UA agrees to reserve network resources. Alice will handle resource reservation in the direction Alice-to-John, but needs John to handle the John-to-Alice direction. Alice indicates this by sending back a 183 (Session Progress) response to John, asking him to start resource reservation and to confirm to her as soon as the John-to-Alice direction is ready for the session. Both John and Alice

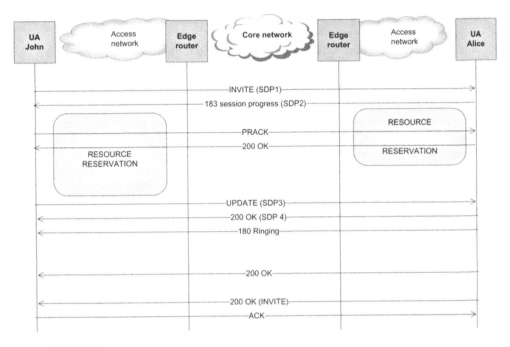

FIGURE 10.8

Call preconditions protect the end user from knowing about the call until it succeeds.

start resource reservation. Let us assume that Alice completes resource reservation in the Alice-to-John direction; she does not alert the user yet because network resources in both directions are needed. When John finishes reserving resources in the John-to-Alice direction, he sends an UPDATE request to Alice. She returns a 200 (OK) response for the UPDATE, indicating that all the preconditions for the session have been met. At this point in time, Alice starts alerting the user, and session establishment completes normally.

10.4.3 Operation

We will now look a bit more in detail at how the SDP exchange works and what are the needed SDP attributes to handle preconditions.

From a user agent's point of view, a precondition is characterized by the following parameters:

- *Type: RFC 3312* considers only the type "qos" (for quality of service). In the future, new types may be defined.
- *Strength:* Indicates whether or not the called party can be alerted if the resources cannot be reserved.

- *Status-type:* Indicates whether the resource reservation needs to be done end to end or segmented.
- *Direction:* Indicates whether the resource reservation applies to one direction (send or receive) or to both.

An end-to-end precondition implies that resources are reserved all along the way between the two parties. A segmented precondition implies that end users need to reserve resources only in their corresponding access networks. From a user agent's perspective, a segmented precondition can be local (if it applies to his or her own access network) or remote (if it applies to a peer's access network). Figures 10.9 and 10.10 illustrate the differences between end-to-end and segmented status-types. The strength tag can have the following values:

- *Mandatory:* Alerting can only occur if resource reservation has been achieved.

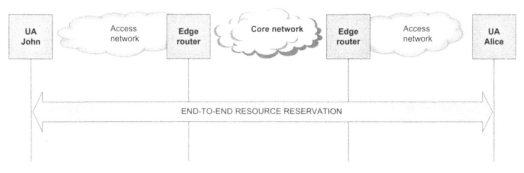

FIGURE 10.9

End-to-end status.

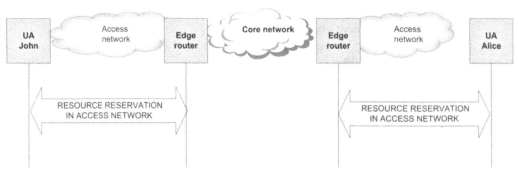

FIGURE 10.10

Segmented status.

- *Optional:* User agents should try to reserve resources, but the session can continue irrespective of whether or not the resource reservation was successfully accomplished.
- *None:* No resource reservation is needed.

The direction parameter can have the following values:

- `sendrecv`: Applies to both directions.
- `send`: Applies to the send direction (from the user agent's point of view).
- `recv`: Applies to the receive direction (from the user agent's point of view).
- `none`: Does not apply for any direction.

We have seen how a precondition is characterized; now let's see how this works.

When John, in our previous example, decides to call Alice using preconditions, he adds some additional media-level attributes to the SDP offer for each media type. One of those attributes is called the desired-status attribute (`a=des`). It represents the desired status for the required precondition. It might look like:

```
a=des:qos mandatory e2e sendrecv
```

What this means is that John requires a `qos` precondition, and that resource reservation must be done end to end and applied to both directions. In addition to the `des` attribute, John must also add another SDP attribute, the current-status attribute (`a=curr`). This attribute represents the actual status of the precondition—that is, the actual status of the resource reservation. Given that John cannot start resource reservation until he has received the SDP answer, the `curr` attribute will indicate that resources are not reserved in any direction. So the complete media-level content of SDP1 would be:

```
m=audio 20000 RTP/AVP 0
a=curr:qos e2e none
a=des:qos mandatory e2e sendrecv
```

The `curr` and `des` attribute must be present in any SDP offer/answer exchange that requires preconditions. The user agent that receives the SDP offer compares `curr` and `des`; if they match (except for the Strength indication, which is sent only from calling party to called party), it means that the precondition is met, and alerting can proceed.

When the INVITE reaches Alice, she will create and send the SDP answer embedded in a 183 response, and start reserving resources in her sending direction. Given that the 183 response contains an SDP answer, it must be sent reliably (that is, it will need to be acknowledged by a PRACK request). The SDP answer reflects the fact that Alice agrees to reserve resources for this session before alerting. She copies the received `des` attribute into the SDP answer, and includes a `curr` attribute that represents her view on the status of the precondition. In addition to those, she adds a new SDP attribute called confirm-status (`a=conf`), which represents a threshold on the status of the precondition. By including it in the response, Alice is indicating that she wants to be notified by John when the pre-condition reaches such a threshold.

SDP2 would look like (only the media-level):

```
m=audio 40000 RTP/AVP 0
a=curr:qos e2e none
a=des:qos mandatory e2e sendrecv
a=conf:qos e2e recv
```

When John receives this SDP, he will know that Alice agrees to reserve resources for this session (otherwise the SDP would have been rejected), so he initiates the resource reservation in his sending direction. The `conf` attribute in this SDP indi-cates to John that when he finishes reserving resources in his sending direction (which corresponds to Alice's receiving direction, as indicated by the `recv` param-eter), he needs to communicate that situation to Alice.

Let us imagine that Alice completes resource reservation in her sending direc-tion. Then she will wait to receive the confirmation from John about the precon-dition status for his sending direction (which corresponds to Alice's receiving direction). When John completes resource reservation in his sending direction, he sends Alice an UPDATE request that reflects the new status for the precondi-tion. SDP3 would look like:

```
m=audio 20000 RTP/AVP 0
a=curr:qos e2e send
a=des:qos mandatory e2e sendrecv
```

We can see that now the current status indicates `send` direction, as opposed to `none`, as appeared in SDP1.

At this point, Alice's UA knows that the precondition has been met, so she will include SDP4 in the body of the 200 (OK) response to the UPDATE, and ringing will start. SDP4 would look like:

```
m=audio 20000 RTP/AVP 0
a=curr:qos e2e sendrecv
a=des:qos mandatory e2e sendrecv
```

As we have seen from the example, the SIP preconditions extension requires that two additional SIP extensions are supported by user agents: the PRACK and UPDATE methods. Therefore, the INVITE requests that require preconditions must additionally include the `100rel` tag in the Supported header field, and should include an Allow header field with the "UPDATE" tag.

10.5 SIP INTEGRATION WITH POLICY CONTROL: MEDIA AND QOS AUTHORIZATION

10.5.1 Motivation

In SIP communication scenarios, SDP is typically used to describe the desired session characteristics. SDP also allows a user agent to indicate that QoS requirements must be met in order to successfully set up a session. However, we have seen that a different protocol, RSVP, is used to request the resources required to meet the end-to-end QoS of the media stream. Therefore, there is a need to assure that the resources requested through the resource reservation process match the resources that were requested and authorized as part of the SIP/SDP session establishment process. In other words, we need a mechanism to link the SIP and transport layer to ensure that policies are correctly enforced. *RFC 3313* defines such a mechanism and will be described in the next subsection.

It is worth mentioning that this mechanism is again in contrast to general Internet principles, which completely separate data from applications. Thus, this solution is not applicable to the Internet at large, but does find a lot of applicability scenarios in networks under a single administrative domain. The SIP extension needed to implement these functions will then be defined as a private (P-) extension.

10.5.2 **Architecture**

RFC 3521 and *RFC 3313* define the reference architecture for applying SIP sessions set up with media and QoS authorization, which is depicted in Figure 10.11. The following list describes the elements in the architecture.

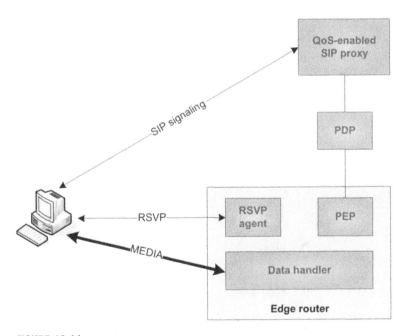

FIGURE 10.11

SIP sessions can be set up with media and QoS authorization.

- *End host*: It is the user's device. It comprises a SIP UA, an RSVP client, and a media tool.
- *Edge router*: It is the router connecting the end host to the rest of the network. It includes the following three components.
  - Policy enforcement point: that is the point where the policy decisions are enforced
  - RSVP agent
  - Data handler, which includes the packet classifier, packet scheduler, and the admission control module
- *QoS-enabled SIP proxy:* That is, a SIP proxy that has the capability to interact with a PDP for the purpose of retrieving the media authorization token, as we will see later on.
- *Policy decision point:* The point where the policy decisions are made.

Figure 10.12 depicts, at a high level, how the media authorization process works. During SIP session establishment, the QoS-enabled proxy will check if the user is authorized to receive QoS. If he or she is, the proxy will contact the PDP and obtain an authorization token. The authorization token is stored in the PDP together with the negotiated session description.

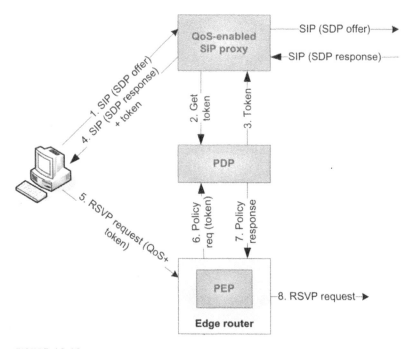

FIGURE 10.12

High-level view of the media authorization process.

The proxy includes the token in the response back to the UA. The token contains all the information needed for the end host to perform resource reservation. Therefore, the end host initiates the resource reservation, including the token in the RSVP message requesting QoS. When this message is received by the edge router, the PEP will forward the token, together with the requested bandwidth, to the PDP. The PDP will check if the corresponding requested bandwidth is within the limit of what was negotiated in the SDP exchange. The PDP uses the token as the key to find the stored negotiated SDP. If the check is passed, the PDP sends back a positive response to the PEP, which reserves the resources and forwards the RSVP message.

10.5.3 Implementation

In order to carry the token in the SIP signaling, a new header is defined: P-Media-Authorization. This header includes a P-Media-Authorization-Token, which represents the token in a specific format. In RSVP signaling, the token is conveyed in an RSVP object called policy data—more specifically, in the Policy-Element field within that object, as defined in *RFC 2750*, which is an extension to the base RSVP protocol defined in *RFC 2205*.

10.5.4 Example

We will now see an end-to-end example for a session setup with media/QoS authorization and resource reservation. The call flow is shown in Figure 10.13. We will assume that:

- John wants to set up a multimedia session with Alice.
- Both John and Alice have contracted QoS with their service provider.
    1. John sends an INVITE to his QoS-enabled outbound proxy (proxy A). The INVITE request includes the SDP offer. The SDP offer contains the description of the media that John desires to use for this communication, and the bandwidth ("b" parameter) requested.
    2. When the outbound proxy receives the INVITE message from the UAC, the proxy authenticates the caller and verifies that the caller is authorized to obtain QoS.
    3. Proxy A forwards the INVITE.
    4. Alice's inbound proxy (proxy B) receives the INVITE. It authenticates the originating proxy and authorizes the call.
    5. Proxy B sends a policy-setup message (AuthProfile) to PDP-B including the media description. PDP-B stores the authorized media description in its local store, and generates an authentication token that points to this description.
    6. PDP-B returns the authorization token to proxy B (AuthToken).
    7. Proxy B places the token in the INVITE message and forwards it to Alice's UA.

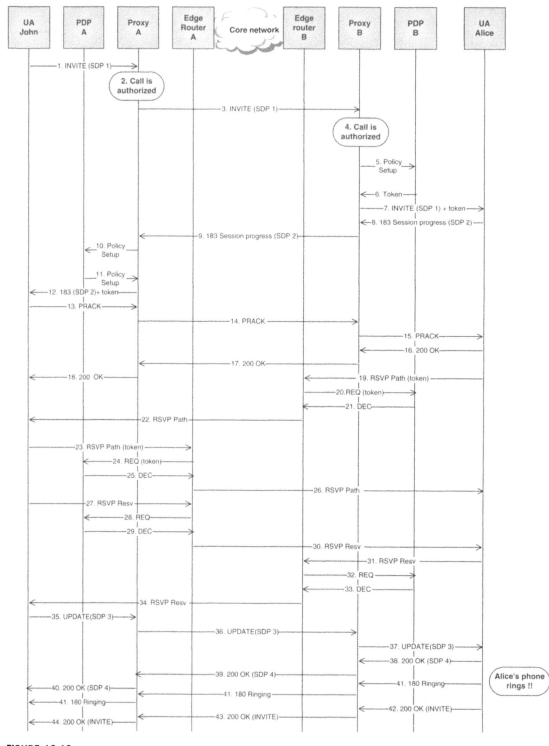

FIGURE 10.13

The call message flow.

8. Alice's UA sends a 183 response (including the Source Description Protocol response) reliably.

9. Proxy B forwards the response to proxy A.

10. Proxy A sends a policy-setup message (AuthProfile) to PDP-A including the negotiated media description. PDP-A stores the authorized media description in its local store, and generates an authentication token that points to this description.

11. PDP-A returns the authorization token to proxy A (AuthToken).

12–18. Proxy A forwards the 183 response to John's UA. Then a PRACK transaction takes place to confirm delivery of the 183 response.

19. As soon as Alice has sent the 183 response (step 8), she can request QoS by sending an RSVP Path message that includes the received token as a policy element.

20. The edge router B, acting as PEP for UA-B, upon receipt of the RSVP Path message, sends a COPS message (REQ) to PDP-B. PDP-B checks the authorization using the stored authorized media description that was linked to the authorization token it returned to proxy B.

21. If the authorization is successful, PDP-B returns an "install" decision (DEC).

22. Edge Router B checks the admissibility of the request, and, if admission succeeds, it forwards the RSVP Path message toward John.

23–26. As soon as John receives the 183 response (step 12), he can start requesting quality of service by sending an RSVP Path message. So, steps analogous to steps 20, 21, and 22 take place, but now on the originating side.

27. As soon as John receives the RSVP Path message (step 22), he sends an RSVP Resv message to reserve resources on the network.

28. The edge router A, upon receipt of the RSVP Resv message, sends a COPS message (REQ) to PDP-A. PDP-A checks the authorization using the stored authorized media description that was linked to the authorization token it returned to proxy A.

29. If the authorization is successful, PDP A returns an "install" decision (DEC).

30. Edge router A checks the admissibility of the request, and, if admission succeeds, it forwards the RSVP Resv message toward Alice.

31–34. As soon as Alice receives the RSVP Path message, she sends the RSVP Resv message in order to reserve resources on the network. So, steps analogous to steps 28, 29, and 30 take place, but now they are on the terminating side.

35–40. As soon as John receives the RSVP Resv message, he sends an UPDATE to Alice to indicate that the preconditions are fulfilled. The UPDATE is acknowledged.

41. As soon as the UPDATE is received, Alice's UA starts ringing.

42. Alice accepts the call, and the media is established.

10.6 SUMMARY

This chapter introduced many concepts. As a summary, for the process to apply QoS in SIP communications, readers should remember:

- The user agents (e.g., calling party and called party) ask for resources through SDP in SIP signaling.
- SIP proxies in the control plane then *permit* the media plane to allocate these resources.
- The clients must still *request* the routers in the media plane to actually *allocate* these resources.

The architectures around QoS are well known, though they have not yet been widely deployed. Broadband accesses and an Internet with increasing capacity have made these architectures not needed in many cases so far. However, with the advent of IP multimedia services for wireless, bandwidth-restricted accesses, these ideas recover importance, and we will see that they will play a crucial role in the IMS architecture for mobile operators.

10.7 RESOURCES

This chapter makes reference to the following IETF RFCs.

RFC 1633, "Integrated Services in the Internet Architecture: an Overview," Braden, R., et al., 1994.

RFC 2205, "Resource ReSerVation Protocol (RSVP)—Version 1 Functional Specification," Braden, R., et al., 1997.

RFC 2211, "Specification of the Controlled-Load Network Element Service," Wroclawski, J., 1997.

RFC 2212, "Specification of Guaranteed Quality of Service," Shenker, S., et al., 1997.

RFC 2474, "Definition of the Differentiated Services Field (DS Field) in the IPv4 and IPv6, Headers," Nichols, K., et al., 1998.

RFC 2475, "An Architecture for Differentiated Services," Blake, S., et al., 1998.

RFC 2597, "Assured Forwarding PHB Group," Heinanen, J., 1999.

RFC 2748, "The COPS (Common Open Policy Service) Protocol," Durham, D., 2000.

RFC 2750, "RSVP Extensions for Policy Control," Herzog, S., 2000.

RFC 2753, "A Framework for Policy-Based Admission Control," Yavatkar, R., et al., 2000.

RFC 2998, "A Framework for Integrated Services Operation over DiffServ Networks," Bernet, Y., et al., 2000.

RFC 3260, "New Terminology and Clarifications for DiffServ," Grossman, D., 2002.

RFC 3312, "Integration of Resource Management and Session Initiation Protocol (SIP)," Camarillo, G., 2002.

RFC 3313, "Private Session Initiation Protocol (SIP) Extensions for Media Authorization," Marshall, W., 2003.

RFC 3521, "Framework for Session Set-up with Media Authorization," Hamer, L-N., 2003.

RFC 3588, "Diameter Base Protocol," Calhoun, P., 2003.

RFC 4032, "Update to the Session Initiation Protocol (SIP) Preconditions Framework," Camarillo, G., and P. Kyzivat, 2005.

RFC 4261, "Common Open Policy Service (COPS) Over Transport Layer Security (TLS)," Walker, J., and A. Kulkarni, 2005.

Core Capacity Planning and Traffic Engineering in IP and MPLS Networks

11

This chapter, taken from Chapter 6 of *Deploying IP and MPLS QoS for Multiservice Networks: Theory and Practice* by John William Evans and Clarence Filsfils, addresses core capacity planning and how traffic engineering can be used as a tool to make more efficient use of network capacity. This chapter has benefited enormously from the input of Thomas Telkamp, Director of Network Consulting at Cariden Technologies, Inc. Thomas's work formed the basis of the capacity planning section.

11.1 CORE NETWORK CAPACITY PLANNING

Capacity planning of the core network is the process of ensuring that sufficient bandwidth is provisioned such that the committed core network service level agreement (SLA) targets of delay, jitter, loss, and availability can be met. In the core network where link bandwidths are high and traffic is highly aggregated, the SLA requirements for a traffic class can be translated into bandwidth requirements, and the problem of SLA assurance can effectively be reduced to that of bandwidth provisioning. Hence, the ability to assure SLAs is dependent on ensuring that core network bandwidth is adequately provisioned, which is in turn dependent on core capacity planning.

The simplest core capacity planning processes use passive measurements of core link utilization statistics and apply rules of thumb, such as upgrading links when they reach 50 percent average utilization, or some other such general utilization target. The aim of such simple processes is to attempt to ensure that the core links are always significantly overprovisioned relative to the offered average load, on the assumption that this will ensure that they are also sufficiently overprovisioned relative to the peak load, that congestion will not occur, and hence the SLA requirements will be met.

There are, however, two significant consequences of such a simple approach. Firstly, without a network-wide understanding of the traffic demands, even an approach that upgrades links when they reach 50 percent average utilization may not be able to ensure that the links are still sufficiently provisioned when network element (e.g., link and node) failures occur, in order to ensure that the committed SLA targets continue to be met. Secondly, and conversely, rule-of-thumb approaches such as this may result in more capacity being provisioned than is actually needed.

Effective core capacity planning can overcome both of these issues. Effective core capacity planning requires a way of measuring the current network load, and a way of determining how much bandwidth should be provisioned relative to the measured load in order to achieve the committed SLAs. Hence, in this section we present a holistic methodology for capacity planning of the core network, which takes the core traffic demand matrix and the network topology into account to determine how much capacity is needed in the network in order to meet the committed SLA requirements, taking network element failures into account if necessary, while minimizing the capacity and cost associated with overprovisioning.

The methodology presented in this section can be applied whether DiffServ is deployed in the core or not. Where DiffServ is not deployed, capacity planning is performed on aggregate. Where DiffServ is deployed, while the fundamental principles remain the same, capacity planning per traffic class is needed to ensure that class SLA targets are not violated.

11.1.1 Capacity Planning Methodology

We distinguish the following steps in the process of capacity planning:

1. Collect the core traffic demand matrices (either on aggregate or per class) and add traffic growth predictions to create a traffic demand forecast. This step is described in Section 11.1.2.

2. Determine the appropriate bandwidth overprovisioning factors (either on aggregate or per class) relative to the measured demand matrices, which are required to ensure that committed SLAs can be met. This step is described in Section 11.1.3.

3. Run simulations to overlay the forecasted demands onto the network topology, taking failure cases into account if necessary, to determine the forecasted link loadings. Analyze the results, comparing the forecasted link loadings against the provisioned bandwidth and taking the calculated overprovisioning factors into account, to determine the future capacity provisioning plan required to achieve the desired SLAs. This step is described in Section 11.1.4.

This capacity planning process is illustrated by Figure 11.1. The steps in the capacity planning process are described in detail in the sections that follow.

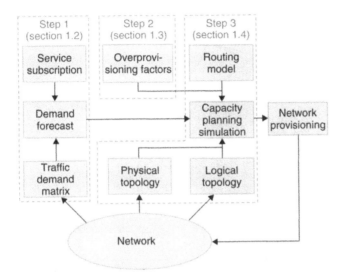

FIGURE 11.1

Capacity planning methodology.

11.1.2 Collecting the Traffic Demand Matrices

The core traffic demand matrix is the matrix of ingress-to-egress traffic demands across the core network. Traffic matrices can be measured or estimated to different levels of aggregation: by IP prefix, by router, by point of presence (POP), or by autonomous system (AS). The benefit of a core traffic matrix over simple per-link statistics is that the demand matrix can be used in conjunction with an understanding of the network routing model to predict the impact that demand growths can have and to simulate "what-if" scenarios, in order to understand the impact that the failure of core network elements can have on the (aggregate or per-class) utilization of the rest of the links in the network.

With simple per-link statistics, when a link or node fails, in all but very simple topologies it may not be possible to know over which links the traffic impacted by the failure will be rerouted. Core network capacity is increasingly being provisioned taking single network element failure cases into account. To understand traffic rerouting in failure cases, a traffic matrix is needed which aggregates traffic at the router-to-router level. If DiffServ is deployed, a per-class of service core traffic matrix is highly desirable.

The core traffic demand matrix can be an internal traffic matrix (i.e., router-to-router, or an external traffic matrix (i.e., router to AS), as illustrated in Figure 11.2, which shows the internal traffic demand matrix from one distribution router (DR), and the external traffic demand matrix from another.

The internal traffic matrix is useful for understanding the impact that internal network element failures will have on the traffic loading within the core. An

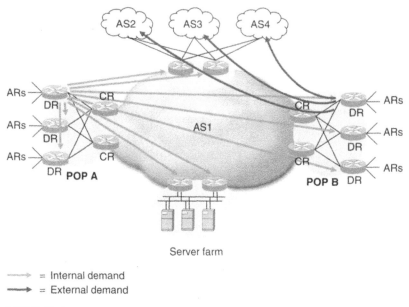

= Internal demand
= External demand

FIGURE 11.2

Internal and external traffic demands.

internal matrix could also be edge-to-edge (e.g., DR to DR), or just across the inner core (e.g., CR to CR); a DR to DR matrix is preferred, as this can also be used to determine the impact of failures within a POP. The external traffic matrix provides additional context, which could be useful for managing peering connection capacity provision, and for understanding where internal network failures might impact in the external traffic matrix, due to closest-exit (a.k.a. "hot potato") routing.

There are a number of possible approaches for collecting the core traffic demand matrix statistics. The approaches differ in terms of their ability to provide an internal or external matrix, whether they can be applied to IP or MPLS, and whether they can provide a per-class of service traffic matrix. Further, the capabilities of network devices to provide information required to determine the core traffic matrix can vary depending on the details of the particular vendor's implementation. Some of the possible approaches for determining the core traffic demand matrix are discussed in the following subsections. Further details on the options for deriving a core traffic matrix are provided in *Best Practices for Determining the Traffic Matrix in IP Networks* by Thomas Telkamp.

IP Flow Statistics Aggregation

The Internet Protocol Flow Information eXport (IPFIX) protocol has been defined within the IETF as a standard for the export of IP flow information from routers, probes, and other devices. If edge devices such as distribution routers are capable of accounting at a flow level (i.e., in terms of packet and byte counts), then a number of potential criteria could be used to aggregate this flow information—potentially locally on the device—to produce a traffic matrix.

Where the Border Gateway Protocol (BGP) is used within an AS, for example, each router at the edge of the AS is referred to as a BGP "peer." For each IP destination address that a peer advertises via BGP it also advertises a BGP next hop IP address, which is used when forwarding packets to that destination. In order to forward a packet to that destination, another BGP router within the AS needs to perform a recursive lookup, firstly looking in its BGP table to retrieve the BGP next-hop address associated with that destination address, and then looking in its Interior Gateway Routing Protocol (IGP) routing table to determine how to get to that particular BGP next-hop address (for further understanding on the workings of BGP, see the further reading section at the end of this chapter). Hence, aggregating IPFIX flow statistics based on the BGP next hop IP address used to reach a particular destination would produce an edge router to edge router traffic matrix.

MPLS LSP Accounting

Where MPLS is used, a label switched path (LSP) implicitly represents an aggregate traffic demand. Where BGP is deployed in conjunction with label distribution by the Label Distribution Protocol (LDP), in the context of a BGP MPLS VPN service for example, and each provider edge (PE) router is a BGP peer, an LSP from one PE to another implicitly represents the PE-to-PE traffic demand. The distribution routers in the generalized network reference model we use in this chapter will normally be provider edge (PE) routers in the context of an MPLS VPN deployment. Hence, if traffic accounting statistics are maintained per LSP, these can be retrieved, using Simple Network Management Protocol (SNMP) for example, to produce the PE-to-PE core traffic matrix.

If MPLS traffic engineering is deployed (see Section 11.2.3) with a full mesh of traffic engineering (TE) tunnels, then each TE tunnel LSP implicitly represents the aggregate demand of traffic from the head-end router at the source of the tunnel, to the tail-end router at the tunnel destination. Hence, if traffic accounting statistics are maintained per TE tunnel LSP, these can be retrieved, using SNMP for example, to understand the core traffic matrix. If DiffServ-aware TE is deployed (see DiffServ-Aware MPLS Traffic Engineering section) with a full mesh of TE tunnels per class of service, the same technique could be used to retrieve a per-traffic class traffic matrix.

Demand Estimation

Demand estimation is the application of mathematical methods to measurements taken from the network, such as core link usage statistics, in order to infer the traffic demand matrix that generated those usage statistics. There are a number of methods that have been proposed for deriving traffic matrices from link measurements and other easily measured data (see Further Reading at the end of this chapter), and there are a number of commercially available tools that use these, or similar, techniques in order to derive the core traffic demand matrix. If link statistics are available on a per-traffic class basis, then these techniques can be applied to estimate the per-class of service traffic matrix.

Retrieving and Using the Statistics

Whichever approach is used for determining the core traffic matrix, the next decision that needs to be made is how often to retrieve the measured statistics from the network. The retrieved statistics will normally be in the form of packet and byte counts, which can be used to determine the average traffic demands over the previous sampling interval. The longer the sampling interval (i.e., the less frequently the statistics are retrieved), the greater the possibility that significant variation in the traffic during the sampling interval may be hidden due to the effects of averaging.

Conversely, the more frequently the statistics are retrieved, the greater the load on the system retrieving the data, the greater the load on the device being polled, and the greater the polling traffic on the network. Hence, in practice the frequency with which the statistics are retrieved is a balance, which depends on the size of the network; in backbone networks it is common to collect these statistics every 5, 10, or 15 minutes.

The measured statistics can then be used to determine the traffic demand matrix during each interval. In order to make the subsequent stages of the process manageable, it may be necessary to select some traffic matrices from the collected data set. A number of possible selection criteria could be applied; one possible approach is to sum the individual (i.e., router to router) traffic demands within each interval, and to take the interval that has the greatest total traffic demand, (i.e., the peak). Alternatively, in order to be sensitive to outliers (e.g., due to possible measurement errors), a high percentile interval such as the 95th percentile (P-95) could be taken, that is the interval for which more than 95 percent of the intervals have a lower value.

In order to be representative, the total data set should be taken over at least a week, or preferably over a month, to ensure that trends in the traffic demand matrices are captured. In the case of a small network, it might be feasible to use all measurement intervals (e.g., all 288 daily measurements for 5-minute intervals), rather than to only use the peak (or percentile of peak) interval; this will give the most accurate simulation results for the network.

In geographically diverse networks, regional peaks in the traffic demand matrix may occur, such that most links in a specific region are near their daily maximum, at a time of the day when the total traffic in the network is not at its maximum. In a global network for example, in morning office hours in Europe, the European region may be busy, while the North American region is relatively lightly loaded. It is not very easy to detect regional peaks automatically, and one alternative approach is to define administrative capacity planning network regions (e.g., United States, Europe, Asia), and apply the previously described procedure per region, to give a selected per-region traffic matrix.

Once the traffic matrix has been determined, other factors may need to be taken into account, such as anticipated traffic growth. Capacity planning will typically be performed looking sufficiently far in advance that new bandwidth could be provisioned before network loading exceeds acceptable levels. If it takes 3 months to provision or upgrade a new core link, for example, and capacity planning is performed monthly, then the capacity planning process would need to try to predict at least 4 months in advance. If expected network traffic growth within the next 4 months was 10 percent, for example, then the current traffic demand matrix would need to be multiplied with a factor of at least 1.1. Service subscription forecasts may be able to provide more granular predictions of future demand growth, possibly predicting the increase of particular traffic demands.

11.1.3 Determine Appropriate Overprovisioning Factors

The derived traffic matrices described in the previous section are averages taken over the sample interval, hence they lack information on the variation in traffic demands within each interval. There will invariably be bursts within the measurement interval that are above the average rate; if traffic bursts are sufficiently large temporary congestion may occur, causing delay, jitter, and loss, which may result in the violation of SLA commitments even though the link is on average not 100 percent utilized. To ensure that bursts above the average do not impact the SLAs, the actual bandwidth may need to be overprovisioned relative to the measure average rates. Hence, a key capacity planning consideration is to determine by how much bandwidth needs to be overprovisioned relative to the measured average rate, in order to meet a defined SLA target for delay, jitter, and loss; we define this as the overprovisioning factor (OP).

The overprovisioning factor required to achieve a particular SLA target depends on the arrival distribution of the traffic on the link, and the link speed. Opinions remain divided on what arrival distribution describes traffic in IP networks. One view is that traffic is self-similar, which means that it is bursty on many or all timescales (i.e., whatever time period the traffic is measured over the variation in the average rate of the traffic stream is the same). An alternative view is that IP traffic arrivals follow a Poisson (or more generally Markovian) arrival process. For Poisson distributed traffic, the longer the time period over which the traffic stream is measured, the less variation there is in the average rate of the traffic stream. Conversely, the shorter the time interval over which the stream is measured, the greater the visibility of burst or the burstiness of the traffic stream. The differences in the resulting measured average utilization between self-similar and Poisson traffic, when measured over different timescales, are shown in Figure 11.3.

For Poisson traffic, queuing theory shows that as link speeds increase and traffic is more highly aggregated, queuing delays reduce for a given level of utilization. For self-similar traffic, however, if the traffic is truly bursty at all timescales, the queuing delay would not decrease with increased traffic aggregation. However, while views on whether IP network traffic tends toward self-similar or Poisson are

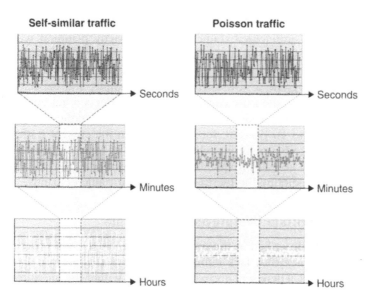

Self-similar traffic   **Poisson traffic**

FIGURE 11.3

Self-similar versus Poisson traffic.

still split, this does not fundamentally impact the capacity planning methodology we are describing. Rather, the impact of these observations is that, for high-speed links, the overprovisioning factor required to achieve a specified SLA target would need to be significantly greater for self-similar traffic than for Poisson traffic.

> *Caveat lector:* A number of studies, both theoretical and empirical, have sought to quantify the bandwidth provisioning required to achieve a particular target for delay, jitter, and loss, although none of these studies has yet been accepted as definitive. In the rest of this section, by way of example, we use the results attained in the study by Telkamp to illustrate the capacity planning methodology. We chose these results because they probably represent the most widely used guidance with respect to core network overprovisioning.

In order to investigate bandwidth provisioning requirements, a number of sets of packet level measurements were captured from an operational IP backbone, carrying Internet and VPN traffic. The traces were used in simulation to determine the bursting and queuing of traffic at small timescales over this interval, to identify the relationship between measures of link utilization that can be easily obtained with capacity planning techniques (e.g., 5-minute average utilizations), and queuing delays experienced in much smaller timeframes, in order to determine the overprovisioning factors required to achieve various SLA targets. By using traces of actual traffic they avoided the need to make assumptions about the nature of the traffic distribution.

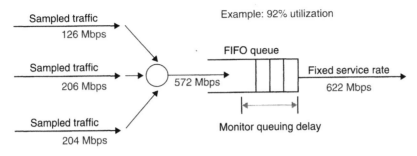

FIGURE 11.4

Queuing simulation.
Source: Adapted from *Traffic Characteristics and Network Planning* by Thomas Telkamp.

Each set of packet measurements or "trace" contained timestamps in microseconds of the arrival time for every packet on a link, over an interval of minutes. The traces, each of different average rates, were then used in a simulation where multiple traces were multiplexed together and the resulting trace was run through a simulated fixed-speed queue (e.g., at 622 Mbps), as shown in Figure 11.4.

In the example in Figure 11.4, three traces with 5-minute average rates of 126 Mbps, 206 Mbps, and 240 Mbps respectively are multiplexed together resulting in a trace with a 5-minute average rate of 572 Mbps, which is run through a 622 Mbps queue (i.e., at a 5-minute average utilization of 92 percent). The queue depth was monitored during the simulation to determine how much queuing delay was experienced. This process was then repeated, with different mixes of traffic; as each mix had a different average utilization, multiple data points were produced for a specific interface speed.

After performing this process for multiple interface speeds, results were derived showing the relationship between average link utilization and the probability of queuing delay. The graph in Figure 11.5 uses the results of this study to show the relationship between the measured 5-minute average link utilization and queuing delay for a number of link speeds. The delay value shown is the P99.9 delay, meaning that 999 out of 1000 packets will have a delay caused by queuing that is lower than this value.

The *x*-axis in Figure 11.5 represents the 5-minute average link utilization; the *y*-axis represents the P99.9 delay. The lines show fitted functions to the simulation results for various link speeds, from 155 Mbps to 2.5 Gbps. Note that other relationships would result if the measured utilization was averaged over longer time periods (e.g., 10 minutes or 15 minutes), as in these cases there may be greater variations that are hidden by averaging, and hence lower average utilizations would be needed to achieve the same delay. The results in Figure 11.5 show that for the same relative levels of utilization, lower delays are experienced for 1 Gbps links than for 622 Mbps links; that is, the level of overprovisioning required to

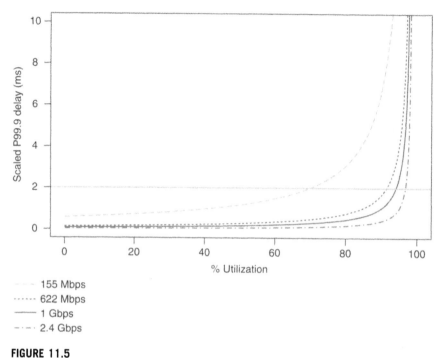

FIGURE 11.5

Queuing simulation results.
Source: Adapted from *Traffic Characteristics and Network Planning* by Thomas Telkamp.

achieve a particular delay target reduces as link bandwidth increases, which is indicative of Poisson traffic.

Taking these results as an example, we can use them to determine the over-provisioning factor that is required to achieve particular SLA objectives. For example, if we assume that DiffServ is not deployed in the core network and want to achieve a target P99.9 queuing delay of 2 ms on a 155 Mbps link, then from Figure 11.5, the 5-minute average link utilization should not be higher than approximately 70 percent or 109 Mbps (i.e., an OP of 1/0.7 = 1.42 is required), meaning that the provisioned link bandwidth should be at least 1.42 times the 5-minute average link utilization. To achieve the same objective for a 1 Gbps link the 5-minute average utilization should be no more than 96 percent or 960 Mbps (i.e., OP = 1.04).

Although the study by Telkamp did not focus on voice traffic, in similar studies by the same authors for VoIP-only traffic (with silence suppression) the OP factors required to achieve the same delay targets were similar.

We can apply the same principle on a per-class basis where DiffServ is deployed. To assure a P99.9 queuing delay of 1 ms for a class serviced with an assured for-warding (AF) PHB providing a minimum bandwidth assurance of 622 Mbps (i.e.,

Number of hops	Delay multiplication factor
1	1.0
2	1.7
3	1.9
4	2.2
5	2.5
6	2.8
7	3.0
8	3.3

FIGURE 11.6

P99.9 delay multiplication factor.

25 percent of a 2.5 Gbps link), the 5-minute average utilization for the class should not be higher than approximately 85 percent or 529 Mbps. Considering another example, to ensure a P99.9 queuing delay of 500 µs for a class serviced with an expedited forwarding (EF) per-hop behavior (PHB) implemented with a strict priority queue on a 2.5 Gbps link, as the scheduler servicing rate of the strict priority queue is 2.5 Gbps, the 5-minute average utilization for the class should not be higher than approximately 92 percent or 2.3 Gbps (i.e., OP = 1.09) of the link rate. Note that these results are for queuing delay only and exclude the possible delay impact on EF traffic due to the scheduler and the interface FIFO.

The delay that has been discussed so far is *per link* and not end-to-end across the core. In most cases, traffic will traverse multiple links in the network, and hence will potentially be subject to queuing delays multiple times. Based on the results by Telkamp, the P99.9 delay was not additive over multiple hops; rather, the table in Figure 11.6 shows the delay "multiplication factor" experienced over a number of hops, relative to the delay over a single hop.

If the delay objective across the core is known, the overprovisioning factor that needs to be maintained per link can be determined. The core delay objective is divided by the multiplication factor from the table in Figure 11.6 to find the per-hop delay objective. This delay can then be looked up in the graphs in Figure 11.5 to find the maximum utilization for a specific link capacity that will meet this per-hop queuing delay objective.

Consider for example, a network comprising 155 Mbps links with a P99.9 delay objective across the core network of 10 ms, and a maximum of 8 hops. From Figure 11.5, the 8 hops cause a multiplication of the per-link number by 3.3, so the per-link objective becomes 10 ms/3.3 = 3 ms. From Figure 11.6, the 3 ms line intersects with the 155 Mbps utilization curve at 80 percent. So the conclusion is that the 5-minute average utilization on the 155 Mbps links in the network should not be more than approximately 80 percent or 124 Mbps (i.e., OP = 1.25) to achieve the goal of 10 ms delay across the core.

11.1.4 Simulation and Analysis

After obtaining the demand matrix, allowing for growth, and determining the overprovisioning factors required to achieve specific SLA targets, the final step in the capacity planning process is to overlay the traffic demands onto the network topology. This requires both an understanding of the network routing model—for example, whether an interior gateway routing protocol (IGP), such as IS–IS or OSPF, is used or whether MPLS traffic engineering is used—and an understanding of the logical network topology (i.e., link metrics and routing protocol areas) in order to understand the routing through the network that demands would take and hence to correctly map the demands to the topology.

There are a number of commercially available tools that can perform this function. Some can also run failure case simulations, which consider the loading on the links in network element failures; it is common to model for single element failures, where an element could be a link, a node, or a shared risk link group (SRLG). SRLGs can be used to group together links that might fail simultaneously; to represent the failure of unprotected interfaces sharing a common line card or circuits sharing a common fiber duct, for example. The concept of SRLGs can also be applied to more than just links, grouping links and nodes which may represent a shared risk, in order to consider what would happen to the network loading in the presence of the failure of a complete POP, for example.

The results of the simulation provide indications of the expected loading of the links in the network; this could be the aggregate loading or the per-class loading if DiffServ is deployed. The forecasted link loadings can then be compared against the provisioned link capacity, taking the calculated overprovisioning factors into account, to determine the future bandwidth provisioning plan required to achieve the desired SLAs. The capacity planner can then use this information to identify links which may be overloaded, such that SLAs will be violated, or areas where more capacity is provisioned than is actually needed.

11.2 IP TRAFFIC ENGINEERING

Capacity planning, as discussed in the preceding section, is the process of ensuring that sufficient bandwidth is provisioned to assure that the committed core SLA targets can be met. IP traffic engineering is the logical process of manipulating traffic on an IP network to make better use of the network capacity, by making use of capacity that would otherwise be unused, for example. Hence, traffic engineering is a tool that can be used to ensure that the available network capacity is appropriately provisioned.

We contrast traffic engineering to network engineering, which is the physical process of manipulating a network to suit the traffic load, by putting in a new link between two POPs to support a traffic demand between them, for example. Clearly, network engineering and traffic engineering are linked; however, in this section we focus on the options for traffic engineering in an IP network. The outcome of the capacity planning process described in the previous section may drive the need for traffic engineering within a network.

In IP-based networks, traffic engineering is often considered synonymous with MPLS traffic engineering in particular, which is described in Section 11.2.3; however, there are other approaches in IP networks, including traffic engineering through the manipulation of IGP metrics—which is described in Section 11.2.2.

11.2.1 The Problem

In conventional IP networks IGPs such as OSPF and IS–IS forward IP packets on the shortest cost path toward the destination IP subnet address of each IP packet. The computation of the shortest cost path is based on a simple additive metric (also known as weight or cost), where each link has an applied metric, and the cost for a path is the sum of the link metrics on the path. Availability of network resources, such as bandwidth, is not taken into account and, consequently, traffic can aggregate on the shortest (i.e., lowest-cost) path, potentially causing links on the shortest path to be congested while links on alternative paths are under-utilized. This property of conventional IP routing protocols, of traffic aggregation on the shortest path, can cause suboptimal use of network resources, and can consequently impact the SLAs that can be offered, or require more network capacity than is optimally required.

Consider, for example, the network in Figure 11.7, where each link is 2.5 Gbps and each link has the same metric (assume a metric of 1). If there were a traffic demand of 1 Gbps from R1 to R8, and a traffic demand of 2 Gbps from R2 to R8, then the IGP would pick the same route for both traffic demands (i.e., R1/R2 → R3 → R4 → R7 → R8), because it has a metric of 4 (summing the metric of 1 for each of the links traversed) and hence is the shortest path.

Therefore, in this example, the decision to route both traffic demands by the top path (R3 → R4 → R7) may result in the path being congested, with a total offered load of 3 Gbps, while there is capacity available on the bottom path (R3 → R5 → R6 → R7). Traffic engineering aims to provide a solution to this problem.

The problem of traffic engineering can be defined as a mathematical optimization problem; that is, a computational problem in which the objective is to find the best of all possible solutions. Given a fixed network topology and a fixed source-to-destination traffic demand matrix to be carried, the optimization problem could be defined as determining the routing of flows that makes most effective use of (either aggregate or per-class) capacity.

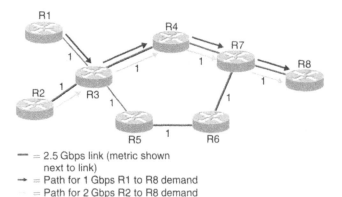

— = 2.5 Gbps link (metric shown
     next to link)
→ = Path for 1 Gbps R1 to R8 demand
    = Path for 2 Gbps R2 to R8 demand

FIGURE 11.7

Traffic engineering: the problem.

In order to solve this problem, however, it is important to define what is meant by the objective "most effective:" This could be to minimize the maximum link/class utilization in normal network working case conditions (i.e., when there are no network element failures). Alternatively the optimization objective could be to minimize the maximum link/class utilization under network element failure case conditions; typically single element (i.e., link, node, or SRLG) failure conditions are considered.

In considering the deployment of traffic engineering mechanisms, it is imperative that the primary optimization objective is defined in order to understand what benefits the different options for traffic engineering can provide and where traffic engineering will not help, but rather more bandwidth is required. Other optimization objectives are possible, such as minimizing propagation delay; however, if considered these are normally secondary objectives.

If we apply the primary optimization objective of minimizing the maximum link utilization in network working case (i.e., normal operating) conditions to the network shown in Figure 11.7 then the solution would be to route some subset of the traffic over the top path (R3 → R4 → R7) and the remainder over the bottom path (R3 → R5 → R6 → R7) such that congestion on the top path is prevented. If, however, we apply the primary optimization objective of minimizing the maximum link utilization during single network element failure case conditions, then on the failure of the link between R3 and R4, for example, both traffic demands R1 to R8 and R2 to R8 will be rerouted onto the bottom path (R3 → R5 → R6 → R7), which would be congested, as shown in Figure 11.8.

The figure illustrates that traffic engineering cannot create capacity and that in some topologies, and possibly dependent on the optimization objective, traffic engineering may not help. In network topologies that have only two paths available in normal network working case conditions, such as ring-based topologies,

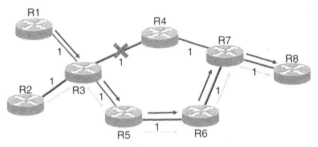

FIGURE 11.8

Failure case optimization.

it is not possible to apply traffic engineering with a primary optimization objective of minimizing the maximum link utilization during network element failure case conditions; there is no scope for sophisticated traffic engineering decisions in network failure case conditions; if a link on one path fails, the other path is taken. In these cases, if congestion occurs during failure conditions then more capacity is simply required. More meshed network topologies may allow scope for traffic engineering in network element failure case conditions.

The chief benefit of traffic engineering is one of cost saving. Traffic engineering gives the network designer flexibility in how to manage backbone bandwidth to achieve proper SLAs. The more effective use of bandwidth potentially allows higher SLA targets to be offered with the existing backbone bandwidth. Alternatively, it offers the potential to achieve the existing SLA targets with less backbone bandwidth or to delay the time until bandwidth upgrades are required. The following conditions can all be drivers for the deployment of traffic engineering mechanisms:

Network asymmetry: Asymmetrical network topologies can often lead to traffic being aggregated on the shortest path while other viable paths are underutilized. Network designers will often try to ensure that networks are symmetrical such that where parallel paths exist, they are of equal cost and hence the load can be balanced across them using conventional IGPs, which support load balancing across multiple equal cost paths. Ensuring network symmetry, however, is not always possible due to economic or topological constraints; traffic engineering offers potential benefits in these cases.

Unexpected demands: In the presence of unexpected traffic demands (e.g., due to some new popular content), there may not be enough capacity on the shortest path (or paths) to satisfy the demand. There may be capacity available on non-shortest paths, however, and hence traffic engineering can provide benefit.

Long bandwidth lead-times: There may be instances when new traffic demands are expected and new capacity is required to satisfy the demand, but is not available in suitable timescales. In these cases, traffic engineering can be used to make use of available bandwidth on non-shortest path links.

The potential benefit of different approaches to traffic engineering can be quantified by using a holistic approach to capacity planning, such as described in Section 11.1, which is able to overlay the network traffic matrix on the network topology, while simulating the relative network loading taking into account different traffic engineering schemes. A network-by-network analysis is required to determine whether the potential TE benefit will justify the additional deployment and operational cost associated with the deployment of these technologies.

Traffic engineering can potentially be performed at layer 2 (i.e., by traffic engineering the underlying transport infrastructure) or at layer 3. In focusing on layer 3, in the following sections we consider possible approaches for IP traffic engineering, and consider traffic engineering at layer 2 to be an inception of network engineering when considered from a layer 3 perspective.

11.2.2 IGP Metric-Based Traffic Engineering

The tactical and ad hoc tweaking of IGP metrics to change the routing of traffic and relieve congested hotspots has long been practiced in IP backbone networks. For a long time, however, this approach was not considered viable for systematic network-wide traffic engineering and it was often cited that changing the link metrics just moves the problem of congestion around the network. If we consider the network from Figure 11.7, by changing the metric of the link from R3 to R4 from 1 to 3, as can be seen in Figure 11.9, the traffic demands both from R1 to R8 and from R2 to R8 are now routed over the bottom path (R3 $\rightarrow$ R5 $\rightarrow$ R6 $\rightarrow$ R7), which is now the least cost path (cost of 5). In this case the congestion has moved to the bottom path.

If, however, the metric of the link from R3 to R4 was changed from 1 to 2 (rather than 1 to 3), then the top path (R3 $\rightarrow$ R4 $\rightarrow$ R7) and the bottom path (R3 $\rightarrow$ R5 $\rightarrow$ R6 $\rightarrow$ R7) would have equal path costs of 5, as shown in Figure 11.10.

Where equal cost IGP paths exist, equal costs multipath (ECMP) algorithms are used to balance the load across the equal cost paths. There are no standards defining how ECMP algorithms should balance traffic across equal cost paths, and different vendors may implement different algorithms. ECMP algorithms typically, however, perform a hash function on fields in the header of the received IP packets to determine which one of the paths should be used for a particular packet. A common approach is to perform the hash function using the 5-tuple of

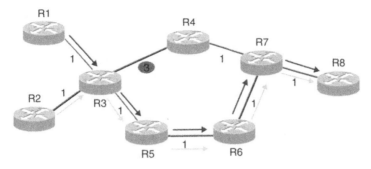

FIGURE 11.9

Changing link metrics moves congestion.

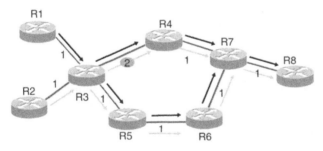

FIGURE 11.10

Equal IGP path costs.

IP protocol, source IP address, destination IP address, source UDP/TCP port, and destination UDP/TCP as inputs. The result of such a hash function is that load balancing across equal cost paths would be achieved for general distributions of IP addresses and ports. Such approaches also ensure that packets within a single flow are consistently hashed to the same path, which is important to prevent resequencing within a flow due to the adverse impact that packet reordering can have on the performance of some applications.

If such an ECMP algorithm were used in the example shown in Figure 11.10, and assuming a general distribution of addresses and ports, the 3 Gbps aggregate demand from R1 and R2 to R8, would be evenly distributed with approximately 1.5 Gbps on the top path and approximately 1.5 Gbps on the bottom path, and therefore the bandwidth would be used effectively and congestion would be avoided. Hence, the mantra that tweaking IGP metrics just moves the problem of congestion around the network is a generalization that is not always true in practice. For some symmetrical network topologies and matrices of traffic, ECMP algorithms may be able to distribute the load effectively without the need for other traffic engineering approaches at all.

In recognition of the possible application of metric-based traffic engineering, there has been a significant recent increase in research in the approach of systematic (i.e., networkwide) traffic engineering by manipulating IGP metrics. Further, IGP metric-based traffic engineering has been realized in the development of automated planning tools, which take inputs of the network logical (i.e., IGP) and physical topology, together with the network traffic demand matrix and derive a more optimal set of link metrics based on a defined optimization goal. These optimization goals may be to minimize the maximum utilization on aggregate, or per class.

IGP metric-based traffic engineering provides less granular traffic control capabilities than MPLS traffic engineering (see Section 11.2.3). The effectiveness of IGP metric-based traffic engineering is dependent on the network topology, the traffic demand matrix, and the optimization goal. For the proposed AT&T WorldNet backbone, it has been found that weight settings performed within a few percent of the optimal general routing is where the flow for each demand is optimally distributed over all paths between source and destination. Optimal distribution may be defined by the solution to the maximum multicommodity flow problem, where the total flow summed over all commodities is to be maximized. Other studies conclude that in the six networks they study, metric-based TE can be 80 to 90 percent as efficient as the theoretical optimal general routing. Further, they surmise that the greatest relative difference in performance between IGP metric-based traffic engineering and traffic engineering via explicit routing (such as provided by MPLS traffic engineering) occurs in large networks with heterogeneous link speeds (i.e., where ECMP cannot be readily used to split traffic between parallel circuits with different capacities).

11.2.3 **MPLS Traffic Engineering**

Unlike conventional IP routing, which uses pure destination-based forwarding, Multiprotocol Label Switching (MPLS) traffic engineering uses the implicit MPLS characteristic of separation between the data plane (also known as the forwarding plane) and the control plane to allow routing decisions to be made on criteria other than the destination address in the IP packet header, such as available link bandwidth. MPLS TE provides constraint-based path computation and explicit routing capabilities at layer 3, which can be used to divert traffic away from congested parts of the network to links where bandwidth is available and hence make more optimal use of available capacity. Label switched paths (LSPs), which are termed "traffic engineering tunnels" in the context of MPLS TE, are used to steer traffic through the network allowing links to be used which are not on the IGP shortest path to the destination.

Note that, as well as being used to solve the traffic engineering problem, MPLS TE has other applications including admission control, route pinning, and MPLS TE fast reroute. Route pinning is the ability to explicitly define the exact path that a particular traffic flow may take through the network.

MPLS TE Example Tunnel Establishment

Consider the network in Figure 11.11, where every link is 2.5 Gbps and each has the same metric (assume a metric of 1), and where a single MPLS TE tunnel of 1 Gbps is already established from LSR1 to LSR8, using the path LSR1 → LSR3 → LSR4 → LSR7 → LSR8, because it is the shortest path (path cost = 4) with available bandwidth. In this example, it is assumed that the entire network has been enabled for MPLS TE, and that the full bandwidth on each interface is used for MPLS TE.

The following subsections describe an example sequence of events, which considers the establishment of another TE tunnel, a 2 Gbps tunnel from LSR2 to LSR8.

Event 1: Resource/Policy Information Distribution

Each router within the network floods information on the available bandwidth resources for its connected links, together with administrative policy constraint information, throughout the network by means of extensions to link-state based IGP routing protocols such as IS–IS and OSPF.

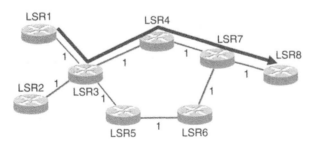

— = 2.5 Gbps link (metric shown
next to link)

➡ = 1 Gbps tunnel from LSR1 to LSR8

FIGURE 11.11

MPLS TE example tunnel establishment.

As TE tunnels are unidirectional, each TE-enabled router maintains a pool of available (i.e., currently unused) TE bandwidth in the egress direction for each interface that it has. Considering LSR3 for example, because the tunnel from LSR1 to LSR8 has already reserved 1 Gbps of bandwidth on the interface to LSR4, LSR3 will only advertise 1.5 Gbps worth of available bandwidth for that interface. For all of its other interfaces, LSR3 will advertise 2.5 Gbps of available bandwidth.

Event 2: Constraint-Based Path Computation

All of the routers within the MPLS TE area will receive the information on the available network resources, advertised via IS-IS or OSPF. With MPLS TE, tunnel paths can be specified manually, but more commonly are either dynamically calculated online in a distributed fashion by the TE tunnel sources (known as tunnel "*head-ends*") themselves or determined by an offline centralized function (also know as a tunnel server or path computation element) which then specifies the explicit tunnel path a head-end should use for a particular tunnel. With either approach, constraint-based routing is performed using a constraint-based shortest path first (CSPF) algorithm to determine the path that a particular tunnel will take based on a fit between the available network bandwidth resources (and optionally policy constraints) and the required bandwidth (and policies) for that tunnel.

This CSPF algorithm is similar to a conventional IGP shortest path first (SPF) algorithm, but also takes into account bandwidth and administrative constraints, pruning links from the topology if they advertised insufficient resources (i.e., not enough bandwidth for the tunnel), or if they violate tunnel policy constraints. The shortest (i.e., lowest cost) path is then selected from the remaining topology. Whether online or offline path calculation is used, the output is an explicit route object (ERO) which defines the hop-by-hop path the tunnel should take and which is handed over to RSVP in order to signal the tunnel label switched path (LSP).

We assume online path calculation by the tunnel head-end, in this case LSR2. There are two possible paths from LSR2 to LSR8, either the top path (LSR2 → LSR3 → LSR4 → LSR7 → LSR8) or the bottom path (LSR2 → LSR3 → LSR5 → LSR6 → LSR7 → LSR8). As the tunnel from LSR2 to LSR8 is for 2 Gbps, there is insufficient bandwidth currently available (1.5 Gbps only) on the links from LSR3 → LSR4 and from LSR4 → LSR7 and hence the top path is discounted by the CSPF algorithm. Therefore, in this example the bottom path is the only possible path for the tunnel from LSR2 to LSR8, and output of the CSPF algorithm is an ERO which specifies the IP addresses of the hops on the path (i.e., LSR2 → LSR3 → LSR5 → LSR6 → LSR7 → LSR8).

Event 3: RSVP for Tunnel Signaling

The Resource ReSerVation Protocol (RSVP), with enhancements for MPLS TE, is used to signal the TE tunnel. RSVP is used differently in the context of MPLS TE than it is for per-flow admission control. RSVP uses two signaling messages, a Path message and a Resv message.

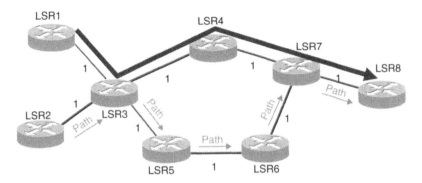

— 2.5 Gbps link (metric shown next to link)

➤ = 1 Gbps tunnel from LSR1 to LSR8

FIGURE 11.12

MPLS TE example tunnel establishment: Event 3a.

The Path message carries the ERO and other information including the requested bandwidth for the tunnel, which is used for admission control. An RSVP Path message is sent from the tunnel head-end to the tunnel tail-end, as shown in Figure 11.12, explicitly routed hop-by-hop using the ERO.

At each router that receives the Path message, an admission control decision is made to verify that the outbound interface that will be used to forward the Path message to the next hop defined by the ERO has sufficient resources available to accept the requested bandwidth for the tunnel. This admission control decision may seem redundant as the CSPF algorithm has already picked a path with sufficient bandwidth; however, it is required because it is possible that the head-end router may have performed the CSPF algorithm on information which is now out of date, for example, if another tunnel has been set up in the intervening period since the tunnel path was calculated.

If the admission control decision is successful, the path message is forwarded to the next hop defined by the ERO, until the path message reaches the tail-end router. MPLS TE supports the concept of pre-emption and a lower priority tunnel may be pre-empted to allow a higher priority tunnel to be set up. If the admission control decision is unsuccessful at any hop, a PathErr message is returned to the tunnel head-end.

Note that where RSVP is used for per-flow admission control, rather than for MPLS TE tunnel signaling, the admission control decision is made in response to the receipt of the Resv message.

If the tail-end receives the Path message, then the admission control decisions must have been successful at each hop on the tunnel path. In response, the tail-end router originates a reservation (Resv) message which follows the path defined

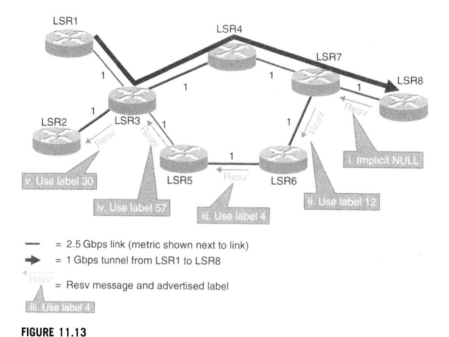

- ——— = 2.5 Gbps link (metric shown next to link)
- ➡ = 1 Gbps tunnel from LSR1 to LSR8
- ◀ Resv = Resv message and advertised label
- iii. Use label 4

FIGURE 11.13

MPLS TE example tunnel establishment: Event 3b—label advertisement.

by the ERO in reverse in order to establish the LSP that defines the tunnel, as shown in Figure 11.13.

At each hop on the tunnel path that receives the Resv message, the tunnel reservation is confirmed. In order to set up the tunnel LSP, the Resv message is then forwarded to the upstream (i.e., closer to head-end) neighbor on the tunnel path, together with MPLS label value that this router expects to be used for traffic on the tunnel received from the upstream neighbor.

In this example, penultimate hop popping (PHP) is assumed and LSR8, as the final hop on the tunnel path, advertises an implicit null label to LSR7 accordingly. LSR7 then advertises label value 12 to LSR6, and so on, until the Resv message reaches the tunnel head-end. This is an example of downstream on-demand label binding with upstream label distribution, where upstream/downstream is with reference to the direction of the flow packets on the LSP.

Event 4: Assignment of Traffic to Tunnels

When the Resv message reaches the head-end, the tunnel LSP has been successfully established and it can be used for traffic forwarding. There are a number of ways to determine when traffic should use the TE tunnel rather than the conventional IGP path. The simplest is to use static routing with a static route defining that traffic to a particular destination subnet address should use the tunnel rather than the conventional IGP route. Some vendors also support the capability to

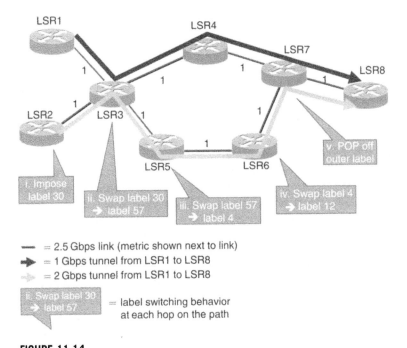

FIGURE 11.14

MPLS TE example tunnel establishment: Event 4—label switching.

automatically calculate IP routes to forward traffic over MPLS TE tunnels, by adapting Dijkstra's SPF algorithm.

Having decided to forward some traffic onto the tunnel, the head-end router, in this case LSR2, assigns traffic to that tunnel by forwarding it on the tunnel LSP. It forwards traffic on the TE tunnel by sending it toward LSR3 with label value 30 as shown in Figure 11.14.

LSR3 receives the labeled packet, and label switches it to LSR5 swapping the label from 30 to 57. Note that LSR3 uses only the label to determine how to forward the packet (i.e., it does not look at the underlying IP destination address). The tunneled packet continues on the LSP until it reaches LSR7, which as the penultimate hop, pops off the outer label and forwards it to LSR8, which is the tunnel tail-end. If a label stack is not used, the tail-end router looks at the IP destination address to determine how to forward the received packet; if a label stack is used (e.g., in the context of BGP MPLS VPNs as per *RFC 4364*), the tail-end router uses the outermost of the remaining labels to determine how to forward the received packet.

Event 5: TE Tunnel Control and Maintenance

Periodic RSVP Path/Resv messages maintain the tunnel state. Unlike tunnel setup, Path/Resv messages used for tunnel maintenance are sent independently and asynchronously.

The tunnel head-end can tear down a tunnel by sending a PathTear message. If a network element (link or node) on the tunnel path should fail, the adjacent upstream neighboring router on the tunnel path will send a PathErr message to the head-end, which will then attempt to recalculate a new tunnel path around the failed element. Similarly, if a tunnel is pre-empted, a PathErr message will be sent to the head-end, which will then attempt to recalculate a new tunnel path where bandwidth is available.

DiffServ-Aware MPLS Traffic Engineering

MPLS TE and DiffServ can be deployed concurrently in an IP backbone, with TE determining the path that traffic takes on aggregate based on aggregate bandwidth constraints, and DiffServ mechanisms being used on each link for differential scheduling of packets on a per-class of service basis. TE and DiffServ are orthogonal technologies which can be used in concert for combined benefit: TE allows distribution of traffic on non-shortest paths for more efficient use of available bandwidth, while DiffServ allows SLA differentiation on a per-class basis. As it was initially defined and has been described in the previous section, however, MPLS TE computes tunnel paths for aggregates across all traffic classes and hence traffic from different classes may use the same TE tunnels. In this form MPLS TE is aware of only a single aggregate pool of available bandwidth per link and is unaware of what specific link bandwidth resources are allocated to which queues, and hence to which classes.

DiffServ-aware MPLS TE (DS-TE) extends the basic capabilities of TE to allow constraint-based path computation, explicit routing, and admission control to be performed separately for different classes of service. DS-TE provides the capability to enforce different bandwidth constraints for different classes of traffic through the addition of more pools of available bandwidth on each link. These bandwidth pools are subpools of the aggregate TE bandwidth constraint (i.e., the subpools are a portion of the aggregate pool). This allows a bandwidth subpool to be used for a particular class of traffic, such that constraint-based routing and admission control can be performed for tunnels carrying traffic of that class, with the aggregate pool used to enforce an aggregate constraint across all classes of traffic. There are two different models that define how the subpool bandwidth constraints are applied:

Maximum allocation model: With the maximum allocation bandwidth constraints model (MAM) for DiffServ-aware MPLS TE, independent subpool constraints can be applied to each class, and an aggregate constraint can be applied across all classes.

Russian doll model: With the Russian dolls bandwidth constraints model (RDM) for DiffServ-aware MPLS TE, a hierarchy of constraints is defined, which consists of an aggregate constraint (global pool), and a number of subconstraints (subpools) where constraint 1 is a subpool of constraint 0, constraint 2 is a subpool of constraint 1, and so on.

The choice of which bandwidth allocation model to use depends on the way in which bandwidth allocation and pre-emption will be managed between tunnels of different classes. It is noted that if traffic engineering is required for only one of the deployed traffic classes (e.g., for EF traffic only), then DS-TE is not required and standard single bandwidth pool TE is sufficient.

In support of DS-TE, extensions have been added to IS-IS and OSPF to advertise the available subpool bandwidth per link. In addition, the TE constraint-based routing algorithms have been enhanced for DS-TE in order to take into account the constraint of available subpool bandwidth in computing the path of subpool tunnels. RSVP has also been extended to indicate the constraint model and the bandwidth pool, for which a tunnel is being signaled.

As described in Section 11.1.3, setting an upper bound on the EF class (e.g., VoIP) utilization per link is necessary to bound the delay for that class and therefore to ensure that the SLA can be met. DS-TE can be used to assure that this upper bound is not exceeded. For example, consider the network in Figure 11.15, where each link is 2.5 Gbps and an IGP and TE metric value of one is applied to each link.

DS-TE could be used to ensure that traffic is routed over the network so that, on every link, there is never more than a defined percentage of the link capacity for EF class traffic, while there can be up to 100 percent of the link capacity for EF and AF class traffic in total. In this example, for illustration we assume that the defined maximum percentage for EF traffic per link is 50 percent. LSR1 is sending an aggregate of 1 Gbps of traffic to LSR8, and R2 is also sending an aggregate of 1 Gbps of traffic to LSR8. In this case, both the IGP (i.e., if TE were not deployed) and non-DiffServ aware TE would pick the same route. The IGP would pick the

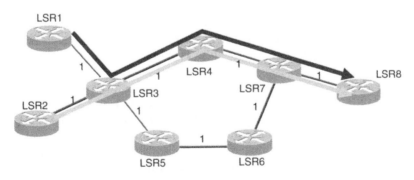

— = 2.5 Gbps link (metric shown next to link)
➡ = 1 Gbps tunnel from LSR1 to LSR8
⇨ = 1 Gbps tunnel from LSR1 to LSR8

FIGURE 11.15

DS-TE deployment example 1.

top route (R1/R2 → R3 → R4 → R5 → R8) because it is the shortest path (with a metric of 4). Assuming 1 Gbps tunnels were used from both LSR1 and LSR2 to LSR8, TE would also pick the top route, because it is the shortest path that has sufficient bandwidth available (metric of 4, 2.5 Gbps bandwidth available, 2 Gbps required). The decision to route both traffic aggregates via the top path may not seem appropriate if we examine the composition of the aggregate traffic flows.

If each of the aggregate flows were composed of 250 Mbps of VoIP traffic and 750 Mbps of standard data traffic, then in this case the total VoIP traffic load on the top links would be 500 Mbps, which is within our EF class per-link bound of 50 percent = 1 Gbps. If, however, each traffic aggregate is comprised of 750 Mbps of VoIP and 250 Mbps of standard data traffic then such routing would aggregate 1.5 Gbps of VoIP traffic on the R3 → R4 → R5 links, thereby exceeding our EF class bound of 50 percent. DS-TE can be used to overcome this problem if, for example, each link is configured with an available aggregate bandwidth pool of 2.5 Gbps, and an available VoIP class subpool bandwidth of 1.25 Gbps (i.e., 50 percent of 2.5 Gbps). A voice over IP class subpool tunnel of 750 Mbps is then configured from R1 to R8, together with a standard class aggregate pool tunnel of 250 Mbps. Similarly, from R2 to R8 a VoIP class subpool tunnel of 750 Mbps and a standard class aggregate pool tunnel of 250 Mbps are configured from R2 to R8.

The DS-TE constraint-based routing algorithm then routes the VoIP subpool tunnels to ensure that the 1.25 Gbps bound is not exceeded on any link, and of the tunnels from R1 and R2 to R8, one VoIP subpool tunnel would be routed via the top path (R1/R2 → R3 → R4 → R5 → R8) and the other via the bottom path (R1/R2 → R6 → R7 → R5 → R8). A propagation-delay constraint can also be specified for the subpool tunnels to ensure that the chosen path exhibits a propagation delay that is smaller or equal to the specified value. In this particular case, there would be enough available bandwidth for both aggregate pool tunnels to be routed via the top path (R1/R2 → R3 → R4 → R5 → R8), which is the shortest path with available aggregate bandwidth, as shown in Figure 11.16, for example.

Hence, DS-TE allows separate route computation and admission control for different classes of traffic, which enables the distribution of EF and AF class load over all available EF and AF class capacity making optimal use of available capacity. It also provides a tool for constraining the class utilization per link to a specified maximum thus ensuring that the class SLAs can be met. In order to provide these benefits, however, the configured bandwidth for the subpools must align to the queuing resources that are available for traffic-engineered traffic.

MPLS TE Deployment Models and Considerations

MPLS TE can be deployed either in an ad hoc fashion, with selective tunnels configured tactically to move a subset of traffic away from congested links, or systematically, with all backbone traffic transported in TE tunnels.

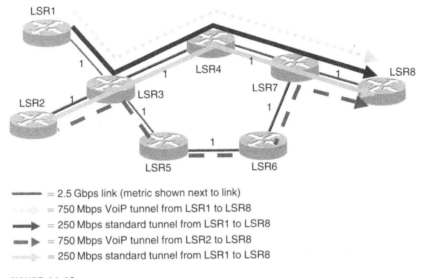

——— = 2.5 Gbps link (metric shown next to link)

······ = 750 Mbps VoIP tunnel from LSR1 to LSR8

——➤ = 250 Mbps standard tunnel from LSR1 to LSR8

━ ▶ = 750 Mbps VoIP tunnel from LSR2 to LSR8

······➤ = 250 Mbps standard tunnel from LSR1 to LSR8

FIGURE 11.16

DS-TE deployment example 2.

Tactical TE Deployment

MPLS TE can be used tactically in order to offload traffic from congestion hotspots; this is an ad hoc approach, aimed at fixing current problems and as such is generally a short-term reactive operational/engineering process. When used in this way, rather than all traffic being subjected to traffic engineering, TE tunnels are deployed to reroute a subset of the network traffic from a congested part of the network, to a part where there is more capacity. This can be done by explicitly defining the path that a tunnel should take on a head-end router.

Consider Figure 11.17, for example; in this case there are two links of unequal capacity providing the connectivity between two POPs: one 622 Mbps, the other 2.5 Gbps. Using IGP metrics proportional to link capacity (e.g., a link cost of 1 for the 2.5 Gbps links and a link cost of 4 for 622 Mbps link, in normal working case conditions), the bottom path would be the lowest cost path and the top path would remain unused.

Thus, even though there is over 3 Gbps of capacity between the POPs, this capacity could not all be used. If, however, two TE tunnels were configured between LSR 1 and LSR 2, one explicitly defined to use the top path and the other the bottom path, then as MPLS TE supports unequal cost load balancing (which normal IGP routing does not), the traffic demand between Router 1 and Router 2 could be balanced over the tunnels in proportion to the bandwidths of those paths, (i.e., 1/5 of the total demand using the top path and 4/5 of the total demand on the bottom path).

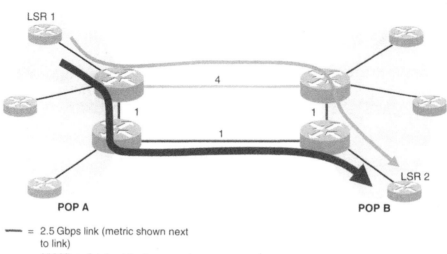

LSR 1

4

1

1

1

LSR 2

POP A   **POP B**

= 2.5 Gbps link (metric shown next
  to link)

= 622 Mbps link (metric shown next
  to link)

= 622 Mbps tunnel from LSR1 to LSR2

FIGURE 2.5 Gbps tunnel from LSR1 to LSR2

Tactical TE deployment—enables unequal cost load balancing.

Systematic TE Deployment

With a systematic TE deployment, all traffic is subjected to traffic engineering within the core; this is a long-term proactive engineering/planning process aimed at cost savings. Such a systematic approach requires that a mesh of TE tunnels be configured, hence one of the key considerations for a systematic MPLS TE deployment is tunnel scaling; a router incurs control plane processing overhead for each tunnel that it has some responsibility for, either as head-end, mid-point, or tail-end of that tunnel. The main metrics that are considered with respect to TE tunnel scalability are the number of tunnels per head-end and the number of tunnels traversing a tunnel mid-point. We consider the key scaling characteristics of a number of different systematic MPLS TE deployment models:

Outer core mesh: In considering a full mesh from edge-to-edge across the core (i.e., from distribution router to distribution router), as MPLS TE tunnels are unidirectional, two tunnels are required between each pair of edge routers hence $n * (n - 1)$ tunnels are required in total where n is the number of edge routers or head-ends. The example in Figure 11.18 shows the tunnels that would be required from the distribution routers within one POP to form a mesh to the distribution routers in other POPs.

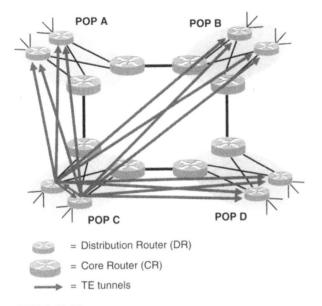

= Distribution Router (DR)

= Core Router (CR)

= TE tunnels

FIGURE 11.18

Outer core TE mesh.

If TE is required for *m* classes of traffic each using DiffServ-aware TE then $m * n * (n - 1)$ tunnels would be required.

Inner core mesh: Creating a core mesh of tunnels (i.e., from core routers to core routers) can make tunnel scaling independent of the number of distribution routers (there are normally more distribution routers than core routers), as shown in Figure 11.19, which illustrates the tunnels that would be required from the core routers within one POP to form a mesh to the core routers in other POPs.

Regional meshes: Another way of reducing the number of tunnels required and therefore improving the tunnel scalability is to break the topology up into regions of meshed routers; adjacent tunnel meshes would be connected by routers which are part of both meshes, as shown in Figure 11.20, which shows meshes within each of two regions. Although this reduces the number of tunnels required, it may result in less optimal routing and less optimal use of available capacity.

To put these options into context, TE deployments may have a full mesh between 120 head-ends, which results in $120^2 = 14,400$ tunnels in total with a maximum of 120 tunnels per head-end and a maximum of 1500 tunnels that traverse a mid-point.

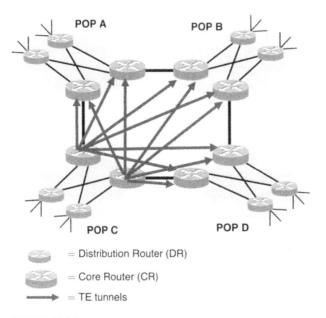

= Distribution Router (DR)

= Core Router (CR)

= TE tunnels

FIGURE 11.19

Inner core MPLS TE mesh.

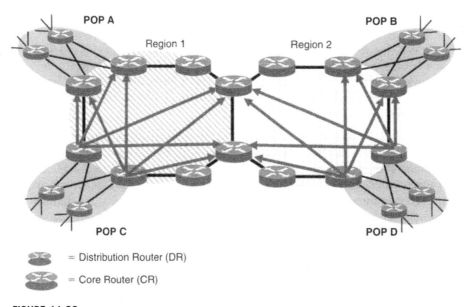

= Distribution Router (DR)

= Core Router (CR)

FIGURE 11.20

Regional MPLS TE meshes.

Setting Tunnel Bandwidth

Having decided on a particular MPLS TE deployment model, the next most significant decision is how to set the bandwidth requested for TE tunnels. The bandwidth of tunnels is a logical (i.e., control plane) constraint, rather than a physical constraint, hence if the actual tunnel load exceeds the reserved bandwidth, congestion can occur. Conversely, if a tunnel reservation is greater than the actual tunnel load, more bandwidth may be reserved than is required, which may lead to needless rejection of other tunnels and hence underutilization of the network.

The same principles of overprovisioning discussed in Section 11.1.3 could be applied to traffic engineering deployments. The bandwidth pools on each link should be set taking the required overprovisioning ratios into account for that particular link speed. For example, if DiffServ is not deployed in the core network and an OP of 1.42 is determined to be required to achieve a target P99.9 queuing delay of 2 ms on a 155 Mbps link, then the aggregate TE bandwidth pool should be set to 155/1.42 = 109 Mbps. Each tunnel (which represents a traffic demand across the network) should then be sized based on the measured average tunnel load (or a percentile thereof, as described for the core traffic demand matrices in Section 11.1.2). This will ensure that the measured average aggregate load on each link will be controlled such that the per-link overprovisioning factor is always met, and hence the target SLAs can be achieved, even when there are potentially multiple tunnels that may traverse the link.

Tunnel resizing can be performed online, by the head-end routers themselves, or by an offline system. When online tunnel resizing is used, algorithms run on the head-end routers to automatically and dynamically resize the tunnels which originate from them, based on some measure of the traffic load on the tunnel over previous measurement periods. Simple algorithms can lead to inefficiencies, however. Consider, for example, an algorithm that sizes the tunnel based on the peak of the 5-minute average tunnel loads in the previous interval; when traffic is ramping up during the day, the algorithm needs to take into account the traffic growth during the next interval, or else it will underprovision the tunnel. Consequently, in the interval following the peak interval of the day, significantly more tunnel bandwidth will be reserved than is necessary, as illustrated by the example in Figure 11.21.

Figure 11.21 plots the total traffic load across all TE tunnels (black line) in a network with a traffic engineering tunnel full mesh during a single day. The corresponding sum of the reserved TE tunnel bandwidth is plotted in grey. The tunnel resizing algorithm used in this case resized each tunnel every 2 hours to a multiple of the peak of the 5-minute average load for that tunnel experienced during the preceding 2-hour period. In order to cope with the rapid ramp up in traffic load before the daily peak, a high multiple needed to be used; in this case the multiple was 1.2 times. As a consequence, the reserved tunnel bandwidth is significantly greater than the actual tunnel load during the period after the daily peak load, due

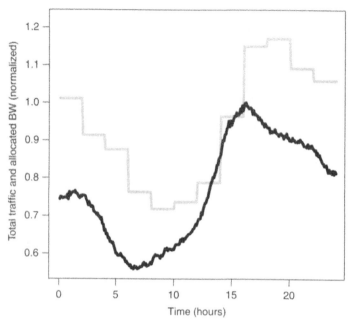

FIGURE 11.21

Automatic tunnel bandwidth sizing.

to the resizing lag. Hence, tunnel resizing algorithms are most efficient when they rely on a longer history of measurements for tunnel sizing (e.g., day, week, or month).

11.3 RESOURCES

The nature of the networking industry and community means that some of the sources referred to here exist only on the World Wide Web. All universal resource locators (URLs) have been checked and were correct at the time of going to press, but their longevity cannot be guaranteed.

Ben Ameur, W., N. Michel, E. Gourdin, and B. Liau, "Routing strategies for IP networks." *Telektronikk*, 2/3:145–158, 2001

Bonald, Thomas., Alexandre Proutiere, and James Roberts, "Statistical guarantees for streaming flows using expedited forwarding." *INFOCOM*, 2001.

Buriol, L. S., M. G. C. Resende, C. C. Ribeiro, and M. Thorup, "A memetic algorithm for OSPF routing." *Proceedings of the 6th INFORMS Telecom*, pp. 187–188, 2002.

Cao, J., W. S. Cleveland, D. Lin, and D. X. Sun, "Internet Traffic tends toward Poisson and Independent as the Load Increases," in *Nonlinear Estimation and Classification*, Springer-Verlag, 2002.

Charny, Anna, and Jean-Yves Le Boudec, "Delay bounds in a network with aggregate scheduling," *First International Workshop on Quality of Future Internet Services*, Berlin, 2000.

Ericsson, M., M. Resende, and P. Pardalos, "A genetic algorithm for the weight setting problem in OSPF routing." *J. Combinatorial Optimization*, 6(3):299–333, 2002.

Fortz, B., J. Rexford, and M. Thorup, "Traffic engineering with traditional IP routing protocols." *IEEE Communications Magazine*, October 2002.

Fortz, Bernard, and Mikkel Thorup, "Internet traffic engineering by optimizing OSPF weights." *Proceedings IEEE INFOCOM,* pp. 519–528, March 2000.

Fraleigh, Chuck, Fouad Tobagi, and Christophe Diot, "Provisioning IP backbone networks to support latency sensitive traffic." *Proceedings IEEE INFOCOM 2003*, April 2003.

Gous, Alan, Arash Afrakhteh, and Thomas Telkamp, "Traffic engineering through automated optimization of routing metrics." Presented at Terena 2004 Conference, Rhodes, June 2004.

Halabi, Sam, *Internet Routing Architectures*. Cisco Press, 2000.

Lorenz, D., A. Ordi, D. Raz, and Y. Shavitt, "How good can IP routing be?" *DIMACS Technical Report,* 2001-17, May 2001.

Maghbouleh, Arman, "Metric-based traffic engineering: Panacea or snake oil? A Real-World Study." *Cariden*, NANOG 27, February 2003.

Medina, A., N. Taft, K. Salamatian, S. Bhattacharyya, and C. Diot, "Traffic matrix estimation: existing techniques and new directions," *Proceedings ACM SIGCOM*, Pittsburgh, August 2002.

Paxson V., and S. Floyd, "Wide-area traffic: The failure of Poisson modeling." *IEEE/ACM Transactions on Networking*, 3(3):226–244, 1994.

RFC 1142, "OSI IS-IS Intra-Domain Routing Protocol," Oran, D. (ed.), February 1999 (republication of ISO DP 10589).

RFC 2205, "Resource ReSerVation Protocol (RSVP)—Version 1: Functional Specification," Braden, R. (ed.), September 1997.

RFC 2328, "OSPF Version 2," Moy, J., April 1998.

RFC 3036, "LDP Specification," Andersson, L., et al., January 2001.

RFC 3209, "RSVP-TE: Extensions to RSVP for LSP Tunnels," Awduche, D., et al., December 2001.

RFC 3630, "Traffic Engineering (TE) Extensions to OSPF Version 2," Katz, D., K. Kompella, and D. Yeung, September 2003.

RFC 3784, "Intermediate System to Intermediate System (IS-IS) Extensions for Traffic Engineering (TE)," Smit, H., and T. Li, June 2004.

RFC 3785, "Use of IGP Metric as a Second TE Metric," Le Faucheur et al., May 2004.

RFC 3906, "Calculating Interior Gateway Protocol (IGP) Routes Over Traffic Engineering Tunnels," Shen, N., and H. Smit, October 2004.

RFC 4124, "Protocol Extensions for Support of DiffServ-Aware MPLS Traffic Engineering." Le Faucheur, F. (ed.), June 2005.

RFC 4125, "Maximum Allocation Bandwidth Constraints Model for DiffServ-Aware MPLS Traffic Engineering," Le Faucheur, F., and W. Lai, June 2005.

RFC 4127, "Russian Dolls Bandwidth Constraints Model for DiffServ-Aware MPLS Traffic Engineering," Le Faucheur, F. (ed.), June 2005.

RFC 4271, "A Border Gateway Protocol 4 (BGP-4)," Rekhter, Y., T. Li, and S. Hares (eds.), January 2006.

RFC 4364, "BGP/MPLS IP Virtual Private Networks (VPNs)," Rosen, E., and Y. Rekhter, February 2006.

RFC 5101, "Specification of the IP Information Export (IPFIX) Protocol for the Exchange of IP Traffic Flow Information," Claise, B. (ed.), January 2008.

Sahinoglu, Z., and S. Tekinay, "On Multimedia Networks: Self-similar Traffic and Network Performance." *IEEE Communications Magazine*, 48–52, January 1999.

Tebaldi, C., and M. West, "Bayesian inference on network traffic using link count data." *J. Amer. Statist. Assoc.*, 93(442):557–576, 1998.

Thomas Telkamp, "Best practices for determining the traffic matrix in IP networks V 2.0." *NANOG* 35, Los Angeles, October 2005; available at *www.nanog.org/mtg-0510/telkamp.html*

Thomas Telkamp, "Traffic characteristics and network planning." *NANOG* 26, October 2002; available at *www.nanog.org/mtg-0210/telkamp.html*

Vardi, Y., "Network Tomography: Estimating source-destination traffic intensities from llink data." *J. Am. Statist. Assoc.*, 91:365–377, 1996.

Zhang, Y., M. Roughan, N. Duffeld, and A. Greenberg, "Fast, accurate computation of large-scale IP traffic matrices from link loads." *ACM SIGMETRICS*, pp. 206–217, San Diego, June 2003.

Zhang, Z.-L., V. Ribeiro, S.Moon, and C. Diot, "Small-time scaling behaviors of Internet backbone traffic: An empirical study." *Proceedings IEEE Infocom*, San Francisco, March 2003.

Index

Note: Page numbers followed by italic *f* denote figures; those followed by *t* denote tables

Printed and bound by CPI Group (UK) Ltd, Croydon, CR0 4YY

03/10/2024

01040317-0013